An Actor Succeeds

An Actor Succeeds

CAREER MANAGEMENT FOR THE ACTOR

TERRANCE HINES and SUZANNE VAUGHAN

SAMUEL FRENCH ✴ HOLLYWOOD

NEW YORK ✴ LONDON ✴ TORONTO

First Edition

Library of Congress Cataloging-in-Publication Data

Hines, Terrance
An actor succeeds: career management for the actor/by Terrance
Hines and Suzanne Vaughan.—1st ed.
p. cm.
1. Acting—Vocational guidance. I. Vaughan, Suzanne. II. Title.
PN2055.H56 1990   792'.028'023—dc20   89-84949

ISBN: 0-573-60603-X

Cover design by Heidi Frieder

Printed and bound in the United States of America

Published and distributed by
Samuel French Trade
7623 Sunset Blvd.
Hollywood, CA 90046

This book is dedicated to my son
Ethan Aric Hines
1972-1981

. . . some of us have shorter roads to travel

CONTENTS

PART ONE: GETTING THE JOBS

PART TWO: CHOOSING THE JOBS

PART SIX: APPENDIX

Acknowledgments

To Patricia . . . for her patience and understanding during the years of Saturdays and Sundays that I was holed up like a Trappist monk.

To Linda Cappel and Brenda Marshall . . . for the endless hours of transcribing and editing interviews.

To my first coach in Hollywood, Ivan Markota . . . who taught me that Hollywood is equal parts art and business!

To those gracious interviewees for their time, energy, and faith in the project.

To Ed and Rita, my parents, for supporting my career choice.

To Colleen, my doctor sister, and Laurie, my lawyer sister, for reading sections of the book at my insistence, even when they really didn't want to!

To my clients, God bless them, for allowing me to grow and learn.

And lastly, to my editor, Joshua Karton, whose insights and tenacity cannot go unmentioned.

INTRODUCTION

The aim of this book is to influence the actor who has already taken the first small steps of beginning a career and is now experiencing the first real opportunities. It assumes you've got a foot in the door—that you are being (or are about to be) "sent out" for roles in features or television. On the other side of that door are the casting directors whom you will meet and for whom you will read. Now you are facing the actor's most difficult work—getting work.

When I first conceived this book two and a half years ago, I intended it as a resource book for my management clients and as a guide to their choices as they achieved each plateau of success in the development of their careers. Since the first hurdles to be jumped are meeting and reading with casting directors, I wanted my actors briefed, before they actually met these people, with the casting directors' insights, preferences, and prejudices. I knew my actors had the edge over their competition when they'd done this homework—not merely preparing the character, but being prepared for the process of cold reading, of interviewing, of dealing with professionals who expect that you, as they, are doing this for a living and are in it for the long haul. I wanted my actors to be pre-acquainted with the style of the young casting directors, who are the wave of the actor's future, as well as with some of the anchors of the profession, those who've set the standards and trained the others.

I also wanted to impress on my clients from the outset that in this business, "paying your dues" doesn't just mean surviving the inevitable rejections, but, even more, comes to mean the process of developing and expanding your relationships within the film, television, and theatre communities. Each new job or opportunity is based on the last, and the buyers of your talent, whether or not they hire you at a particular time, remember you as much from the quality of your professionalism as from the quality of your work. I wanted my actors to have the concrete advantage that results when their professional relationships have been based not on taking or using others, but on the mutual confidence and long-term trust that support and replenish a successful career. For the last decade, I have managed the careers of some of Los Angeles' top young talent, from Lisa Bonet to Lukas Haas, and it has involved endless hours of conversations and feedback from casting directors. But, additionally, I've also taught acting and auditioning for over twenty-five years, and I train all the clients I manage, so I know the actor from this side as well. And what I've seen, nine times out of ten, is that when there is a choice between two actors for the same job, talent and training being equal, the production company will always hire the second choice if the first choice has been perceived as "difficult." As one of the interviewed casting directors points out, "It's important to cast 'nice.'" On the other hand, *all* the interviewed casting directors emphasize that they want to see the "real you," and phoniness repels them. Clearly, something more than just talent or hard work or determination attracts—and then holds—their attention. Is there a key to the kind of career that not only succeeds, but also survives?

THE SURVIVAL OF THE FITTEST: "It is not the strong that survive, but those able to adapt to their environment." This is the fundamental principle of Charles Darwin's Theory of Natural Selection. When applied to the species known as *actors,* Darwin's theory sums up how and why some actors survive in the entertainment industry and some do not:

—Variety is characteristic of every group.
—More actors of each kind are born than can possibly obtain jobs and survive.
—There ensues a struggle for survival, a competition for space. In the life of a career, it is an active kill-or-be-killed competition.

—Some of the variations exhibited by actors enhance their chances of survival. Some of the variations are handicaps that bring about their elimination.

—The survival of the fittest is the survival of those of the species who demonstrate the successful variations which best adapt them to their environment.

The last step of Darwin's theory—that successful variations are transmitted to succeeding generations—is what convinced me that the audience for this book expands beyond my own roster of clients and includes not just other actors but parents, for example, who are trying to manage their child's career, or others in this industry who benefit from a greater understanding of the process by which actors are cast.

Once a career is moving in the right direction, the responsibility of maintaining professional relationships, and establishing new ones, only increases. Rules change, players switch. Those who reject your work may in turn be replaced in a short time by someone who loves your work. An assistant or secretary whom you treated with respect becomes tomorrow's casting director—and a buyer of your talent. As a career becomes more established, the actor will have to learn what is necessary in engaging the services of an attorney, an accountant, a publicist— so interviews with experts in these fields are also included in this book. But even once all these relationships are in place, major stars will still find themselves needing a new teacher or coach for a specific skill for a specific role. Or having to change agents or find a new manager. Or wanting to read for a role for which they know they'd be perfect, but the casting director, whom they've never met, would never think of them for this role since this particular casting director wasn't even born when these stars won their Academy Awards. Even if this casting director is familiar with these actors' reputations, the actors are still, once again, back in the position of wanting to meet and read for a casting director they don't know. The learning process in the arts, and in the business of the arts, is never finished. Studios are bought and sold, executives spend their creative lives in revolving doors, and casting directors move back and forth from television to film, gaining casting partners and assistants and parting from them time and again. The struggle for the actor to successfully adapt to this ever-shifting environment is unrelenting. So this book offers direction in additional adaptation skills—for example, obtaining unemployment, where the wrong choice can result in losing hard-earned money. Or stunt work, where the wrong choice on the actor's part can result in literal life-or-death consequences.

And finally, this book concerns itself not just with the consequences of rejection, but also with the consequences of success. What happens when you are so surrounded with the trappings of power that you become insulated from the mainstream? How do you keep your work meaningful to the audience on whom your success depends? John Biroc is a college theatre professor in Southern California, who is also a doctor of psychology with a career as a psychotherapist. He conducts seminars for the entertainment industry. (He is also a "regular guy" who coaches Little League.) He remembers dropping off a script one day to a former student who was doing quite well at the time:

He was running out the door and he grabbed me by the arm and said, "Come on, we're going over to see Dom DeLuise." I said, "Terrific." So we get into his Porsche, rrrrmmmm!, and go screaming out of Twentieth Century Fox up Century Park East. We're driving along, and I said, "How long have you had the Porsche?" And he said, "Oh, for about six months now; I really love it. I had a Rolls-Royce before; I hated the Rolls-Royce!" I said, "Why did you hate it?" He replied, "Because it's not me. I'm not a Rolls-Royce person; I'm a sportscar person." "Then why did you get a Rolls-Royce if you don't like it?" And he looked at me dumbfounded and he said, "Get a Rolls-Royce?! I didn't get it, they gave it to me!" "Who's they?" "The studio. As long as I'm on the series, they supply the cars for me. Any car I want. Any car. It could be a Lamborghini, it could be a Ferrari." "This is above and beyond your salary?" And he said, "Yeah, and they keep trying to give me more money and I keep turning them down, and I told them I wanted a production company, so they supplied a production company for me." All just given to him, above and beyond the normal salary.

The last acting I did was on GENERAL HOSPITAL. And I

can't remember the name of the star, but I was in his dressing room. He was not on that day. And he had piles of teddy bears and gifts and boxes that he hadn't opened yet from fans, and pictures of himself all over the walls. And I thought to myself, "What does this tell somebody? When everyone treats you with such adulation? What does this say?" . . . In a television show I did one time, I played a bartender, and the actress, who was very successful, lit up a cigarette during the rehearsal, and she went to flick her ashes and there was no ashtray. And she said, out loud, "Could I have an ashtray?" and there were six ashtrays that came from different directions—bang, bang, bang, bang, bang, bang—like that. She flicked her ashes and bang, bang, bang, six ashtrays were gone. Tremendous amount of power. This could really go to your head. And this, compounded with relationships—my God, trying to relate to someone and thinking that you're some extraordinary person when you're a human being who has feelings and cries, who has feelings of guilt, all those other things—gets lost in this mishmash. Someplace.

So, throughout this book there is a repeated emphasis on establishing a solid, grounded base of support that can withstand the strains of success, an emphasis on observing the day-to-day process of this business, on reading the trade papers, on studying both your craft and the structure of your industry, and on carefully seeding and tending your professional relationships, while preserving the integrity of your personal ones amidst the emotional turmoil inevitable in the fluctuations of a successful career.

Although much of the advice in this book will prove true at any stage of your career, and wherever you are having that career, the focus is on career management for actors working in film and television in Los Angeles. There are significant differences between how actors are represented on the East and West Coasts. In California, the majority of actors are signed to only one agent. In New York, an actor often works through many agents, and the manager is the one who fields the calls from the agents asking for actors for an audition. Particularly with young clients, New York managers may have several hundred clients, and the actor may never see the manager after the first signing. In Los Angeles, ten to fifteen clients in the adult- or child-actor categories should be a manager's limit. New York is still where most casting occurs for commercials, and commercial agents may be booking several commercials a week, working from a roster of hundreds of clients, and have no connection with these actors either personally or with their acting careers in film, television, or theatre. California offers more opportunities for non-commercial work—what are called "theatricals," which refer to film, television, and theatre. California also has strict laws for minors, monitoring tutors and parental supervision and working hours, which New York either doesn't have or doesn't enforce, so the treatment of parents in New York is quite different from in California. Unless otherwise specified, when this book refers to casting directors and agents, it is referring to theatrical casting directors and agents working in Los Angeles. The advice on managers and their function in an actor's career, unless otherwise specified, also refers to career management in Los Angeles. (Reference in this book to *any* of these professions or job descriptions—manager, agent, casting director, actor, etc.—signifies both female and male, and when a pronoun is necessary to stand for one of these terms, *he* is meant to signify both *he* and *she*.)

Actors swarm into Los Angeles from all over the country, New York included. In addition to whatever is particular to how the business is run in Los Angeles, there is also the unique nature of the place itself. It is easy to be lulled by the soft swaying palms and the months of summer sun. In the development of this book, I received invaluable help from my editor, Suzanne Vaughan, who among other careers and accomplishments is an actress with extensive stage background. She constantly assumed the role of the young actor or actress, newly arrived in "Hollywood," fresh off the bus from Smallstown, U.S.A. She challenged me to answer her concerns, encouraging me to see each question clear through to its possible resolutions. Her relationship to this book became an important and integral part of its growth.

Whether you are in New York, Los Angeles, or Turtle Creek, the love of your work, if you are an actor, can never be based in the outward signs of success. They are just too changeable and difficult to rely on. At the end of each day, you must sit and evaluate the small success or gain you have made that day and rejoice in it, understanding that its full benefit to you may not be felt for years. Some days will seem like baby steps, but it's imperative to learn how to appreciate even the smallest advance forward, for there will also be days of retreat and rejection. They'll say it isn't personal—but it is. Rejection is cold, sharp, and, most often, painful. It is always on the lookout for a victim. With the proper training and support structure and perspective on your career, you will be able to face it head-on, stare it down, and walk right past it.

—Terrance Hines
North Hollywood, California
September, 1989

PART ONE

GETTING THE JOBS

CHAPTER 1

READING WITH
THE CASTING DIRECTOR

The first step an actor takes toward gaining a role in film or television usually involves reading a scene with a casting director or with the casting director's assistant, who sometimes "pre-reads" you before presenting you to the boss. You may have already met the casting director in a "general interview," where you were just being seen to evaluate your physical appropriateness for a specific part, or where you were just being met . . . in general. But it's this reading, with or for the casting director, that presents the first step in gaining the casting people's respect for you as an actor. And, without that, you won't have the chance of going further—of reading for the producer, director, or the network executive.

GET THE SCRIPT AHEAD OF TIME

This first reading is called a "cold reading" because the material is being read aloud "cold"—without having been seen or studied before. But you seldom get an actual cold reading anymore because of SAG's ruling that scripts and/or "sides" be available twenty-four hours in advance of the call. You can read the script at the casting office or take it home to work on it or to get private coaching. Still, there are times when scripts or sides might not be available—for example, on a project where secrecy is a part of the publicity, or where the producers have legitimate concerns about piracy. In such cases, the scripts are numbered, coded, and rarely given out ahead of time. The degree of secrecy surrounding a Steven Spielberg project is illustrated by the story of the bonded messenger who was sent to New York to deliver a Spielberg script to a famous couple. The messenger arrived at their front door with the script in a locked briefcase handcuffed to his wrist. He waited in the hallway while the actors read the script. When they finished, he locked the script into the briefcase and flew back to Los Angeles.

So, unless the script is being delivered to you, always pick up the material ahead of time. Otherwise, you'll be placing yourself in a position where you have little time to read it and even less time to make choices, thereby doing a disservice to both your talent and the material.

PREPARING FOR THE COLD READING

You must be able to break down the material quickly. Your first reading should be silent and swift. However, take enough time to get the basic situation and the flow of the material.

The second reading should be done out loud, reading both characters. Read it slower and try to determine where the scene is going. Is the scene an argument? A love scene? How do the characters feel?

The third time, read it out loud to get a sense of the visual. Where does it take place? What is the room like? How does *this* affect how the characters feel?

On the fourth time through, make a character choice that will work for you. If it's a comedy, play it so that the jokes are set up and the punch lines hit with clarity, enunciation, and volume. Some actors can play comedy very easily without much rehearsal; others need to keep repeating the lines until they've discovered the underlying rhythm which must steer the delivery.

If the material is a serious piece and the honest emotion is not at your fingertips, don't fake it. Sometimes the emotions that you consider necessary or appropriate for making the material work may simply not be available to you. Play what is real for you at the moment, even if it means no tears where the script calls for them. As long as you are playing something real, the casting people can see your talent, even if you're not playing the scene exactly the way you think you should.

If strong feelings come easily to you, then you may want to play a "cover"—to play against the obviousness of those feelings once they are flowing. It is important during the reading not to play the result of the scene—for example, knowing that it is a sad scene, starting out heavy—as if you had already experienced the whole scene. You, like your character, must take what happens moment by moment, and this often means in real life trying to delay or deny or dismiss what is happening to you, especially if it's bad. If you're sobbing at the beginning of the scene, how much emotional distance have you given yourself to travel? It is the journey that gives an audience the opportunity to be emotionally moved, not the result. Consider going with the idea, for example, that you are determined not to let these horrible experiences you're talking about really matter and that everything will be okay. The audience's sympathy tends to go out to the character who is struggling valiantly not to collapse, as opposed to the character who is wallowing in self-pity. Meryl Streep uses this technique to great effect in the scene in which she is forced by the Nazis to choose between her son and daughter in SOPHIE'S CHOICE.

Actors as a rule are much more afraid of dramatic readings than comedic ones. Serious material requires an immense amount of trust in your ability as an actor. The trust required to take the risk of putting yourself into such an extremely vulnerable position is the result of a lot of training and hard work. I've observed over the years that having led an unhappy personal life is no guarantee of great dramatic facility in actors. People who are comfortable with themselves and who've lived in a household in which the parents respected and helped them can get just as involved with their feelings, often because they'll know afterwards that it wasn't real. They can go home to real people whom they feel know and support them. Keep in mind that good acting is often simply a matter of solving problems.

WAITING

Once you arrive at the casting director's office, in all probability you will find yourself waiting for your turn, sometimes well past your scheduled appointment time. Your hands get colder and wetter. The butterflies in your stomach start a basketball game. To stay in touch with the scene and the character, take a stereo headset with a classical music cassette to relax you or a rock music cassette if you want to stay loose and energized. While you listen to the music, visualize the street or the doors of the room where the scene takes place. Run the scene in your mind and see the faces of the people you'll be talking to. Don't be afraid of your feelings once they begin to flow. Don't be afraid to look foolish to those in the hall with you. Everyone prepares in his own way.

Once you are inside and reading, you may find yourself abruptly waiting again if the telephone rings. If casting directors take calls during your reading, it's because they may be making deals with name actors or solving problems that won't wait. Stay in the scene and in character—and don't take it personally. It also may be possible when the phone call is finished to ask to start again.

DON'T APOLOGIZE

From the moment you walk in the door for an audition, you should exude the desire to be there—that you belong there. You must be willing to explore the limits of your acting instrument. Take risks. You can't do this if you're feeling apologetic. (Unless you're late, you haven't done anything wrong . . . yet.) Prepare a verbal résumé so that when you're asked, "What have you done?" you won't feel apologetic about what you haven't done. Talk about your plays, your favorite roles, movies-of-the-week (MOWs). Emphasize study if your credits are not extensive. We all started small. One month ago, the woman you're talking to might have been the secretary.

If you make a mistake during the reading, even get a fit of giggles during a dramatic scene, include it as the character's choice and go on. Never stop when an accident happens. Accidents incorporated into a reading are so often precisely what make the audition glow with organic behavior—that quality so admired in the work of an actor such as Gene Hackman, who seems to be saying the words as if out of his own mouth, spontaneously, for the very first time. Accidents create this opportunity by providing the character with surprises beyond what the actor already knows from having read the script. So don't ignore them. Deal with them, respond to them in character, and keep on going.

Sometimes no amount of preparation prepares you for what can be thrown at you when you arrive at a reading. Let's say you've been asked to come in and read for a specific role and the sides are not available. All you know in advance is that the character is gentle, sensitive, philosophical, but with a real zest for living. Using these scraps, you've explored and created a full life for this character. You arrive at the reading to discover that sides are still not available, and you're being given a scene from the script of this production company's last project, "just to see what you can do with it." Unfortunately, the character you'll be reading is described as a "cab driver, blue-collar, gives new meaning to the term 'brain dead.'" You have several options: 1) Not read. 2) Ask to use the phone and call your agent. 3) Consider that all the other actors there will be laboring under the same circumstances and decide to go for it. If number three is your choice, ask the casting director for advice on how to approach the character because the dialogue is completely opposite of the character for whom you're being considered. Remember that casting directors are not the writers or the producers, so the choice of the material being used to read you may be out of their control. No matter how unfair the situation seems, do not take it out on the casting director. Once you are gone, what remains, beyond any specific sense of you as the character, is how you've defined your level of professionalism.

After you've read, if you feel that you haven't made the right choice or you don't feel there has been a response, then ask to read it again and read it with feeling and involvement. You may be asked to read a second time to see if you can take direction. It means they saw something . . . good sign. They may want to see if you have other interesting character choices available. The ability to take direction is paramount to your career. If your first choice has been effective and the casting director decides to take you to the producer, you now have an obligation to the casting director, who is putting his integrity on the line for you. Give the same quality and effort to the second reading. You want to do well for yourself, your agent, and your manager, but now you also have the opportunity to make the casting director look good. After all, the casting director's job is to get the best people to the producer or network and not to let the good people slip through.

PLAY OFF THE PERSON YOU ARE READING WITH

During the reading, you should be looking at the person you are reading with. You must see what is happening with the other person and adjust your reading to his behavior, especially to what is going on in his eyes. Eye contact is very important to the casting director because it is through your eyes that the casting director can see the honesty, truth, and depth of your performance. I remember once having a client read with Robert Duvall, who has a way of looking at you with his eyes, almost as though he is looking through to the back of your head. He is so vulnerable and so open that when he started to talk to my client about her life, she was able to trust her feelings, and she started to cry and allow herself the same vulnerability. Without having to officially "begin the reading," they just segued their conversation right into the scene.

You will find some casting directors have acting experience and can be fun to read with, bringing a real joy to the process. These casting directors will make up for those others who read so flatly that you feel you're trying to play a scene with someone doing a Jack Webb imitation. You must be prepared to bring your own special excitement to the audition process, no matter with whom you find yourself reading. Some casting directors, who may give the actor little to play off in the reading, purposely do not allow themselves to be vulnerable because their job requires them to focus on the actor, not give a performance. Would you want a casting director more focused on his own acting than on yours? The good casting directors will find a way to get an actor to open up. Some have a way of talking to you in emotional images that actually help you prepare for the risks in the reading, or they'll get you talking about personal experiences that allow you to open up and respond. The ideal casting director will redirect you if your choice in the reading has been valid and honest but isn't what the producers or writers have specified, although the choice to take this extra time with you may depend on the rightness of your look.

USE THE WORDS THE WRITER HAS GIVEN YOU

Keep in mind when you are thinking about changing lines or adding to the script that a writer has spent a lot of time and energy on this material and will not be happy if you change it. This is especially true in comedy, where the jokes are written very specifically to set up the laugh. Often the producer is also the writer—how do you think he got to be producer?—and is not appreciative of your "improvements" to the script. Remember also that the casting director has now heard the script numerous times and knows if you're rewriting.

When you're preparing for the reading, try to find the lines that trigger the flow of your emotions. I call these lines "the hook." If all you have to work with is on the order of "The file is in the cabinet" or "I'll get it, sir," then you must trigger the flow of your imagination until you've created something interesting in the character's "private" life, something you can take with you into the scene, even if you're never talking about it. Perhaps you are having trouble at home, or your girlfriend/boyfriend has abandoned you. Perhaps your father has just surprised you with a new stepmother. Perhaps you are planning on a new career . . . If the character is nameless, the actor should give himself a name. Where were you born? What did you eat for dinner? It's important to personalize all of these particulars of situation and character. It's amazing how many actors don't. They just wait around for their cues. But even the perfect script, by itself, cannot endow you with a fully fleshed-out character. Actors are faced with a less-than-perfect script ninety-nine percent of the time. It's important to learn how to bring out through the material, however it's written, a belief in the truth of your character, a commitment from you to an actual life. This is what involves the audience and allows them to feel they are observing a real, three-dimensional human existence, not a flat pasteboard imitation. A good actor is working at all times on at least two levels: what he says and hears (the lines) and what he's thinking as he's talking and listening. In the case of live theatre and four-camera television, there is the third level of awareness of the audience. And the great actor is operating on even more levels than these three.

WHO HAS THE FINAL SAY IN CASTING?

You must realize that many people have a vote in the casting process. Directors have certain people they like to work with. Network casting people (those at ABC, NBC, CBS, and FBS) can have different choices from those of the casting director that the producers have hired. The networks have the final say in talent choices for MOWs and series roles. They control the funds that developed the show or they control distribution, so their input is very decisive. More than one producer has found his casting choices rejected by the networks at their Friday afternoon sessions.

While the actor cannot control the casting, ultimately it is within his grasp to control much of the audition process. For example, if you are a typical New York actor, then you are used to preparing outside, and when you enter the room you begin the scene immediately with little or no small talk with the casting director. In L.A., the first part of the audition usually involves the casting director getting to know you through a series of questions. While this conversation may relax some actors, you may find it dissipates your emotional preparation. Decide how you prefer to read and be willing to ask to read first, before any conversation with the casting director or producer, if that is how you feel you read the best. You will be able to exert far more control over the interview/reading if you are careful to:

BE ON TIME—or better yet, be early. Allow time to get to the interview, making allowances for traffic and parking. Don't waste your agent or manager's time getting complicated verbal directions to an interview. Buy a map book and learn how to read it. Be sure to call if you can't get there or are going to be late. And don't bring an entourage of unnecessary people with you.

BE PREPARED—including memorization.

BE FLEXIBLE—in case you have to throw your preparation aside.

BRING EXCELLENT PICTURES that look like you and an updated résumé that has recent credits, written in if necessary. In fact, have pictures and résumés with you at all times. You never know when you'll have an interview. For child actors, be sure that the work permit, Social Security card, and guild membership cards are also with you at all times and up-to-date.

HAVE SOLID, CREATIVE CHOICES ready for the casting director.

BE COURTEOUS, but not overly friendly or inappropriately familiar. This is a job interview, not a social situation.

WEAR THE APPROPRIATE CLOTHING specified by your agent. If the interview/reading is for a child and nothing is specified, play clothes are fine.

BE OBSERVANT AND AWARE of what is happening in the room. Be prepared to adjust.

BE VULNERABLE and open to your own feelings. Create inner images of what is going on in the scene. Don't be afraid to take risks.

PRACTICE LISTENING—the kind of active, responsive, animated listening you employ in your real life when you are fully engaged with what you're hearing and don't know what you're going to say next.

KEEP YOUR EYES OUT OF THE SCRIPT and don't read the other person's lines.

LOOK DIRECTLY INTO THE EYES of the other person.

MEMORIZE THE FIRST AND LAST LINES of the scene so that you open and close on the other actor's eyes with your own personal signature.

THANK THOSE CASTING for their time.

KEEP A RECORD of the interviews—listing time, place, date, studio, advertiser (if it is a commercial), and clothing.

FEEDBACK

There is no direct ratio between the amount of time you've spent at the interview/reading and whether or not you'll get called back or hired. You can wait two hours to see a casting director and only get to read half a page. The casting director on your next appointment may not read you at all; instead, you talk about salmon fishing and end up getting the part. Sometimes casting directors will read half a page and be satisfied that they know if you're right for the project—which to you may seem totally ridiculous and, in some cases, it may very well be. But in other cases, they may have a very specific look in mind, and the minute you walk through the door, long before you open your mouth, they know if you will satisfy the niche they have to fill. That may be all they have time for. Not every single audition is going to be fair. That's just something you will have to deal with as an actor. Keep in mind that they may see fifty to sixty actors per day, five days a week, 300 days a year. That's a lot of actors, and the casting director can't help but develop what he feels is a practiced and efficient eye. Also keep in mind that, with this kind of schedule, even if the casting director loves your reading, if you're not what he needs for the part he is not going to have time to reassure you that, yes, you will indeed work again, sometime, someplace. And it may well be through him. If your reading was excellent, even if you weren't hired, these people cast other projects and they will remember you. They keep files like libraries and have excellent memories. They will perhaps call to request you in the future because of the quality of previous readings. Every single interview is a brick in the path to your success. No matter how long this road is, how wide it may become, whether it weaves to the right or the left, it's very important that each brick be laid carefully and that you learn a way to feel positive about the experience that each reading has offered you.

Even once you have the role, the feedback you get may feel insufficient or bewildering. You may, for example, have just done a scene for episodic television, felt it went beautifully, and when it was over all you heard was, "Okay, let's go on to the next scene." Particularly in television, speed is an economic necessity. Three to four times the number of script pages must be shot per day than on a feature film. If you walk in front of a camera, they're apt to print it. There's no time for the rehearsals or the number of takes you would like to get. You know you're doing okay if they print it and go on to the next scene! After you've done a handful of small parts, you may begin to feel discouraged that anybody can progress further from these kinds of roles. Unfortunately, you seldom find out that you've made any kind of impression on a producer or director, when you've worked for them only a few times, until much later when you get a surprise call for an interview for a co-starring or recurring role on a series and you find out that this producer or director suggested you! Don't ever rule anything out.

If you aren't called back, you're going to want to know why. If you are called back but then don't get cast, you're going to want to know why. But once your agent or manager gets feedback from the casting director and it's passed on to you, you may still be left wondering why. For example, you learn that a casting director found your reading "boring." Does this mean you should have danced on his desk? He might have been horrified, but at least he wouldn't have been bored. If you get the commentary that the reading was boring, you might examine the energy level you used. Evaluate the reading in the following terms: Did you feel good about yourself personally? Did you have the time to prepare? Did you prepare properly? Did you really want that role? Were you willing to take the kinds of risks that allowed the casting director to see your feelings unfurl freely and honestly? Did you enjoy meeting that person? If you can answer yes, then your reading couldn't possibly have been "boring." If you had a problem in any of the areas above, then that's how it may have come across—as "boring." On the other hand, the casting director may not have been able to put his finger on exactly what was wrong, or may have known but could not articulate it, so he uses the catchall word "boring."

You must learn how to accept feedback and to understand it. A good agent, manager, and parent can help to put it in proper perspective. It's not your whole life or the end of the world if they didn't find you "special enough" or didn't like what you did or the choices you made. Besides, killing yourself or quitting the business isn't going to help make you be any more "special." The feedback you get from a casting director is one person's opinion—and it is an opinion that is based on information provided by the writer who has described a particular type, and you may not be it—regardless of how well you read. Often the reason you don't get a role is entirely beyond your control. You might have been too young or too old, too tall, too short, not beautiful or handsome enough. These should not be allowed to get in the way of your work. You should get feedback from your agent and manager, and it should be discussed between you what it means and how it should be interpreted. It is the only way to grow and improve.

Some criticism will be very useful and some will not. Negative criticism will not help you. And if it's vague as well as negative, you're best advised to ignore it. Being told someone thought you were "lousy" doesn't help you know what to do about it, other than to feel even lousier. In an effort to soften the blow, casting directors sometimes relay criticism to agents which is so couched in euphemism and encouragement that all that comes through is the evasiveness, and the actor is left wondering if the casting director has confused him with someone else. (See Chapter 4 for a glossary of euphemistic criticisms commonly employed by casting directors.) Sometimes even the use of the word "criticism" may not be helpful, since that word has a negative connotation that can set off defense mechanisms. In its place, I use the word "feedback," which can embrace positive as well as a negative information. Feedback can be easier to digest than criticism.

CHAPTER 2

INTERVIEWS WITH CASTING DIRECTORS

The theatrical casting director works extremely long hours. The job is often underpaid, and casting directors can be under pressure twenty-four hours a day. They frequently feel powerless if only the producer and director can say yes to the hiring of an actor. The casting director is only part of the screening process. But, because they are the first turnstile of entry into that screening process, they do in fact wield a great deal of power. The good ones love actors and feel a genuine need to help and develop talent. For them, to discover someone or to give the actor his first job is what really matters.

Good casting directors have the ability to understand what the director wants but also have an intuitive sense of the material and can steer the actor closer to what the director wants while still allowing the actor his own creativity. They also provide the actor with an environment in which he can take risks. Above all, they have respect for talent. (There are times when the system backfires and an actor doesn't make it past the first reading with a casting director, only to meet the director or producer much later and hear, "You're perfect! How come I never saw you for my project?" It happens rarely, but it does happen.)

To get the interview rolling, a casting director is likely to ask an actor: "Who are your acting teachers—past and present? Have you done any theatre—in New York or in L.A.? Do you have any stage training? If so, where?" But you are just as likely to find yourself talking about where you're originally from and/or what made you decide to become an actor or about some interest totally outside of show business that you discover you and the casting director have in common. Casting directors are interviewing and reading actors in order to find *people*, the right *person* for the role.   Remember to talk to them as if they were people, too . . . because that's what they are.

In the interviews which follow, we sought advice, opinions, and information from professional casting directors on a variety of questions and issues, including:

- What do you look for in an actor or actress?
- How do you deal with a bad script?
- Can an actor ask you to recommend an agent?
- Must the actor dress identically for a call back?
- What should an actor never do in a reading?
- What's your pet peeve in dealing with actors? agents? managers?
- How do you keep track of everybody whom you see and read?
- Do you have a preference for seeing actors from certain agencies?
- What should the actor spend money on?
- What would you change about the casting process?

We asked these and other questions of the following casting directors:

1. **Mary Gail Artz**
2. **Cody Michael Ewell**
3. **Mali Finn**
4. **Bob Harbin**
5. **Marc Hirschfeld**
6. **Caro Jones**
7. **Elizabeth Leustig**
8. **Bob MacDonald**
9. **Robin Stoltz Nassif**
10. **Barbara Remsen**
11. **Renee Rousselot**
12. **Sally Stiner**
13. **Stanzi Stokes**
14. **Judy Taylor**
15. **Mary West**

1. MARY GAIL ARTZ
INDEPENDENT CASTING DIRECTOR;
FORMERLY DIRECTOR OF FEATURE CASTING,
DISNEY STUDIOS

I moved to Los Angeles in 1971. After Immaculate Heart College, I went to work in the mailroom at Warner Bros. for about a year and then got a job as a receptionist for Diane Crittenden and Karen Rea in the casting department. It was a great way for me to start because I was right in the middle of everything—business affairs, and all of their calls, and I could see who was drifting in and out. Then Vivian McRae was going off on her own to become the head of television, and I became her assistant for about two years. Then I left to work in features. After about eight months as a reader at Warner Bros., I went out on my own as an independent casting director. I'd met Gretchen Rennell in New York, and she got me the interview at Fox for casting LUCAS. It was Gretchen who called to ask me if I wanted this job at Disney. Although I had cast HALLOWEEN II and did some of the principal casting on BAD BOYS, I think it was LUCAS that allowed me to get to this place.

WHAT QUALITIES DO YOU LOOK FOR IN AN ACTOR YOU REALLY RESPECT?

I like people who come in prepared. They don't make excuses. They give a reading, they have a lot of faith in what they're doing, and they're not too intimidated to say, "This is what I decided to do. What do you think?" They're there to do the work and so are you. That kind of attitude always impresses me. It's attractive to me when people come in with a strong enough sense of themselves that they can be honest—they can ask questions about what they don't know. They're not expecting that something is going to be done for them or given to them.

I also think having a sense of humor is very important. I don't know how people can live without it. It's very difficult being an actor, and just to stay in the game, I think you have to have a good sense of humor in addition to this strong sense of who you are.

Also, I think I'm very attracted to intelligence. In combination with intuition, it's what allows actors to glean something from reading the sides that connects to what's happened to them in their own emotional life, so that then they're able to give that scene a little more. I find a lot of actors don't observe. Often they don't listen. They don't remember your name or listen to directions. They've taken the sides home and worked on them, but they've turned it into something so set in their minds that it can't be flexible. And if it can't be flexible, it's because they don't really own it. After two pages of dialogue in the reading, they're still looking down to make sure they're getting all the words. That's not what a cold reading is all about. Once you've got the sense of what's going on, I'd much rather be looking at your face. When people come in to read, I try to say to them, "Do you feel comfortable? Do you have any questions for me?" Then I let them read the scene first and if they're way off base, I'll try to steer them a little closer. If there's a reason why they went off base, I'll ask them. If I'm interested in them, I'll start it over and see if they can get a little closer to what I'm looking for.

HOW SHOULD AN ACTOR READ YOUR CRITICISM?

At the end of our meeting, I say, "Thank you. It was a pleasure to meet you." I never say, "You should get out of the business" or, for that matter, "You should stay in the business, but you should take acting lessons." I don't impose. I don't offer suggestions about people's careers, so actors should not read these kinds of things into my remarks.

DO YOU ALLOW YOURSELF TO BECOME VULNERABLE TO WHAT'S GOING ON IN THE READING?

I remember once a girl came in who had a man's name, so I wasn't expecting a woman, and when she came in I was sort of taken aback. She was unusual looking. We ended up talking about childhoods, the way people grow up, and how they relate to their parents. It wasn't just rattling down someone's résumé. Our interaction told me something about her. But, by the same token, this kind of exchange doesn't tell me if she's a good actress.

DO YOU HAVE TECHNIQUES THAT YOU USE IN INTER-VIEWING ACTORS?

No, I'm not aware of any.

BUT ISN'T WHAT YOU JUST DESCRIBED A TECHNIQUE—INVOLVING AN ACTRESS IN TALKING ABOUT SOMETHING FROM HER REAL LIFE, SHARING SOMETHING OF YOUR REAL LIFE, AND THEN MOVING DIRECTLY INTO THE SCENE ONCE SHE'S TOTALLY INVOLVED? SOME CASTING DIRECTORS WILL DO THAT.

Not me. It would never even dawn on me to do that. I don't know whether that's good or not. Certainly, I've been around other people who give a tremendous amount of advice to actors. But I would prefer to have them leave with the thought, "Well, I talked to her and that's what I did." Period. There have been times when I've been surprised, or pleased, or very touched by actors' readings. But other times, when they ask me if they're coming back, if I know it's not going to work for this project, I have to be able to tell them, straightforward, "Sorry. It's not going to work for this project."

HOW DO YOU REMEMBER ALL THE PEOPLE THAT YOU MANAGE TO SEE?

I've got a good memory, thank God! I do have a filing system. I keep a complete picture file, and I use cards to take down information on people. And then it's all grouped according to age.

AFTER THE ACTOR HAS READ AND LEFT, WHAT'S LIKELY TO OCCUR?

The conversations run the gamut: "She was great." "She was interesting. Let's bring her back." "Will she look good with him?" "Will he look good with her?" "Is she maybe too tall or too big?" "But I like the way she read it. Let's get her back." So sometimes you run right out and you bring her right back, then and there. Or maybe it's three days later. Sometimes, the producers or the director are on the fence. So you have to put a big question mark by the actress or actor's name and bring them back. If I believe in an actor, I really push the producer and the director. I'm fully willing to say, "You're wrong. I think you should give that person another chance. Let me get the film that influenced me to bring him in here in the first place."

FROM YOUR STANDPOINT, HOW DOES AN ACTOR TELL IF HE HAS A GOOD AGENT?

You need to ask certain questions about your agent: Does your agent have good relationships with casting directors? Is he truly knowledgeable about what's going on currently in the business? Does he send you out on appropriate projects? Does he give you the right information? Is he someone you trust and whom you think other people like and respect? A lot of people can do the job of agenting and casting, but, above and beyond that, there's a kind of indefinable quality that makes or breaks the relationship between actor and agent.

IF THE ACTOR'S CAREER WERE A PIE, SLICED UP INTO SEVERAL SEPARATE PIECES, ON WHICH SECTIONS SHOULD THE ACTOR BE SPENDING HIS MONEY? WHAT PROPORTION OF THE ACTOR'S ENERGY AND INCOME WOULD YOU SUGGEST BE DEVOTED TO WHICH PIECES?

Ninety-seven percent of the pie has to be allocated to persistence. You have to *really* want to do it. *Have* to do it. That's ninety-seven percent. The remaining three percent after that is one percent for your pictures and one percent for your clothes. I think some actors should also spend money on therapy. If they don't need it, put that extra one percent into the pictures, not the clothes. I'm impressed with good photographs. Clothes? It's always the girl or the guy who comes in here in a T-shirt and a pair of jeans that I like, but again, that's my taste. A lot of actors let clothes wear them, and what that always indicates to me is that they don't like themselves just as they are. I got this picture yesterday, and the girl in it looks great. Who knows where it was taken? Obviously, it's not in a studio; it's not out of doors. It doesn't look professional to me. She's a USC student and hasn't really done much of anything. But I'm curious about her. Much more than I am about the guys who have the jean jacket with the collar up and the no-shirt look, like they're posing for something.

WHAT ABOUT TAPE?

I think it's important to have tape as long as it looks professional and not like it's made in your backyard. The quality has to be good—the sound, the image. It should be short and cut together well. I saw a tape the other day I liked that consisted of clips from just three things. There was music behind it, it was very short, very well done, it had the actor's name at the front, and his name was brought up again at the end. I always tell an agent, "Send over some film that's *appropriate.*" It cannot be ten years old because the director and producer will conclude, "That was ten years ago, so it doesn't count." It should be appropriate for the character that you are up for, because otherwise, again, they're going to use the tape to *eliminate* the actor. It's best to show something appropriate or don't show it at all, because then they still have some curiosity or at least some doubt in their minds about you. If I want the actor to stay in the running and I'm really pushing for him, I'm going to look at that film very carefully before I show it to the producers to make sure they're not going to get a wrong impression. I'll say to the agent, "You're going to have to trust me." It's in my hands, and the agent doesn't know the director or the producer as well as I do.

IS IT IMPORTANT FOR AGENTS AND MANAGERS TO GET FEEDBACK FROM THE CASTING DIRECTORS ABOUT THEIR CLIENTS?

I think so. But not a lot of them ask for it. I can't call every agent after I've seen every actor and give them feedback, but if the agent calls me, I try to be as specific as I can about why it didn't work, or if it did work, why the actor is being called back. A lot of times, agents don't call to find out this information. That's a call they should make. It's hard. Sometimes it didn't happen, just didn't work, and admittedly, I don't know why. Maybe the actors didn't do their homework, didn't understand the scene or the character, maybe they're too old, or they're too this or too that. It's something the director needs to tell me. Unfortunately, when twenty actors are still out there in the lobby waiting to read, I can't sit with the director and insist he get very specific about why he didn't care for this last one, but at the end of the day, I'll usually say, "Okay, let's talk." And then, by the end of the day, hours later, he may have forgotten the impression that someone made or didn't make on him. The director or producers may often just be able to say, "We love this person. Bring this person back." It's not as if they can clearly explain for those who didn't make an impression, "I didn't like her because . . . " I can only guess sometimes, and that's a problem. Often, there's a lack of concrete information for me to give the agent or the manager about his client. Because we don't sit and talk after every person. Sometimes there is that leisure, but sometimes there isn't. If they're running late on interviews, discussing why a reading was or wasn't successful throws the whole schedule off, and they won't do it.

WHAT DO YOU ENJOY MOST ABOUT THE CASTING PROCESS?

I love the possibilities of casting. It's making a complicated dish with different combinations of herbs. Getting all these actors together in a group and making them fit. I think that's exciting! I love meeting actors. I think they have a lot of courage. They walk around with their hearts on their sleeves, or their pants down, or whatever, and I sometimes feel quite honored when they bare their souls. When people come in and read a scene, they put light in the dark corners. They add texture. It's like taking something that's flat and hidden, and all of a sudden, you realize "Whoa! I didn't know that was there." You read twenty people in a day, you hear fifteen readings, and then somebody comes in and they wake you up. It's startling and unexpected and you never know when that's going to happen. You have to really love watching movies and television and going to theatre, because that's your homework, so when you leave the office after the casting sessions, you continue to work. You work hard at this job. You could be doing it all the time. You could go to the theatre every night, read the papers and magazines constantly and watch tapes all night at home.

WHAT ARE YOUR PET PEEVES?

People who won't come in and meet and people who are submitted who aren't right. I understand why an agent wants to do that. The agent needs to get that client a meeting or the actor needs to be seen, even he's wrong for the part. But I think that's a mistake, because it's shifting the agent's responsibility to his client onto me when, in fact, the agent should be dealing with the client directly on this matter. I also don't like it when agents call and ask me to see an actor, and then they change the appointment three or four times. I finally say, "Forget it. I don't want to see that person anymore." Also, why do actors come in and announce to the director that they haven't read the material when they came and picked up the sides the day before?! What they want is more information from the director. Fine. But then why not simply say to the director, "You know what? I'd like a little more information from you, if you're willing." When the actors pretend they don't know anything about the script, the director then asks me after they've left, "Didn't you tell them what this was about?" I'll say, "Yes," but by that time the damage has been done.

HOW DO YOU GET VALIDATED FOR A JOB WELL-DONE?

During the process of casting, validation comes from the director and producer, who'll tell me if I'm going in the right direction or not. They're the ones I'm in contact with the most. Then, as we move towards the end and have narrowed everything down to first-choice and second-choice situations, the people at the studio start getting to know the actors by looking at their tapes or their screen tests, and I'll start to get feedback from them. You don't hear it directly from the top that they're pleased with your work, but it eventually filters back to you. My friends also give me support. And actors will come in and compliment me on things that I've done in the past.

2. CODY MICHAEL EWELL
INDEPENDENT CASTING,
TWENTIETH CENTURY FOX

When I was in my late teens, I was involved with a small rock band in Fort Worth, Texas. I hung out with the guys, and they got a contract with Columbia Records. I became their road manager. I traveled on the road, managing them for Columbia. I left, went to college at Texas Christian University and then the University of Houston in mass communications and public relations. I opened a theatrical agency in Houston. I had contracts with universities in Oklahoma, Louisianna, Arkansas, and Texas to provide entertainment for homecoming dances and benefits. If the musical agents with William Morris, IFA, and CMA had a major act coming through the area, they would call me up and say, "Look, we've got a free night on this date. We'll give you the band for $5,000." I would take it and go sell it to a college for that night for $10,000.

I met the producer, Cash Baxter, when he was doing CANDIDE on Broadway with Celeste Holm. I invited him to the office one day and he said, "New York — that's really where you should be." I closed everything up, and I called him and said, "I want to come to New York," and he set up everything for me. He got me interviews with agents. The first job I had there was writing bios of the actors in Playbill *for a press agent. This press agent was working on the Tony Awards, and at the banquet after the telecast I met Jeff Hunter. He had Barbra Streisand, Raul Julia, John Travolta, Irene Daly, Elaine Stritch, Donald Madden. I worked with him for a few years and then was hired by Ann Wright to work as a commercial*

*agent in her New York office. She transferred me
out to L.A. in 1974. A couple of years later, I went
to Bill Cunningham's agency, and after a couple
of more years, I burned out being an agent. I
moved to San Francisco to get my head together. I
met a girl I'd known in New York. Karen Keiser
had been a casting director with Young and Rubi-
cam Advertising. She had gotten into the EST thing
heavy, moved to San Francisco to be a follower of
Werner Ehrhard, and I saw her in a restaurant.
She asked what I was doing I told her, and she
said, "What do you want to do?" I said, "I don't
know!" She said, "Have you ever thought about
casting?" "Yeah," I answered, "but I don't know
anything about how to get into it." She said, "Well,
I have a friend, Noam Pitlik, a director, who's
currently working on BARNEY MILLER, and
they're looking for a casting director. Do you want
me to set something up?" I said, "Fine." I flew down
here, I met Noam Pitlik, and they asked me to cast
a prospective script to see what my ideas would be
like. They liked what I did in the casting of this
phony script and they hired me. So I did the last
three seasons of BARNEY MILLER, and that's how it
started.*

*[AUTHOR'S NOTE: Cody Michael Ewell's casting
credits also include the television series MR. BEL-
VEDERE, RAGS TO RICHES, and SISTER KATE, as
well as movies-of-the-week NITTY, SHOOT DOWN,
and THE LADY FORGETS.]*

WHAT IS IT ABOUT CASTING THAT EXCITES YOU?

As an agent, you're very restricted because you can only work
with the clients you represent. You get a call and someone says,
"I'm looking for this particular kind of thing." You may not have

it on your client list, but you know an actor who's perfect for it and who happens to be signed with someone else. So your hands are tied and you can't always work on the projects you want to because you don't have the clients to meet that need. In casting, you can work with every actor in town. Unless you're a packaging agent, your creative input in being able to work with the producer, director, costume, and hair people is nil. You're not involved in the whole construction of a project as you are when you're casting. Casting is a much more creative outlet than agenting—at least, for me.

WHAT DO YOU LOOK FOR IN AN ACTOR?

I expect actors to be punctual for the appointment. If someone isn't punctual, I get crazy. If you have a reading, you've gotten your material in advance and you know exactly what you're going to do. I expect people to be prepared with the material but also to have done research finding out as much as they can about what it's about, how their character fits into it. Show me that you've done more than just come in, pick up a piece of material for five minutes, and then just spew it off. That doesn't mean anything to me. I spend a lot of time doing my homework. If someone has done his homework, it impresses me. I look for someone who knows how to handle himself professionally at an audition, especially if he's coming in for the producer/director. I like it when they're polite but they don't try to ingratiate themselves with the people in some sort of silly manner or try to make small talk. When they come in, they're introduced, they ask questions about what they're going to do, they get the answer, do the reading, and go on. I'm looking for people who have that something that will bring a spark to what they're doing. Someone who takes the material and sees something in it or something in themselves that they can bring to this role. I hear many actors saying, "Gee, we couldn't get the material in time." Well, I'm sorry, that's not my fault if you couldn't get over there because your tennis lesson got in the way. I find that, more often than not, people will just come in the door, five minutes before the appointment, and pick up the material. Then when it's time for their appointment, I'll come out to see if they're ready and they'll say, "No, I need more time." That makes me crazy.

WHY ARE FULL SCRIPTS NOT AVAILABLE?

There is a certain financial aspect to it. When I do a movie-of-the-week or a pilot, generally full scripts are available for those. In an episodic situation, it's very difficult because the scripts for those shows are physically not available until the day they start working so that what I'm casting from is either an outline, or a conversation that I've had, or material written specifically to audition actors. On BARNEY MILLER, I never ever had a script until the day we went to the table—after the show was cast. The same guys are doing MR. BELVEDERE. I never have a script on that show prior to going to the table, so I simply have to cast from old BELVEDERE scripts that might parallel. Or I have to read with scenes that they specifically write for me to use. Most of the time when scripts are not available, it's because they don't exist.

I have a general rule that when I do a movie of the week, I ask for thirty to fourty scripts from the producer, which costs $200 to $300. I know who I will allow to have those scripts. Major names. Agents call in and say they'd like to have one, and I make the choice at that point. Do they have the kind of clients who will fit this project? Is it going to be a waste of time giving that script to somebody? Sometimes I've given scripts to small agencies. It depends on the project. And if I run out of forty, I'll ask the producer for twenty-five more. Some producers provide them easily to me. Some are hesitant because of the expense involved.

IF YOU COULD CHANGE THE PROCESS, WHAT WOULD YOU DO?

I would like producers to give us more time to prepare for them. Here's a good example. After I walked in tonight, the office called and said that NBC wanted to send me a script for a pilot that they want to start casting on Friday morning. It's a half-hour pilot for Sandy Duncan. They're sending me the script tonight! Now, how much preparation is that? I understand the parameters within which they have to work. They have a delivery date. Fine. I understand that, but the fact is, if I could change anything and I had the power to do it, I would want more time to prepare things because I think that, in the long run, I could do a better job. Even when I have what I consider to be a fairly good amount of time to work on something, there's always the feeling that, "Oh, there's got to be somebody around the corner that I've missed." I think you especially have that feeling when you're under the gun and you really don't have a lot of time to prepare on pilots and movies-of-the-week. Episodic is even worse because you generally don't have scripts and you don't have a lot of preparation time. There are many answers that actors would like to get from me that I don't have because I'm not being provided the information. It makes me feel ill at ease, knowing I can't help those people. They're trying to do the research. They're asking me questions that will help them, and I can't give them the answers because they haven't been given to me and I probably can't get them, either. I would also like to be able to have more direct contact with producers. That's the nice thing about producer Len Hill. I can get to him wherever he is. If he's in a network meeting, he'll take my call.

I was involved in a movie-of-the-week recently where the producer started us off, and we had one casting session. We found a couple of roles out of that one session, and then he decided he wanted to go skiing. He went off and said, "You continue to work on this, and work it out the best you can. I'm going skiing." I couldn't ask him questions. I couldn't get his opinion. Nothing! He was gone. You really need to have direct access to these people, because what happens is that they will leave the decisions in your hands, and then you make the decision and it's wrong and you're screwed. That bothers me. I wish we had more direct contact with the directors because many directors are working on several projects at the same time and will call up and say, "Okay, we have eighteen roles to do on this, and I'll give you an hour on Friday. We'll do it then." You know, you physically cannot do that. You cannot run actors in and out. It's not fair to the actors to treat them that way, and it's not fair of this person to come in and say, "You have an hour to do this." Give me more time. And, if you're hiring me because you think I'm good, fine; but don't expect me to do the impossible. Don't expect me to cast a show with eighteen characters in it in an hour. It can't be done.

WHAT IS YOUR CASTING PROCESS?

The first thing I'll do is put out a breakdown. I want to get as much input from every agent as I possibly can. I want to get as many photographs in my office as I can. The day they come in, we put them in files according to characters. I'll go into that file and I'll pull out all the actors that I know could do that role in a breeze, and I'll put them aside. Then I'll go through the file and look at people I don't know, and if there is someone that intrigues me by their looks or their credits or that I've heard one of my peers mention, I'll set aside a time to read these people to find out if I can bring in somebody new—not new to the industry, but new in the sense of their relationship to me. Then I do something which is kind of interesting. There are agents in town who will come up with very good ideas, but there are also other ideas that they don't come up with. I'll challenge them to find where it is that they say, "Oh, yeah, I missed that!" Because breakdowns are not infallible. You can't say everything about a character in a breakdown. I talk to someone and I'll say, "Well, here's the way it will work with so-and-so," and that will prompt them into coming up with some more ideas. After I get all the pictures, I'll go to the agents that I really feel have the strongest clients for this project.

Agencies have personalities and a feeling. There are certain agencies that I know have more actors who are classically trained. They've worked at Yale Rep or Williamstown, or they have that East Coast kind of sophistication about their acting as opposed to somebody who's trained differently. There are agencies that reflect that kind of thing. I'll call the agents that I know reflect the personality of this project I'm working on and get verbal input from them. They may not have been able to come up with this through the breakdown. After I do the general readings, if there's anyone out there that I found for any of the roles who are new or are surprises I've come up with, I'll add those to the group that I clipped together of the people that I know could do the role in a breeze. When the director or producer says to me, "All right, we're going to do a session. I want to see six or eight people for each role." I might have thirty people put aside, and I'll narrow that down to my top six people. If they say, "We'd like to see more," I'll go back to that group and pull out the next six in line.

With children, it's a lot different because children change so quickly. Someone whom I used a year ago might not be the same now. I'll try to pre-read actors before I bring them in unless the actor is someone who has guest-starred on every show in television or has starred in half a dozen movies-of-the-week. Children change, and sometimes they're not adapatable to certain things. Children are more instinctual about what they do. If they identify with what's happening, they obviously can do it better. Many adult actors will say to themselves, "I don't really identify with that, but I can study and research and get my head into it." Kids either feel it or they don't. I'm talking about the young ones. If I'm doing a project that has a lot of kids, then I pre-read most of them prior to bringing them in for the director.

DO YOU ENJOY WORKING WITH MANAGERS AND HOW DO YOU SEE THEIR FUNCTION?

It depends on the manager. I see their function as career guidance. One of the things that bothers me about managers is that they're hiding behind the guise of career management in trying to negotiate contracts. A manager should help decide whether you should take this project or not, regardless of what it's paying you. There are managers who will say, "Yes, you should take this if we can get this amount of money." The law says a manager cannot negotiate a contract, cannot make a deal. Where, in the long run, is this going to help you make another step up? There are some managers I really have an affinity for, and others I really think are looking to make a fast buck. Generally, I have no problem with managers. If the manager is fair and treats his client fairly and makes wise decisions, I have no problem with him.

WHY DO YOU SURROUND YOURSELF WITH CERTAIN KINDS OF PEOPLE IN YOUR OFFICE?

It depends on the personality of the casting director. There are many casting directors who are intimidated by anyone they fear is going to take their job away. Agents, too. When you go in as an agent or casting director, you hire an assistant. Some people are the kind of people who want to hire people that they know they can train and bring up to make valuable to their operation. Then there are some who want to hire lackeys because they don't want to have to fear that this person is going to climb the ladder and take their job. So it really is how secure you are about yourself. Peter Verano, my assistant, says to me, "When am I going to get my own show?" I tell him, "When I think you are ready for it. And when you are ready for it, I'll be the first one to give it to you." I'm not intimidated in the least because I know that they're coming to this office because it is my office. And if I've been smart enough to bring someone into my operation and train that person in my style, then that can only speak well of me. And if this person then goes out of my office and gets his own work and goes on his way, fine. I am aggressive and ambitious enough that I like people who are the same way and want to go on to other things. Lackeys don't give me any excitement. It's the people who will contradict you and say, "No, you're wrong and here's why . . ." and point it out to you. If their point is valid, it's a point well-taken.

One of the reasons I hired Marsha as a receptionist is because she's worked for a lot of good casting directors and knows how to handle what she does very well. She knows the terms, contracts, agents and their assistants. She came with that background and something else which was even more appealing to me—her lack of desire to go any further than where she is sitting. In the past four years, I have probably been through twelve people in that job. I had one who said to me, two weeks after she was there in her first job in the industry and I had just turned a job down because I was too busy, "Why did you do that? I could have done that. I could have cast that one for you!" Receptionist is a very important job. She's responsible for making sure all the work calls go out, the contracts are correct, the scripts arrive to the actors with the revisions, wardrobe has been contacted, and everything is coordinated to make sure that everybody working is on time. Marsha is not a "yes" person. I mean, I'll point something out to her, and I'll tell her she did it wrong, and she'll say, "No, you're wrong. This is the way it should be done. Call the union and find out." And I'll say, "Okay," and call the union and, of course, she's right. I like that. It's very hard to find good people. That's why I've been through too many. Peter watches a lot of films and television, and in a casting session the director says, "Gee, you know, we've been looking for this one role and we haven't hit it yet—like the guy who played Ann-Margret's father in da-da-da-da in 19—, you know." Between myself and Peter, we can say, "Oh, you mean so-and-so." And he'll say, "Yes, that one." We constantly have an answer because we're both involved in film and television.

HOW DO YOU MANAGE TO REMEMBER THE NAMES AND FACES?

If I interview someone and like what they've done, I'll put them in a particular file, depending on the type. I'll go to those files and look. I may not remember the name of the person, but I'll remember the face, interview, and résumé. Nine times out of ten, it's in the mind. If someone comes in and is ingratiating as an individual in a general interview, coupled with their good reading, being on time and prepared, and having done the research, when it comes together, it's like a dream. You work to find these kinds of people. They stand out in your mind. We did THE LAST FLING with Connie Sellecca and John Ritter, and there was an actor I had interviewed many months before that, a young kid with hardly any roles in television, and a few theatre credits. The first casting session on this particular role, we went the wrong direction on it. The director had a different opinion than the producer, and we took one person's word over the other and went the wrong direction. They said, "No, no, this is the direction we want to go." They redirected my mind, and for some reason as I was sitting there, I said, "That guy! That kid I saw six months ago. He's perfect for this." I remembered his face. I could see it in my mind and I could remember that he had very few credits. All I had to do was go to the file and pull it. I knew it the minute it came up that that was him. I brought him in and he got the part. If you're impressed enough with somebody, you don't forget them.

I have a Rollcall computer here because I work more out of here at home at night than I do at my office. I'm starting to categorize people and put them into age groups and then cross-reference them so I can find them. It's not my favorite way to work because I like my personal input. I like that conversation with the agents. There are so many parameters that make things work. I might say one word that was not in a breakdown that could totally click somebody else's name into this agent's mind. They'll say it, and I'll say, "That's brilliant. Let's go with that." A computer is not going to do that for you. It's pretty cut and dried. You still have to talk to people.

WHEN YOU'RE LOOKING AT PICTURES AND RÉSUMÉS, WHAT POPS OUT AT YOU?

Well, in the picture, my eyes will go directly to their eyes. If their eyes are not focusing directly on mine, I lose contact with them immediately. I'm sure every agent in the world who's ever been worth their salt has told their clients, "When you get your pictures, make sure you have good eye contact." You always hear that, constantly, but it's very true, and maybe that's my agent training, but that's the one thing I do when I'm going through that stack of pictures like a deck of cards. When one comes up that is looking me in the eye, I stop at it. And when one comes up that looks honest or that doesn't look like it was airbrushed into tomorrow, or doesn't look like this is somebody representing themselves in an unfamiliar situation, I get interested. You can tell when someone is comfortable. You can tell when someone has had a good picture taken they felt comfortable doing or when there's a frozen smile or there's something that's not real. It's the eye contact that gets me every time, and the simplicity of the photograph. I don't like studio photographs. I don't like indoor shots. I think those are very boring. Nine times out of ten, the photographers don't know how to work with black and white or color indoors. They don't know how to light somebody to make the picture flattering. I like natural photographs, outdoors, sunlight, with something that sparkles in the background. You know, this ivy that you see out here—that's a perfect background for photographs because it will bleed out in the background. You'll see something, but you won't know what it is, and the actor is framed against that . . . a very straight-on, honest head shot is what attracts me.

AND ON A RÉSUMÉ, WHAT STANDS OUT TO YOU?

Unfortunately, I am a victim of a system in which I work, so my eyes will go directly to what an actor has done in episodic television. If I'm doing an episodic show, I look to see how many guest-star roles, co-star roles, or feature roles they've done. That's not to say that I would rule out an actor because he doesn't have the credits if I find other interesting things on the résumé. It's a natural instinct to see how much episodic TV they've done. If they have no episodic TV, then I look at theatre. I'm not saying that theatre falls third on my list, but when I'm working on episodic, I want to know that the person is experienced enough to be able to handle themselves on a set. On these one-hour shows that are on seven-and-a-half day schedules, you don't have time to go in there with somebody who doesn't know what they're doing or somebody who is going to be intimidated by that size crew or the enormity of some of those sound stages or the complexity of what they're facing. So naturally I look to see what they've done in that area. And theatre—obviously if they've got good theatre credits, that's interesting. If I'm doing a comedy, I'll look to see if they've done comedy plays. If I'm doing drama, nine times out of ten, I'll look to see if they've done comedy plays, because if they can do the comedy, they can do the drama that we do in episodic TV.

IS IT A POSITIVE EXPERIENCE FOR YOUNG ACTORS TO BE IN THE BUSINESS?

It's a positive experience to me if they have a strong family unit behind them and a loving, wonderful home that does not put acting number one. If the kid is dedicated enough, he will get a job and continue to keep his career moving. There has to be a real strong sense of family unity and love. It pains me to see children treated badly by their parents when they're on auditions. It happens constantly. It's unfortunate when children walk out the door and the mother says, "How did you do? Did you get the part? Did you smile? Did you go in and do what I told you to do?" The child is immediately bombarded with all these awful things, not "Okay, let's go home and have some dinner and watch some TV or something." Nothing positive. It's all negative. I saw a child recently. It was horrible. I went out to the reception area to bring somebody in and I called out the child's name. Apparently he or she, I forget what it was, was involved in a conversation with another child and didn't hear. So I called the name again and again the child didn't respond. Now I didn't know the child, so I was looking around the room. The mother had been off in another part of my office and came in and heard me calling the child's name for the second time. She went over to her child and said, "Get in there NOW!" She kicked the child! I just wanted to slap this mother around a little bit because it just was so painful to see that. These are kids. These are children. These are not robots. These are not adults who have careers. These are kids who want to play. And generally, this is play, even to the most professional kids. They know they can still go off and be a dentist if they want to later on in life. This is a sure way to make money and have a good time and maybe miss a few hours of school. I love to see kids get started and move on up—like Robby Rist, whom we used in a WIZARD episode. It's wonderful to see how Robby is coming along since he was a tiny kid. When I was an agent in New York, there were many kids working commercially who are out here working now. The Baios are a good example. They were with us in New York and we used them in commercials, and now Scott's directing episodes of his own series.

It's wonderful to see how these careers move and the kids grow up. It's the ones that were treated properly by their families that do make it. The ones that don't are the ones who were mistreated. They've got such a bad taste for what happened in their early life that their major concern as they get older is to get away from this aspect of it because it will get them away from their stage mother or stage father. They might love acting, but their psyches have been so badly treated that they will walk away from it. I think we may lose a lot of talented adult actors because they were treated badly as children.

ACTORS FREQUENTLY FEEL POWERLESS AND THAT THE CASTING DIRECTORS AND STUDIOS CALL ALL THE SHOTS.

Actors do have a tendency to feel that everyone on the production side of things holds the power. Young people don't understand the power that they have. If it were not for them, we would not have shows. We are at the mercy of the people we bring in. As a casting director, I am as strong as the actors that I am able to get into my office. If I don't treat them well and give them the proper tools they need to do a good job, then I look bad. More than anything, I want actors to know that they are powerful. If the facts be known, they run this whole thing. A lot of young people are very intimidated when they come into a room with eight to ten people. That's natural. I am intimidated every time I do a casting session when we go to network readings and we've got thirty people sitting there. I've been through them for years, but it's still intimidating. I can imagine for someone just coming into it what it must be like. If they could just remember that they are a very important part of what is going on in this room—maybe the most important part, it might make them feel more secure and help them to do a better job because they know they are a part of this. They're not on the outside looking in, and they should feel the strength they have and let it work for them.

3. MALI FINN
INDEPENDENT CASTING DIRECTOR,
FEATURES AND PILOTS; FORMERLY WITH
LYNN STALMASTER & ASSOCIATES

I was a theatre major at the University of Minnesota, and then I taught theatre at all age levels. I've been out here in Los Angeles for six years. I worked as an assistant to Michael McClain. Then I was with with Lynn Stalmaster, first as an assistant and then as an associate, for three years. We worked together on OUTRAGEOUS FORTUNE, AMAZING GRACE AND CHUCK, THE UNTOUCHABLES, BIG SHOTS, BUCK JAMES, RENO AND YOLANDA, KID GLOVES, and SWITCHING CHANNELS.

WHAT QUALITIES DO YOU LOOK FOR IN AN ACTOR?

I look for someone who is relaxed and who does not have a façade. Someone who has warmth.

HOW DO YOU MANAGE TO REMEMBER ALL THE PEOPLE YOU SEE?

I use a couple of different systems. I have a huge book of "name" people. I hate that distinction, but that's very much a part of this business. We will be called upon to cast a lead, and so I have to have alphabetized lists. Then each time I meet someone, I make out a card and put the date and the agent, approximate age, all of those things, and then comment on the actor after the interview, and keep those filed. In addition, I keep a picture file. When I do a show, I will go through lists, cards, and photos, and that gives me a pretty thorough background for searching for all the roles.

SHOULD AN ACTOR DRESS AND READ THE SAME WAY ON THE CALLBACK?

I don't think you can make any generalizations about that. I've heard a lot of actors ask that. I don't think every reading can be the same because I think situations vary. Sometimes an actor will come in and read with me and next time he may read with Lynn. Or the director. And that will make the reading different. Sometimes an actor will come in and read with me, and then if he's going to see a director, the director might say some things to him just before the reading that will be keys to what the director is looking for. I think that an actor has to be ready to adjust. I don't think that clothes are that important. Because this town is very visual, very image-oriented, certainly if you are trying out for someone who is sophisticated and you come in a pair of jeans and a sweatshirt, that's probably going to work against you. But I don't think the exact costume is the essence of what the reading is all about or whether or not the actor is going to be selected.

HOW SHOULD AN ACTOR READ YOUR RESPONSES?

I think a lot of times what can happen is that an actor finishes a reading, and you find yourself saying something like, "Good," because it's a comfortable way to end an interview, but then that actor walks out thinking, "Well, I did a good job." So I don't give specific comments after each reading, because I would rather be giving positive comments, and a lot of times the readings are not good. I very seldom say to someone right after an interview, "You're going to have a callback." I would rather not give any kind of false impression. I suppose in the long run if somebody did something where tears came to my eyes or I was overwhelmed, I would have to sit back and be honest and say, "You know, that was terrific!" and they would know it.

If I feel someone is off to a bad start, I will always stop and let him do it again. Especially with younger actors because they'll come in and the first time they want to rush through, they're so excited. Their energy rushes them through the reading. Then I say, "Okay, now you've calmed down, you're settled into this a little bit, let's do it again." When you're seeing twenty to twenty-five people in an afternoon, I don't know how you can be expected to read an actor once in a scene and make a snap judgement. I don't think that's possible.

HOW DO YOU FEEL ABOUT AGENTS AND MANAGERS REQUESTING FEEDBACK FROM YOU?

I think it's very important. The clients need it. There are too many games played in this area, and a lot of times there's hemming and hawing. There's a way to state that someone wasn't right that is soft-pedaling the actual response. It's always a cop out, saying the person wasn't physically right. Well— almost always. This town is very physical and very visual, so there are times, unfortunately, when that's absolutely the case.

HOW DO YOU DEAL WITH A BAD SCRIPT?

I find ways to generate some enthusiasm. I can remember an instance a year ago when I was given a bad script to work on and what I had to do was say, "Oh, look, this is going to be a good opportunity to review Hispanic kids from twelve to fifteen." I find other aspects of the casting that will excite me. I've got to find something to make me feel positive about the experience, and usually I can find something that will give me that enthusiasm to work 100 percent.

WHAT EXCITES YOU ABOUT CASTING?

It's very close to the preliminary work that a director goes through in theatre, and that's an exciting process for me. When you take the script and analyze and begin to visualize relation- ships and people, that's the process of directing I like. It's the preliminary stages that got me into casting. I love actors and I like the puzzle of finding ways to place people. Most of the experi- ences working with directors have been very positive. I like the mutual energies. I like the idea that one of the things I can do is help a director cast a film more efficiently.

HOW WOULD YOU MAKE THE PROCESS BETTER?

I prefer working on features to television because there is time. I think that sometimes there's a momentum that a producer has when he has to get a script going in a month and a half in order to make sure the studio will give it a green light. I dislike working on features or television when they are thrown together. I like the idea of having time to research and sit back and get away from the script a little bit, and then move into it, and then to look at all the possible resources. I like to know if we're looking for a black child that we've not only covered actors, but we've been to the Inner City Cultural Center and to the Afro-American Center. We've been out searching and have been thorough about it. It's important to me to have time.

Another part of the process that doesn't make any sense to me is how fast interviews end. British directors tend to take more time with actors. I'll work with a British director who will say, "I can only see two people" or "I can only see eight people today!" That exhausts me because there's such concentration, and I want to be able to give the actor his time. I appreciate that. There needs to be more time spent in an improv situation. You can get three or four actors together and see the relationships. Agents begin to object, of course. There are SAG rules that say you can have only so many callbacks, but I think that's all working against the creative process. I think you should be able to have as many callbacks as are necessary and bring people together, so that four or five people are reading together before decisions are made. I know that is time consuming and that there are a good many directors who get so involved during that casting period, location scouting, and doing all of the other things that are necessary for pre-production that they might not want to take time to do that. There are some directors that do.

HOW DOES YOUR PROCESS WORK——GETTING A SCRIPT AND GETTING IT CAST?

It varies depending on the project and on how much time. What I like to be able to do is read a script and to do a character analysis. And then pull back from it, making sure that I listen very carefully to the director's concept because the point of view and those images are what we have to be looking for. At that point, if I had questions or if I felt I wasn't understanding something, I would want to discuss those things to make sure that I knew exactly where we were going and how he envisioned the whole piece. Then I like to look at each kind of casting challenge and say, "Now what are all the resources and where can I look to find these people?" We don't put out a breakdown on a good many shows, so what I do is look for my own resources and go through all of my own materials. Even if we don't put out a breakdown, we're obviously hearing from agents. It's just accumulating as many names, as many possibilities, and going to readings.

HOW ACCURATE ARE THE BREAKDOWNS THAT ARE PUT OUT COMPARED TO WHAT YOU'RE REALLY LOOKING FOR AND WHAT YOU END UP WITH?

At Lynn Stalmaster & Associates, we wrote our own breakdowns, and usually I looked to a writer or director for clarification. That's something that Lynn and I felt out because we worked together on every project. He might have said, "This is a director who doesn't have to approve the material" or "This producer wants to read everything very carefully." Sometimes we had the writer write descriptions. We tried to make things as accurate and simple as possible so that we would get a wide range. If you're too specific, you're not going to get enough of a choice. We tried to simplify the breakdowns so that it was not a lot to assimilate because I don't think agents read a lot. I think they read the age because they're working very fast. Having worked as an agent, I realize the pressure is immense!

WHAT HAVE YOU LEARNED FROM THE PEOPLE WHO TRAINED YOU AS A CASTING DIRECTOR?

One thing that I've learned from Lynn is that the quality of time given to the actor is very important. He has an incredible concentration and focus on each person who comes in. He may not spend a lot of time with them, but he gives them his full attention while they're there. I think he makes each actor feel very special, which I think is important. Actors are herded around and their lives are full of daily rejections, so I think that what we've got to do is make our atmosphere as comfortable as possible for the actor so that he can feel free to give—to be as creative and relaxed as he can be. Lynn is very good at that, and it's not always an easy situation to go in and see him because of his reputation, but he helps people feel very relaxed. Prior to working with Lynn, one of the things I always did as a teacher was look for the positive instead of looking at a kid and labeling him. You know, that's going to be the bad kid in the group. I would try very hard to find something positive so that we have something to structure the relationship on. But he's taught me that you can meet a good many people on an open call or you can meet people back to back in an afternoon and, even if you don't have a lot of time to give them, still give them your full concentration.

WHAT'S YOUR PET PEEVE ABOUT CASTING?

So much of what's done in this town has to do with types. I think it's sometimes far more interesting to cast against type than to map out exactly what you're looking for and then narrow it down to those actors who fit that bill. I think everything is too visual. I look at a lot of theatre actors who come out of training and a lot of actresses who come in to interviews. They're maybe ten pounds overweight for the camera and they're wearing their little thrift shop kind of theatrical costumes and they give a wonderful reading, but unless they learn to adjust to what's accepted in terms of the visual here, they're just not going to get anyplace in the city. Maybe they'll be able to do some theatre or go off to New York, but at this point I've just started being very brutal and straightforward and saying, "You've got to lose ten pounds if you're going to be in front of the camera. You should find somebody to redo your hair. Forget the '40's look and buy one hot outfit to wear to all these readings so that you look like a million bucks." I'm hopefully helping people adjust to this place, and if they're going to be here, they're going to have to do that.

EVERY ONCE IN A WHILE I'LL SEE "PLEASE SEND ME YOUR CLIENT LIST" IN THE BREAKDOWN. WHY DO YOU ASK FOR THOSE THINGS?

Because that's another way that I go about coming up with ideas. I have a huge book, and I would take that home one night and go through it. It's another way to come up with people who might be good possibilities.

HOW IMPORTANT ARE THE *ACADEMY PLAYERS DIRECTORY* AND THE COMPUTERS AT SAG AND AFTRA? DO YOU USE THOSE THINGS?

All the time. Because people move around so much from agent to agent. There are a lot of people who aren't in the *Players Directory*, so you have to use the contact numbers at the guilds.

DO YOU USE THE *PLAYERS DIRECTORY* AS PART OF YOUR PROCESS IN TERMS OF SEARCHING?

Not usually. Unless there's something very specific or if I'm looking for kids. Except that I find with children, a lot of times their pictures are not updated, and so they'll look one way in the *Players Directory* and then they'll come in and they're three years older. The picture is very misleading. I would prefer not to thumb through and try to come up with ideas by looking at the *Directory*. I think it's arduous and time consuming.

THE NETWORK IS AN INTIMIDATING ATMOSPHERE. WHY DON'T THEY PAIR ACTORS TOGETHER AND HAVE THE LEADS WHO ARE ALREADY CAST READ OFF THESE ACTORS COMING IN?

I've been in the situation at Lynn Stalmaster & Associates where we did a pilot, and the lead in the pilot was there to rehearse the day before with people and read with them. It was a wonderful experience. When people were cast, he called them and welcomed them into his family. This is a man who is a real creative soul.

BECAUSE OF PAST POOR PERFORMANCE, DO YOU EVER REFUSE TO SEE ACTORS AGAIN?

We all have bad days, so I would always let an actor come back. There are so many things that can affect a reading: a traffic jam before the person gets there, a fight with someone. Maybe the actor was out partying the night before and didn't spend time preparing. Well, that's just his problem, but if the reading is bad, there are just too many things going on. I would never say, "That's that actor" and give him a big black mark on his card and say, "I'm not going to see him again." It depends on the level of the actor. If I read an older actor two or three times for two or three varied roles and felt that the actor had no range, or simply didn't have the skills that were necessary after those two or three readings, then I suppose at that point I would probably not have the time to see him again. I'm not going to label him a bad actor. Kids are different. They change so much, you've got to be very careful. An eleven-year-old can walk in and sell Wheaties at one interview and maybe be far too commercial. A year later, perhaps he's taken lessons or he's just relaxing and is much more natural. You've got to be careful about bringing these kids back again and again. Sometimes agents will say, "You know my client. Why do you have to read him?" I want to read an actor in every role. Every role is different. If I've seen an actor play something two or three times and it's very similar, I wouldn't have him in to read. Hopefully, I'm not bringing an actor in for something I've seen him do two or three times!

HOW DO YOU GET OUT OF THE BOX WITH THE CASTING DIRECTOR? LET'S SUPPOSE HE'S PLAYED THAT ROLE THREE OR FOUR TIMES AND HE REALLY WANTS TO BE BROUGHT IN ON A ROLE THAT'S AGAINST TYPE. CAN HE CHANGE YOUR MIND?

With me, that's not a problem. I don't want to typecast, so if I know that an actor has played something and perhaps feels boxed in, I would jump at the chance to find something that would be different for that actor to play.

DO YOU BRING IN ACTORS WHEN THE BREAKDOWN SAYS YOU HAVE ALREADY HIRED SOMEONE?

I don't do that. We didn't do that at Lynn Stalmaster & Associates, either. If one of the lead roles is cast, I put the name of the role and the actor's name there because that might be an incentive, somebody that other actors would be excited to work with.

DO YOU GET REPEAT BUSINESS FROM PRODUCERS?

As a newly independent, I'm not in a position at this point to answer that. Because so many of the projects that Lynn Stalmaster does are people that he's worked with, he's established a relationship over a number of years.

WHY DON'T CASTING PEOPLE AT THE PRE-READING SUGGEST TO THE ACTOR WHAT IT IS THEY'RE LOOKING FOR IN TERMS OF A CHOICE FOR THE READING INSTEAD OF ALLOWING ACTORS TO JUST GUESS WHAT IT IS THEY WANT?

It depends on when the reading takes place. If it's a pre-read before we've been in a session with the director, then even though you have heard a director's image, that image is not altogether clear or it's expanded at a later time. Once a director gets with the actors and he hears the words, then he begins to say things that clarify the character much more. You can take that information and go back. I would not want to be too specific prior to those readings with the director because there are so many choices to be made. We only know what that director wants by two or three statements, and that's so preliminary that you really have to wait until you hear what he begins to say once he begins working. That's when the character becomes clearer. I will share all of that information with an actor.

WHEN YOU DO A TEST DEAL, DOES THE LOWEST MONEY MAKE A DIFFERENCE?

Never would make a difference. If you're doing a test deal, you can either make a deal within the budget or you can't. If you can't make a deal within the budget, then obviously that person is not even going to test.

HOW DO YOU GET VALIDATED FOR A JOB WELL-DONE?

It's all personal. I know if I've done a good job, and I don't need anything else. I do need credit because that's part of the business. I want to be a business person as long as I'm out here working in what is both a business and an art. But at the same time, everybody likes to have someone else say, "A job well done." But I know when I've done it.

DO YOU, AS A CASTING DIRECTOR, SOCIALIZE WITH AGENTS, MANAGERS, AND ACTORS?

I socialize with people I like. I don't have a lot of time to socialize, and I'm not involved in a lot of industry gatherings.

DO YOU GO TO PLAYS OR SHOWCASES?

Yes. I love them. It's another chance to see actors and that's good.

DO YOU EVER SEE PEOPLE ON GENERAL INTERVIEWS?

Oh yes. As a matter of fact, I have big buckets of pictures, and what I will do at least once or twice a month is just go through those and pick a stack full and say, "Get these people in to see me." It makes me feel better. I'm afraid I'm going to miss someone, and I want to make sure that I'm seeing as many new people as possible.

WHAT'S GOING TO CATCH YOUR INTEREST ON A RÉSUMÉ?

My eyes go to theatre because my background is theatre; I look to see where they have studied. I detest résumés that have the names of plays without the names of directors or theatres, because those plays could have taken place anywhere. They could have been in community or regional theatre. I gravitate toward theatre. Once I've taken a look at the types of roles they've played and the theatres—and I know the reputations of regional theatres—I will look at the training. I know where the good trainers are. I know Hobbs is up in Washington, and I know John David Luce is in Evansville, and I know a lot of the academic people in the Midwest. I know the reputation of the schools there fairly well, since I taught for twenty years. After that, it depends on the project. If it's film, obviously I want to see if they have any experience, but that never is a prerequisite.

WHAT DO YOU WANT TO SEE, OR NOT SEE, ON AN ACTOR'S TAPE?

I think that the most important thing is that the tape is well done. Too many times beginners put something on tape and don't ask advice, or haven't researched how to do a tape, or don't ask the right questions. They tend to put on scenes that are not their scenes or too much of an episodic show or feature film. The point of a tape is that someone wants to come in and see something quickly and have it well edited and make sure that the scene highlights your character, so that they know who they're looking at. A good piece of tape has to be varied and show a wide range.

IS THERE ANY SINGLE CHARACTERISTIC THAT SUCCESS-FUL ACTORS HAVE IN COMMON?

I think that everyone who succeeds in this town must be tenacious. When I came here, everyone said, "You're a woman, you're in your mid-forties, you're not going to make it in this business. Go do something else." The only way I got my foot in the door was to be tenacious enough to call a casting director two or three times every two weeks until, finally, after three months she said, "What the hell do you want?" I said, "I want to learn what you do. May I come in and just intern with you and find out what casting is all about?" I had to make that happen, and I think that actors can't sit back and wait for other people to do the job for them. They've got to feel they're involved. That does not mean overstepping. You've got to work this out with your manager or your agent—how those relationships work best. It doesn't mean stepping on anyone's toes in terms of a business relationship. It does mean an actor works on his craft. An actor takes responsibility by constantly taking lessons or working out or gathering with people and reading plays, but most of all by being involved and not just sitting back and waiting for roles to come. I think an actor must be like a dancer. You've got to be constantly working at something. It doesn't necessarily mean spending money for expensive classes. Maybe a group of actors get together and just do some improvs. There are a lot of young actors now in this town who are beginning to form theatre groups, which I think is very healthy. There are more New York actors here who are used to doing things with people during the day. They're not used to going to the beach or sitting around and waiting for phone calls. They're used to getting out and walking the pavement and making something happen. In doing that, you also make contacts, and that's very important. I think many agents would probably get upset if actors went around making casting telephone calls, and I know that some agents feel that actors are just harping at them, constantly calling. But that's just common sense—you can be tenacious without stepping on anyone's toes. You've got to find ways to make things happen for yourself. You can't put your life into someone else's hands. You're responsible.

4. BOB HARBIN
INDEPENDENT CASTING DIRECTOR, *L.A. LAW;* FORMER MANAGER OF CASTING, NBC

I went to college at Ball State University in Muncie, Indiana, where I majored in acting, costume design, and American literature. I started as a messenger for Arnold Rifkin and Nicole David and worked my way up from messenger boy to receptionist to assistant to executive assistant to subagent. And then I discovered that I didn't get a kick out of agenting, and I wanted to try something else. I went with Mary Goldberg, who was kind enough to hire me for three weeks when she was casting AMADEUS. Then there was a position available at NBC. It was a cut in salary, but I took it for the chance to learn and work in a network. I just applied myself, put in a lot of hours, and put up with a lot of junk. I was primed for L.A. LAW to come along. I worked with Karen Hendel on FATAL VISION, assisted on CELEBRITY. I actually cast a short-lived series called HOT PURSUIT with Harry and Renee Longstreet, who are terrific producers. Currently, I'm working on a movie-of-the-week that I'm real proud of. I'm also the winner of the 3rd Annual Artios Award for Outstanding Achievement in Dramatic Episodic Casting for L.A. LAW: THE SERIES.

[AUTHOR'S NOTE: Bob Harbin's casting credits also include the Steven Bochco series DOOGIE HOWSER, M.D., and the movies-of-the-week DAUGHTER OF THE STREET, LADY IN A CORNER, and EXILE.]

WHAT QUALITIES DO YOU LOOK FOR IN AN ACTOR?

Basically, it boils down to their commitment to what they're doing. I like someone who believes in himself enough to relax and be himself, not come in and give you a programmed response or something that's very safe that he's used over and over. I like someone to just come in and be real. Then it's purely a gut response to their treatment of the material.

HOW DO YOU REMEMBER ALL THE PEOPLE YOU MANAGE TO SEE?

I keep pictures. I've got pictures from seven years ago. It's not everybody that you get excited about, and you keep different pictures for different things. I keep stacks in the cabinet behind me so I can run to them desperately. I don't keep 3 x 5 cards on actors because all that changes. I don't know if I want a computer. That seems to make it all very analytical.

WHAT ADVICE WOULD YOU GIVE ACTORS ABOUT PICTURES?

When I look at a picture, my eyes go first to the eyes. I think that's where the honesty is, if there is any. There are a lot of bad pictures. Actresses come in and say, "Oh well, you know — the photographer wouldn't give me what I wanted." I wonder who paid for the pictures! Pictures are very important as a sales tool. It's important that they look like you. If I'm calling someone and I have a picture, it's because I thought there was something in the picture that interests me or seems right for that project or that role. Unless you can produce that quality in the room with me, what's the point? It makes me want to say, "Excuse me, are you same person?"

IF AN ACTOR COMES IN FOR A CALLBACK, SHOULD HE DRESS AND READ THE SAME WAY?

If he has no other clothes, yes. I think that's dependent on the actor and the casting director. I know a lot of actors feel that's a luck factor. "I wore the blue dress for the casting director and he liked me. I'm going to wear the blue dress for the producers." It also gives them a sense of security. If it got past me, then it's certainly a safe thing to wear. I think that's fine. As long as they wash it between times. On the other hand, the reading is what got you to the next step and I think that's something that should be discussed. If the casting director thinks that something needs to be changed, he'll tell you. Let's face it. My job is to get someone hired. When I take someone to the producers, I don't want to look like a fool. So I'm taking people that I believe in and trust. They should do exactly what they did in the room with me and should follow any instructions or guidelines that I might be able to give them before they get to the producers. Do not go home and dream up, "Oh God, if I'd done that, I would have been so much better." Nine times out of ten, you'll be getting yourself in trouble. You'll go over the top and it'll be a mess.

WHAT DO YOU SAY TO AN ACTOR AFTER THE READING?

I don't say a lot. If they have done something really nice, I certainly try to tell them that. If they have done something wrong, and I think they're talented enough to make that change, we make the adjustment within the room. If I think they're God-awful, I usually just say, "Thank you," and let it go at that. If I think there's something more worthwhile to find out or if I'm intrigued, I'll take the time. Sometimes I sit there holding my breath, waiting for it to be over and then get them out the door. I will thank them for their time because they've taken their time to come see me. I'm not their acting coach or their agent or their manager or their mother. They have come selling a ware to me. I'm either buying it or I'm not. And there are times when someone has given a lovely reading, but they were totally wrong and you also try to tell them that. "Thank you, that was very nice. I will certainly try to use you for something else, but you're wrong for this." I try not to lose sight from the first readings to the twentieth. I purposely schedule my readings so that my morning is mixed. I'll see five or six different people for each role. That way, I don't get totally bonkers. It's important to me that I keep attentive. You don't know when someone wonderful is going to be there. And just because it's number thirteen out of twenty, you might miss it because you're looking out the window or thinking about lunch. That helps keep me a little sharper. I do all the readings myself, which keeps me in touch. I'm not free to just sit there. I'm part of the process. It's helped me to gauge if the actor is giving something. I like reading the actors, but I try not to get involved. Although I studied acting in college, I'm not there to get the role. I have no desire to be an actor.

WHAT DO YOU DO WITH A BAD SCRIPT?

You cry. You hope that the project will be canceled and you'll be paid off! If you're an independent, you have certain choices. If you're at the network, you don't. If you're offered the job, you always want to read the script before you accept. If it's a bad script, you certainly have the choice to say yes or no. If it's someone that I know, I'll say, "You know, I just don't think this is something I can get involved with and give you my hundred percent." Which is quite honest. I wouldn't be able to. If it's someone that I don't know, then I'd say, "I'm going to be too busy" or "I'm going to see my mother." Just any way to get out of it. But if you don't have the choice, and you are going to work on it, then you try to believe that if you can cast it in the right way, the cast can come off better than the script. I think that happens a lot. You see it all the time. The script is just drivel, but the show survives, and you have to think it's the casting of the people that makes the words somehow work.

WHAT EXCITES YOU ABOUT CASTING?

I really like actors. I admire the fortitude that it takes to walk into a stranger's office, having heard God knows what about them before you walk in, and then going into that office and basically stripping away to your emotions. I'm not so sure that I could do it and do it honestly, and yet that's what I ask of these people when they come in. If they're not being honest, you sort of dismiss them or you call them on it and try to get something better. I think it's exciting to see someone's words come to life. When you read a novel, you have in your mind a picture of what that character should be, and as you get further into the novel, you have your own little cast in your mind. I think it's fascinating to have someone totally against what you have in your mind come in and read the words and you realize, "Oh, my God! That's something that I didn't even see! That's wonderful."

Everybody has their own little cast in their mind, especially the producer, the director—and they're all different.

WHAT WOULD YOU CHANGE ABOUT THE PROCESS TO MAKE IT BETTER?

I wish there weren't so many egos involved—if the actor could walk in and give you what he has to give you and if the casting director did not pull any power trips on the actors. If both sides could realize that they need each other, that we're all there to get the best person for whatever reasons, it would prove much simpler. We all get too self-important. We're here to put a product on the screen. We're not curing any diseases or doing brain surgery. We're making people in Iowa laugh or look at a serious topic in a different way.

NOW THAT YOU'RE INDEPENDENT, HOW DOES YOUR PROCESS WORK—FROM GETTING A SCRIPT TO GETTING IT CAST?

On an episodic show, you get the script, and hopefully you have a chance to read it before you discuss it with the production staff. You send it out to Breakdown Services, and the agents submit. When I read a script, I always go through the people that I've held onto for one reason or another to see who might be right. Even though the breakdowns say written submissions only, you always get a day full of phone calls to weed through. I'm not offended by that. There's no way to stop it. Sometimes it depends on the person who's calling. There's a big difference in agents and managers in that respect. Some people are there because they really believe that a client is right, and some are there to get a job and a commission. Some don't know why they're there.

An agent calls and says, "Oh God, I'm so excited. Finally there's something on your show for so-and-so." I may disagree, but that's fine. That's somebody getting involved. Then you try to weed out the calls. "Oh, see so-and-so, they're perfect." "Why are they perfect?" "Well, they just are." "Well, why? Why do you believe in them?" "I just think you should meet them." You sort of smell a fish there. Don't waste my time. I usually give agents one or two shots, and if they are sending you people who are good, then I trust them the next time. Everybody deserves a shot. The most wonderful actor in the world may have come into town last night and went to dinner at Love's Barbecue. At the next table was an agent from a very small agency. The actor signed with that agency that night. Just because an agency is small doesn't mean that they can't still have a sense of what's good or what's bad. I think they deserve a shot.

HOW ACCURATE ARE THE BREAKDOWNS?

You do have control over that. Unless they're terribly swamped or you are, they call you and read the breakdown to you over the phone. If you have time, they will bring you a copy of it the next day and you can change or add to it, however you'd like. There are times that they'll leave out an age and you don't pick it up, and then everybody is calling to see how old so-and-so is, and that's regrettable.

WHAT HAVE YOU LEARNED FROM THE PEOPLE WHO TRAINED YOU AS A CASTING DIRECTOR?

When I went into casting, Joel Thurm and Karen Hendel taught me the most. Joel is one of the brightest casting people that I've met. He's someone that everyone has an opinion about, a strong opinion. They love him or they hate him. We've had our disagreements, but he knows his business and he's honest. Sometimes to the point of being blunt. I learned a lot about networks and how they work. Karen Hendel taught me how to recognize a real actor and not just a commercial person. She's a humanitarian and a wonderful judge of talent. Gail Eisenstadt, bless her soul, was terrific. She took her work very seriously, but she also said, "Come on, we've got to have some fun." And if that means in the middle of the afternoon, you've got to stop work and do something crazy, then you have to do that. All of those things have been very valuable to me. They've shaped my own beliefs. In turn, you hope that you can influence others.

WHAT ABOUT YOUR PET PEEVES?

I don't like name-droppers. I have difficulty with people who think they're more important than they are. I've had actors who've condescended to read for the producers come in five minutes before the reading to pick up the material, thinking they really didn't need to look at it, and give God-awful readings. I've worked with a group of producers who are fabulous. If someone comes in and has done eight features and gives a lousy reading, these producers will say, "We're sorry. We can't use you." They're not impressed by that stuff.

HOW IMPORTANT IS THE *ACADEMY PLAYERS DIRECTORY*? AND THE COMPUTERS AT SAG AND AFTRA? DO YOU USE THEM?

The *Directory* is very important. There's nothing more frustrating than to try to find an actor and they're not there and not listed with SAG, or they've moved agents and haven't bothered to call SAG and let them know.

THE NETWORK ATMOSPHERE IS INTIMIDATING. WHY BRING ACTORS IN BY THEMSELVES? WHY DON'T YOU BRING ACTORS IN PAIRS OR WITH THE PEOPLE WHO ARE ALREADY CAST?

Many times the stars won't do it. There are some wonderful actors out there who are intelligent enough to know that if that person is co-starring with them, it's sure as hell a lot smarter reading with them and having some input than it is to let other people just decide and show up on the set. Sometimes I pair people up if I've got a family that we're casting. When we have callbacks, we'll have the husband read with all the wives. It's better because you have an actual actor there reading. Often, it's just a matter of availability, as to whether they're willing to do it. I know SAG just passed a ruling on it. You have to have someone reading with the actors who is capable of reading. They're trying to get away from the casting director or the associate or the assistant with the monotone reading.

WHAT ABOUT THE ACTORS WHO GET BOXED INTO A CATEGORY? HOW DO THEY GET OUT OF THAT?

I think there comes a time when they have to refuse to go in on those roles. That's a decision between the actor and agent. It's true, a casting person will see someone do a role and say, "Oh, that's just who I need. I have a role just like that." And you'll have them in, which is not necessarily a good thing to do. I make a practice of having people in who are not right for the role. Oddly enough, when I take people to the producers for a role—and I've got a wild card—that's who they go with.

My production staff is wonderful that way. It doesn't work on every show. You couldn't get away with that on your "pretty" shows. You're either pretty and have a certain style about you or you're not hired. Our show deals with real people, so they want to keep it that way. But sometimes it's the agents who will call and say, "Excuse me, he's played Thug Number 3 eighteen times. Why can't he play Thug Number 3 for you?" And I'll say, "Because he's played Thug Number 3 eighteen times! I want someone different."

WHEN YOU PRE-READ AN ACTOR BEFORE TAKING HIM TO THE PRODUCER, DO YOU SUGGEST CHOICES THAT YOU THINK THE PRODUCERS ARE LOOKING FOR?

I may not tell them a lot about the role because I want to see what they bring to it. They may bring something to it that I didn't see.

As long as I'm the one at the bottom of the pole choosing who comes in, as long as they have entrusted me to do that, then I think it's fun to challenge their ideas for a role. Scripts come in written for thirty-five-year-old men. It's wonderful to say, "Where can I put a woman in here? Why couldn't this be a woman?" And bring them women and no men and have them say, "Oh, you've changed this, haven't you?" They're very accepting of that, and it works a lot of times. That's the only reason I would not tell an actor what they're looking for.

WHAT KIND OF JOB DOES THE ASSOCIATION OF CASTING DIRECTORS DO?

It's an infant organization. Bottom-line casting is a very important aspect of any production. We're lobbying to get recognition for the job that is done. How many times when an actor accepts an award do they mention, "Thanks to the casting person who brought me in," or to the agent who's been supporting him all this time or to the manager?

WHY DID YOU DECIDE TO GO INDEPENDENT?

At the network, there wasn't enough hands-on casting. Too much supervising, pulling strings from behind. I like to be down there doing it. I'm not a watcher. I like to play. Lori Openden, bless her heart, really pushed to get me this job because she believed in me. We remain very close friends. I consider her my mentor and I call her for advice on a regular basis. It was a very fortunate thing for me to get L.A. LAW. It has become a hit. Beyond being a popular show, it's also a critically acclaimed show.

HOW DO YOU GET VALIDATED FOR A JOB WELL-DONE?

There's really not enough good things I can say about Stephen Bochco, Gregory Hoblit, Terry Louise Fisher, and everyone else on the production staff. They have been more than generous with their praise. I can't tell you the number of phone calls and cards that I receive from actors saying, "Thank you for the break."

I got a phone call from a woman in New York City who just said, "I don't know who you are, and I know you don't know me, but I love your show. I just hunted you down and wanted to tell you that." You hang up the phone and your face lights up. It was nice, because someone took the time to do that.

WHAT DO YOU SAY TO THE ACTOR WHO HASN'T HAD A JOB IN SO LONG THAT HE'S THINKING OF LEAVING THE BUSINESS . . . OR HIS AGENT?

If you're not getting work, there's got to be a reason. You could be lousy and need to get out of the business and go into real estate! Maybe you just need to work a little more on your craft, take lessons, and audition for plays. Maybe you're trying to go from under-fives to leads on episodic television—and to do that you're going to have to turn down some under-fives. If you're not working a lot and are trying to make a major change, get out there and do a play. Keep yourself involved. Keep the energy flowing. Being seen—that's the actor's responsibility. It's also his responsibility to make sure his pictures are good and his résumés are updated. I don't think that you sit back and expect somebody to work for you and become a nuisance. Don't call on the phone every time with "Did I get any feedback? How did I do? Was I wonderful? Did they like me?" You did what you do. You have to trust that the people working for you are doing just that— working for you. An agent is there to get you work. It takes two to do what one used to do. Managers have become a very big force because agents no longer have time to maintain personal involvement with their clients. And actors, being the breed of people that they are, need that attention; therefore, they go to someone else to get it.

5. MARC HIRSCHFELD
INDEPENDENT CASTING DIRECTOR,
LIBERMAN/HIRSCHFELD; FORMER DIRECTOR
OF TALENT & CASTING, EMBASSY TV

I was born in Newark, New Jersey. I went to college at Syracuse University as a film and psychology major. I graduated in 1978 and came out to Los Angeles in 1979 and started working as a "gofer" for Embassy Television. I started in the casting office as a temp and enjoyed the work and meeting people. I acted in high school and so appreciate actors. I stayed at Embassy for seven and a half years, where I cast MARRIED WITH CHILDREN, 227 with Marla Gibbs, E/R with Elliott Gould, A.K.A. PABLO, SQUARE PEGS, IT'S YOUR MOVE, KIDS INCORPORATED. Those are the original series I've cast. Episodic casting includes: SILVER SPOONS, THE FACTS OF LIFE, WHO'S THE BOSS, THE JEFFERSONS, ONE DAY AT A TIME, DIFF'RENT STROKES. I worked on the Embassy film, THIS IS SPINAL TAP with Rob Reiner; the "Schoolbreak Special," BABIES HAVING BABIES directed by Martin Sheen; a movie-of-the-week called THE LANEL JEETERS STORY; THE FACTS OF LIFE GOES TO AUSTRALIA, and more pilots than I could ever mention. I received an Outstanding Achievement award in Daytime Casting for BA-BIES HAVING BABIES at the 3rd Annual Artios Award Ceremonies.

WHAT QUALITIES DO YOU LOOK FOR IN AN ACTOR?

A natural quality is the most important thing. That means not stagey or affected. I look for a warm, sincere, real quality to a performance. In comedy, there's the John Ritter school—his THREE'S COMPANY pratfalls. But bigger-than-life comedy can come out of a real base. I like for an actor to bring part of himself to the role. I'm surprised when I meet someone in a general interview and they're warm and funny, and then as soon as they start reading, this wall goes up. Something happens, and they either try to be a different person or try to disassociate themselves from the character. I cannot relate to it at all. They lose their sense of humor and the warmth. I don't understand it.

HOW SHOULD AN ACTOR READ YOUR RESPONSES?

An actor will come in and read for me. If I see something interesting, even if they're a little off what I'm looking for, but I get a sense that they've made some strong, interesting choices about a character that are not totally out in left field, and they seem to have an intelligent idea of what the character is or they touch on something, I will take them to the next step. I may give them a note, something to think about that may not be in the script, background on the character, and ask them to do all or part of the scene again. I give them additional information and try to lead them in the direction the producers want to go with the character. I avoid giving line readings. At the end of the reading, I say, "Thank you very much," and they leave. I will usually wait for an agent or manager to call me for feedback, which I am happy to give. If I think they've done something unusually spectacular or exciting or terrible in the audition, I'll let the manager or the agent know.

I had an actress in for a casting session once, and she was wearing a very short skirt and no underwear. After she left, the producers and I kind of looked at each other like, "Oh my God!" you know? And, "What was that about?" I called the agent afterwards and said, "I don't want it to go any further, but your client wasn't wearing any underwear. That was very odd." I let the agent deal with it the way he wanted. That's an extreme case. Another time I had an actress in to read for a part, and when she came in, she was arrogant and rude to me and the producers before the audition started. Just rude! She read and she was wonderful. We didn't go with her. We went with another actress who was equally as good but didn't come with all the excess baggage. I called the agent and said, "Listen, she couldn't have been meaner." He said, "Her father just died and they were very close. She was upset!" I accepted that. There was another role that came up and I said, "I'll have her in again." She came in, and the exact same thing happened. She was nasty and belligerent, a horrible person. She read and she was wonderful. When she left the room, the director said, "She would be great for the role because she's a terrific actress, but I'd hate like hell to have to work with her for a week!" So I called the agent and said, "Now look, the first time is fine. I understand it. But she's got some problems, and you'd better deal with them. This is why she didn't get the role. I want her to know that because she's a good actress." I will call an agent or manager with feedback like that. I'll also give positive feedback if I'm very excited about an actor or I've seen an incredible change or improvement in an actor. I'll call and give that kind of feedback as well.

Inappropriate behavior deserves a call to the agent or manager. I've heard of casting directors who tell everyone they did a brilliant performance, and then you never hear from them again. I will say, "Thank you very much," and reserve my opinion, especially if it's early on in the process, because I'm still searching for what I want in the role. My interpretation of what the character should be is cumulative. I'm looking for various interpretations. Three separate interpretations may be great. But one will be appropriate for this particular role. If I say, "Great job," and have only one of them back, the other two are asking, "Well, how come I didn't get a callback? I think I did a nice reading." If the agent calls me for feedback, I'll say, "He was terrific. I just didn't think he was right for this particular project, but I'll keep him in mind for something else."

In selecting people to take to the producers, I take people who have made separate and unique choices—all valid and special, but, giving my producer, writer, and director a range of choices. I think writers have a certain vision, a prototype for the role. They write for that. A lot of producers write stereotypes like "the bald-headed old codger." They have a vision of the role. I like to cast against type. I'll bring in the type that they want and a couple of alternatives. Almost inevitably, they will do a complete turnaround in the room because they will get excited by a person who is not their vision but is better than plugging into one of the stereotypes. Once the casting process starts, most producers throw away all those preconceived notions of the type they wanted when they start to see the range of possibilities. That's my job—to stimulate the process.

HOW DO YOU REMEMBER ALL THE PEOPLE YOU SEE?

Several ways. The *Academy Players Directory* is very useful. I have binders from various projects I've been working on with lists of the actors whom I've had in, whom I've met, and who've been suggested. I have picture and résumé books and general interview books categorized male/female and age range. I have videotapes. I also use agents as a resource. I have been working on a computerized file cabinet of actors whom I've met. I'm computerizing every actor I've ever met onto a data base—sex, race, age range, what city they live in, and any minor notes to stimulate my memory. "Met on this date for this project." So if I am looking for male, white actors from twenty to thirty, it gives me an absolute laundry list, everyone from Rob Lowe to John Doe. And they're all mixed together. I take that as a resource, and I search through and select from that laundry list who might be appropriate for this role. That system will never replace the personal contact, but it provides us with a data base that will allow us to avoid having things slip through. There are times I go "Damn!" afterwards. I forgot all about that person.

My system is very personal. The notes that I put in are things like "blonde-haired kid on FACTS OF LIFE." I may not remember the episode, but if I say that to myself, it'll trigger things. The computer would be similar to breakdowns for agents and managers.

A lot of actors seem intimidated by the fact that I'm becoming computerized. I can assure them that it is to their benefit. First of all, everyone is on that list and they're not differentiated. The beginning actor whom I've met is indeed next to the Robert DeNiros. The second thing is that it's a resource for me so I won't forget them. If I've met them on a general interview or seen them in a play or seen their tape, they're in there. It's like a big file cabinet.

IF AN ACTOR HAD TO CHOOSE BETWEEN YOUR DEFINITELY SEEING HIS TAPE OR YOU'RE GETTING TO MEET HIM PERSONALLY IN A GENERAL INTERVIEW, WHICH IS GOING TO HAVE THE MORE IMPACT ON YOU AND ON YOUR MEMORY OF HIM? IN OTHER WORDS, HOW IMPORTANT IS THAT TAPE?

Tape is very important. I've met actors, and I take a look at their résumés and they've done guest roles on this show and that show, and I'll say, "Geez, I'd love to see that episode," and they respond with, "You know, I never got around to getting that" or "I never got around to editing that together." I'm thinking to myself, "Why the hell not?" If that was a wonderful piece of work and a wonderful project, you'd be an idiot not to have a copy of it! Not only for professional reasons, but for your own personal use. I've hired actors without meeting them, just on the basis of their tape. I have both a 3/4-inch and 1/2-inch machine, and I use them constantly, as you can see by the box of tapes right there that I'm about to view. I don't think it can ever hurt you. It can only help. It's a great way for a casting director to see your work. I do general interviews, but to tell you the truth, after I meet with someone, I'll think "Gee, he's a real nice person, but I don't know exactly how I can use him." If I can see one of his tapes, that will give me a better idea of how he views himself and roles that are representative of his work. It should be of decent quality. I remember one actor's tape—it was the worst dub I've ever seen in my life! You couldn't see it, you couldn't hear it, it was not clear what was going on! It's important to have both formats (1/2-inch VHS and 3/4-inch). 3/4-inch is still the industry stan- dard. I saw one tape an actress had—but all the roles were her playing hookers! I've seen tape that was done in a studio—a monologue that was wonderful—and that's acceptable to me as well. It's important on a tape to identify who you are—put a card on the front of the tape with your picture on it and attach a picture and a résumé. Before the tape begins, show a still picture of the person represented and then their name underneath, especially if there are a lot of people in the scene! You should get a real sense of the character in the scene, but it shouldn't go on for a half hour!

WHAT ABOUT THE PICTURE AND RÉSUMÉ FIRST CATCHES YOUR ATTENTION?

The picture and the résumé are the most important tools the actor has. It's your calling card—a producer and casting director's first contact with you. I always encourage actors to have current pictures and résumés professionally done. Spend the money, even if the damn things cost $1,000, which is excessive! One job will pay for all the pictures and résumés you will ever have printed. It's an important investment. I look for personality in the picture; it comes through the eyes. I think actors should shop around. They should network with other actors, see their pictures, and go to several photographers and see their portfolios.

You shouldn't have an old résumé with a million things written on it; one or two recent things are fine. It shows me, "Gee, this guy is working." If you have a sloppy résumé with five typewritten things and the rest of it is all hand written and crossed off, and then there are typos—if you spell "Ambassy Television" instead of "Embassy" or "Peter Boners" instead of "Peter Bonerz," I mean, how closely did you work with him? I have pet peeves about misspelling and cover letters. I'll get cover letters all the time that go, "Dear Mr. Hirshfeld: I would love to appear in your series, DIFF'RENT STROKES." DIFF'RENT STROKES has been off the air for a year now, over a year. They saw my name at the end of the credits of a rerun, so they figure that the show is being done. If they don't have the wherewithal to know what's going on in the industry or to know that the show is no longer in production, I don't find them professional.

WHAT EXCITES YOU ABOUT CASTING AND WHAT ARE SOME OF YOUR PET PEEVES?

It excites me to put together an ensemble of actors who work well, and to see the range of choices that the actors make. Five different actors can come in and do a role five completely different ways. It's amazing to me and I find it very stimulating and exciting. I may read a scene 500 times. Then that 501st person comes in and makes a choice that is completely unique— one you never saw before or envisioned.

Producers, production companies, casting directors, and the writer all share a vision of what a project is going to be. It comes out of a lot of meetings and discussions about what the series or film is about. It can be too many cooks when the network gets involved. The less network interference, the better. They're an important partner because they have certain goals, but I think that they can be destructive to a project if their involvement is more arbitrary than collaborative. They have an investment in the project. I've found that the more of a laissez-faire attitude a network has, the more exciting a project can be. The network will sometimes give notes on a script that is weak, and it will make that script stronger. They can be a valuable contributor to the process. The network trusts the producers' vision, and if the network buys that project on the basis of that vision, they should say, "Okay, we're excited about your vision, we share it. Now go and do it." The network should have enough trust to let them move forward with it.

WHAT ABOUT PET PEEVES WITH ACTORS?

Actors should get the sides early if they're available. Most of the time, they are. Five out of ten times, the actor shows up five minutes before the interview, never having seen the material. They don't know what the character is about or the project. They have done absolutely no homework. They should get the script early and know their lines and the character. They should know the names of the casting director and the producers, what sort of things they've done in the past. It's going to give the actor a sense of the kind of comedy or drama these producers are involved in. Take the time to research and find out a little about the project.

Tardiness on the part of the actor is hardly ever an excuse. Always bring a picture and résumé. I don't think it's necessary for an actor to dress for the role. We had someone who came in recently for the role of a security guard and he had the badge and the little hat on, all that stuff. Producers resent that and think, "Oh God, I didn't have the imagination to see you could be a security guard. You had to lay it out." An actor should only indicate through his appearance the nature of the part. He doesn't have to dress for it. If you're going to play a blue-collar workman, you shouldn't come in a three-piece suit. You should come in a pair of jeans and something casual. You don't have to come in with the "Little Joe's Garage" thing tacked on and greasy hands. And believe me, I've gotten that before! If you're reading for a businessman, come in a suit with a tie. Something that indicates, but doesn't beat us over the head with it.

After you've finished the reading, do not go, "Oh, Jeez, that was terrible. Can I do it again?" That makes me crazy. If I want you to do it again, I'll ask. The thing to do beforehand is to say, "Listen, I've made a choice as far as the way I see the role. If you think I'm going in the wrong direction, tell me and I'll stop and readjust." That gives the casting director or the producer the option. First of all, they know that you're an intelligent actor. You've made creative choices about the role. You are directable. It gives them the option to direct you. When you go, "Jeez, can I do that again?" it shows me that you haven't made any clear choices and you are insecure about the choices you have made. I don't want to hire an actor like that, because if you're down on the floor, there are going to be rewrites. I want to know that you are confident enough as an actor that you can take those rewrites or whatever they throw at you. I want to know that you are a secure and confident individual, not easily flustered.

WHAT HAVE YOU LEARNED FROM THE PEOPLE WHO HAVE TRAINED YOU AS A CASTING DIRECTOR?

Eve Brandstein trained me. She taught me that it's really important to treat the people you come in contact with as human beings. It becomes less of a job, less of an ordeal, if you enjoy what you're doing. There is real value to the relationships that you cultivate and the people you come in contact with. Actors, producers, and directors all appreciate respect. They'll look forward to working with you if you treat them with some decency. I've had actors do favors for me on a number of occasions where I've asked them to—an actor of considerable stature do a small but important role in one of my series. It may only be one line, but it's an important joke or an important set-up. They've done it for me because they like to work with me, Embassy, or the producers. Relationships are important in this business. I'm not talking about false relationships, I'm talking about real relationships that have some sort of basis, not this Hollywood bullshit. What you put out there comes back to you. I don't want to work with an actor whom I don't like. Life is too short. I want to work with nice people! This cast that we have now on MARRIED WITH CHILDREN is the nicest group of people that I've ever put together into an ensemble. They go whale watching, bowling together. Why go with an actor who will make their lives, my life, and the producers' lives miserable? It's just my philosophy of life. Otherwise, I'm not going to enjoy coming in to work.

HOW DO YOU GET VALIDATED FOR A JOB WELL-DONE?

If the show is a success, most of the credit goes to the producers. When the project begins, it's completely collaborative between the writer and the casting director. If you have a strong script and a lousy cast, the show will not go forward. However, a strong cast can elevate a mediocre script. Within this company, sensitive producers are aware of what good casting does for a show and will acknowledge that. Like most jobs, it's self-satisfaction. Incidentally, the way I validate actors is by treating them as human beings. That would seem to be all you have to do. That's all I have to do for them to go, "Oh, my God, you're a really nice person." Apparently, some casting directors out there are less than kind to actors, which I find amazing. If you treat them like human beings and not like so many cattle, and you take an interest in them, I think they appreciate that. Your enthusiasm for them will translate to the project. That support is important, and I find they will return the kindness. Occasionally, I'll get an appreciative actor who thanks me.

HOW CAN AN ACTOR PUT HIMSELF IN CHARGE OF HIS CAREER?

I think actors need to focus in on their goals. They need a game plan. They can't just go blindly. If they're new actors, that means finding a teacher to study with, networking and finding out who's out there, auditing a lot of classes, and deciding who they work with. They have to decide to invest the time, money, and energy, both physical and emotional, in their career. That means not sitting by the phone but getting out there, being aggressive without being obnoxious, sending out pictures and résumés, investing the money to get professional pictures and résumés. Getting involved with theatre in L.A. is becoming more and more the way to be seen by the industry—deciding that this is going to be a course of action and not just sitting back and letting things happen to you. Being in control of your life.

6. CARO JONES
INDEPENDENT CASTING DIRECTOR,
FEATURES

I went to college for a year, and then I came to New York to train as a singer. I sang opera and with symphonies and then toured with OKLAHOMA for a year. I started casting with the U.S. STEEL HOUR and was with them for six years. After that, I did some independent films and came to Los Angeles where I worked for Filmways and then became an independent casting director. After that, I had a three year stint at Paramount doing a lot of television. I started my film career as an independent with the original ROCKY. I've done SAVE THE TIGER with John Avildsen, CROSS CREEK with Bob Radnitz, and WHEN YOU COMING BACK, RED RYDER with Martin Scorsese. I also did KARATE KID I and KARATE KID II. I cast CAN'T BUY ME LOVE, which was done on $1.7 million and has grossed $30 million so far.

WHAT DO YOU LOOK FOR IN AN ACTOR?

Charisma. Colors. Knowledge of what they're doing. The ability to probe a character and discover all the different colors that are there. Because I work in feature films, I look for the ability to sense a beginning, middle, and an end. I don't want to see the character all on one level. Those qualities make your auditions very incisive. We're always looking for that special, wonderful, exciting, charismatic quality that signifies a star. It's indefinable, but you sense if it's there.

WHAT'S IMPORTANT TO YOU IN A RÉSUMÉ?

I look at film credits first on a résumé because I'm working in film. Then I look at television and then theatre and training.

Training is very important to me, especially *where* people have trained.

HOW DO YOU MANAGE TO REMEMBER THE NAMES AND FACES OF ALL THE ACTORS YOU SEE?

There are two answers to that. One, if they make an impression, you don't forget them. If they have talent, you'll never forget them. Secondly, if I'm feeling problematic about how many I'm seeing at once, I make notes and refer to them. I keep files and interview sheets from every production we do. They're all on file and in books.

IF AN ACTOR COMES IN FOR A CALLBACK, SHOULD HE DRESS THE SAME WAY AND READ THE PART THE SAME WAY HE DID THE FIRST TIME, OR SHOULD HE CHANGE BOTH TO GIVE YOU A DIFFERENT WAY OF LOOKING AT HIM?

That's up to the actor. If the actor feels comfortable in the clothes that he wore and if he has a callback, obviously something was right about it. I wouldn't arbitrarily select that as something he has to do, but if he is comfortable and feels that's part of the character that he worked out before he came in, then fine. Do that. In answer to the second question, retain everything you had in the first interview or audition and add to it. Because there was something there that made them call you back, but the reason you're coming back is so they can see more. So now you have to give more.

HOW DO YOU KNOW WHAT THAT "MORE" IS? HOW SHOULD AN ACTOR KNOW THAT HE'S NOT CHANGING THE WHOLE THRUST OF WHERE IT'S GOING?

If you're an actor, you've made choices, so you know what you did. You can try to find out from the director areas in which something should be added to illuminate the character further. It doesn't hurt to ask questions, especially of the director.

SHOULD AN ACTOR ASK QUESTIONS IN THE READING, AND WHAT KIND OF QUESTIONS SHOULD HE ASK?

If he's going to be working on a picture, he's going to have a million questions to ask the director. That's part of the process of making a picture. He should start by establishing that rapport. Frequently, directors will ask what you think of the script. If it's not a very good script, say, "It's fine," and don't go into it. But, if it's a script you're really interested in doing, then you should say, "I found this interesting, but what's going to happen here? And why?" Discuss it intelligently. It's all part of probing for the character.

HOW CAN AN ACTOR READ YOUR RESPONSES IF YOU'RE PLEASANT AND JUST SAY "THANK YOU?'

That depends on who is doing the talking. I had people say, "You are wonderful! You are brilliant!" They go all out and they don't mean one word of it. They just feel they want to send the actor off feeling good. Then I have other people who will say, "That was nice. I liked it. Bye." The actor will go out the door and they'll say, "He was brilliant! Where did you find him?" Do you know what I mean? You must consider that it is only one person's opinion. Your ability to see humor in someone may not be as developed as someone else's. I would tell an actor two things: If he feels he's done a good job, as good as he can do in a reading situation, then he should say, "Thank you very much for the opportunity," and leave—accept whatever they say. If he feels that he did a poor reading, got off on the wrong track and really blew it, I think he should say, right then and there, "I really felt that wasn't what I wanted to do and it was bad. May I please do it again?" Don't go out the door and shoot yourself when you get around the corner. Ninety-nine times out of a hundred, they'll say okay.

AS A CASTING DIRECTOR, DO YOU HAVE A PREFERENCE FOR CERTAIN AGENCIES BECAUSE OF A RELATIONSHIP YOU MAY HAVE WITH THEM?

That would not influence my choices. But it's like having friends. You have your friends, and I have my friends. Some people are easier to deal with than others or make for a more pleasant association. Again, that would never have an effect on my choice of talent or seeing talent. I feel that everybody is in this because they love and want to find talent and want to give you the best possible person they represent. Therefore, you owe them the respect of carefully considering their submission. I have found, through the years, that you never truly know where or from which source a brilliant talent is going to come. I firmly believe that.

IF YOU, AS A CASTING DIRECTOR, ARE INTERVIEWING PEOPLE AND YOU CANNOT BRING THE RIGHT PEOPLE TO THE PRODUCERS, WOULD THEY FIRE YOU?

I think it does happen. Sure.

DOES THAT MEAN YOU DIDN'T DO YOUR JOB AS A CASTING DIRECTOR OR THAT YOU DIDN'T UNDERSTAND WHAT THEY WANTED?

That's a hard question to answer because there are all these temperaments involved. Generally, your best situation is where the director or producer has asked for you and has a lot of respect for your opinion. That makes working so much easier. If you're thrown into a network situation where somebody has brought you in and the people there don't know you, you'll be working uphill. They may be critical of your choices because they don't know you. To trust you means they have to trust that final decision, and if it falls through, the boulder rolls down hill. So while your choices might be very good, they might not trust your judgement because they're insecure in some respect.

HOW MUCH INFLUENCE DO YOU REALLY HAVE?

Depends. You're a catalyst between talent and buyers. I think in certain instances you have a lot of influence. In others, you don't.

It depends on who you're working for and how much they respect what you do.

WHAT DO YOU DO WHEN YOU GET A BAD SCRIPT?

Figure out how I can make it better by booking actors who make you forget what it is they're doing. That's really rough because the really good actors usually read it and don't want to do it. That happens a lot. But it's a great challenge. I've done films for people where critics have said that the actors are so superior that you forgot it really wasn't a very good script.

**BEYOND THE USUALS—TALENT, HARD WORK, ETC.—
IS THERE SOMETHING SPECIAL THAT MAKES FOR A
SUCCESSFUL ACTOR?**

Learn to be an agreeable person to have around. In the twenty-five years that I've spent in this profession, the people that are around years later, with staying power, are people that you like to be with, and work with. I see it more and more. They're not necessarily the most super-gifted, but they're people who know their craft and are very pleasant to be around. Bring vitality and joy to your job because almost everybody in this business is in it because they love it. And if they see that quality in a young person, it's irresistible. It really is.

7. ELIZABETH LEUSTIG
INDEPENDENT CASTING DIRECTOR,
FEATURES

I was born in Troyes in France. My father was in the Army, so we moved around. We spent five years in Morocco, five years in Germany, and then came back to France. That's when I started cutting out pictures of actors and actresses. My mother caught me and threw everything away. But I had my little secret way of putting folders in groups, and I'd hide the pictures in between my notebooks in school so my mother wouldn't find them. I went to The Sorbonne to study German because I was going to be a translator. In my family, everyone speaks German. I was always attracted by the movies, and I saw a film by Godard in which there was a girl who was a translator in Rome, and she spoke French, German, Italian, and English in the film, so that's why I was going to become one. I got involved with Jean Luc Godard because he was making social movies. Since I was a student, I was a liaison between him and the students. We distributed the little shorts, which were to be used for discussions. You'd watch them, and then you'd talk about what were the social problems of France. They were a great bunch. I loved the way they lived and thought—the freedom. I moved to the States just because I wanted to see a foreign country. When I was in L.A., I met my husband and we moved to New York where he was an executive. He decided to drop it all and go study acting with Lee Strasberg, which he did for three years. I was able to really follow the whole process and audit some of the classes as well as attend the rehearsals in the Actor's Studio for the plays. So little by little all these signals were put into my life, especially the desire to be in that environment.

I always loved movies and found that I understood more than I ever suspected about them. We moved to L.A. and I went to work at the Los Angeles Actors Theatre as assistant to the producer. The last few months that I was working in the theatre, I saw APOCALYPSE NOW and I thought, "I want to go work with that guy." I quit the theatre and decided to go to a casting seminar that Mike Fenton was having for actors. I thought, "Okay, it's not for me, but here and there I'll be able to ask a few questions." Jennifer Schull was one of the people he invited, so after the talk I went to Jennifer and I told her that I would love to work as a volunteer in casting. She took my phone number and my name, and three weeks later I hadn't heard anything, and I saw a flyer that said they were having open calls to create the extra casting at Zoetrope. I called Barbara Johnson, who was in charge of putting this together, and volunteered and she told me to come in the next day. Jennifer was there and said, "That's the girl I was telling you about," and that's how I started. And after two months of volunteering, Jennifer said "That's enough. Now you have to start getting paid." Barbara left and Susan Landell had been hired two weeks before I arrived on the scene, so she and I took over as extra casting directors on ONE FROM THE HEART. Then Suzie left, and I worked on alone until we all got loaned out to FRANCES. Jennifer would give me small parts to cast in her movies, so by the time I got to FRANCES, I had twenty-five parts to cast and was able to suggest whomever I wanted to for the leads. I had the extra casting to do, too. That was my journey into main casting. When Zoetrope closed, Jennifer Schull, Janet Hirshenson, and Jane Jenkins formed a casting company and asked me to join them as their casting associate; so I went with them, worked with them for two years, and then

*went on my own. The films I've worked on the last
year or two include GLEAMING THE CUBE, THE
BEAR, SHAG, JIMMY REARDON, SWEET LIES,
CRITTERS, HONEYMOON, DEFENSELESS, CHECK-
ING OUT, SCENES FROM THE CLASS STRUGGLE IN
BEVERLY HILLS, DANCES WITH WOLVES, as well
as a few European projects.*

WHAT QUALITIES DO YOU FIND APPEALING IN ACTORS YOU'VE SEEN OVER THE LAST COUPLE OF YEARS?

I like honesty and passion and commitment. All kinds of things
contribute to your personality and your creativeness. So that's on
a personal level of growing. Then I think it's important to go with
a good agent; and if you're going to have a manager, you should
go with someone who is in sync with you in terms of how they
see what you want to accomplish, the kind of work you want to
do. I think it's important to go after the quality of the material.
The money should be number two.

I also look for intelligence in actors, someone who is sharp
and committed. Talent is obviously important. To me, talent is
being able to make people feel. When I come out of a movie or
play and I've been through something emotional, then to me
that's talent. (Obviously, I'm not talking about coming out of a
play angry because I saw a lousy show. I'm talking about feeling
fulfilled, satisfied.)

HOW ABOUT ANY OTHER AREAS IN TERMS OF RESPONSIBILITY?

Punctuality is important. It makes an impression on the producer
and director. If you don't show up for the interview on time,
they're going to wonder if you're going to show up on time at the
set, and they can't afford that waste of money. Another thing that
is pretty important is that the actor not be impossible to be with.
Every time I cast, some of my suggestions are rejected because
they say, "He's too much trouble." That keeps you from getting
the part.

HOW DO YOU FEEL ABOUT STUDYING?

I think it's very important. I think you've got to really go for the best teachers because you can learn bad habits from less talented teachers. But I also think that studying is not only going to class. I think it can be taking a trip somewhere in the desert so you can listen to yourself and grow and learn about something else. It's opening different senses.

WHAT ARE THE MARKS OF A GOOD TEACHER IN YOUR MIND?

If the teacher makes you understand the process that helps you get to an emotion that you can communicate. Teachers give you insights into how to get to the places you have to get at. I've done cold reading workshops, and I think I was trying to make them see the values that could be in that scene that they would have to focus on and go for. A lot of actors didn't realize what was in the text. You have to be able to understand what a writer has written and what are the values, emotions involved, what is going on in the human being. There are teachers who will help you get there once they've clarified to you what could be the potential of the scene and all the nuances of it.

HOW DO YOU MANAGE TO REMEMBER ALL THE PEOPLE THAT YOU SEE?

I take notes. Somebody will just strike me and then it's in my head. I have a notebook for the movie, and I take notes of all my meetings. After an actor leaves, I write a few lines, things that have to do with physical appearance as well as their energy. I used to just note physical things when I first started. Now I need to know the kind of temper and energy a person has.

For example, Donna Mitchell is an actress who I saw for JIMMY REARDON, and it was the first time I read her. I brought her back in on GLEAMING THE CUBE because my notes said, "Forties, brunette, beautiful woman, blue eyes, intelligent, reading very good understanding of all the nuances of the character, soft-spoken but can also get firm. Always with a feeling that she cares for you. She has a certain warmth; even if she gets tough, you know she's a person who could be a help. You don't have to be threatened by her." These are the kinds of things I write.

It's taken a while to evolve my note taking. When I first started, they were not obvious to me. I keep all my cast lists on the plays I see. I have another notebook where I keep the cast list and the bios on the actors I like. Every movie that I see, I write down in my book the cast, the production company, the director, and the stars. I really love this. I wouldn't do it if I didn't love it, because it's all consuming.

I also have a big file cabinet in my home of pictures as well as boxes and boxes in my kitchen and in my bedroom. I have a few in my car, and if you look in the bathroom I have about five of them! So I keep boxes. Now I also have another kind of book. The book of lists. On my lists I've got different categories: leading men, leading women, comedians, minorities, Europeans, musicals, characters, young, middle-age, older. The lists are important because I look at them before every movie. I have the *Academy Players Directory,* which I think everybody should be in with the right, up-to-date picture. It should be a picture that looks like you—not glamorized. The purpose is to get the best person, and all this information I get should help to gear me toward the right person.

That goes back to responsibility of an actor. He's not just paying the $45 to make his agent happy. He's going into a book that hopefully is going to be seen by me or a producer. I think it would be wonderful if everybody was in it because then it would be the ultimate source. I know everybody isn't in it. This year I am shocked by the number of people I am looking for who are not in it. I go to SAG, and SAG is not up-to-date, and I lose people that way. I lose track of people. The first place we look for somebody is in the book, and after that it's SAG, and if he's not in SAG, we ask our contacts. And after that we try AFTRA. I have to try to remember, "Where did I see him?" You have to be a detective. When I am making lists of suggestions for specific parts for specific movies, I'll go through the book. Maybe I'll just need three names, but if you're one of those three names and you end up with a part, you will have been happy to have been in the book.

IF AN ACTOR COMES IN FOR A CALLBACK SHOULD HE DRESS AND READ THE SAME WAY HE DID THE FIRST TIME?

I think it all depends on the part that's being cast. If the part has anything to do with a certain look, if the actor dressed right the first time around, then he should come back the same way. If it's something that doesn't have a lot to do with clothing or make-up, I don't give a damn. I'm more for the core. But there are a few times when we need to see the shape of the person—most of the time it's a girl. If she walks in and I need to see her shape because she'll be in tight pants in the movie or there will be remarks about how good-looking she is, then obviously she should be good-looking. If she comes to me and she's in a tent dress, then obviously I'll tell her I need to see another picture of her. If she comes to me in the sexy thing they do now, you know, with the leggings, and I see it, and the part requires that, then that's the way she should come back.

HOW ABOUT THE READINGS?

If the essential qualities of the character were put across to me in the audition and I call them back, that's because I want those same qualities to be in there on the callback. When the actor comes and does a reading for me, what I like is commitment. If they commit, even if they go after the wrong values, if I see that this is an intelligent actress who has made a choice that could be valid but does not fit in with my director's point of view, but I see she went for it and did a job that was interesting for me, then I will have her read it again. I will be likely to say, "Okay, those are the qualities I would like you to do when I bring you back for the director." If they hit it right away, I'll probably not tell them because I guess I assume that they will do it that way.

I had hired an actor once, and I saw him a year or two later in a play. He was very good. A year after that, I brought him back to my director because I knew his work, so there was no reason for me to check him out. When I brought him in, he was drunk. I will never call that guy again. It's looks as if I don't know my actor. If someone is going to do something fairly daring (and here I'm talking basically about behavior), then I would like to know before, because I know the director or the producer better than the actor does, and they may be receptive or they may not. If they're not, then I would like to know before and have a chance to stop it if it's not what I want.

Somebody sat on my lap for the director. The part was going to be like that in the movie, but it was going to be a man and the girl came in and right in front of the director she sat on my lap. I'm fairly shy, so I was totally uncomfortable, and I think there is no way that that didn't come across. And I would have liked to have known before, because if it is something that is going to invade someone else's territory, I like to be alerted. Some people can be receptive and others cannot. If I bring people to the director, it's because I believe they could do a good job. Every time I bring an actor or actress in, I want that person to get the job. Obviously, I have to bring in more and more, but I'm always trying to side with the actor or the actress. Therefore, if they're going to do something that removes me a little bit from it, I like to know.

WHAT'S INAPPROPRIATE BEHAVIOR TO YOU?

Rudeness is number one. It's a collective effort and we need everybody's cooperation.

HOW SHOULD AN ACTOR READ YOUR RESPONSES?

If they're good, I will tell them. I'll say "That was great, I really liked your reading. I want to bring you back." If they don't do a good reading, then I'll say "Thank you. We'll see what happens. I'll talk to my director and we'll see what happens." If I give a positive compliment, it means I was impressed. But I'm not going to tell them they're bad if they're bad. With agents I'm a lot more open. Because it is removed. I'd say "Honestly, she did a lousy reading." There is a big agent in town on the last film I was doing, I saw his girl twice, and he called me. I said, "You know, I think she has to develop her acting." And he said to me "She was just offered a lead. I'm going to make you eat your words." I said "Fine, I'd be delighted. But honestly I can only give you my feeling, and I feel that she's not an actress yet. I'd like you to prove me wrong because the girl is lovely and beautiful and I would love her to be able to act."

With most agents, I have a nice enough rapport that I can tell them what I feel. If they scream at me, then I may not have a tendency to tell them what's on my mind. Because I don't want to be screamed at for nothing. I usually listen to it, but there are not many people who scream at me. There are a few.

WHEN YOU'RE IN A READING, DO YOU ALLOW YOURSELF TO BECOME EMOTIONALLY INVOLVED?

I can't escape it! Barbara Williams can tell you. She was the girl in THIEF OF HEARTS. It wasn't too successful a movie, but she can tell you I was crying at the end of her reading. Kathleen Lloyd came in on TABLE FOR FIVE for the part that eventually went to Millie Perkins. Fortunately, I was not the only one crying. The writer was crying with me. We both were sniffling. It's great when you do it. I'm always embarrassed to cry, but at the same time that's what I'm looking for if it's a dramatic part. I love it because that's what they're supposed to accomplish.

DO YOU THINK IT'S IMPORTANT FOR AGENTS AND MANAGERS TO OBTAIN FEEDBACK FOR THEIR CLIENTS?

Yes I do. Because I feel that we're all after the same thing, which is how to make it so that actor or actress gets a better handle on his or her career. If the agent and the manager are on one side of the coin, I'm on the other side. I may know something they never get to see. So I think it's very important that we are able to give the criticism to the agent, so he can relay it to the actor and, therefore, work on improving things. But that also requires that the agent or manager are interested, and not all of them are. As the years go by, I realize that you are on the same wavelength with a certain crowd of people, and those are the ones I'm more interested in working with. They are the ones with whom I'm more inclined to share information so that their clients can learn and they grow from it.

WHAT DO YOU DO WITH A BAD SCRIPT?

It depends if I need money or not!

HOW DO YOU HANDLE ONE IF YOU GET ONE?

It's very difficult. I usually say "I don't get it and I would not be comfortable dealing with it." There is material that I would not be comfortable with. That's the hardest thing to say. I am not comfortable with a dumb script. If it's totally dumb and it's being made for the basest reasons, then I say, "This is not the kind of material that I'm comfortable with." I may also know that the director who started the project was someone who had some intelligence, but then he got fired, so someone else took over and it went nowhere. It went in a direction that I'm less happy with.

There are some things that I just cannot do. Recently I was approached with a script, and I found the women in it were presented completely as sex objects and nothing else. Nothing else. Everytime a woman appeared, it was only to show the nipples through the wet T-shirt. I was not interested. But fortunately, the producers were intelligent and nice, so that when I met with them, I told them what I resented about the script, and because they had been so involved in the rewrite of another aspect of the script, this had been overlooked. They thanked me for pinpointing it to them, and were considering changing it. The sleazy ones are harder to deal with.

WHAT EXCITES YOU ABOUT CASTING?

The fact that you are really creating a moving painting which you later refine. What excites me the most is that as you refine the character, it's a collaborative process with your director, with your producer, with the writer. I'm part of this creative process of understanding and sometimes refining what this movie is saying, what this character is about. You really dissect the qualities of the characters. Sometimes you get several actors, and each of them will have something different because they're all unique. You go into this discussion of what is most important. What do you want to accomplish in your story? So I'm really a part of the build-up of the picture in terms of the human elements, and to me it's these human elements that become super important. Filmmaking is a complex thing, but you cannot do a great movie without wonderful actors, so I have a big responsibility. I hope people will listen to me. They don't always. So really you build up the whole emotional texture to a movie and I think it's wonderful. You're part of a puzzle.

WHAT WOULD YOU CHANGE ABOUT THE PROCESS?

The part that bugs me the most is the cheating in deal making. I would like it if people were more honest because my idea of a good deal is a deal that's fair to both. To me that's the most painful part of the job because you stop dealing with the creative side. I've worked with someone who thinks a good deal is a deal where he's going to squeeze it to discount prices. That's not my idea of a good deal. I've had the other side where an agent will be asking for an outrageous amount and doing a star trip on people when it's totally ridiculous. I have agents who cheat. They'll give you the wrong quote. I had an agent recently where I made a deal, and then I sent a memo that reflected the deal made, and then I sent a contract which reflected it. Nobody ever lifted a phone, a finger, or gave me a call. The thespian reported to location, and two days before that person was going to shoot, the contract comes back and there's an addition—an addition that I could never have given. This was a particular point I would never have given since it never even existed in my territory of possibilities. So I called the agent and was told, "Yes, you gave it to me." And I told him, "No, I couldn't." And he said, "Yes, you gave it to me." And I know I couldn't. I couldn't have. And I'm very careful; I take great notes because I know how important it is. And then

I said, "Well, I sent you a deal memo. How come you didn't pick up a phone?" "Well, we thought it was a typo." "A typo that's a deal breaker?!" Because that's what I'm told, it's a deal breaker. "Well, I just thought it was a typo!" And I said, "You have my contract and it said exactly the same thing, and you still aren't picking up a phone?" "Well, we thought it was understood." Now I know that I'm being bullshitted. My producer is being bullshitted into a situation where it's basically too late to replace the actor or actress. They've gotten into a position that's a power position that's unfortunately too costly to us and we have to give in. Now that kind of bullshit to me is in a world I don't like to live in. The result of it is that both my producer and myself have been advised by our lawyer to avoid that agency, and therefore, their clients are going to lose jobs. So to me that's the worst because I think it should never get there. They got a little something more than we could give them for this particular picture, but we are all in it in the long run. They've lost a lot more than they've gained.

WHAT HAVE YOU LEARNED FROM THE PEOPLE YOU'VE TRAINED WITH AS A CASTING DIRECTOR?

Jennifer Schull is a fantastic teacher because she's always courteous, attentive, fair, very honest, thorough, and committed. I was super lucky to start with her. I think she's fantastic. Best training I could get. Jane and Janet were nice follow-ups. We all went to the same school with Jennifer. So there was a great group atmosphere. Jennifer had to go to Columbia, so I went on with Jane and Janet who were open to me getting more and more involved and taking more and more responsibilities.

HOW DO YOU GET VALIDATED?

If my actor or actress does a great job in the movie, that's how it happens. I like to feel that I can go to sleep feeling I did a good job. So if I go see a movie and my actors are doing the job, when I'm leaving the film and thinking, "They did a good job," that's where it's at.

IS IT OKAY WHEN AN ACTOR BRINGS YOU SOMETHING?

It's wonderful, but I would never want anyone to think it's a bribe. But it's wonderful! Because you know when they do that, that you've also added something to them in terms of the feeling in their life. Usually one or two people will do that every movie. And I tell you it feels great every time. Because you know the person was happy. The kind of gifts I don't like are those pads of papers, notepads, with a picture of the actor and the name and the phone number on them. That I don't like because I feel that that is bribery. That's pushing. I like a gift that comes from the heart. If it's buying your way in, then no, I'd rather you not send me any gift because you get exactly the opposite from me. If I get a notepad that has your picture and phone number and your name on it, I won't call you. Because something is creepy about the method. It may work with some other people. You should just know with me you shouldn't do it because I don't like it. Or pencils that have your name on them. I don't like something that's a tool to advertise yourself being given as if it were a present.

WOULD YOU REFUSE TO SEE AN ACTOR AGAIN BECAUSE OF PAST POOR PERFORMANCE? HOW DOES AN ACTOR GET OUT OF A CATEGORY HE'S GOTTEN BOXED INTO WITH YOU?

I am aware that there is typecasting happening. We all succumb to it. If anyone tells me he's been typecast, I will give him a shot at reading something else unless he's totally the wrong type for it, or I need a real WASP G.I. and the guy is ethnically very obvious, or I need a short, short guy because it's a poignant story and someone is suggesting a 6'2" guy, then I will say no. Otherwise, I hope I would be open to give it a shot. A past performance that was lousy, it's harder for me to forget. I have prejudices. Cathy Lee Crosby had done those animal shows, she was more a personality than an actress, so she was an easy person to have prejudices against, easy to dismiss as an actress. Her agent bugged me so much that I thought I've got to get her in. I told my director—and fortunately my director was open enough—I said

"Look, this agent is bugging me. I've got to get rid of this. Would you mind if we read her together?" He said "Okay, if you would like." I said "Yes, I would. It would make my life easier!" And we did and she was excellent. I was ready to go with my prejudices, but she did a wonderful dramatic reading. Now if I'm asked to bring her in, I can go totally honestly to my director and say "Look, she did a very good reading for me." It took pushing from the agent, and I'm glad he pushed me. I knew her from that animal show—as a beautiful woman with a body and not as an intelligent actress. I'm glad that I gave in to the agent because the girl did a fantastic job with us. She didn't get the job for a totally different reason, but she did a great scene.

TALK ABOUT READINGS.

I think that readings are essential for casting directors. When we go to directors or producers suggesting people, we have to feel fairly confident about their abilities. It's the basis of our credibility when we go to the director and we say, "This guy can do the job." I've had cases where you're dealing with young people, and the agent has this idea that the actor or the actress should go straight to the director. Any 16-, 17-, 18-, 19-year old . . . it's not like there's a huge amount of work around on which to judge. I've had cases where I could see nothing of the work, and the agent was pressing like hell for me to go straight to the director. I think it's bullshit. I said no. Sometimes, too late, the agent gives in. I think that any casting director should have the "right" to read a person. I think that if you are an actor, you should always be available to read because it's a sample of your work. I would hope that the mentality of the young people would be towards sharing and making people know of their ability, rather than playing political games that have to do with getting to the producer and overstepping the casting director. I had the case recently of a kid who was all of twenty-one, and I was not allowed to have him read for me. I said, "Sorry, I'm not going to bring him in." But as soon as I gave the part to someone else, miraculously, I'm allowed to see the kid. Fortunately, he ended up with the part because the first deal didn't go through. I mean,

I just don't understand his behavior. He could have had the part to start with. He didn't have to wait three or four weeks for the deal to fall through with the other kid if I had just been allowed to see him. But I am not going to give in to someone trying to bulldoze me when I'm trying to have a certain integrity in my work and my director is hiring me and my producer is hiring me on the basis of my opinion and my taste. I read articles by casting directors being too young in this town for the tastes of a number of people. Okay, we're too young. Agreed. Therefore, obviously, there is some information we still don't have yet. I would just hope that the actors are always willing to read, first of all, because it's their business, and secondly, if they don't do it, then how can I go with any confidence and talk about it?

I'm for the actors. When they're in my office, they can ask me any question they want. Anything I can do to help, I will. Because if they do a good job, I look good. It's just that simple. If I bring in five actors and all of them are different, but they are all valued options, then I've got a producer and a director telling me, "Great!" When they go in front of my bosses, I only want them to perform well. Because of the power-tripping in this town, there is erosion to the availability of readings. I would hope that actors would still be willing to do them. It's important to have the experience of reading because you've got to deal with your nerves. I have one actress in mind. Excellent actress. She's been on stage for the last six or seven years I've been in town. I've seen her on stage, but she gets so few auditions that every time it's blown, almost every time. I bring her in because I've seen her on stage, and I know what she can do. But she blows it in the damn auditions because she's got such nerves that it overcomes her. Well, if she were used to coming in, more and more, eventually she would get rid of those nerves. She could adjust to it. She could develop a certain way to deal with it. So I think it only helps the actors in the long run. They also refine their skills by being in the audition situation, and I think reading for casting directors could almost be seen as a rehearsal for reading for the directors and the producers. If you looked at it that way, then it's a great opportunity. Obviously you get the risk of being rejected by the casting director, but I know I'm gentle.

8. BOB MacDONALD

INDEPENDENT CASTING DIRECTO[]
FEATURES, WITH PERRY BULLINGT[]
FORMER DIRECTOR OF CASTING
FOR CANNON FILMS

I was editor of the Daily News, *the student newspaper at Western Washington State University. While I was standing outside my office one day, the vice president of A&M records walked in, looking for someone to hire as a college representative because they wanted to tap the college market. I got the job and worked in Seattle for A&M Records for six months. They brought me to Los Angeles to put together a college promotional publicity department. I went all over the country and hired campus representatives from seventeen major universities and directed the whole project. I then went back and got my B.A. in Economics. After that, I wanted to come back, so I called a friend of mine, David Geffen, and he turned me on to a job as an associate producer in the pop A&R division at Capitol Records. I worked there for several years with such artists as Linda Ronstadt, Bobbie Gentry, and Helen Reddy. I began meeting people in film and television and began to grow away from the music business. There's a lot of resentment at a record company for a twenty-two-year-old executive.*

I became an agent trainee at Henderson-Hogan, a small, prestigious agency, and after four years, I was made vice president and remained there another two years, representing such clients as Michael Learned, Dick Cavett, Conrad Bain, Carrie Nye, David Keith, Craig Wasson, and Sam Jones. The reason I left agenting was that I had gotten into my mind that I was responsible for the livelihood of 100 people. You can't function that way as an agent. Joe

Cardon, a writer-director who was a client, had a script that a foreign production company wanted to produce. We didn't do this particular script we were working on, however. We ended up doing a film called THUNDER ALLEY, which was marginally successful. It took us three years to get it made. Columbia wanted to option it, but Cannon was the first company that said, "Okay, let's just do it now."

While Joe was in post-production on the film, I was taking other projects of his around town, and they called from Cannon and asked me to come in and work for one week on a re-shoot of EXTERMINATOR II. It was four years since that one week. I have recently left Cannon and become an independent casting director for feature films.

WHAT QUALITIES DO YOU LOOK FOR IN AN ACTOR OR ACTRESS?

On a general interview, I'm not really looking for anything. As far as casting for a specific role, what I look for in an actor is the physical aspect and a positive attitude. In a reading, I look for a variety of choices. You know immediately when the person walks in whether it's going to happen or not. And as good as their reading may be, if they're not physically right for the part, they're not going to get called back.

I like a sense of humor in everybody. Niceness, politeness. The chip-on-the-shoulder routine does not appeal to me in the slightest. Usually, the kind of people who have chips on their shoulders are not going to get very far with me. It's a defense thing which an actor builds up after struggling for years and years and facing rejection. I understand that. But young actors coming in and acting like James Dean and having no sense of humor do not turn me on. The producer of SPLASH at a symposium at UCLA said that the most important thing in casting is "cast nice."

HOW DO YOU REMEMBER ALL THE PEOPLE YOU SEE?

My mind. I have files of all the people who have starred in feature films. They're very complete. I use the *Players Directory* to spark my memory. I have a computer coming in called STARARCHIVES, which is very sophisticated. You can pull up color print from a film. It's got update information and you subscribe to it.

WHAT ARE YOU LOOKING FOR IN AN ACTOR'S PICTURE?

You need two different head shots. Don't use your glamour shot to get a feature film interview. You may be beautiful, but have a more real kind of shot. For television, have one of those perfect glamour photographs—touched-up, whatever, that will look nice on the little box. People with awkward features become movie stars—more generous noses, eyes, mouths, this kind of thing.

WHAT ABOUT WHEN YOU ARE LOOKING AT AN ACTOR'S TAPE? WHAT'S IMPORTANT TO YOU?

If it's an important role and we ask to see tape on you and you send us an episode of SEARCH FOR TOMORROW, forget it! I have seen more actors lose jobs based on their tapes than get them. If you don't have good tape, don't send it just because you have it. We're more careful about it now, because it's happened a few times . . . some wonderful people were not hired because of their tapes . . . but have gone on to star in other films for other people. We just didn't have the time to pre-screen, to get involved in discussions about appropriateness with the agent. If the director wants to see film and there's no film, then the person gets eliminated from the part. An actress that starred in STREET SMARTS for us just got a lead in a big film, and we were not allowed to send tape of the film because the film hadn't been released and the agent kept saying, "It's all based on her performance in this film." She wound up getting the part anyway without showing the tape.

**WHAT HAVE YOU LEARNED FROM THE PEOPLE WHO
TRAINED YOU?**

To look for the best in every actor, to appreciate the fact that even
though an actor may be excellent, he's not going to necessarily
get the part. There are no answers. There are only questions.

**WHEN YOU SIT IN SESSIONS WITH DIRECTORS WHERE
YOU ARE TALKING ABOUT THE SCRIPT OR YOU WATCH
THEM WORK WITH ACTORS, WHAT IS IT THAT YOU GET
FROM WATCHING THE PROCESS?**

Andre Konchalovsky is really the only director who's been able
to teach me anything in terms of that. He's very specific about all
of his characters. When he worked with Eric Roberts on RUN-
AWAY TRAIN, he said, "I want a puppy dog" because Jon Voight
kept putting the character down. He kept explaining that to the
actor, and no one seemed to be able to do that very thing, but
Eric Roberts did it perfectly. He'd be like a puppy who would
come up and growl and fight and then you'd hit it and he'd
whimper away and then come back wagging his tail—that kind
of thing. He uses animal characteristics when he's directing. He's
so helpful to the actors. He gives them everything. To know him
is to want to work with him. I'm frequently surprised as to how
specific he can be. Some of it is so complex that I don't retain all
of it day to day. Each session with him is an entirely new
experience. He uses different images and different ways of
evoking your emotions. We'll really work with those actors that
we believe are physically right for the part. We're not teachers.
We're pickers, choosers. The actors are here on time, and they're
really anxious to do their best for the role. I'm not saying that all
the films we're doing are masterpieces. But they are movies, and
to get a part in a film means a lot. I only work with film directors.
They will ask an actor, "What films have you been in?" and they'll
be looking at a résumé for films. They don't want to hear about
how you had an option to do a pilot and you're waiting to see if
it gets picked up. Their whole frame of reference is films.

WHAT EXCITES YOU ABOUT CASTING?

I'm a part of the creative team that puts together the production—that really excites me. I like to be involved in high-quality projects and also to give opportunities to new actors who have never starred in a feature before. There's a lot of excitement in that. For example, the girl who stars in Norman Mailer's TOUGH GUYS DON'T DANCE, Deborah Salin, had never done a film or a television show before. She graduated from Northwestern three years ago, stayed in Chicago, did theatre, came out here, and beat out so many star names for that part. Perry Bullington, my associate, found another young fellow, Jesse Dabson, at a workshop, and he got a starring role. He didn't belong to SAG, didn't have an agent or anything, and he read against a lot of top name people and he got the part. So it's fun to find new people. I enjoy that. I love to be able to put actors to work. It makes them so happy. I get joy out of that myself. Having been an agent, it's nice because the actors are so nice to me. The niceness factor is a variable when you're an agent, depending on where the actor is in his career. At one point they're working for you and then, all of a sudden, you're working for them. Once they cross that hump, they're gone because it's just too impossible to deal with. I always say to actors when I do a workshop: "I know a lot of actors think that casting directors are against them, but we're only as good as you are. When we bring you in on a role, we want you to get it. You make us look good. Without you, we wouldn't have jobs. We're for you, not against you. So try not to add that to all of your nervousness, sitting out in the waiting room with other actors. Just be confident that we're bringing you in because we think you can do the part."

IF AN ACTOR COMES FOR A CALLBACK, SHOULD HE DRESS AND READ THE SAME WAY?

Yes. That's just the way it is. It's just a show biz myth or something. I have never seen anybody not do that. Actors will read better for us than for the director. And that's a major disappointment. We make them feel so much more comfortable.

When they get a callback, they are actually getting closer to the job. That makes them more nervous. Then we have to go through this explanation, "Well, he was great before, I don't know what happened." At Cannon, we had fun with everybody we worked with there. We laughed with the directors. We could either be laughing or crying. We chose to laugh and make the best of it. It was actually a happy place to work.

TALK ABOUT CRITICISM.

If an actor is good, I'll definitely tell him that he's good. Whether he's right for the part is another thing. If he does a good reading, I'll tell him I'll have him back for something else. When you criticize an actor, you're taking on a responsibility. Then they feel free to call you and start asking you questions. I don't have time. I'm not their parent.

I will talk to their agents about them. If it's somebody I care about and who is really a good actor but who just didn't pull through for me, I'll ask, "What happened to this person? Why did he come in and light up a cigarette and blow smoke in the director's face for starters?" At Cannon, I had an experience with Andre Konchalovsky, who is an absolute health nut, and this one actress I was crazy about just completely let me down. But I care about her. I care about talent, and I care about people more than anything. I will never tell anyone to get out of the business or that they're untalented. I will never take on that responsibility. It's not my job. They will have to find that out themselves through rejection or through their managers and their agents. I'm looking for people who are right, not people who are wrong. If an actor gives a good reading and the director doesn't like him, I will follow him out and tell him that I felt he was good and the director is shortsighted in this case. I certainly see a lot more talent than any director does.

TALK ABOUT YOUR PROCESS.

I don't read with actors. I cannot read and make any kind of judgement at the same time. I cannot make a fair assessment, so I have actors who come in on a volunteer basis or, like at Cannon, I'd use one of the assistants. Whenever anyone came to read at Cannon, they're treated very nicely. They're always reading with the correct gender, and they always read with someone who gives them something. I don't believe in the type of casting where you put the actor in the worst possible circumstances, and if he can make it work, then he'll be able to do the part. I just don't believe that's true. Put him in the best possible circumstances, since a reading is a bad circumstance to begin with.

They come in and say hello. I take a look at their résumé and talk about their background, just try to make them feel at ease. I don't just whip them in and out. I'm very kind to actors and very fair.

At Cannon, Perry and I were very popular. We didn't have a bunch of executives yelling at us all the time. We had almost total autonomy. The decisions were usually between us and the director. Sometimes Menachem [Golan, Chairman of the Board of Cannon Films] would give some directions. He was open to discussion as to whether we felt that a person might or might not be right for the part. It was a real comfortable working situation. We had fans—certain actors and actresses we'd brought in and in and had finally gotten them leads in films. We kept at it until they got something. We wore the other people down. The only problem was that sometimes we had such a strong relationship with the actor that he'd come in and address everybody like we were friends. In the office he'd be very comfortable with us and would direct his focus towards Perry or me, and that was a big mistake. When you're brought in to read for a director, look at the director, talk to the director. You can look back and forth, but don't sit there and talk to me the whole time. Directors are very sensitive, very fragile. That can work against an actor, so they should really zero in on the director. Otherwise, it's very disturbing to the director. I can feel it, and I will say something to the actor to bring him back to the director.

CAN YOU GIVE ME SOME EXAMPLES OF WHAT

YOU WOULD CONSIDER INAPPROPRIATE BEHAVIOR IN A SESSION?

No one likes to wait for anything, but this is a very dynamic business and directors can be called into meetings. I could get an important phone call. I'm in the middle of negotiations with major star deals all the time. I'm interrupted from time to time. It's a fluid, dynamic business. Sometimes you're going to have to wait, actors, and accept that! Don't complain about that. Actors, don't come in and complain to me. They give the receptionist a hard time. I like my receptionist, and that person can actually have an effect. If someone gave her a bad time, I'd think that person may give somebody on the set a bad time. Don't come in with excuses about your appearance or that you had too many interviews that day. Don't keep a director waiting. Ever. I don't want to know how long it took you to park. A lot of actors come in and think the more time they spend in the room, the better the audition is going. It is not true at all. Come in. Be totally professional. Don't be overly familiar with anybody. An actor can be that way with me when he's with me, but not with someone he's never met before. I'm not going to say that about Barbara Hershey or Jill Clayburgh or Eric Roberts or Rebecca DeMornay. They can be whatever they want to be when they come in. Just be totally professional, friendly and nice. Everybody appreciates a sense of humor.

WHAT'S THE FUNCTION OF THE AGENT AND MANAGER FROM YOUR STANDPOINT?

The agent's job is to submit his clients for roles and to make the deals. A lot of agents function as managers. Smaller agents can do that if they have the time. I believe strongly that you need all the help you can get when you're at the bottom, and you need all the help you can get when you're at the top. There's a middle ground if you're with a Henderson-Hogan or STE. Then you probably don't need a manager because they're trustworthy agencies. It depends on the needs of the actors. I had a few clients when I was an agent who parked themselves in my office. You wanted to say, "Go get a manager." If they get a manager, the first thing the manager does is take the client away from you. The manager's job is to keep the client off the agent's back!

A lot of clients would come to me from Harvard or Yale. They studied drama, got degrees, starred in every production on Earth, but knew nothing about the business. They come to New York, and they can't even get a bit part on a Broadway play or a TV series, and this upsets them. Some schools will bring in people. When we were at Cannon, Perry had gone to Dallas to talk to students. Within the universities' drama departments, I'm sure if they just talked about the reality of the business, those departments would disintegrate. The realities are very harsh. They're so ill-prepared for the show business aspect of it. I understand the university's point of view. People wouldn't pursue it if they knew what they were up against.

Actors will say to me, "I went to my agent's office. I just gave him a hundred pictures and it's two months later and there are only ten left and I haven't had an audition." I say, "Don't complain about that. Go get more pictures. That means they're working for you. If you give them a hundred pictures and two months later there are ninety-five there, you're not being submitted for anything." And they always go, "Oh, I never thought about that."

HOW DOES AN ACTOR TAKE PERSONAL RESPONSIBILITY FOR HIS CAREER?

There are some actors this would never apply to because they have no career and will never have a career. On the other hand, there are actors who went to college, majored in drama, went on to theatre in New York. Stage-trained, they have all their tools sharpened, they're ready to work, and ready for professional interviews. There are also people who come to Hollywood and say, "I'm going to become a star overnight." They take a commercial casting workshop. They look in the mirror and think, "I can be a star." In terms of taking responsibility, showing up for your appointments, being prepared, we always have material available. Agents can always get the scripts one way or another. Know why you're going in and what you're going in on. Whoever your agent is, try to have a good relationship with him. Don't burn your bridges. As an agent, I found I worked hardest for clients that worked the hardest for themselves. It really is a partnership even though the actor is getting ninety percent and the agent is only getting ten percent. I was very motivated by those who did showcases and plays and would do everything they could to promote their career. They're not saying you can't have the commission—you should have gotten this for me. Well, that's not the way it is. If they can't get things for themselves, I don't want to be their agent.

WHY DO YOU THINK SO MANY ACTORS GET INTO EMOTIONAL OR PSYCHOLOGICAL TROUBLE, NOT FROM FAILURE, BUT FROM SUCCESS?

Many actors whom I have interviewed have come from broken homes, Army traveling families, people whose parents have been stationed all over the world or all over the United States. They never stay in one place and have to make new friends over and over again. They become actors because they want to get outside of themselves and be other people. They're very unhappy and troubled individuals. They are generally the most talented people. And when the money and the success comes in, they can't handle it, so they turn to drugs. A lot of actors have a failure-wish, and a lot of times people choose to be actors because they know they'll never make it, and it will be an excuse for them to be waiters the rest of their lives. They don't want to be successful. The very thing they don't want to be, they become. Then they have to destroy it. Because they don't know what to do with it. When you're successful, you don't know who your friends are unless they're family or old friends. A lot of genuinely good, successful people who make a lot of money seem to deal with it fine, so I think it's upbringing and a good value system that seems to make the difference. I'm sure a lot of actors are jealous of the fact that there are so many children of actors who have become successful. The reason: they don't have to go through the process of telling their parents they want to be actors. No middle-class family is going to say, "Oh, great, be an actor." Girls can do it more easily. Sixty-five percent of the members of SAG are women. Children of actors are raised in an environment where acting is okay. They're used to the strange hours of their parents. They have strange lives. They have a lot to draw on just by watching their parents growing up. They have a basic understanding of the whole industry, so they are at a distinct advantage. The name value has a lot to do with getting them work. They are often better prepared to deal with Hollywood.

9. ROBIN STOLTZ NASSIF
DIRECTOR OF CASTING, ABC

I studied at UC Santa Barbara and then graduated from Berkeley with a degree in theatre arts specializing in technical theatre, costuming, and lighting. I spent two years as a costumer for Norman Lear's company, Tandem Productions, and then I got a job in the FERNWOOD TONIGHT casting offices as a receptionist. Over the next six years, I worked on casting until I became a casting director in 1982, and then from 1982 to 1984, I was a casting director at Tandem/TAT Productions, which became Embassy. I cast THE FACTS OF LIFE, ONE DAY AT A TIME, and SILVER SPOONS.

In 1984, I came to ABC, where I am now Director of Casting. I supervise the casting of almost all the comedy pilots, all prime-time on-air series, and that involves any new additional characters they add to the existing shows. From time to time, I help Donna Rosenstein, ABC's Vice President of Casting, with ideas for films, and I have worked on several of the drama pilots as well. I just finished a pilot season where some of the projects I worked on included THE WONDER YEARS, ROSEANNE, ANYTHING BUT LOVE with Jamie Lee Curtis, FLAMINGO KID, and LIVIN' LARGE for Stephen Cannell, as well as supervising our hits, PERFECT STRANGERS, WHO'S THE BOSS, HERO OF THE CLASS, HOOPERMAN, GROWING PAINS, FULL HOUSE, and MR. BELVEDERE. I am married to an agent.

WHAT QUALITIES DO YOU LOOK FOR IN AN ACTOR?

I look for personality, confidence, and a great look. I think it's important for the actor to be himself in the interview. Shyness is not a good attribute. Confidence I like, especially when I give them sides and they say, "I'd like to do this. Great! I can't wait to get into it." If they go out, work on it, come in, have an attitude, make choices and do it—that's confidence. I look for someone who has something special about the way they look that jumps out at me. I'm not saying I look for someone who's an 8 x 10 glossy, but someone who has something unique about his or her appearance that will make other people stand up and take notice.

HOW DO YOU REMEMBER ALL THE PEOPLE YOU MANAGE TO SEE?

I have little appointment sheets with the actor's names, and I take notes on them. I keep these in a notebook and refer to it constantly. Every three months, I go through it and put the actors' names onto a master list that is broken down into leading women 20-30, character women 20-30, etc. That list goes into a master book. It's a list of all the actors that I've met that I like. It's broken down into age groups, character, and leading ladies and men. When I'm casting a project, I open to the category that I'm looking for and pull names out. I keep every picture and résumé of everybody that I like. I have them in a separate file and if I forget the person's face, I look up the name. They're all in alphabetical order.

IF AN ACTOR COMES IN FOR A CALLBACK, SHOULD HE DRESS AND READ THE SAME WAY?

Absolutely. The reason he's coming in for the callback is that they liked what he did before. To get the best results, he should do what he did the first time, and that means read the same way unless the director tells him to do something differently.

IF THE ACTOR DOESN'T GET DIRECTION FROM YOU OR THE DIRECTOR, AND HE'S COMING BACK FOR THE SECOND TIME, AND HE'S WORKING ON THE MATERIAL AND COMES UP WITH ANOTHER BEAT OR MOMENT OR

SOMETHING ELSE INTERESTING, SHOULD HE PRESENT IT?

I think it's risky. I think he should do exactly what he did that the people liked before. That's why he's back there. If he comes up with something brand new, forget it. Of course, if we're talking about an actor of the caliber of Robert DeNiro, I would probably make an exception. I say stick to what is tried and true, but be prepared to change direction if you get comments. You should be prepared to swing with the punches.

HOW SHOULD AN ACTOR READ YOUR RESPONSES?

Actors get feedback and criticism from their agents and managers based on conversations with me. In the room after the actor is finished, I usually say, "Thank you very much. I really appreciate you reading for me." And if I thought it was absolutely wonderful, I will say, "That was a very nice reading." And if I didn't think it was so great, I won't say anything. I don't mislead actors. I don't say, "Oh, that was wonderful!" if they didn't do a good job. If an agent calls me and asks for specific feedback and says, "It's very important that I know how this actor did," I'll try to be as honest as I can about what I saw. But I would never say that person doesn't have any talent. I'll say, "I think they need to work on cold reading, or interview technique, or their choices, or just present a stronger attitude."

DO YOU FEEL IT'S IMPORTANT FOR AGENTS AND MANAGERS TO OBTAIN FEEDBACK FOR THEIR CLIENTS?

I think it's important and I gladly give it. I know that agents love to get feedback on their actors, and I know that actors live for it. They want to know what they've done, and they want to know how they can improve and what they can do differently. It's very important that agents follow up. I'm more than happy to give feedback or criticism if it's requested. I will not offer it. I will not call somebody up and say, "Oh, this is the worst thing I ever saw."

Sometimes I call up if I'm really blown away by somebody and I'll say, "That girl was great! Where did you find her?"

WHAT DO YOU DO WITH A BAD SCRIPT?

I don't let people know how I feel. I read the script and try to discover what the writers are looking for, read the breakdown, and have a consultation with the casting director. I ask them what they're looking for, and I just keep my eyes open for that type of actor. I don't say, "You know, this is terrible and I can't stand working on this." I just do it. If I love it, I'll say, "God, this is so much fun," but if I don't like it, I keep my mouth shut.

WHAT EXCITES YOU ABOUT CASTING?

The most exciting thing about casting is discovering new talent. Someone that no one has taken a chance on before. Someone will walk into my office, brand new, and I see something there, and I take them into Donna Rosenstein, and she goes crazy over them. It's wonderful! You give them a piece of script to read and they're great!

WHAT WOULD YOU CHANGE ABOUT THE CASTING PROCESS TO MAKE IT BETTER?

Marc Hirschfeld, who was my partner, and I took cold reading classes when we were casting directors together because we thought it would be helpful to give something to the actor when they were reading with us. Often, casting directors give nothing to the actor. The actor doesn't even get eye contact with them, no feeling, nothing to react off. I think it's very important for an actor to be able to give the most when he's reading. I think it would be very valuable for all casting directors to take a cold reading class. I would highly recommend it. We did it, and it really changed the way we related to actors. I think that, whenever possible, an actor should be put on tape. An actor has a much better chance on tape than coming before a live group of people, which will tend to make him very nervous. It's not a natural situation. It would be my choice to try to put more people on tape and have less in-person readings. You can't do that when you're casting a major project and you have 200 people to read. I really like it when a production company says, "Look, we're going to do film tests of the actors and send it over to you to look at." I love that. Because the actors aren't nervous, they're not stuttering or upset. They have time and you can really see what the product is going to be like.

You can see that I have tape all over my office. If I don't know an actor, or I haven't seen him recently, the first thing I say to an agent is, "Send me tape on him. I'd like to see what he's doing, what he's up to." Or if I don't know an actor as being a comedy actor, I'll say, "Send me comedy tape on him," and if they don't have it, it's a little hard for me to know his work, especially if he's not the kind of person who's going to come in and read for me. So it's real important to have a current tape of what you've done lately and have it well edited—concise, varied, with different types of things on it. The ideal tape is probably about seven minutes long, has maybe three or four different bits on it, a couple of minutes each, so that the casting director gets a good idea of what the actor can do.

HOW DOES YOUR PROCESS WORK?

Basically, we supervise casting directors hired by the production company. We are not casting directors with the network. We make sure that they look at all types. We may run into somebody that they don't know about, and we supplement their knowledge. If someone appropriate comes into my office when I'm casting a project, I will have them read for me, and, if I like the way that they read, I'll send them over to meet the casting person. If the casting person passes on them, then they pass on them. But at least I had some input.

WHEN YOU GET A SCRIPT FROM A PRODUCTION COMPANY, WHAT DO YOU DO WITH IT?

I read it, break it down, and make a list of actors that I think would be right for the project. Then I call the casting director and go over my ideas with him or her. I say, "These are my ideas. If you like them, great. If you don't, fine." Because I don't push anybody down anybody's throat! And I don't think ABC operates that way. One of the reasons I like ABC is because they let the production companies have creative control. We never have said to someone, "No, you can't bring that actor to the network." That doesn't happen. We might say, "We'd like you to bring more than one choice."

WHY DO YOU SAY "BRING MORE THAN ONE CHOICE?"

Sometimes the talent that they're bringing in has a reputation for being a certain type of actor, and it might be more interesting to have another actor coming in that offers another quality. It's better to have several actors, and then everybody can make a more creative decision. If there's more to choose from, it gives you more to talk about and therefore more options.

WHAT HAPPENS AFTER THE DOOR CLOSES AND THE ACTORS GO HOME?

Everybody tries to come to an agreement as to which actor is best for the role in terms of acting ability and looks. If we have a choice between a look and acting ability, we'll go with the acting ability. The basic criteria is—who's the best actor. That decision doesn't come easily. Sometimes it comes immediately. Sometimes we can be in a room for an hour and still not have an idea. Then we have to go back to the drawing board and come up with other actors. They might have loved the actor, but not everybody in the room felt that that actor was right for that part. Perhaps we'll go to New York or Chicago for a search.

WHAT'S THE FUNCTION OF THE AGENT AND THE MANAGER FROM YOUR STANDPOINT?

I think that agents and managers should be in contact with the network. There are very few agents that really use us as a resource, and they should, because, if they're having a problem getting an actor in, or they really feel somebody is right for a part, I can often help. I can call and say, "Maybe you should consider so-and-so because I've seen him do such-and-such and he might be right." Then the casting director might say, "Oh yeah, you're right, he did do that and he would be right. Okay, I will see him." Agents are suppose to call the networks and casting people. The function of managers is to keep their clients happy and make sure the client is getting the proper treatment by everybody.

WHAT HAVE YOU LEARNED FROM THE PEOPLE WITH WHOM YOU'VE TRAINED?

When given a choice between acting and looks, go for acting. Actors get treated like cattle, so try to go out of your way to make actors feel comfortable.

WHAT'S YOUR PET PEEVE ABOUT ACTORS?

I can't stand it when an agent sends an actor in to meet me and they have absolutely no personality. They answer my questions with one word, and they look straight ahead and have no life. It happens about five percent of the time. I have actors in here and I have no idea why they're here. They don't seem to want to be here. They don't seem to know why they're here. I go out of my way to make people feel comfortable, but there are certain actors who are wonderful but should not go on personality interviews because they don't have a strong personality. I've even heard this about some of our most famous actors—that they don't know what to say to people on a one-on-one situation, but when they get on the screen, they're magic. Those people should probably just go in for readings. Not go in and sit and chat because an interview situation is basically to see an actor's personality and hopefully to have that personality be interesting and stimulating.

Also, an actor should *always* check his message machine. There've been so many times when I've tried to find actors and they haven't checked in with their answering machines, and they've ended up losing parts because they're not in contact with either their managers or their machines.

WHY DO YOU ASK FOR CURRENT CLIENT LISTS FROM AGENTS?

So that when I'm casting, I'll have an additional resource. When I run out of ideas, I might look at a client list to come up with names. The name triggers an image. An actor will call me and say, "I'm thinking of signing with such and such an agency. Who do they represent?" I'll flip through and see who they represent.

HOW IMPORTANT IS THE *PLAYERS DIRECTORY* AND THE COMPUTER AT SAG AND AFTRA?

The only sure way to find an actor is the *Players Directory* and calling SAG and AFTRA. If I look in those places and can't find the actor, I sometimes give up. Every actor should have his picture in every issue of the *Players Directory* and should be on the SAG and AFTRA computers. A lot of times actors may be on the computers, but they haven't updated their agents and the previous agent won't refer you.

WHAT JUMPS OUT AT YOU FIRST FROM AN ACTOR'S PICTURE?

When I look at a picture, my eyes go first to the actor's eyes. If I look at a picture and the person's eyes seem expressive, then I like the picture. And if the eyes are kind of dead—if there's nothing behind the eyes—then it's not too interesting to me.

IT CAN BE VERY INTIMIDATING WHEN YOU GO INTO THAT NETWORK ROOM. WHY DON'T THEY PAIR ACTORS UP WITH THE ONES THAT THEY'VE ALREADY CAST?

We always ask the production company to bring in the actors that are already set, to read with the actors who are auditioning. Sometimes the actor is not available because of other commitments. When the actor is available and willing, it makes it much easier for everybody. As far as pairing up, that's up to the individual casting director and how he or she wants to do it. I like it when I see the interaction between actors. I think it's more fun. It gives a lot more depth and vision to what you're looking at.

BECAUSE OF AN ACTOR'S PAST POOR PERFORMANCE, DO YOU REFUSE TO SEE THEM AGAIN? WHAT IF THEY HAVE DONE THE SAME TYPE OF ROLE FIVE DIFFERENT TIMES AND THEY'RE BOXED INTO A CATEGORY? HOW CAN THEIR AGENT OR MANAGER CHANGE YOUR MIND?

I try not to stereotype people. I always give an actor a second chance. If an agent calls me up and pitches somebody and I haven't thought of them in that role, I try to have an open mind about it. If somebody comes in and does a bad reading, maybe his mother died yesterday. If an actor calls me and begs to come back in again because of a specific circumstance that happened, I usually say yes unless I'm not available.

DO YOU BELONG TO THE ASSOCIATION OF CASTING DIRECTORS?

Yes. What it's doing is promoting pride in the casting business. It's a support group for casting directors. They can talk about problems they have and how to get more work. They talk about what to do to raise the image of casting directors. I think it's a mutually beneficial society for everybody that's involved with it. I think the more that people join it, the more beneficial it will become. It's a way for casting people to talk about their problems, hopes, and dreams, and I hope it will make a difference in the business.

WHEN YOU PRE-READ, DO YOU SUGGEST TO THE ACTOR WHAT IT IS THAT THE BUYERS ARE LOOKING FOR?

I usually say, "Do you have any questions?" If they do, then I answer them and then they read. If I'm going to send an actor over to the director or the casting person, I might say, "When you read for so-and-so, keep in mind that such-and-such or you might try this . . ." I don't give them line readings. I might give them some kind of idea of what they might do differently to be more of what the individual casting person is looking for.

DO YOU GO TO PLAYS AND SHOWCASES?

Yes. All the time. If I go to something that's absolutely dreadful, I'll leave at the intermission. If I go to something that I halfway enjoy, I'll stay. And if I go to something that I really enjoy, of course I'll stay. I try to get out to the theatre at least once or twice a week.

HOW DO YOU GET VALIDATED FOR THE JOB THAT YOU DO?

When an actor calls and thanks me for helping him get a part or when he tells me that he got a part I had something to do with—that's validation. When my boss tells me the pilots look great and thanks me for my contribution.

DO YOU AGREE WITH SOCIALIZING BETWEEN CASTING DIRECTORS, NETWORK PEOPLE, ACTORS, AGENTS, AND MANAGERS?

That's a personal choice. Some people like to do it. Some people don't. I don't go to lunch with actors. I find that actors become very dependent on you if you start doing social things with them. It can get out of hand, so it's just not a good idea.

10. BARBARA REMSEN
INDEPENDENT CASTING DIRECTOR

I was born Barbara Dodd in New Brunswick, New Jersey. After graduating from Douglas College in 1951 with a B.A. degree in English and Drama, I moved to New York and went to work as a receptionist at NBC. Some of my co-workers were Grant Tinker, Meredith Wilson, Dave Garroway and Fred Coe. I was on staff with Fred Coe from 1952 to 1956 and worked in all capacities of production on both PRODUCER'S SHOWCASE and PLAYWRIGHTS 56 with Paddy Chayefsky, J.P. Miller, Delbert Mann, and Dominick Dunne among others. I also acted in YELLOW JACK (Eva Marie Saint, Rod Steiger) and STATE OF THE UNION (Joseph Cotten, Margaret Sullivan).

The shows went off the air in 1959 and I came to California. While working as a production assistant on a play, WINESBURG, OHIO, I met actor Bert Remsen and we were married in 1959. Our daughter Ann works with me in casting, and our other daughter, Kerry, is an actress.

I formed my independent casting company, Barbara Remsen and Associates, ten years ago. Since then we've cast over twenty-five features including THE BEAR (Gary Busey), JAKE SPEED (Wayne Crawford, John Hurt, Karen Kopins), TRUST ME (Adam Ant, Talia Balsam, David Packer), and UFORIA (Cindy Williams, Fred Ward, Harry Dean Stanton). Among the numerous ABC and CBS "Afterschool Specials" they cast, ARE YOU MY MOTHER (Michael York) and JUST A REGULAR KID/AN AIDS STORY have received Emmy nominations, as has PBS/Wonderworks WORDS BY HEART (Alfre Woodard). Another PBS/Wonder-

works show HIROSHIMA MAIDEN (Susan Blakely, Richard Masur, Stephen Dorff, Tamlyn Tomita) aired in May, 1988.

Most recently we did the nationwide talent search and casting for a movie-of-the-week, ANGELS '88 (Aaron Spelling/Fox Broadcasting).

I'm a member of C.S.A., Women in Film, SAG, AFTRA, and the Academy of Television Arts and Sciences, and I frequently speak at AFI, Actors Center, and SAG Conservatory.

WHAT QUALITIES DO YOU LOOK FOR IN AN ACTOR?

The first thing I look for in an actor when he comes into my office is a positive approach to life. I like positive people in every aspect, whether we're talking about acting or anything else. I look for people who seem to want to act because it makes them happy, not for some underlying reason like fame or fortune. I don't like negativity, and if I spot it, it clouds my feeling toward the individual. When I'm talking to an actor, I really want to see what kind of person he is. After so many years, I have an instinct and I know whether an actor is playing a game with me or whether he really is what he seems to be.

WHAT SHOULD AN ACTOR TELL YOU ABOUT HIMSELF DURING AN INTERVIEW?

He doesn't need to tell me much unless I'm asking him specific questions. If I'm pressed for time, don't tell me too much. If there's something I pick up on or you pick up on—fine. For example, if you come into the room and you see a picture, mention it: "Gee, I love that." Or start a positive conversation. Just don't sit there like a bump on a log.

WHAT SHOULD AN ACTOR ABSOLUTELY *NOT* DO IN AN INTERVIEW?

Whether he is a minor or an adult, he should not come in with a predetermined attitude that he is absolutely right for the part. With kids, the thing they should *not* do is act. They should not come in playing a little scene and looking too perfect. We shouldn't feel that they've been preened by parents or whomever is in the outer office. If they're very young, they shouldn't come in that prepared. I like spontaneity, especially in young people, because it's either there or it isn't. Minors shouldn't be running around and not paying attention. We don't have a lot of time, and we're trying to find the right person. The one thing I dislike most is the child who has been prepped and made perfect. Child actors shouldn't be perfect little people. All the naturalness you're looking for in the part will have been erased by so much coaching. You don't want that. They should be like kids coming out of school. We're looking for naturalness in adults and definitely in children. Parents are to blame when they force their children into this business. When I work on any project with children, the minute it comes to the point where the child is being considered, the producer always wants to know about the parents.

Also, don't be phony. It doesn't work when a sexy girl comes in and is much more involved with her looks than what she does with her reading. I mean, we're not that stupid. Don't "come on" to anybody. Don't try to be something that you're not. Don't come in late. If you have two interviews and you're running late, don't go to the second one. You won't be at your best. I only want to see people at their best. If you're running late, just call. I realize things happen to make you late, and I understand completely.

IS THERE ANYTHING PARTICULAR YOU LOOK FOR ON A RÉSUMÉ?

Theatre should be on an actor's résumé. I started in the New York school, where theatre is a very important element. I like to see theatre experience on every actor's résumé. Are they studying? That demonstrates a commitment. In New York, I read résumés from top to bottom because it's theatre to film. In L.A., bottom to top. I start at the bottom because I want to see that training and background, then get into episodic TV and film.

SHOULD AN ACTOR PUT EXTRA WORK ON HIS RÉSUMÉ WITHOUT SPECIFYING THAT IT IS EXTRA WORK? AFTER ALL, IT *IS* WORK.

I don't think an actor should mention that it was extra work. We can tell if they are members of AFTRA and SAG. I also don't think it's necessary to list "guest star," "featured," and "co-star" next to the role. Why belittle yourself? Mention you had a nice scene with someone.

ARE GENERAL INTERVIEWS WORTHWHILE?

I don't think they're worthwhile at all. I can't remember the people I've done general interviews with unless they were so specific they went to the same high school I did. I do general interviews when I can, but it's very hard for me to book my time. When I'm not working, I'm looking for work just as an actor is. If I do bring in someone for a general interview, I read them right then and there. I have to know if they have talent.

YOU SEE SO MANY PEOPLE. HOW DO YOU MANAGE TO REMEMBER THEIR FACES AND/OR NAMES TO CALL THEM BACK AGAIN?

Well, between my daughter Ann and myself, we remember a lot of people. I may have seen them do something and say, "Yeah, they were good in that." Unless it's a very specific role, it's always brand new. We bring them in again. I have pictures and résumés in my office, although not terribly well filed. I'm going on computer soon if I can figure out how to work it. I think it will be very helpful for specifics like a certain height or language. Then I don't have to call SAG or AFTRA. Mainly, it's in my mind. I almost never have time to go through all the files. I go in at 7:00 a.m. to get my office straightened up for each working day.

IF AN ACTOR COMES IN FOR A CALLBACK, SHOULD HE DRESS AND READ THE SAME WAY HE DID THE FIRST TIME, OR SHOULD HE CHANGE BOTH TO GIVE YOU A DIFFERENT WAY OF LOOKING AT HIM?

The callback is not for me, but for the writer, director, and producer. They don't know what the actor wore originally, and I could care less. I would say don't wear the same clothes again. Give a reading similar to the one you did before because that's what's getting you in. You might give a little more this time than you did the first time.

IT'S SO HARD FOR AN ACTOR COMING INTO A ROOM TO MEET A CASTING DIRECTOR FOR THE FIRST TIME FOR A PART THAT IS VERY IMPORTANT. WHAT SHOULD A TONGUE-TIED ACTOR SAY AS AN INTRO?

You should use your common sense and be secure with yourself. If a casting person or a producer feels you are intimidated by him, you'll never go any further with that person. I always say, "Look, if you're nervous with me and you can't get past me, you're gonna have a real tough time in this town." If I do spot nerves and insecurities such as "I can't do it, I can't take it because it scares me," I'm not doing you any favors by casting you. How do I know that after you get through all six casting levels and you get on the stage or set, you might not drop dead of fear when the leading actor says, "Oh, my God, you're playing this part!" Just remember, it's not the casting director's interview—it is yours. If you don't like the casting director and you feel you don't read as well for him as you could, then you probably won't get the job. But at least if you go in for that casting director again, if he will have you in, you'll know what to expect. So look at it as experience and don't go ridiculing yourself.

HOW SHOULD AN ACTOR READ CRITICISM?

I don't think he should read criticism at all. I think the minute he leaves the office, he should forget everything and assume he did the best he could. Don't try to imagine why you didn't get the callback or why you didn't get the job. Don't waste your time. Just go outward and upward. Go on to the next thing and look at it as an experience, whether it was a good one or a bad one.

WHAT MAKES AN ACTOR INTO A STAR?

There's a certain magic I spot when an actor walks into the office and opens his mouth. In fact, in one case, I never read the actor. I spotted something, and I loved it. I've never been wrong about somebody I've seen talent in. In other cases, it's as soon as the actor has opened his mouth during a cold reading. Especially if it's something completely different that nobody's even thought of, I'm filled with excitement. When I get excited reading with an actor, you have to believe that I will put my head on the platter for him, and if my people don't believe in him, I say, "Fine, but that person is going to be a star, and I'm going to do everything I can to take him further and tell everyone in town."

DO YOU FEEL YOU CAN SPOT STAR QUALITY, AND IS IT SOMETHING AN ACTOR IS BORN WITH OR CAN IT BE DEVELOPED?

I think star quality can be developed. I think anything can be. I certainly know that when I give you material, my instincts tell me whenever it sounds right and if I feel it, even if you don't. If it sounds right to my ear, then you're right doing it.

11. RENEE ROUSSELOT
DIRECTOR OF FEATURE CASTING, DISNEY
STUDIOS; FORMER DIRECTOR OF TALENT AND
CASTING, CBS

*[AUTHOR'S NOTE: The following interview was
conducted with Renee Rousselot while she was Director of Talent & Casting at CBS. Since the time of
the interview, she has moved to the position of
Director of Feature Casting at Disney Studios.
Many of the questions put to her addressed themselves specifically to the particulars of working for a
network and how casting at the network differs
from feature or independent casting. While at CBS,
she cast the movie-of-the-week UNCONQUERED
and supervised the casting of the television series
WISEGUY and BEAUTY AND THE BEAST. Since
arriving at Disney, she has supervised the casting of
the features BETSY'S WEDDING and WHITE
FANG.]*

*I got a B.F.A. in theatre at Southern Methodist Uni-
versity. I worked as an administrative assistant in a
theatre in Dallas for about a year, and then I
moved to Los Angeles. A few months after I got here,
I went to work with Marsha Kleinman as her assistant. She was in partnership with Susan Bluestein
at the time, and I worked with them for two and a
half years. Susan and Marsha split up, and I stayed
on with Marsha for a while. Then I went with Susan
as her assistant and we became partners six
months before I took this job with CBS.*

WHAT QUALITIES DO YOU LOOK FOR IN AN ACTOR?

If an actor comes in and I really like that actor, it's because he is
unique and has a sense of himself as an individual. It's not

something he's tried to acquire. Any actor that comes in and has a sense of who he is will have that vulnerability. He's not afraid to be who he is. That automatically makes him vulnerable. Someone who comes in and who's not vulnerable and has all these defenses up is not really going to be just who they are. It's like a mask. It's the actor's job to peel that away.

IF AN ACTOR COMES IN FOR A CALLBACK, SHOULD HE DRESS AND READ THE SAME WAY?

I don't like them to dress that way. I don't really know a director or producer who's gone by that. If an actor feels good in those clothes and feels lucky, then go ahead. If he's coming for a callback, I would say, "There was nothing wrong with your reading. Just do it the way you did it before." Or if there's an adjustment that I want to see, I'll tell him. So be open to re-direction from the casting director, producer, and the director.

HOW SHOULD AN ACTOR READ YOUR RESPONSES?

I'll say, "Thank you," or, if I loved the reading, "I love that. It was terrific." If I did not like a reading, I will rarely say that directly to an actor. I will say it to the agent or manager. The reason I don't say it to the actor is that it sometimes creates a strange feeling in the room. If I'm blown away and it's obvious that I'm going to have them back, I will tell them that. If an actor comes in and they're wrong for the part, I'll tell them that, too. I'll tell you something that really irritates me: If I've met an actor five or six times, and I've had them back that many times, and they don't even remember my name. That drives me crazy. They don't even take you in as a person. I guess I have to understand that when they come to an audition, they get very nervous and uptight. But if I call them back that many times on different projects, they should at least remember me.

BECAUSE OF PAST POOR PERFORMANCE, DO YOU REFUSE TO SEE ACTORS AGAIN?

I will never ax a person after one reading. I will always give them a second chance. After the second time, if I just don't see their skill is improved, then I just don't want to see them again. Two or three years down the line, I might be willing to, if I know that they've been studying. After I've seen them a couple of times, I don't want to waste my time seeing that person again. There's so many actors to see.

I don't like stereotyping people. If I see that there's a quality in that person that would lend itself to a different kind of role, then I'd be willing to see that. I'm pretty open on that issue. It can be difficult if a person is really very severe-looking. It's going to be difficult to cast them in a sympathetic role.

HOW DO YOU REMEMBER ALL THE PEOPLE YOU MANAGE TO SEE? DO YOU HAVE A PROCESS?

Sometimes I don't! I just remember people. I have cards that I fill out. I started the card system about three months ago. Before that, every time I had readings or interviews, I always had a list of who was coming in, and I saved all of those. I'll periodically go back and review that. I also keep a big book categorized as to women, men, age groups. Any actor I see in a play or movie or that I meet will be written down in that book. The book is my main source. In the beginning, I tried writing notes, but I don't like that because I just take in a person and will remember them. If I see their name, up comes the image. I'll write down if they have red hair or blonde or sometimes I'll write certain physical things about them that will make me recall that image. If we talk about something unusual, I'll put that down.

WHAT ARE YOU LOOKING FOR WHEN YOU READ SOMEONE'S RÉSUMÉ?

The first thing I look at on an actor's résumé is feature films, then television. I'll concentrate on the most recent things. I'll look to see if they were projects that I liked or had a good director or had other people in the cast that I respect. Training and theatre credits are very important. There's got to be training, skill and a willingness to open up and be vulnerable and let out the individual that's in there. You can do that through training if it's the right kind of training. Develop the basic skills. You have to keep working at your craft. Keep doing work in theatre and somehow you're going to be seen.

HOW MUCH DO YOU RELY ON TAPE IN YOUR OFFICE? WHERE MIGHT IT HURT AN ACTOR MORE THAN HELP?

Tape can be inappropriate in certain situations. It might hurt if the part the actor is up for is different from what's on the tape. If a director and producer, who are not very creative in their thinking, suddenly see a quality in your tape and think, "God, I don't want to see that in the character!" then they're going to freak. I don't think that happens often. Sometimes your tape is very different from a character you're up for, but the producer and director want to see what you look like on tape or film. That would be okay. I try to be clear with the casting director or the producer about what they want and what they are looking for: the actor's work or if they just want to see how he looks on tape. I think it's very important for the agent or manager to say, "How do you intend to use this? Because this is old tape (or for whatever reason), we don't feel it's applicable at this point after having read the script. How are you going to use it so our client doesn't come off in a harmful way simply because it may not work." An inappropriate tape can blow the job for them before they even got a chance to read.

One thing I don't like is when the actor has a tape, and it has the name and then a big montage with music and all that. I hate that. A montage with music does not tell me if that person can act. I don't want to see how they can look five different ways. I want to see whether they can act. I like it when they cut to the scene and they show one piece after another. I don't need all these production values. I get bored with that, and I watch so many tapes that I just want to turn it on, and I want to see the work. I think it's very difficult to tell how good somebody is from tape. I find it difficult enough with the reading, for fear that I could be wrong, I might have missed something. I'm only a set of eyes.

WHAT GOES THROUGH YOUR MIND WHEN YOU SEE TWENTY PEOPLE FOR THE SAME ROLE AND YOU SEE THE SAME SCENE OVER AND OVER AGAIN?

"When is my day going to be over? Why did I schedule this many people today?" As far as the scene goes, what happens is that the more it's read and read, the more it begins to take shape in your head and becomes clearer. When an actor comes in who finds all the beats and nuances, that's the person who's really going to stand out. Every actor will bring something different to it. When you've seen a scene fifty times, it can become very boring. To give the actor the benefit of the doubt and to protect myself, I have to remain open every time an actor walks into the room. Once you've heard a scene so many times, you can usually tell what approach the actor is going to take to the scene in the first few lines, whether the actor is going to grab you or not. It doesn't mean you tune out, however.

WHEN A CASTING DIRECTOR SCHEDULES A READING FOR A PROJECT, WHY DOESN'T HE PICK SCENES WHERE THE ACTOR CAN SHOW DEPTH?

Often no scene like that exists. If I'm casting something and there's a certain scene that has a lot of depth, that's what I would choose for them to read. What's especially difficult is a scene that has a lot of action, and that's the only scene that exists for a certain character. In the end, I will probably have them read that scene. Sometimes, it may be that the directors want a certain quality that they're not going to get in another scene. When I choose sides for a major character, I'll want to get scenes that show different or contrasting qualities.

WHAT EXCITES YOU ABOUT CASTING?

I've been doing it for about six years and I just love it. I love actors. It's a creative process and I like sensing who an individual is when I look at a script, to be able to see what kind of actors will bring the most to that character and make it come alive. They have so many nuances that you just want to watch. If you've shaped them in some way, then when you see it up on the screen, you know, "I was responsible for part of that." It makes me feel part of the performance. I enjoy having someone come onto my playground and do their thing. It's such hard work, and you put in so many hours. It has to be fun because if it wasn't fun to me, it wouldn't be worth it.

WHAT WOULD YOU CHANGE ABOUT THE PROCESS TO MAKE IT BETTER?

Let me make the decisions and cast the movie! The process is never going to work that way because you're always going to have so many people involved in the decision—producers, directors, writers, studio executives.

WHAT DO YOU DO WITH A BAD SCRIPT? HOW DO YOU GET EXCITED ABOUT IT AND MAKE IT BETTER?

You have to do the best possible casting job that you can. It is so hard when you have a bad script because so many people will turn it down. Actors don't want to do it. You get angry about it, but you don't really blame them for not wanting to do it. The only thing you can do is try to make it the best you possibly can. Often you can elevate a script by the cast in it. If you can be persuasive and get good people to do it, you're better off. When I was independent (which I was for five and a half years), then you can just turn the project down.

THE NETWORK ATMOSPHERE CAN BE INTIMIDATING. WHY DO YOU SEND ACTORS IN BY THEMSELVES RATHER THAN PAIR THEM UP WITH PEOPLE WHO HAVE ALREADY BEEN CAST?

In the past, it's been actors reading by themselves. When we have a star cast, we'll want them to come in and read with the other actors. Most of the time, they do. If there are two actors and they're up for two different parts and the scene is together and neither of them has been cast, often they want to read together. We say no and they don't like it. The reason for that is that it's really unfair because you get two actors who are auditioning for parts, and they want to upstage each other. It often splits your focus. You're darting back and forth. This year during pilot season, we had one pilot in which the producers read a whole group of people together. None of them had been cast. They were all auditioning for their parts. They wanted to have this little group reading and we allowed them to do it. It actually worked quite well. The producer is a very well-known Broadway producer. You really got a sense of the whole piece. That particular piece lent itself to that kind of casting because it was more like a play than a television show. With most television shows, it's not going to work.

CAN YOU BE SPECIFIC ABOUT THE DIFFERENCE BETWEEN INDEPENDENT AND NETWORK CASTING?

At the network, I'm not on the line. Here, it's a managerial position. I have projects that I do. During pilot season, I had twenty projects that I was covering. There were casting directors on all those projects and I was overseeing them, making sure that things were being cast the way we wanted them to be. We can be absolutely instrumental in casting in certain things, but one thing I really miss about being on-line is you don't see the process. You know, when you're there casting a project, it's like your baby. You read the script and suddenly see this whole process that comes to life. In being here, you really don't see that process. I mean, you do see something come to life, but you're a little more removed from it. You're not there every day laboring on it.

DO YOU LIKE THE NETWORK?

I do. It's very different from independent casting. It's a great experience just seeing how this whole side of things works.

WHAT HAVE YOU LEARNED FROM THE PEOPLE THAT TRAINED YOU AS A CASTING DIRECTOR?

Negotiating. How to get the best price. How to work out the logistics of billing, all the minor details of deals. If they're deserving and have worked to that point, then actors do deserve certain things, but I don't think you should just give away everything. As far as money goes, it should be based upon how much they've worked. An actor's price is eventually going to go up, but it's not going to be a lot over what they've previously made. It's a matter of being fair.

WHAT'S THE FUNCTION OF THE AGENT AND THE MANAGER FROM YOUR STANDPOINT?

The function of an agent is to solicit work for their clients. That's true for managers, too. Just to be aware of all the parts that are being cast in town and aware whether their clients are right for these parts and then to try to get them a reading.

HOW ABOUT MANAGERS AND AGENTS OBTAINING FEEDBACK?

They should do so. Definitely. I never mind giving feedback to anybody. They should obtain it because they should know how their client performs. The reason it doesn't work is not always definable. If the agent or manager can't accept that and keeps pushing me for a reason, then I resent that in a way. In the beginning stages, you can usually verbalize it quite well. However, when you've been looking for an actor for a long time or you've read a hundred people for the part, it really becomes undefinable. You don't even know what you're looking for, but you'll know it when you see it. That's when it becomes difficult to say what it is that didn't work. Maybe the reading was fine but not special.

HOW DO YOU GET VALIDATED?

Casting directors rarely get validation. I worked on a miniseries for Showtime which hasn't aired yet. Someone saw that and called me and raved about how wonderful they thought the cast was. I really appreciated that because it's very rare that a casting director hears that. If there's a bad casting choice and it's not the casting director's fault, we will still get blamed for it. If it's a great casting choice, even though it may be the casting director's choice, everybody else will take credit for it.

12. SALLY STINER
INDEPENDENT CASTING DIRECTOR,
TWENTIETH CENTURY FOX

I grew up in Canton, Ohio, the eldest of five children. After attending Kent State University and studying early-childhood education, I moved to Florida and worked at Walt Disney World (Fantasyland) for a year. Then I moved to New York and tried to get a job with a talent agency. Here was this young naive person from Canton, Ohio, who didn't have a clue about the business. I would go in an apply for jobs everywhere, but nobody would hire me bacause I looked like I was going straight back to the farm. They thought I would never last in New York City. I got hired as temp secretary at ICM after they had their big fire. I was at ICM working in this huge room, cement blocks for walls, with Sam Cohen and Billy Bartz, the hottest agents in the business. They had a card table and a telephone because of the fire. That was my introduction to the business. I was very lucky because I got a card table beside the personnel director of ICM. My first job was with Bo Stacey in the amusement area, which is a separate area of ICM—a big, big dollar area. I did that for a while and then went into the commercial area, where I really started to get my feel for talent. I worked with the off-Broadway people and the Broadway people. Everybody works freelance there, so you were always meeting new people.

I loved it, but I was tired of the city. So they transferred me from ICM in New York to L.A. That's where I got into the television area. I worked with Gary Rado and Yul Shanker. Then I hooked up with Sylvia Gold, who's a little dynamo, and got some incredible training. Ina Bernstein was right where I was. All the agents told me, "You don't want to get into casting," and all the casting people said, "You don't want to be an agent." So I did what I wanted to do, and I became a casting director. I worked my very first job experience with Dody McClain, who is the finest woman I think one will ever meet. I adore her. She trained me. She comes from the old school, which is the best school. I worked with her on a movie-of-the-week with Jim Garner, and then we did the series MAVERICK. Then I went off and worked on a film with Tom Laughlin, where I met Lisa Bonet. I did the feature MYSTERIOUS STRANGER, which never got off the ground. Then Michelle Farberman hired me to help her with a film, ROCK AND ROLL ALIENS, with Pia Zadora and Ruth Gordon that's never been released. Then I did a movie, MONSTER IN THE CLOSET. My boyfriend was killed, and I had to take a step back in the industry. I was able to hook up with Tim Flack and start over again. God knows I would never want to relive my life again and have that tragedy, but career-wise it was terrific because Tim introduced me to comedy, where I finally found my true love. I worked with Tim as an assistant on COSBY and MADELINE and I was hooked. I then went over to NBC with Tim, and I was an executive there in charge of comedy.

WHAT QUALITIES DO YOU LOOK FOR IN AN ACTOR?

I'm looking for somebody who arouses my interest. It's a presence. You know it when they walk in the door. Once you communicate with them and see their work, you can spot that spark, that star quality. Sometimes you look at an actor and you think, "Uh-oh, this is going to be boring." Then they read, and all of a sudden this whole essence unfolds. You are enticed to do a little more digging.

HOW DO YOU DEFINE STAR QUALITY IN AN ACTOR?

There's an aura. It can be developed on rare occasions. Most of the time, it's organic. You can see star quality with someone who's never done a thing. When you watched James Garner in dailies, even with no training, he was wonderful. You can see a lot in the eyes. I never trained as an actor, but I always look in the eyes. It's giving support and I know I'm going to get it back. It's not enough to be good looking. Sometimes you see something exciting in a person, and then they read and it's terrible. They need more training. With a cold reading, I look for a sense of the person, not how they hit every word. You don't expect an actor to give a performance, but you love it when they do. You could be blind, deaf, and dumb, and it is so obvious that this is the person. I don't always need the dialogue—there're things I just know.

ARE GENERAL INTERVIEWS IMPORTANT?

I love to do tons of general interviews. I'm always looking for new people. The creative part of casting is finding the interesting characters. Today I came up with a guy who was the world's kick-boxing champion. I can go into my producer and director and say, "Hey, here's an interesting way to go. I know it's not written that way, but he's a very special talent." Some casting directors don't have generals. I don't understand. You constantly try to put interesting people in projects. If you're going to use the same talent in every picture, it's going to get very boring. Seeing and trying to find new faces is a big casting challenge. There's a lot of creativity there. It's exciting to find someone who's really unique and special and you're able to put them in their first role.

WHAT'S THE ROLE OF THE CASTING DIRECTOR?

Casting is a service. That was put in my head when I was trained a long time ago. You are a service to your producer and director. Fran Bascom, my mentor, was from the old school, which had a great approach. It wasn't the "let's do it fast" kind of Hollywood casting. Casting can be a very thankless job. You'll hear that over and over again. I'm here to provide my producer and my director with the best possible talent. If I think there's a role I can do a little better with, it's my job as the casting director to suggest it. Open up my mouth and say, "This is going to work," or "No, that's not going to work." I'm the one whose experience they draw on. I know the talent out there in this town. Not only do I have to know if an actor is talented, but I have to know if he had a drug or drinking problem on his last set. I need to keep my ear to the ground. Are they going through a major divorce and crazy right now? I had a situation where an actor was perfectly fine on his last three films, and all of a sudden, he was a major drunk. The producer called and said, "Didn't you know that?" I can only do so much. I can't babysit an actor after he's hired.

SHOULD AN ACTOR PUT EXTRA WORK DOWN ON HIS RÉSUMÉ AND NOT SPECIFY THAT IT IS EXTRA WORK?

It's only fair that you put down that you were an extra. To have a line of credits on your résumé that looks like you've done every show in town is giving the wrong impression. List your credits as co-star, guest starring, featured, extra. Be specific and be honest.

SHOULD AN ACTOR GIVE THE SAME READING ON A CALLBACK AS HE DID ON THE FIRST AUDITION, OR SHOULD HE CHANGE IT TO GIVE THE CASTING PEOPLE ANOTHER WAY OF LOOKING AT HIM?

You bring an actor back because he's doing it right, or you would have given him some other direction. It just kills you when he comes in for the second time and changes everything. Then when he walks out the door, the producer and director just look at you. "What can I say? He did it differently for me." This is a very critical thing because a lot of actors do this and I don't understand why. Obviously, we liked what he did or we wouldn't have called him back. So why change everything unless he has been redirected by one of us?

LET'S TALK ABOUT INAPPROPRIATE BEHAVIOR THAT SHOULD HAVE BEEN BROUGHT TO LIGHT BEFORE THE READING BEGAN SO THAT THE PEOPLE WERE WARNED ABOUT WHAT THE ACTOR WAS GOING TO DO.

I was casting HEART OF THE CITY, a Michael Zinberg Fox project. I was interviewing for street gang types, and I was trying to find a female gang leader—a very tough woman. I had all of these people coming into my office being tough and hard. This actress came in, and she had a towel on her hand. Curious person that I am, I kept watching this towel. I just waited to see what was about to happen. In the middle of the reading, she pulled a hatchet out. That's when I really felt I should get out of the industry. I invite all of these strange people into my office, that's insanity. Maybe this person was really insane, how do I know? That was pretty frightening. I had a gun pulled on me. Whose to know if this person is desperate and really is serious. You really put your life out on the line. There was a director who asked me, "Do you mind, Sally, if you just stand there while I interview these stunt men and have them come in, and I just want them to put their arm around you and drag you across the room?" This one stunt man forgot his strength. He was 6'8", he grabbed me around the neck and choked me. I was terrified; I turned purple.

HOW WOULD YOU LIKE TO SEE THIS PHYSICAL BEHAVIOR HANDLED, SHOULD THE ACTOR CHOOSE TO DO SOMETHING WHERE IT MAY APPEAR AS IF HE WERE THREATENING YOU AND/OR OTHER PEOPLE IN THE ROOM?

There's two schools of thought. One, people who like props and two, those who don't. I don't like props. I like to see what the actor can do, and I think that props are a distraction. When I was at the network, this guy came in, he pulled a pepperoni out of his pocket, and handed it to me. That had nothing to do with the project. You sit there and it distracts from the reading because you're thinking to yourself, "Why in the hell did this guy hand me this pepperoni?" You get into the pepperoni rather than the reading. So, I think that there should maybe be a quick discussion about the use of props, especially hatchets, pepperoni, and guns. I think anybody in their right mind is going to react. I think you should try to help the actor as much as possible. If this is going to help with his performance then you need to work with it in a certain way. You have to let somebody know if you're going to pull out a hatchet. I had an actor friend who got very upset because he went in to interview with an agent and he had staged the entire production before he got into the office. He had planned on using the agent's desk. Now, he had also asked an actor to come in and do it with him. Well, when he got into the office the agent told him, "No, you can't use the desk." He did not know what to do at that point. The other actor totally upstaged him. That's who the agent became interested in, and my friend was so thrown that he didn't do his best work. The desk is my stage. That is where I do my work. If somebody comes in and re-arranges my desk in a reading, I spend my entire day trying to find the papers on my desk. I cannot sit there and re-arrange my desk. I love an actor to use his stage. They're free to go wherever they want to. I prefer them to stand and move in a reading. I'm a water freak, and people would come in and pick up my glass and toss it around. I don't want to drink my water out of that. That is my stage. And that is my territory.

HOW DO YOU FEEL ABOUT THE PRODUCERS WHO CHANGE THEIR MINDS ABOUT THE APPROACH TO THE CHARACTER AT THE LAST MINUTE?

I feel it's unfair to just throw a change at the actor when he walks through the door. I think the actor should speak up because it isn't a reasonable situation to put him in. The only thing you can do is give him time to make the adjustment. The casting director may be under pressure, but you have to be fair to yourself as an actor. You're the product. I firmly believe you should take your time. You might even have to come back another day, although the stark realities of the business are such that we sometimes cast in one session, especially when we're doing television.

SHOULD YOU BE HONEST ABOUT YOUR NERVOUSNESS AT A READING?

I think that if you're scared, you should express how you feel. I believe in honesty. I think letting it out releases a lot of anxiety and makes you feel freer to open up. It's worked with actors who have come in and said to me, "Look, I'm scared." I said, "Oh, you should be. I'm a vampire."

WHAT DO YOU TALK ABOUT TO BREAK THE ICE?

Before you meet an actor, you have his picture and résumé in your hand, and that tells you a lot. That's the purpose of it. I ask a lot of personal questions. I always ask where they're from. There's a couple of reasons for that. It makes me feel a little closer to the actor and helps me remember him. I feel a personal note between the two of us. It helps me to get to know the person and lets the person relax so that he's comfortable in letting himself go in the reading. You get to know a lot about the actor when he starts talking about his home. There's always a lot of feeling and animation. I get a lot of good stuff out of that for both of us. You're doing your job, finding out about the actor, but you're also putting him at ease. I'm sure actors say later, "We talked about Ohio and Thanksgiving dinner and autumn leaves. What does that mean?" That's how I get to know them. I look at their credits. But it's the person that intrigues me.

I had a special thing happen in my office. An actor came in. I'm having a crazy bad day, and I'm talking to him, going through this and that. He stopped all of a sudden, looked at me and said, "How are you today, Sally?"

He really wanted to know. I almost passed out in my chair because that's so rare in an interview. For a moment, I couldn't speak. I felt so bad because I rarely stop in a session. But I was stopped in my tracks. He made my day because he cared about me as a person.

HOW DO YOU APPROACH CRITICISM AFTER A READING?

I try to say to the actors, "That was a great reading, but it's not

going to work for this project because of size, look, whatever." I
might also say, "Come on, let's try it again. We're getting off to a
bad start here." Often the actor felt that and just didn't know how
to stop. I always tell an actor in a reading if they're getting off to
a bad start to stop and say, "That sucked eggs," or whatever. "Let
me start again."

HOW DO YOU REMEMBER ACTORS?

I have extensive files, and I sleep with my *Academy Players
Directory.* I look at old interview lists. We're such list-makers. I
even do that in my personal life.

WHAT'S YOUR PET PEEVE?

My pet peeve is when an agent loses a client and won't tell you
where he went. I think they're being jerks and it's just disgusting.
We get it all the time. You're so tempted to say, "Gee, I'll do you
a favor sometime, too." It's so petty. Let's cooperate and work
together.

  When I was at a network, I had an instance where an
agent said, "I've got this great kid and you've got to see him—but
he won't do television." "Could I read him?" I asked. "No." "Well,
could I have his picture?" "He's only going to do leads in films,"
said the agent. And I said, "What has he done?" "Nothing."
"Where did he come from?" They found him on the street and
decided he was going to be a movie star. So that was it. I wasn't
allowed to see him, only allowed to hear his name. Finally, a year
later, I saw his name. They had submitted him for a TV project I
was working on. I brought him in to read. The kid didn't have a
clue what to do in the reading or how to meet people. The agent
had never sent him out. They must be kidding if they think a
producer would hire someone that green. He had a nice look, but
his people weren't doing their job.

HOW DO YOU GET VALIDATED?

On my current series, HEART OF THE CITY, the producer will

come up to me and say, "Sally, that was an excellent session. Thank you." It's not the norm. It's usually, "Hurry up. Can we get so-and-so, and is there anybody else?" There's panic, fear, and terror. Everybody's running around like a crazy person. People do forget to say, "Good job" or "Thank you." So you have to enjoy discovering talent. I often go home and say, "I did a good job."

Actors rarely call and say, "Thank you. I enjoyed working on the show." I've put people on series who have never said, "Thank you." On this series, Robert Desiderio takes the time to come over and say, "I love the job you're doing. Excellent cast." It's wonderful when an actor comes to me and says he loves the cast. It's important to everyone in this industry to get acknowledged. On a larger scale, it's special and important in all facets of our lives.

HOW DO YOU DEAL WITH YOUNG, INEXPERIENCED PRODUCERS?

Young producers are scared to death. Some don't have a clue. Those are the worst. They're indecisive and don't know what they're looking for. They want to see every actor in town. It's your job to bring in the best talent right away. The whole series or film could be cast in one session if everyone knew what he was looking for and what to do. Some of these producers just want to meet actors, and that is the most frustrating thing. You've gone out and done your work. You feel great about who your choice is, and they say, "Let's see a few more people." Eventually, what you're doing is bringing in bodies.

13. STANZI STOKES
INDEPENDENT CASTING DIRECTOR,
FEATURES

I always wanted to be an actress. I spent my early years traveling and studying acting. I majored in drama in college, was lucky in getting into various theatres, went to Europe, and worked in professional theatre over there and in Canada. Once I started to pursue film, I found that I was afraid of the camera and, through lucky flukes, got into casting. Sally Denison was the first person to give me a break in casting. I worked with her as an assistant for about two and a half years. I met her in my hometown on a film called BOUND FOR GLORY. She was casting extras at the time, and I worked with her. I moved to Los Angeles and she got her first job casting speaking roles on I WANT TO HOLD YOUR HAND and hired me as her assistant. I went on from there.

MENTION SOME OF THE FILMS YOU'VE DONE IN THE LAST COUPLE OF YEARS.

TERMINATOR is the one I get the most compliments on. A STRANGER'S KISS was a very small movie, but did very well critically. RETURN OF THE LIVING DEAD was kind of a hoot. YOU TALKING TO ME was released by United Artists, BURNING LOVE by Tri-Star, BILL AND TED'S EXCELLENT ADVENTURE by Orion, CASUAL SEX distributed by Universal, and FEDS by Warner Bros.

IN YOUR OPINION, HOW CAN AN ACTOR TELL IF HE HAS A GOOD AGENT ?

If he gets out on interviews! If he's getting in doors, getting seen. One of the things I always ask actors is how often does your agent ask for pictures. If it's often, you know they're submitting you a lot. Whether you get in on everything they submit, at least you know you're getting your picture out. If you're with an agent for two years and he never asks for more than the first 100 pictures, then you have to worry. A sign of a good agent is being accessible to the client—an agent whom you can talk to and see what's going on, or whom you can call if you hear of something you want to tell them.

WHAT QUALITIES DO YOU LOOK FOR IN AN ACTOR?

Basically, an openness. The actor should be able to come in here and be himself, as relaxed as possible. I know it's a nervous situation. Certain people just have something. It's intuition that's involved in casting. Two people may do a good job reading, but one person will just have that quality. You know by instinct.

WHAT HAPPENS WHEN AN ACTOR COMES THROUGH YOUR DOOR? WHAT'S THE SEQUENCE OF EVENTS?

First, I like to take a minute or two to sit and chat with the actor and put him at his ease. I go over the résumé and find something to talk about. I'll pick something off his special skills, or something he's done in the past or where he went to school and ask him to tell me a little more. This is also to see the actor as himself before he starts to read. Then I ask him if he has a certain way he plans to do the reading or does he have any questions. Does he want direction first? Usually people say, "Gee, if it's okay to do it twice, I'd rather do it my way first," so I always take the time. Sometimes the person is right on anyway, and other times we go through it a second time, and I'll give them a little direction just to see if they can run with it. That's very important. If they've done it a certain way and I say, "Okay, read the line with a different emphasis," I look to see if they can follow that. I'm looking for versatility!

HOW DO YOU REMEMBER ALL THE PEOPLE YOU MANAGE TO SEE?

I have a very good memory. I'll meet an actor and he won't even remember who I am, but I'll say, "Yeah, you read for me three years ago on such-and-such film!" I don't remember every single actor who comes in, but the ones who do a good job I'll remember for years. The ones who do a good job come back in a second time, and then of course, I'll remember them even more. I keep files and very extensive notes, When I go onto the next picture, I go back to the film before, to all my notes, and see who might be right from what I've seen before. Half the time, I'll just remember right away, but still I go to the notes just in case I've forgotten anybody. I keep pictures of everybody that I've liked in their readings. I watch a lot of television and see films. I watch TV in my bedroom, so I keep a notebook next to my bed. I have a notebook in my purse, too, so that when I go to a film, I can jot down if I really like someone. I'm the person in the movie theatre who's left at the very end as the credits are rolling. I go to a lot of theatre including Equity waiver. And to showcases. I like to find new talent. I do a lot of independent films where they give me the opportunity to find new talent.

TALK ABOUT CRITICISM. HOW SHOULD AN ACTOR READ YOUR RESPONSES?

Whenever I do give criticism, I try to keep it as positive as possible. I don't come down hard on actors, but if I see the spark of something right and they do the reading totally wrong, I'll tell them. I'll say, "Listen, pull it back. You were too big," and give them as much re-direction and feedback as possible. If an actor reads for me and I really don't see anything there, then I usually just say "Thank you," and that's it. I can't take the time to give a full criticism, but if I see the spark there, I'll take the time.

HAVE YOU EVER HAD A SITUATION IN WHICH THE ACTOR READ SO BRILLIANTLY THAT YOU BECAME EMOTIONALLY INVOLVED?

I've had a few of them. I get goosebumps or I cry. Even if it's a comedy. I get tears in my eyes because I get so excited. When I hear a wonderful reading, the actor gets a callback, and I make sure to tell the director before the person even reads that this person gave me goosebumps. They're already coming in with this positive reaction from the director. A couple of times there was magic. That's what makes it all worthwhile.

WHAT EXCITES YOU ABOUT CASTING?

The actors. I love the creativity involved, and that's again why I like where I am right now. I do independent features where I am given the chance to be creative. If I were in one of the jobs where I was literally just making lists all the time and using the same people over and over, I'd probably get out of the business. The actors make it worthwhile. I think they're wonderful, like children, and I love to help mold them.

HOW CAN ACTORS TAKE MORE RESPONSIBILITY FOR MOVING THEIR CAREERS FORWARD?

Too many actors will get an agent, and then they'll sit back and wait for that phone to ring. I think the most important thing is to get out there and get seen. Even if you have a good agent, get out there and do things. Try to get into theatre. Casting people do go and there's always the chance that somebody is just looking for your type. Take classes. Always be out there trying to promote yourself. That doesn't mean calling the casting director—which is a no-no! But if you hear something, don't be afraid to submit yourself. You can have your agent on the résumé, of course, so we can reach you. That's something that the actors in New York do a lot. I know it has been discouraged by a lot of people here in L.A., but it can't hurt to send in your picture if you hear of something. The more times that picture crosses my desk, the more attention I'm going to pay to it. When the second one comes through, I go "Wait a minute, I've already seen that," and then I'll find out why I got two and then say, "Hmmm, maybe I should see this person." That's why managers double submit. It's great. Those little postcards with the little pictures on them are great, too.

DO YOU HAVE ANY PET PEEVES?

Punctuality is one of my major ones. Even when I have a solid day of interviews, I will only run fifteen minutes late unless the producer or the director calls. Of course, I have to take the call, and that might put me half an hour off. Otherwise, I'm very punctual. So I get mad when I'm on time and the actor isn't. I always make sides available to the actors ahead of time, at least a day in advance if not more. And the actors who show up right at their appointment time and have not picked up their sides and say, "Oh, I need five minutes to look at my sides" do not make a good impression on me, especially if I'm ready for them. If I'm running a little late, then I'll never know. But it infuriates me. I go to the trouble to make the sides available. If somebody is working the day before, we'll tape it to the door in case they come afterwards, or we'll leave it downstairs with the reception- ist. We will go out of our way to make sure actors have their sides. And if they don't care enough to come and pick them up in advance and prepare a little bit, I get very upset. I don't expect them to be memorized. Actors get too set in their ways if they memorize, and then it's too hard to give them re-direction. I need them to be familiar with their lines and be able to look at me and make eye contact.

Some actors come in and aren't themselves. Don't try to be what you think I want you to be. I don't like that. I want you just to be yourself.

IF YOU HAD A PIE AND SECTIONS OF IT WERE DEVOTED TO DIFFERENT AREAS IN AN ACTOR'S CAREER IN TERMS OF WHERE HE SHOULD SPEND HIS MONEY, WHAT WOULD OCCUPY THE LARGEST PIECES OF PIE?

Studying is important because there's always something you can learn. I have actor and actress friends who are major names and still go to class.

Pictures are awfully important. I think a good picture should look like the actor. So many actors try to go for the glamour shot. They love the ones that make them look great, then they walk in the door and don't look like that. It's an immediate negative reaction on my part, because I'll have brought them in because of the way they look in their pictures. If they get a glamour shot done and send that in, they should look like that when they come in. The best pictures are the ones that are very natural, not a lot of fancy lighting and airbrushing. If you don't feel comfortable smiling, look the way you're most comfortable. Half the time I prefer a picture where the actor is not smiling, or maybe just half smiling. But these big teeth smiles I usually just hate! It looks too commercial. The kind I like is where the camera has apparently just caught you in a moment where you're just yourself. The actor should research his photographer. If you see a friend's picture that you like, find out who that photographer is. Go in and make sure you look through their photographer's books and make sure they don't ask their subjects to pose or look fake or glamorize them too much. I like to see actors dressed comfortably for the part. Casually. Hair is important. If you had your picture taken at a certain length of hair, keep it that way. I know that can run to expense, but you've got to keep the hair as close to it as possible. If that means recutting or reperming or recoloring, keep on top of that. Of course, money should go for the little postcards. And the *Academy Directory* is very important. I use it a lot. Producers and directors use it a lot. The computerized systems are a way that actors should start getting their faces in front of a casting director. I'm using a computer system almost as much as the *Academy Directory*. As more actors sign up, I'll be using it even more.

I think tapes are really important. I know it's another money expense, but it's one that should definitely be done if you have enough stuff to put on a tape. Always make sure that the tape is only five minutes long, at most, and put your best stuff first, since a lot of times, we'll watch two or three minutes and that's it, because we go home with stacks of tape at night. If you have, say, three things of one type of role and then of another type, don't lump them together. Give variety early on in the tape. So if you've got some comedy, put that first, then a nice dramatic role, and then maybe something off-beat. I find too many people lump all the same types of roles together, so if we're only to watch two or three minutes, then all we see is that one type. We don't get the variety. Sometimes tape can hurt you, so make sure if you or your agent or your manager submit tape that it is something that's appropriate. The last five films I did were comedies. When people would submit tapes that were heavily dramatic, it showed me, yes, you can do drama, but it's so different from comedy that it really hurts. A few actors who normally don't read for casting directors anymore ended up having to come in and read for me if they wanted to be up for the movie because I looked at their tapes and was not that crazy about what I saw because it wasn't comedy. Once in a while, I will just want to see tape for one minute to see how the person photographs!

Also, if you've only got two seconds on screen, don't put it on your tape. Only use a scene where it's something where we can see what the work's like. Otherwise, it's useless. So it's almost better not to have a tape until you've got something where you got a few scenes. Don't put anything on there you're not proud of. Make sure it's something that you want seen. Don't put it on just to have something on your tape, because sometimes that's the difference between getting in the door or not. Don't tape a scene in class or go to one of these places where they will tape you doing a scene; it's useless. For that, I can see you in my office. I want to see the finished work, a finished product. A couple of other things that are really great are to put a little picture on the outside of the tape, because if I'm looking at a couple of hundred tapes, I want to know right away who I'm looking for as the tape starts—or right at the beginning of the video, have your picture with your name and agent on it. That's just wonderful! Some of the places that are putting together tapes now really do a wonderful job. Sometimes they do a little collage right at the beginning of snippets of everything, and then you watch it. It makes it a little more interesting.

WHAT HAVE YOU LEARNED FROM THE PEOPLE WHO HAVE TRAINED YOU?

One of the main things I've learned from Sally Denison, who is the only casting person I really trained with, is creativity. She is wonderfully creative and open to new ideas. She taught me to take a chance and go with people who may be a little offbeat from the original description in the script or from the director's description of the character. So often those are the people that get the parts. It's something not quite standard, normal, and predictable. It makes it exciting. I watch my directors a lot and listen to them. I've learned how to give direction and work with actors and how to re-direct.

HOW DO YOU GET VALIDATED?

Putting together a good cast in my reward. Getting the people whom I've gone to bat for cast. The producers and directors are wonderfully supportive. They will compliment me a lot. The people I'm working with right now are incredible. When I started bringing people, they were just so supportive. People don't realize how much just a little bit of positive "God, you're doing a great job" or "Boy, we love those faces" really helps. The bottom line is putting together an interesting and wonderful cast. That's why I do these boards in my office. I put all the pictures of my current cast up and then I sit there and it gives me a lift every morning.

BECAUSE OF PAST POOR PERFORMANCE BY AN ACTOR, DO YOU EVER REFUSE TO SEE THAT ACTOR AGAIN?

I will always give somebody another chance. One of the worst things for me is attitude problems. "I shouldn't even be here" or "Why am I reading for you?" I have had a couple of cases in the last year where an actor has come in and had such a terrible attitude with the producer and director. I was thinking, "Oh, my God!" but I still gave the actor another chance. The agent and the manager had talked to me and assured me that the actor had changed his ways. And, when I saw the actor again, he had changed his attitude and realized what he was doing. I'm always willing to give another chance unless somebody really burns me badly. I will usually give somebody two chances, unless it's just the most God-awful reading that I know there's no talent there. An actor may not feel that great that day. He may have three appointments and not be totally on. If I see even just a spark, I'll give him a chance again.

IF AN ACTOR IS BOXED INTO A CERTAIN CATEGORY, HOW CAN HE GET OUT OF IT?

With me, it's easy. Because that's what I love to do. I like to put somebody who's been stuck with one category and never had a chance to do something else into a different category. That's the fun. That's the creativity of giving somebody the chance to do something he's never done.

DO YOU GET REPEAT BUSINESS FROM PRODUCERS AND STUDIOS WHO LIKE YOUR WORK?

For a while I was doing all horror films. TERMINATOR really wasn't a horror film, but then I had RETURN OF THE LIVING DEAD for Hemdale. Then I did this movie I don't like to talk about too much, SILENT NIGHT, DEADLY NIGHT, which was a Santa slasher movie, and I did MOTEL HELL, so for a while people would say, "Gee, you're the horror-movie lady!" I read horror books. That's my light reading. I actually like to cast horror films. Now five films in a row have been comedies. I work with the same people quite often. One producer will mention me to another producer or a production manager. They like to have someone nice to be around and who agrees with the essential direction that the film is going to take. Once in a while, though, I've felt very strongly about going a different way, and I'll stand up, too.

IS IT IMPORTANT FOR AGENTS AND MANAGERS TO OBTAIN FEEDBACK?

When I first started out, I did not give specific feedback. I'd either say, "It was a good reading" or "No, it just wasn't right for this," and I wouldn't give anything specific. I didn't want to hurt the agent's feelings. In the last three or four years, I've become very specific. If I didn't like an actor's reading, I make specific notes. I'll be specific with an agent and say, "Okay, I thought it was a weak reading. When I gave the actor the direction, he couldn't take it. We tried it a couple of times. Maybe he should go to a class." I'll sometimes be right down to it and say, "I really don't see any potential for this actor!" or "He didn't do the greatest reading, but I do see some potential."

Sometimes an actor will do a good reading, but for one reason the look or age will be wrong. I will tell the agent, "Listen, this person was good, but he's five years too old." Glynnis, my assistant, makes a copy every day of the interview list so she can read off my notes exactly. She knows me well enough now, so she's able to give trustworthy feedback.

That's a skill too: To be able to put down in writing what you see and it's something I've learned over the years. I teach classes now, and I had to learn to be able to vocalize and give direction. Some directors know what they want but can't convey it to the actor. I've learned to convey what I want in the most specific way possible. If I go see a play and I see an actor that I really like or see one in a showcase or class, I'll often call the agent the next day and say, "Listen, I saw your person. I can't use him right now, but I really think he's a talent." It helps a lot, too, for agents to get that little extra boost. Because that will make them work a little harder for their client.

DO YOU ENJOY TEACHING?

I love it. I wonder if someday I will want to be a director because I love that side of it. I go as much with direction as possible because that again is the creative aspect. I enjoy the teaching, and I may end up going into it because I love to share whatever knowledge I have. I go to speak to groups and at seminars. I like to because more people know what to expect when they walk in my door. That's why I think this book will be good. People will know a little more about what I want and hopefully know, too, that they can just relax, that I'm a nice person and I'm not going to jump down their throat.

14. JUDY TAYLOR
CASTING DIRECTOR,
FENTON-FEINBERG & TAYLOR CASTING

I went to Stephens College and graduated in 1973. I came to Los Angeles two months later and interviewed for different production jobs in personnel departments. I ended up interviewing with Fenton-Feinberg Casting. They'd formed their partnership about a year before. I went to work as their secretary for four years and then was their assistant for a couple of years and have been casting ever since as a part of the company. We're independent and a small outfit and it's nice.

[AUTHOR'S NOTE: Judy Taylor's feature film casting credits include INDIANA JONES AND THE LAST CRUSADE; THE FRESHMAN; BACK TO THE FUTURE I, II, AND III; BIRD ON A WIRE; HONEY, I SHRUNK THE KIDS; ARACNIPHOBIA; and BEACHES in addition to television movies-of-the-week such as BLIND RAGE.]

HOW DO YOU REMEMBER ALL THE PEOPLE YOU MANAGE TO SEE?

The most obvious system is the filing of pictures and résumés. I don't keep pictures and résumés that are mailed in from people I've never met. If I see them in a play or on television or in a film, it tends to stick in the recesses of my brain. I find that it's easier to remember talent when I've met them in relationship to a particular project. I have general interviews when the time lends itself. I've gotten pretty good at it with practice and time. When you're looking for something really specific, the second that person walks through that door, you have an immediate reaction whether they're close to what you're looking for or not.

Obviously, calling on the phone is not a good idea. I love the note system and the postcards saying, "Watch me Tuesday,

I'm on something." I make notes on their picture and résumé at the time that I meet them if there's something in particular that stands out. I keep those pictures and résumés in file cabinets in my closet. Alphabetized. The file grows and grows. Another thing I'll do is, once the project is completed, I'll go through and I'll pull out pictures of people I know and add them to the collection.

DO YOU HAVE SPECIAL TECHNIQUES THAT YOU USE THAT PERHAPS YOU'RE UNAWARE OF TO BRING OUT THINGS FROM ACTORS WHEN THEY COME IN TO READ?

I rarely read people in my office. I know that a lot of casting directors do. I like to think that I can tell from the meeting and by who has sent this person to me and what their résumé says to me, whether or not they're capable of handling certain kinds of roles. I'll know whether they're ready for a supporting role or whether I need to test them out on a smaller role first. I tend to read people when I'm doing a project such as a BACK TO THE FUTURE on which, even though there are obvious choices for the lead, the director says, "I want to have an open call. I want to canvass major cities throughout the country." Then you're in a position where you, as the casting director, have to take the responsibility of reading everybody who comes in because there might be somebody who has done nothing but might have that talent just waiting there. My first effort is to try to put them as much at ease as possible so that I don't get an acted reading but just kind of see what kind of natural sense I can get from them, especially if it's a young person playing a young person. Nothing is more exciting or fresher than for them to just be themselves, which I realize is the hardest thing for them to do. But I try not to direct them too much in my reading because I'm not a director and I don't claim to be. I don't want to give them misdirection so that when they come in to the director, he says, "No-no-no-no, that's not right." So I kind of get a feeling of their own instincts. And if I see that they need to pick up cues or try it in a different way, I will experiment, but I try not to get into it too much because I don't really think that it's necessarily a casting director's forté.

DO YOU ALLOW YOURSELF, AS A CASTING DIRECTOR, TO BE VULNERABLE TO THE READINGS?

Oh absolutely. I am affected enough by it that that's probably part of the reason that I don't read too often. I think the actors are probably more comfortable in a reading situation sometimes than the casting directors that they're reading with. Actors want to come into my office and do scenes or monologues, and I'm more comfortable at a distance when I can view them on a stage. They could probably do it in a closet if they had to, but I want them to be funny and to make me laugh if it's a funny scene. I don't want to feel the pressure of laughing just to put them at ease. I think I'm very vulnerable and willing to be moved in whatever way. I did have an instance on BACK TO THE FUTURE where I met an actor who came in to read for the father and he was it! When he came in, he was rather bumbling and ill at ease and his hair was kind of flopping down in his face. I remember thinking, "This is George McFly."

His name was Crispin Glover, and he got the part. I remember when he read the scene, I wanted to get down on my knees and kiss his feet. I felt like, "This is it!" You know, if people don't agree with me on this one, then I don't know what I'm doing.

HOW ABOUT READING WITH CHILDREN?

I have kids of my own, so I try extra hard to put them at ease because I think I've experienced on occasion kids who are uncomfortable in this situation. I think it's easy to tell the kids who really want to do this and kids who have been pushed into it for whatever reason or think they want to do it but maybe really don't somewhere in their heart of hearts. When I'm interviewing and reading kids, I try extra hard to talk to them about school or their friends, as I'm sure most casting directors do. I don't think that's any real trick. I think we would all want them to be as comfortable as possible because that's how you're going to get the best reading. I don't think I'm necessarily moved by them more than adults, but, boy, when a kid is really on the money for something, that's pretty exciting because a lot of times you'll be meeting kids who haven't done that much, so it's a true discovery situation.

WHAT QUALITIES DO YOU LOOK FOR IN AN ACTOR?

The most important thing for me is their own commitment to their craft. What disappoints me the most is when I meet an actor or an actress, and I sense from them that they think they have it and there's no need to really hone their craft or study or do plays or constantly keep themselves in tune. I do think it's a God-given gift and there's a certain amount of talent that's innate, but that lack of commitment worries me and tends to make me think a little more about how serious they are about what they do. It's such a competitive field, and if I sense a real earnestness, a real commitment to the craft, that's the quality that's most important to me. A lot of times it's evident in the résumé. I think there has to be a certain amount of confidence in an actor when you meet them and a belief in themselves. You can tell when they're taking it really seriously and are devoted. I think they have to be to maintain. I'm sure there are instances when they haven't had to be and they've made it anyway. What impresses me the most and what I look for is the ability to be themselves and not to feel like they have to act in an interview or in a reading. I'll even give them the benefit of the doubt on that one if I think they're working hard.

A sense of humor is important, too. But a lot of times you don't get that in an interview. I'm one of these people who think anybody who has a sense of humor and can do comedy can also do drama, and I would never hesitate to bring them in for a dramatic role. If you have one mastered, the other one can't be far away. I don't know that there's necessarily a flip side. If you're a great serious actor, you don't always have a funny bone.

WHAT ARE YOU LOOKING FOR IN A RÉSUMÉ PHOTO WHEN YOU'RE FLIPPING THROUGH A WHOLE PILE OF THEM?

I want a great headshot that is really representative of how you look when people see you walking on the street, not glamorous or made up, or too much of a character. We want your face to look very much like the way you look when you're sitting there talking to me. If I'm looking at the person and there's very little resemblance to the picture—it's frustrating. If you're in a position to get pictures taken and you don't have an agent or manager to look at the proof sheets with you and you're pretty much on your own, I think I would just get as good a head shot as possible—not go to any great expense. Invariably, what will happen when you do get represented, they won't like your pictures. I'm very sensitive to the fact that it's a very expensive process, so I always say when I meet actors who aren't with an agent, "Don't spend a lot of money. Get something of good quality, something that's going to be focused, and then get a couple of hundred made up. Then wait until you have somebody who's taking a real interest in your career, and then maybe it behooves you to spend a little more money and get two or three different head shots—one that you might use for a sitcom situation and several for features. All of them should be as representative of you as possible.

HOW ABOUT THE RÉSUMÉ? WHAT STANDS OUT TO YOU?

When I look at a résumé, I usually go to the training first. There are two reasons I do that. The most obvious one is to see how committed they are and how long they've been studying. It tells me instantly where they're from. When I'm interviewing, I like to start with, "Are you a native Californian?" We can get off on a whole other tangent just discussing where they grew up and where their families live. I don't look for feature credits, even though we primarily cast movies. If an actor comes in and hasn't done any movies or very little television, we don't just automatically say, "Well, forget it." As long as they've studied and have good stage credits, we're just looking for somebody who is going to be comfortable and know what they're doing. The proper measure is how much they've studied, who they've studied with, and for how long. Sometimes you'll meet people who've decided to go into this after they've gotten a Bachelor of Science degree and God knows what. But then that situation speaks for itself, and they're obviously really committed if they've decided to ditch all of that and attempt to do this. Those people are usually always studying with somebody right away because they want to see if they're going to be able to survive.

HOW MUCH ARE YOU RELYING ON ACTORS' VIDEOTAPES NOWADAYS BEFORE CALLING THEM IN FOR A READING?

We existed without tape for a long time, and I don't remember that it was that difficult. Producers and directors usually have access to either a 1/2-inch VHS or a 3/4-inch videotape machine. When we have to get tape, it saves us from having to order the actual film and go sit in a screening room and mark it. Tape is now an added luxury. I will say to actors who come in and have a good track record that if they have a tape, I look at it more for the enjoyment of being able to view them in their element. It's not like I have to see your tape before I bring you in for a reading. It might be more valuable when it's somebody whose work I haven't seen. As a way of convincing me that they're ready for certain kinds of roles, a tape could be helpful. I look at it more as the icing on a cake. I find that it can be overwhelming. You can spend a whole afternoon, if you've got the time, just viewing tapes. I enjoy doing it, but I find that I kind of wind up limiting myself to the ones I need to see. If I happen to have time, we have a movie viewing session, and we all sit in there and look at tapes and have a great time. Your tape should be put together so that it is representative of the different kinds of roles you can do. If we know it's going to be seven or eight minutes, then it's very easy to run in there because you say, "Well, that's a relatively short span of time." The production values should be good because it will only hurt you if we look at a tape that's put together poorly or isn't lit well or focused properly. It leaves a bad taste in everybody's mouth and, nine times out of ten, has nothing to do with the actor's performance. It's just that it's difficult to watch, and you're angry that you took the time and that it was not fruitful. I wouldn't rush out and have somebody videotape a scene. I would wait until you have something that you're really proud of—because you don't know who's going to be sitting in the room with me. I might have tapes here and Mike and Jane and Valerie and everybody happens to be there and this is your chance.

IF AN ACTOR COMES IN FOR A CALLBACK, SHOULD HE DRESS AND READ THE SAME WAY?

I would leave that up to the actor. Some believe in their lucky suit. They'll come in in the same thing. What I usually stress to actors when they ask me this question themselves is that if you're going in for a professional person, it can only enhance your reading and the way that the director is envisioning you to go with that. If you're going in for an attorney, wear a jacket. Or if you're a woman, wear a dress and heels. I do it in my business. If I'm meeting with an important producer or director, I dress differently than when I'm with you today in my Levi's and tennis shoes. I don't think you have to take it to the extreme on the other hand and go rent a uniform if you're reading for a cop. I think that only distracts from what you're really there to do. And as far as what you wear when you come for your callback, I'd say I'd leave that up to the actor. If he's more comfortable and it means something to him to wear the same clothes, then, fine.

As far as the reading, I try to advise the agent when I call to set up the callback. If the reading was right on the money, I might say something like, "Don't change a thing. Just tell him to do exactly what he did. He was wonderful, the director loved it, and he's just looking at two different physical types. Don't change a thing." Or if the director wished he'd taken more time and didn't give the direction to the person at the time of the first reading, then I might say, "Tell him to take his time." I would want to help the actor out in that respect. I don't think I would take it upon myself to give any specific direction that the director hadn't already indicated at the time of the reading. I wouldn't want to be responsible for him blowing the audition because he did just what I told him to do and it was the wrong thing.

But what I would urge actors to do is if they're in a callback situation and they have a burning question or even a not-so-burning question, to ask. Maybe the reading went great but they think, "Gee, I wonder if . . ." I think they owe it to themselves to take the time to ask the director when they come in for the callback, "Is there anything you want me to do differently? Do you think it would work if I did that?" I would also urge them to think about what's really important to them because you don't want to go on and on with four or five questions. The director might have a room full of people he's waiting to read and be under a lot of pressure, so, as much as he would like to take the time, maybe he doesn't have the liberty. I feel badly for actors when they leave a reading and they're kicking themselves and saying, "Why didn't I do that? Why didn't I ask?" You only go around once and I say you owe it to yourself to ask those one or two most important questions before you jump into that. Especially in a callback situation. Even on a first reading, if you look through the sides and you have a real question, it's important.

HOW SHOULD AN ACTOR READ YOUR RESPONSES?

When actors read for me, they will get a good sense of how I feel. I'm pretty honest. I might have them do it two or three times, or I might say, "I don't know that you're really right for this part, but we might give the reading a try." I try not to mislead and just say, "Thank you and that was great," and have them walk out the door. I think they would be able to interpret pretty much what I said and have a good feeling about how it really went. I don't know that I would be able to say it was awful. I would find that too difficult. I might just say, "I don't know if this is the right project or the right part, but we'll see."

Interpreting the director's feedback is sometimes confusing because they all work differently. Some give immediate feedback after the actor walks out the door and some don't. Some don't immediately tell us how they feel. They like to think about it for a while and maybe we'll have a wrap-up at the end of the whole reading session, in which case you don't get specific feedback on every actor. You'll probably only discuss the two or three that the director was really taken with. Or the one. So in that case, when agents call me and say, "How did so-and-so do?" I can only answer from my point of view and say, "Well, he read very well, but the director didn't seem to respond to him, and I don't really know specifically why. At the end of the session, he only discussed the people that he was really interested in."

If I get specific feedback from the director, I will not hesitate to give it to the agent. I will leave it up to him to interpret it with his client. I think it's a grab bag at best because there are too many people for it to filter through. Actors are seldom going to have the luxury of the director looking right at them and saying, "This is what I liked about it and this is what I didn't like about it." You only get that in a theatre situation where you're being directed and rehearsed on a daily basis and working up to an opening. You just don't have that luxury now. You have to rely a lot on your own instinct when you leave the room as to whether it was a good reading. You have to learn to be honest with yourself because sometimes you're going to get it and sometimes you're not. I constantly get calls from agents, "How did they do? What did they say?" I find that I rarely have something specific to say from my notes except my own comments.

IS IT IMPORTANT FOR AGENTS AND MANAGERS TO OBTAIN FEEDBACK FOR THEIR CLIENTS?

I think it's important to their clients, and that's something that they should do for them. I think I'm influenced a lot by the fact that I'm married to an actor, and I know how important it is to him to get feedback. If there's feedback to be given, I'm more than happy to give it to agents or managers, and I don't blame them or begrudge them for making the phone call. There'll be days when I'm so busy and I'll see a certain person has called and know instantly why they've called because I just had their client in to read the day before. I may be too busy to get back to them that day. When you're doing pilots and you're at the beginning and you're going to have a two-month casting process, it's going to be forever and a day before the director starts getting specific and calling people back. You might not know for a matter of weeks how it's going to go for this particular person.

WHAT EXCITES YOU ABOUT CASTING?

I think the casting of the supporting or smaller roles. That's one of the few places where a casting director's talent can really come through. The perfect example is in casting the leads in a movie. If it's a leading man and a leading woman and they want lists, I might be able to do the lists much quicker than somebody else who isn't a casting director, but ultimately, if they gave themselves enough time, the list would probably be very similar.

When a director gives us a concept for a good supporting role or even a role that has just one scene and you don't have all kinds of money to spend, you really need to get creative, it's your chance to introduce new talent to this director and to give somebody a shot. It's ultimately the director's choice. Our power only comes once we have the concept. We decide which six actors get to the director, and beyond that, some directors want our input more than others. When a director is very open and wants to hear your ideas and how you think, that's exciting. You feel like you're making a contribution. Some directors do that and others don't. You bring them talent and they look and it's their own choice. If it's a director you have the flexibility with, then you can do a little experimenting. You could bring someone in who's not quite what they describe but that I know could do what they want. When they get excited about things like that, that's gravy for us.

WHAT WOULD YOU CHANGE ABOUT THE CASTING PROCESS TO MAKE IT BETTER?

You want plenty of time to prepare, but by the same token, there's a danger when you have too much time to prepare. You'll lose the choices that are really the most right for the project if you're not forced into making a decision. For me, the magic wand would be having a set time period to cast so that you know when your start date is and you know when you need to make a decision. You have enough time to explore all the possibilities but not so much time that you lose sight of the vision and people start disappearing before your very eyes.

I wish I had a director who could communicate exactly what he wanted to me and whom I had a real rapport with. I can take those chances and not worry that they're going to think I've got a screw loose. Someone who will look at it as an adventure. We need to see these people and open ourselves up to the different possibilities.

A very practical one is to have the kind of budget that you would like to have because what's really frustrating is to know you need a certain caliber of actor for a certain role and then be limited by the numbers. It sometimes gets very frustrating on our part. Your director is begging you for a certain thing, and the dollars aren't providing it. I like it when we have a real say in the cast budget. A lot of times, the budgets aren't realistic, and, if we can give advice, it helps.

WHAT HAVE YOU LEARNED FROM THE PEOPLE WHO TRAINED YOU?

I came out to California after I graduated from college, and I didn't really know anything about the film business. I was a theatre major and I knew I wanted to get into production. I was lucky enough to get a temporary position with Mike Fenton and Jane Feinberg as their secretary. I could type very well, and I knew I could handle phones, but I had no aspirations of being a casting director at that time. I've been with them almost fourteen years now, so everything I learned, I learned from them. They were able to mold me to the way that they work. They compliment each other as a partnership. Mike has given me a very good sense of the business as far as making a cast budget and negotiating deals. He's very good on the creative end as well, but the business end is something I knew that I could get from him. Jane is very creative in her casting. She's taught me about not being afraid to expand upon the director's concept. To take that risk. If there's an actor you have a gut feeling about and he's not exactly what the director asked for, but you have this feeling that he could go for it, that's when it can be the most exciting and I've seen Jane do it.

At some point in the fourteen years I've been here, I've

looked at the two of them and thought, "Boy, if I learn the business side from Mike, I'm going to always feel confident and comfortable in the way I go about negotiating deals and doing budgets. And be able to have Jane's willingness to really experiment and take chances and not be afraid. I remember when she met Debra Winger, she felt it instantly. We weren't casting URBAN COWBOY, but they called us and said, "We can't find the girl." Jane and Mike made up a list and both of them felt very strongly about Debra Winger and really went to the mat for her and said, "Just test her and give her a shot." The rest is history.

When I met Tim Hutton, he was seventeen. I remember he walked in, and I ran to Jane and Mike and said, "I just met Tim Hutton, Jim Hutton's son, and he's really good." They looked at me and said, "Judy, you're all excited." They could tell it meant something, and they really believed it, too, which says a lot for them and our relationship. We immediately started sending him out on things. We put him in a TV movie called FRIENDLY FIRE. He went in and read and when the director said, "This kid is terrific," it just reconfirmed that you have to trust those instincts and take those chances and not be afraid.

Maybe actors are less likely to let you down in that situation in a strange way because you haven't read them. You're excited about them as a person. They feel a greater sense of responsibility to be prepared when they've got to read for the producer because they know you're on the line. You're hanging all the way out there. So maybe that makes a difference.

IN TERMS OF INVESTING NON-MONEY ITEMS IN YOUR CAREER, WHAT WOULD BE IMPORTANT?

First, objectivity, because I think actors have a tendency to think it's always something they did and that's the reason they didn't get the part. Maybe they wanted somebody with different color eyes or hair. You have to be able to tell when you did it well and when you did poorly.

In Los Angeles, an agent is very important. Also a sense of humor. In every walk of life, it will only work in your favor.

Attitude would account for a small percentage. I don't

want to see somebody with a chip on his shoulder.

I think when you reach a certain point in your career that a support team can be very important. I wouldn't want an actor to necessarily overload himself in the beginning. I think a manager can be very helpful in guidance and lending that support. I think beyond that, unless you're making a certain amount of money or have a schedule that's really difficult to keep track of, you may be overextending yourself and what you need.

I think the first thing an actor needs would be classes. What actors have to be the most responsible for is—once you get the opportunity, you make the max out of it. The only way you can do that is to have studied and done your homework. Take the time to get prepared, because the opportunities are only going to present themselves so often and the talent, ability, and preparation have to be there when the opportunity does arise. If you get these great opportunities and you're not ready and you haven't taken the necessary steps, then why bother? Make sure you're with an agent that you feel good about. It's a very personal relationship, and, in a business like this that's so competitive and where you're so reliant upon that person, you need to take charge. Instead of complaining or feeling neglected or whatever actors tend to do, they owe it to themselves, I think, to work it out until they're with the person they really feel comfortable with— who sees them the way they want to be seen and envisions the same kind of career moves and the same kind of future for them that they see. Otherwise, I would think that you'd just be butting heads. It would save a lot of heartache studying and getting yourself together. No one can do that for you. That's the bottom line.

15. MARY WEST
INDEPENDENT CASTING DIRECTOR, MINISERIES, MOVIES-OF-THE-WEEK, FEATURES; PARTNERED WITH ROSS BROWN

HOW DO YOU REMEMBER ALL OF THE PEOPLE YOU MANAGE TO SEE?

When a person walks through the door, I write down my first thought. Maybe they remind me of somebody I was in sixth grade with. I always have a typed sheet on anyone coming in on a good day. I write down, "Sat in front of me in the sixth grade and a little like Harry Hamlin." Then when I look at the notes, the actor will immediately fall into place.

I have a computer but I don't use it. It freaks me out. I'm afraid I'm going to touch a button and erase everything. If I can't remember, then what good is it going to do me? You can't take a computer to a play with you.

I have a list of every submission sheet that I've received on any project that I've done. I don't save the pictures because we get thousands. I keep the top submission sheet that comes in. We keep them in volumes. So if an agent calls me about his submissions, I can open the book to that submission sheet and discuss the actor. I keep all the submissions until the project is completed. We have a room in there that proves that! I can always go to that agent's submissions, unless they are preposterous. Ross Brown and I each go through the submissions that come in, each of us separately three times, every single picture, because early in the morning I could really miss somebody. And early in the morning is when he is really on the mark. It helps having a partner who's as different from you as night and day. It's these wonderful checks and balances that protect the actor.

IF AN ACTOR COMES IN FOR A CALLBACK, SHOULD HE DRESS AND READ THE SAME WAY?

Sure, unless I have asked him to do something differently. A great

many producers are men and they tend to say, "I liked the girl in
the red sweater." Women producers and directors will say, "Nice
quality." They'll go for the emotional aspect, the persona. This is
like reverse chauvinism. So again, my notetaking is very important in this instance because there might be three girls who come
in in a red sweater. I found that men tend to identify with a
definite specific like the red hair or the pink tennis shoes or the
girl with the funny laugh. It's very important not to mention the
quality of the attitude to the actor or to the agent. If they had a lot
of energy, and I give this note to the actor, they'll come in like
they're on something—energy for days. I had this kind of
experience on THE DAY AFTER. You bring an actor back and
you learn not to rave to the producers. The actor comes back and
on the line "Oh, my God, my children are dead!" this time he puts
his fist through the wall. The front door is gone. The door of the
producer's office suddenly has the actor's fist through it. You feel
like such a jerk because you raved about this guy and you want
the floor to open up and just swallow you. First dates are great.
Second dates are trying to live up to whatever the magic was that
made the first date work. Interviews are blind dates for everybody concerned.

HOW SHOULD AN ACTOR READ YOUR RESPONSES?

Generally as the truth. If I'm reading and I know the actor is not
going to get a callback, I'll tell him. I'll say, "It's not going to work
on this one."

WILL YOU TELL HIM WHY?

You mean like, "You're cross-eyed?" Maybe I would say, "You
weren't connected in the reading." That's terminology I would
use. Communication is everything. That's what I'm about. I have
to be able to communicate with an actor.

**MARY, AS AN ACTING TEACHER, SOMETIMES YOU'RE
STARTING THE READING AND YOU KNOW THEY'RE OFF
ON THE WRONG FOOT BECAUSE THEY'RE NERVOUS.**

YOU GET ABOUT TEN LINES IN, AND YOU KNOW IT'S NOT GOING TO GET ANY BETTER. YOU KNOW THEY'RE NOT IN TOUCH WITH WHAT'S THERE. I WOULDN'T SEE ANYTHING WRONG—I KNOW MY ACTORS WOULD APPRECIATE IT—IF YOU STOPPED AND SAID, "WAIT A SECOND, YOU'RE JUST NOT CONNECTED, YOU'RE NOT IN TOUCH WITH WHAT'S REALLY NECESSARY TO MAKE THIS SCENE REALLY GO SOME PLACE. NOW LET'S STOP AND YOU THINK ABOUT WHAT'S REALLY GOING ON HERE." YOU CAN TALK ABOUT WHATEVER IT IS AND THEN BEGIN AGAIN. AND AFTER YOU'VE GIVEN THEM THAT SECOND CHANCE, IF THEY STILL DON'T DO IT, WELL, IT'S OVER.

Actually, there are a number of actors that if I'd said, "You're just not connected," they would have connected with my jaw. It's very important to talk to someone prior to reading them. If I feel the actor is trying to be the character rather than be comfortable within his own skin, I might say to him, "I think there's a little bullshit happening here." And if they say, "I don't know what you mean," I say, "Well, it might be me." I'm not trying to be Irene Dunne in my office, "Come in, come in." It's my job to make someone as comfortable as I can. The actor and I are a team like in a rowboat. If I'm taking him in to my producer, he gets in the rowboat with me and we both have an oar. If he's the only one doing the rowing, we're going to go around in a circle. I've got to meet him halfway so that he knows he can trust me. It's like the old joke where the father says, "Jump, jump, I'll catch you" to the little kid. The kid jumps and the father doesn't catch him and the father says, "See, I told you never to trust anybody." It's a mutual trust. I have to know the actor isn't going to come in really bizarre, which has happened. The callback is the scariest thing for the casting director.

On THE DAY AFTER, an actor came in for the role of the minister after Lawrence, Kansas, had been nuked. We had him in. He gave an extraordinary reading and we were in tears. We brought him back for the producers of this huge project for ABC. A callback for that project was held in the conference room over at ABC. It was properly lit and the table was filled. I wouldn't have wanted to be an actor reading for that. This guy came in. He had gone home and torched his clothing, his shoes, his hair, and his Bible. His eyebrows were singed. He had a Bible that had ashes falling off it. I mean, the man had just lost it. He had gone out and done acid after his initial reading. The reading was the very same quality. It was superb, but the window dressing had changed. He had turned it into this bizarre, trick-or-treat interpretation. He opened his Bible and all these burnt pages fell out. Then he hit his hand against the wall, and you could see where he had put his hand probably in the fireplace before he'd come to the interview. He left a big black handprint on the wall of the conference room over at ABC!

HOW DID THE PEOPLE AROUND THE TABLE RESPOND WHEN THE ACTOR LEFT?

It was worse during. I couldn't leave. I prayed I could leave with the guy. What occurred while he was there was bodies shaking. You could feel the table with people trying not to laugh. The man was like a looney tune. My partner and I looked at each other (I was not Ross' partner at the time). It was my first experience with "What in God's name happened to this man since yesterday?" I looked like a horse in a fire because it was my first project of any responsibility. I felt the tears coming up being my eyes, I was trying so hard not to laugh. One of the other people in the room was feigning coughing. He was a gentleman. None of us knew each other well enough that anyone could say, "You people are really screwed. What have you done?" Later they mentioned it to us after he left. There was a call to maintenance to clean the wall, and that was about it. I never had the actor in again, but I've seen him on things and he's an extraordinary actor.

HOW ABOUT AGENTS AND MANAGERS OBTAINING CRITICISM?

Absolutely. Either one. The majority of the inquiries start early in the morning. I call you to find out if one of your clients is available. You say, "Yes, but we have another offer coming in. Let me check and I'll call you back." You and I have two or three phone calls going back and forth and we're best friends by 11:00 a.m. By 2:00 p.m., I'm on another character. So suddenly you and I can't make contact again, so between 5:00 and 7:00 to 7:30 p.m., my first deal is in the process of being made, so you can't reach me. You think, "My God, my client is like— " so we set up the appointment and the same sort of structure is going on. I'm reading people from say 10:00 in the morning till 1:00. Then I've got a lunch break and then I'm reading people from 3:00 to 6:00. So you're calling me trying to find out, and the next morning I've got readings again. It's very important to try and get feedback within forty-eight hours. My clarity or remembrance is going to be dulled by finding somebody for a different role that might change the impression that your client made on me, so I think the sooner the feedback is requested, the better. I think it's very important that when you call the office, don't just say, "Would you have Mary call me?" Say, "I am calling for feedback on Joanie Smith. Would you please give that information to Mary?" Most people who call the office just leave their names. A lot of people are in the office late. I don't know how any of us have social lives. Don't call me at 7:00 in the morning because I'm not going to be here, but keep after me because I would like to give the feedback. There are some people who don't receive feedback well. "What do you mean by that?" and try to get into a big argument. You don't want to deal with that person as much anymore. You don't want to be as candid. You learn. We all learn.

WHAT DO YOU DO WITH A BAD SCRIPT?

Pray. It might have a lot of nudity and you don't want to ask women if they're willing to bare their breasts. You get tired of that. A script will be bad, meaning maybe the material was very stilted. We get stuff that's more arid than smarmy, you know? Dull. What we do with it depends, of course, on who brought it to us. If it comes from a network, you can't just say, "Take this script and shove it." There are only four networks. But I can't possibly do something that I'm not really happy doing.

For example, a pilot came into the office and I knew it was not for me. It was THE BIG CHILL done in the Catskills with the William Hurt role to be played by Danny DeVito. I couldn't envision it because William Hurt is the only person in the world I would like to meet. I thought, "Hey, I don't know the actors that they're looking for. I'm not ready for this." There's somebody else out there that can do a better job for the producer if I feel that way about the project.

WHAT EXCITES YOU ABOUT CASTING?

As an actress in New York, I was working on the stage. I really loved it. I felt like this was it. I came out here and I worked in film and I felt like I was wearing a disguise. I was so scared and nervous. I thought they didn't like me when I didn't get the job. "They" were a sort of nebulous, invisible person who was making decisions out there somewhere. It was my own shyness, which I think everybody has, which became so enhanced in my own mind that I never realized until I started to cast that acting wasn't for me. Casting is like being a gold miner. Every day I feel like I'm walking into the gold mine and I know there's gold there. Every day I know I'm going to strike gold, whether I do or not. That's what I love about it. Because the gold's there and it's my job to look for it. Because there's so much talent around. It's like each one of us has the ability to say just the right thing or the wrong thing to make somebody do something really weird or funny or interesting and you see something you never saw before. And that moment, that moment when you say, "Wait a moment," is why I love doing this. I love casting more than I ever thought I could love anything. It's just so exciting to be in the process.

WHAT WOULD YOU CHANGE ABOUT THE WHOLE PROCESS OF CASTING TO MAKE IT WORK A LITTLE BETTER?

The fear that's instilled in actors, the fear of approval, of asking questions. Everybody's fear is different, so you can't put your finger on it. It's the preconception that a casting director is there to judge you. The "T" in television stands for time, not talent. So lots of times when we don't have much time, actors think we don't like them and that distressed me a lot, because as much as I wanted to be liked when I was an actress, I don't want actresses to think I don't like them as a casting director. I love actors. I hate actors who don't have empathy. But how could they? Many times I have said to actors, "Would you like to come when I'm doing a casting session?" I've made it available for actors to sit in on it because I'm trying to get actors to come in and work for nothing. But seriously, I think if an actor could just be in on a casting session and see—just sit there and see, really observe what goes on, and realize it's never their interpretation of the character we're looking for. It's the physical circumstances. We might have a 24-year-old playing an 18-year-old, therefore, we've got to get a 22-year-old guy playing the 17-year-old brother. An actor thinks, "Well, I was too tall," or "They didn't like me," or "I chewed gum," and he gets all attitudey. Next interview he goes on, he makes it tougher on himself. Actors can make themselves unlovable.

Another suggestion. Do not bring anybody with you on your callback or your interview. If you have a minor child, do not bring your next-door neighbor because you don't want to drive from La Puenta by yourself. I realize if you've got a lot of children, it's important not to leave the children at home alone so you get busted by the juvenile authorities for being a bad parent. But to take everybody that you ever knew to see how movies are made when you go on a call for a reading is a very good way to really piss somebody off. Like the guy who comes in with the entourage. That happens a lot. They all wear whips and chains these days, spurs, and they always have these kinds of girls who are wearing the white gauze dresses and one earring. Everybody sits around our office, and it's real bad. I mean, real bad. Go on an interview alone or I immediately think, "Unprofessional." An agent reminded me the other day of one of my first interviews when I was interviewing children. I went out into the waiting room and said, "Would the mothers all please go outside, so there will be oxygen?"

Another pet peeve is the actor who calls everybody he knows and tells them what I'm casting—the good-guy actor who wants to have his best friends in the community. So every actor in town starts dropping by the office with his picture. This is an actor who doesn't think he's going to get the job. There are a number of actors who say, "Well, she's got thirty-five roles." Well, there are 2,000 submissions! So more than likely the actor who's been told by his friend to call me has already been submitted by his agent, and I have seen him three times and my partner has seen him three times and have, for whatever reason, not felt that this guy is right for the role per our meeting with the producers and the writer and the director. That's very counter-productive.

DO YOU OPEN ALL AGENTS' SUBMISSIONS?

I haven't got a right to be disrespectful to any agency. But sometimes an agent will come by after work, and he'll have maybe one or two people that he wants to submit and he will push four or five pictures in an envelope through the mailbox. I will come in in the morning, and it will look like trash because it will be all balled up, and we'll throw it away. I just did a picture about Alcatraz and when you put out a breakdown, you put a start date on it. On this envelope from this agent it said "Fourth-class mail!" Now that agent doesn't care about his people. I mean, fourth-class mail! That's shocking. I'm not going to judge the guy, but yeah, that's terrible.

DO YOU HAVE ANY DO'S OR DON'T'S FOR ACTORS SENDING YOU TAPE ON THEMSELVES?

An actor should be very careful not to send out "bad tape" to casting directors. A bad tape is one that uses crude language and is probably taken out of a hard R-rated movie, where the exposition that leads up to the actor coming in—which may be the only tape he's got—is some guy referring to a sexual experience he's just had with the leading lady. Sometimes, in order to justify what's coming up, actors will put things on their tapes that are extremely tasteless. Bad tape also means tape that you can't see, or tape that's been done in someone's living room, or tape that comes from one of those "Come and have yourself put on tape!" places, and, oh God, it's terrible. I don't know where they shoot these things, but there's an echo and when they walk across the room it sounds like they've got horseshoes on. They put a dish down on the table, and it sounds like they've put a boulder down instead. There's shadows cast on the wall behind them. I mean, it would be smarter to just turn around, spot the shadow, and do "animal hands" on it! It's a waste of money for the actor. Actors, skip it! Don't send it to me! I look at it, I see it and I hear the echo and the hum, I hear the boulder hitting the table, and I turn it off. Those are the tapes I don't rewind, so the actor knows exactly where I was when he lost me.

BECAUSE OF PAST POOR PERFORMANCE, DO YOU EVER REFUSE TO SEE AN ACTOR AGAIN?

I would never refuse to see an actor because of past poor performance.

HOW CAN AN ACTOR WHO'S BOXED HIMSELF INTO A CATEGORY GET HIMSELF OUT?

That's a challenge. The first actor I ever read was so green. And I said to him, "Hang in there and study and work and do whatever you have to do, but don't give up. Because it's there." That's all I knew to say to him. You don't know what to say. So I was recently in New York and I ran into this actor on the street and he came up to me and put his arm around me. He told me he'd just gotten a really good part in a play in New York and said, "I really want to thank you. You're the only person who took the time. Everybody else just said, 'Next!'" It was really gratifying because that was five years ago. An actor who doesn't read well doesn't do it on purpose. If he's not ready, I generally will ask if he's studying with anyone, and if he says no, I will call the agent. I never ask the actor why. I talk to the agent and say, "May I suggest this person study?" If the agent doesn't know anyone and says, "Who do you suggest he study with?" I will recommend.

It's the agent's job to see that he's sending out quality people because it's too competitive and there aren't that many people who are real natural. The typical teenager has changed so radically. I used Eric Stoltz in a picture called THE KILLER IN THE FAMILY. He played this sort of gangly, not-too-bright kid. He came in and gave a very interesting reading, not too focused, which was perfect for the role. But I didn't know until the next time I saw Eric Stoltz how focused he was. He was studying. He went to class four times a week! I read him for something else, and I realized what a good actor he was. And he got the part in this other movie playing this sort of unfocused kid, and then he's gone on to do other wonderful things. I think he's a young Peter O'Toole. He's going to go through a period where he's going to think, "I'm washed up, it's all over" because it's that maturity thing and then suddenly, he's going to go from "Hi, Eric," to "Mr. Stoltz." It's scary that some actors go through this, and they think, "Well, I'm going to have to go to Omaha and open a hardware store because it's all over for me as an artist," because the spirit is always there. It's the mind that talks you out of it. And other people's opinions. If you never have the engine tuned on your car, ultimately the car is just going to stop. So an actor who is not getting out there and getting into class is going to have a problem. Do not let fellow actors criticize you because they do it behind your back. One person should be running a class and that's the teacher from whom you're taking the class and from whom you're getting your criticism.

It's also important to change teachers from time to time to get a fresh input.

HOW DO YOU GET VALIDATED?

If I don't get validated, I don't work for them. If I have to pay for my own parking, the hell with them! It's the communication with the actors, it's knowing that things have clicked into place. It's really having a good laugh with somebody. But it's never money. Sometimes that invalidates you. A project will look so good on the surface that I would kill to be on it, and then suddenly you would kill not to do it. Also actors are wonderful for validation. They bring me flowers and things, which is really nice. I love that. I've never had anybody do anything real ostentatious. A Corniche wouldn't hurt. I don't mean the game hen, I mean the car! I had a little kid once, who probably couldn't even write, take out an ad in the trades thanking me for casting him in a movie. I thought that was really weird. That embarrassed me.

IS IT OKAY TO SOCIALIZE WITH AN ACTOR?

It depends if I'm really busy. I wish you could do business over dinner. It's more profitable for me to have lunch with an agent or a manager than with an actor unless the actor is producing a bunch of movies. Robert Redford I'll have lunch with!

DO YOU GO TO PLAYS OR SHOWCASES?

Yes. I've been on location a lot for the last couple of years and have not gone to as many plays as I would like to go to, which I will remedy soon, I hope. It's very important to go to plays because there's a lot of actors who are in them that I've never seen before, and many of them do not have agents so they've never been submitted to me. I've seen so many actors in showcases that I wouldn't ordinarily see. I think they serve a very good purpose.

HOW DO YOU FEEL ABOUT THE SITUATION WHERE AN HONORARIUM IS OFFERED TO CASTING DIRECTORS FOR ATTENDING A SHOWCASE?

If you want me to elaborate on the financial situation, I'll be happy to do so because I think it's lousy. I don't want to get into whether casting directors are getting paid or not because that's none of my business. The people who called me said, "Would you come and do a showcase, and we will give you an honorarium." I swear to God, the first time somebody offered me an honorarium, I thought "What's a burial at sea got to do with a showcase?" That's true! I didn't know what they were talking about! They're going to put me in an urn, okay! Well, hey! So I did this showcase and everyone was so bad. They gave me this envelope kind of furtively, slipped it under my arm as they were walking me to my car. I said, "What is this?" They said, "This is a check." I said, "What for?" They said, "It's from the actors." I gave it back to them, and they said, "What can we do with it?" I don't know. I didn't take it. One week I was asked to do five showcases. I said to each of the people, "I will be happy to come and attend your showcase if you will announce in front of the actors present that I am not accepting money for doing it." Four of the five people running the showcases said no. There's a great deal of emphasis placed on casting directors accepting money. I think it's rather odd that only one of these people was willing to let the actors present know that money that they might have spent to be in the showcase was not going to the casting director. Somewhere along the line there, I think things have gotten a little out of hand here as far as casting directors getting the full brunt over all of this money that we are purportedly receiving for doing showcases, because it's in our best interest to see actors, and it's not in the actor's best interest to pay to get a job.

WHAT HAVE YOU LEARNED FROM THE PEOPLE WHO HAVE TRAINED YOU AS A CASTING DIRECTOR?

Do not editorialize with your face. Don't stick your finger down your throat and go, "Ahhh!" when somebody is terrible. A kid came in to read for me. It was his first reading. In the stage directions, it said, "He is thrown on the floor by the man." This guy pantomined the entire fight with this other person. Threw himself on the floor, was strangled by this invisible person. It was the most amazing thing! But I was not laughing, not doing anything but acting like this was the perfectly normal thing! The producer who happened to be there was on the floor. He was laughing so hard, he fell off his chair. Don't let the actor take over. When you're reading, if someone is trying to get your attention and he grabs your hand while you're holding the script and the script falls out of your hands onto the floor and he stays in character because he's crying "real" tears (put that in quotes, please!) . . . I don't give a damn if the actor stays in character if I'm stumbling around on the floor trying to pick up my script and get the responsibility for his behavior in my office back into my hands.

So I say, keep it very simple. Everything I do I have learned from Ross Brown, who took the trouble and two years at $50 a week to teach me. I spilled White-Out in the typewriter. He threw the White-Out on the floor, and I said to him, "Well, now I can't make any mistakes." He threw the typewriter on the floor and said, "Now you can pay for a new typewriter." I did! He took $5 a month out of my $50-a-week paycheck for two years. He overpaid me. I worked for Ross and Hank McCann, both of whom I have tremendous respect for.

IS IT ALL RIGHT TO CALL THE CASTING DIRECTOR AND ASK FOR SOME RECOMMENDATIONS OF AGENTS?

Not as far as I'm concerned. I'm not in the business of not respecting the agent I'm dealing with. I'm not a reference service for actors. I'm not going to say to a client of theirs, "You're getting rotten representation," because it's none of my business. I might call an agent and say, "Listen, I just met somebody who's with you and I want to know why you haven't submitted him to me or why you haven't talked to me about him." I don't do business with actors or deal with actors. An actor has to be responsible for not being afraid of his agent or manager.

DO YOU NEGOTIATE YOUR OWN DEALS FOR CASTING DIRECTOR JOBS?

No. I ask agents if they will do it for me. I can't get involved. I do not negotiate my own deals because I want to please. We all want to be liked, so I will ask an agent if he will do it for me because if it gets into trouble later on, I don't want to be the one who starts screaming and yelling at the person who can hire me again.

DO YOU HAVE ANY NOTES FOR ACTORS?

Yes. Make sure you have your glasses checked frequently. And contact lenses, too. Contacts that don't fit can make you not see enough and you look real starry-eyed and weird. I have found that contacts can be one of the greatest hindrances to an actor or actress not getting work on film because I'll look at them and think, "This person can work in zombie movies!" Ill-fitting contacts can make you hold your head funny. I'll say to an actor, "Do you pump iron?" and they'll say no, and it's because their eyes are bugging out. When you're nervous, anything that's alien to you tends to become more evident. I care about helping an actor get the job. Anything that I see that's going to be a hindrance, I will bring up. For example, I will ask, "Do you wear contacts?" and, nine times out of ten, they do and they haven't had them checked. How your contacts fit has so much bearing on your demeanor in an office, particularly if there's air conditioning.

WHY DO YOU ASK FOR CURRENT CLIENT LISTS?

Sometimes when there's nothing happening, I want to look like I'm busy. When I'm low on casting, I go through the client lists all the time, and I never talk to an agent without having his client list in front of me. I learned that from Ross. If you're going to call an agent, don't waste that person's time by not having his client list so that you know who he's got.

One agent I always call up and say, "Hey, did Mark Harmon leave you yet?" because Mark Harmon left him about three years ago, and an agent without a sense of humor should go home and open a deli. If I can't laugh and joke with an agent, what's the point? The people you have fun with are the ones you want to work with.

CHAPTER 3

INTERVIEW WITH A WRITER-PRODUCER

MICHAEL SWERDLICK
SCREENWRITER AND ASSOCIATE PRODUCER
OF *CAN'T BUY ME LOVE*
AND FORMER AGENT

I was born in New York and went to college at American University in Washington, D.C. I came out to California to attend law school at Pepperdine University. I met people in the entertainment business and became interested. Right after I took the bar exam, I started in the mailroom at William Morris—bottom rung of the ladder. I moved very rapidly out of the mailroom to become an assistant agent, which is little more than a glorified secretary, but you get involved with a lot of the clients. While I was an assistant agent, I found out that I had passed the bar exam and was now an attorney, but at that point I was already bitten by the bug.

After a year at William Morris, I received an offer from Merritt Blake, who runs Camden Artists, Ltd., one of the best small agencies in town. He offered to triple my salary (the mailroom pays zilch) and get me out there as an agent. So I spent a year and a half with him, making deals, rubbing elbows with some pretty big stars, and getting to look at a lot of young talent. I signed a few young people such as Brian Robbins, who is now on HEAD OF THE

CLASS. I spent a lot of time going to Equity waiver plays and trying to really get to know young talent. My door was always open. I would meet total newcomers, right off the street, all the time.

When I was at William Morris, I read seven or eight scripts a week. I would critique them, do a synopsis, and give it to the agent, since he didn't have time to read scripts. He was at lunches every day. That's how I learned how to write—by osmosis through all the scripts I read. One day I just walked in to Merritt Blake and said, "I'm giving you two weeks notice or a month or whatever you need. I'm gone. I want to write scripts." Of course, everybody thought I was nuts. I didn't own a typewriter, I'd never written before, I had no clue as to what I was doing. My first script, CAN'T BUY ME LOVE, was bought by Disney and released all over the country. I'm a full-fledged writer.

IN ADDITION TO WRITING THE SCRIPT FOR *CAN'T BUY ME LOVE*, YOU ALSO WERE THE ASSOCIATE PRODUCER. THIS MEANT THAT THE WRITER WAS PRESENT IN CASTING SESSIONS AND ON THE SET, WHICH IS NORMALLY NOT THE CASE—UNLESS THE WRITER AND THE PRODUCER ARE ONE AND THE SAME. ADDITIONALLY, YOU'VE BEEN AN AGENT, SO YOU'VE SEEN THINGS FROM THE OTHER SIDE. FROM THE COMBINATION OF THESE THREE VANTAGE POINTS, WHAT DO YOU FEEL IS THE ACTOR'S OBLIGATION TOWARD THE WRITER'S WORK, FIRST IN THE READING AND THEN ON THE SET?

CAN'T BUY ME LOVE is my one experience as a writer, and it was a high-school piece. Three or four of my leads were still in high school, so I decided I wanted to be very open with them and listen to any of their suggestions. I made it a real point of asking each actor how he felt about his role. Actors would come up to me and say, "I love this line, but could I say this word instead of that word? It's more comfortable." We would discuss it, and often times I would feel that their interpretation was as good, if not better, than mine.

In the casting sessions, we met over 200 people, and we'd have some actors come in, and they would rewrite my scene for me. I could tell that kind of thing bothered other people in the room—the producer, the director. I thought it was hysterical because I would see these actors' take on it, and they would come up with the strangest interpretations. It didn't bother me, but, I think when an actor auditions, he ought to stick to the script as best he can. I have no problem with an actor reading off the script and I don't think actors should have to memorize when they're reading for a part. I think it's great that they can stand right there with the script open and take their time and not be nervous.

Most actors when they come in are thoroughly prepared. Occasionally, there were a few embarrassing situations where an actor hadn't even looked at the material. I consider that a little insulting. I spent a lot of time writing the script, I'd hired these casting directors, this is my career we're dealing with. In the casting process, it's best for the actor to be totally honest. Don't try to fake it. We had actresses and actors come in, start into the script, and suddenly say, "Could we start the scene over again?" I had no problem with this. If they want to do it again, we would always let them. If you just got the script three minutes before, the best thing you can do is come in and say, "Listen, can five or six people go in ahead of me? I just got the script five minutes ago." You can always be accommodated. An actor should never walk in unprepared into an audition with the writer, the producer, and the director sitting there. I know how tough it is, especially from being an agent, so I want to give an actor the best possible shot.

As far as being out on location or on the set, I look forward to an actor's opinions on the script. We might change it right there on the set, or we'll try it a few different ways—their way, our way, the cameraman's way—everybody has an opinion and that's fine. But actors also have to realize that there are time constraints. If we have to get thirty-five set-ups done in one day, we can't sit around and have script meetings. On CAN'T BUY ME LOVE, all of the actors were great about this, except one who was just a pain, and it got to the point where this person needed to have a major half-hour discussion over every line. I think an actor has to be more aware of the temperament of the other people who are involved and the temperament of that day's shooting. But on the whole, I think I'm pretty mellow about these kinds of things. I'm not such a great writer that I can't get criticism. I look forward to it.

HOW DO REWRITES FIT INTO THE PERFORMANCES ONCE THE FILMING HAS BEGUN?

On location, there were rewrites are for all types of reasons. It snowed in Tucson for the first time in fifteen years. So, "Michael, let's come up with a scene in the snow!" I came up with a scene that morning—practically right on the spot. Rewrites on the set occur because someone will get an idea, and we had a few on this movie that really helped.

And, on the other side of the coin, rewrites may be required if an actor can't handle the line. We had a scene in this movie where I had a certain interpretation of the scene. I thought it was obvious that the take on the scene was comic. The actor was supposed to be playing it seriously, but it was still comedy because he was making fun of another actor in a serious way, putting down the other actor. The actor who was reading the lines did not get that at all. Finally, five minutes before the shot, I came over and asked if he wanted to talk about it. He was great about it. He said, "Sure, I don't understand it." So I acted it out for him with him playing the other role. He picked it up at that point and played a great scene. At times, an actor will be a little hesitant, and I think the best thing is to ask the director or writer or producer for help. It's better to go into the shot with everybody having a clear understanding and get it right than to have to go back and do it again or to do twenty takes.

In our film, we had Patrick Dempsey and Amanda Peterson as the two lead characters, Ronald and Cindy. I trusted them both so much that they could have spun on their heads and whistled "Dixie" and I would have thought it was great because they just *were* those two characters. They could do no wrong. Whatever Amanda and Patrick brought, it so completely embodied their characters that it just made my work look that much better. Sometimes the actor can make the writer look great.

DID YOUR PERCEPTION OF HOW CASTING DIRECTORS SHOULD PREPARE OR HELP ACTORS CHANGE ONCE IT WAS YOUR SCRIPT THAT WAS BEING CAST RATHER THAN—AS IT HAD BEEN WHEN YOU WERE AN AGENT— YOUR ACTORS BEING CAST IN SOMEONE ELSE'S SCRIPT?

When I was an agent, a lot of times if an actor would get cut off at the casting director level, I'd think, "Some people just fall through the cracks—that's the nature of the business." But our casting directors, Caro and Jack Jones, knew exactly the proper take on each scene in the script. They knew which scenes were supposed to be comedy and which ones were supposed to be serious so that, when they would read an actor, they could really prepare him. Caro prepared the actors for us first by reading the scene with the actor, and then by helping the actor along and talking about the script and giving an interpretation to the role that the actor may not have understood or may not have picked up on. I can write what I think is the greatest scene in the world, but, if none of the actors pick up on it, obviously I'm the one who's wrong at that point.

But I also had people come in and read scenes in my movie completely differently from how I had envisioned them, and I'd find myself thinking, "Oh, yeah, that's the way I saw it." So, I still believe it's very important for casting directors to keep an open mind and to just not go for the stereotypical person who they think may be right. They need to keep an open mind and give the director and the writer and producer a lot of choices.

AFTER CASTING DIRECTORS HAVE GIVEN ACTORS CERTAIN SUGGESTIONS AS TO THE DIRECTION IN WHICH TO GO,

WHAT SHOULD THE ACTORS DO ONCE THEY GET HOME? THEY HAVEN'T YET MET THE WRITER OR THE DIRECTOR, SO ALL THEY'VE GOT IS THE SCRIPT AND THE CASTING DIRECTOR'S SUGGESTIONS.

I think they should be familiar with the material and be ready to ask and answer questions, if need be, about the material. Once you're meeting with the producer and director, you're going to be asked questions along the lines of, "What do you think of the character?" So aside from the reading and from the way that you look, I think you should be prepared for this kind of discussion. And you won't be unless you've read the whole script. If you're going to go through the whole trouble of seriously preparing the character and the scene for the writer, director, and producer, I think you should be well versed in the whole script. If I can work seventy hours a week at William Morris and synopsize eight scripts a week, then an actor should be able to read eight or ten scripts a week, no problem. That's their job. It's like a lawyer having to read twenty-five briefs a week. Or an investment banker reading thirty-five prospectuses a week. That's just their job.

Actors will read the one scene with which they're going to audition and not know anything else about the character. That's why in our movie we had guys who, when they read just that scene, would say, "Oh, I have to be a nerd." Well, a lot of guys came in for the reading dressed nerded-out with the glasses and acting goofy. That's not what we wanted. Those are the guys who blew it right off the bat. We didn't want nerds. We just wanted to get people who weren't popular. There's a difference between a nerd—a total geek—and a guy who's just not popular and is into studying and that type of thing. Those guys hadn't read the script. They came in over-prepared as nerds. We had girls come in dressed as cheerleaders. That I didn't find embarrassing—everybody takes their shot, you know? But if you had read the whole script for this movie, you would have come in as who you are. Because that's what the whole movie was about: Just be who you are. If all you came in as was a full-blown nerd, that's all we could see.

HOW SHOULD THE ACTOR HANDLE A SITUATION ON THE SET WHEN THE DIRECTOR AND WRITER ARE AT ODDS OVER THE INTERPRETATION OF THE MATERIAL?

It didn't happen on CAN'T BUY ME LOVE because Steve Rash, the director, was great. Basically, when the cameras start to roll, the writer can jump up and down and cry like a baby if he wants, but it's the director's movie, and I understood that. I think if it came down to a battle between the director and the writer, I think the writer would probably be on the first plane back to L.A. and would be history. It's pretty much the director's movie once the cameras start to roll.

HOW ABOUT A SITUATION ON A SET WHERE THE DIRECTOR AND THE PRODUCER ARE AT ODDS AND EVERYONE STARTS TAKING SIDES? BECAUSE IN THIS CASE, IT'S THE DIRECTOR, WITH WHOM YOU'RE TRYING TO MAINTAIN A GOOD RELATIONSHIP, WHO IS MORE LIKELY TO BE THE ONE WHO DISAPPEARS—IF IT COMES TO THAT.

That's a tough one. I would be as diplomatic as possible and be nice to everyone and when the cameras roll, just take your best shot!

We had an interesting thing happen in our movie when it wasn't even the director. The producers fired a P.A. She just wasn't doing her job. She wasn't maintaining crowd control, keeping kids quiet on the set, and we had to do take after take because of the noise. Five or six of the actors banded together. "We're leaving. Either you rehire the P.A. or we quit the movie." Big mistake. An actor has to realize this is a business. This is not camp where we're all in a bunk together and we're going to make marshmallows and s'mores. It's a business. And when you have seventy-five people standing around and you have to do take after take after take because someone is not doing his or her job, the actors should realize there's money being spent here. The production manager and the producer and everybody were not happy about having to spend valuable time arguing about something that should never have happened in the first place, and then had already been taken care of.

IF THE DIRECTOR HAS A PENCHANT FOR CHANGING LINES AND ALLOWING ACTORS TO AD LIB, HOW DOES THIS MAKE YOU FEEL AS A WRITER? OR IS THIS SIMPLY A PART OF THE PROCESS YOU HAVE TO LEARN TO ACCEPT?

I think it's just part of the process you have to learn to accept more often than not. My experience on this film was that they came up with a better line. However, I was very lucky. Pretty much what I wrote is on the screen. A few minor things were changed and one-liners were added by actors during the scenes. I think all for the better. Who better to know how to deal with a high-school party than high-school kids? They knew what to say. I thought it was great. I could see how writers could yell. If a writer wrote TERMS OF ENDEARMENT and an actor wanted to change a scene, that's one thing. I think comedy is a little different. If an actor comes up with a line and it's hysterical, we rewrite the comedy. The actor did you a favor. You've got to be open.

WHEN YOU'RE DEVELOPING IDEAS FOR SCRIPTS, HOW MUCH OF IT COMES IN RESPONSE TO INPUT FROM ACTORS? DO YOU GO TO ACTING CLASSES YOURSELF? DO YOU HAVE ACTORS READ YOUR WORK BEFORE IT GOES TO YOUR AGENT?

I don't go to acting classes. I have a lot of friends in the business and friends who are actors who will read my scripts as friends and give me their take on it. But no, I basically don't show anybody my work until I show it to my agent. She's probably the first person who sees it. Maybe one or two close friends along the way will read a rough sixty pages. For the most part with most of the writers I know, I don't think actors get involved.

I know a few writers who go to acting class, but not a lot. Directors go to acting class because they want to see how the whole process works for the actor. But I covered that pretty well as an agent, and it was a lot of fun. Actually, I would like to write a movie about that someday because I think it's pretty funny—some of the things that go on. You know when an actor walks through the door into a casting session who's taking it really seriously, and who's in it because of their pretty faces or because they're a hunk or model type. The actors I respect are the ones who take their work seriously. This is their life. This is what they want to do. (Some take it a little *too* seriously. I had an actor walk in and he was doing guru stuff, mantras, and that scared me a little. I thought demons were going to start popping out. You don't have to go quite that far. Another actor came in and started to do pushups. If that's what gets you psyched, that's fine. It's kind of weird, though, when a guy comes into the room and starts to do pushups!)

WHAT DO YOU TALK ABOUT IN CASTING SESSIONS AFTER THE ACTORS LEAVE? HOW DO YOU DECIDE WHICH ACTORS TO CHOOSE?

We talk about everything. Acting ability, personality, the way an actor came in. Some actors come in like they're asleep. But, first and foremost, we talk about their acting ability. And a lot of times the look. Look is a big part of it. Also, a lot of times, an actor will come into the room (this happened in our movie) and four or five people would show no interest and one person would fight for one particular actor to come back. I think we had two or three people in the film based on people in that room fighting, whether it be me or the director or the producer.

Patrick Dempsey, for example, walked into that room and he was it. I saw him read a couple of times and he was the character. He was Ronald Miller. We loved the way he read and we asked him to read with five different actresses. A total pro. You would ask him to do it a different way and the guy would just do it eight different ways. He turned out to be a consummate professional on the set. Totally prepared.

Amanda Peterson, totally prepared. When we put her on tape, it was, "Do you want me to do this differently?" Asking all the right questions. "How about if I tried this?" She really made us feel comfortable with her right away. But the first time I saw her, I didn't immediately recognize her as the character, Cindy Mancini. Everybody else thought she was great and I had my doubts. There was another actress I thought was a little more interesting. Then Amanda read again, and the second time around it hit me. I missed the boat on this one. But most of the actors I pretty much knew were right for their roles from the beginning. I usually had two or three choices for each character the first time I met everybody, and then we started bringing people back.

When we met Tina Caspary, I knew from the first day we were going to keep bringing her back until we found something in this movie for her. Because there was just something about her. She could act. She was a total professional. And she had real energy. Every time she came in, she was up. And that's great. You get a lot of actors in there that are asleep and you need to wake them up, but Tina was completely the opposite and I thought she would be a great person to be on the set with because she could keep everyone together and the energy level high. It proved true. She was an absolute professional.

I think that's the most important thing for young actors, just be professional. A lot of times I think they read about the Brat Pack punching out people, smashing beer bottles. I think it's a bunch of nonsense. I think they should know that if you treat people like professionals, they'll treat you like one. You always get back what you give out. We had a great group. I couldn't have been any happier with the cast on CAN'T BUY ME LOVE. They all looked around at each other and said, "All right. We're making this movie in twenty-nine days on a 2.7 million dollar budget, and let's just go for it. Let's everybody get into it and do the best we can and work as hard as we can." So Disney bought it and it came out in 1,300 theatres. I think it's because the actors really pulled together.

HOW CAN AN ACTOR TAKE RESPONSIBILITY FOR HIS CAREER?

The toughest thing is to get your foot in the door. Once you have that foot in the door, the most important thing is to take it seriously. When I was an agent, I had young actors and actresses, on their way up, lots of potential, and then they would not show up at an audition. I'd get a call ten minutes before the audition and hear, "I can't make it." It's so unprofessional. You have to be professional. This is going to be your job, and you've to get out there and do it. Get serious about it and show up on time, show up prepared.

If I'm an agent and I leave a script for you in the mailbox in my office, you've got to have it read the next morning. If I come in the next day and see the script still sitting there, I know that you're not going to be prepared for the meeting. This is your job to take it seriously. Don't be an actor if you can't put up with the whole preparation process, because you're wasting your time. Don't waste the agent's time. Don't waste anyone's time! Because this is a business, first and foremost, but it's a business with a lot of great creativity.

Never be afraid to ask questions in the casting session, too. As a matter of fact, this flatters a writer and a director, so be careful that they are legitimate questions. A lot of times, actors come in and you know they've prepared a question just to flatter you. You can see through that. It's as if all night the actor worried, "Now what can I say to the writer to get him to like me?" The actor has picked a totally obscure scene in the film and begins, "You know the scene where . . ." I'll think "Oh my God," and the producer will lean over to me and say, "Prepared question, prepared question!"

CHAPTER 4

THE TOOLS OF YOUR TRADE

PICTURES

Pictures are the single most important sales tool, besides your acting ability, that you have.

Your theatrical headshots should be realistic and look like you because casting directors are expecting what they see in your pictures—not some stranger—to walk in at the appointed time. Beefcake and cheesecake pictures are offensive to casting people. Pictures that don't look like you are worthless. A good headshot shows the actor facing the camera, looking directly at the viewer. The face should fill at least three quarters of the frame, so that the viewer's attention goes immediately to the eyes. The picture needs to stand out from the other 500 the casting director received that week.

A headshot for commercial work must always show you looking happy, perky, and in love with life.

Your name should go on the picture, at the bottom in the center, below the photograph. Your agent and manager's names should not be on the picture, but only on the résumé. The picture should look clean and unencumbered.

In planning what you want your head shot to look like, consider the kinds of roles for which you're usually submitted. Check your log and talk to your agent and manager. Interview them about how they see you. How do you see yourself? Is there a known star you look like—perhaps a younger version? To be described as a young William Hurt or Mickey Rourke isn't all bad.

It is definitely appropriate to use a hair and make-up person. Many of these professionals like to pick up extra cash during slack times, and they bring the know-how and expertise of their film and television work with them. Light makeup is very acceptable, and a good touch-up lab can retouch under the eyes and cover any blemishes that might come through. Avoid heavy, high-fashion makeup. Women should pay particular attention to their hair. The way your hair is styled (curly, french braid, pony tail, perm, etc.) may be the deciding factor in getting you work.

In considering which of the photograpers is right for you, it helps to look at their books to see their composition and lighting. Most will be happy to show them to you. Ask beforehand about the photographer's policy regarding reshoots, payments, number of rolls, cost of enlargements, and canceled appointments. Your agent or manager can often recommend a photographer from whose photos their clients have scored a high average of interviews. Even after all your research, it doesn't mean the pictures will be totally suitable for a long period of time. Pictures are a continuous thing—requiring constant updating and expense.

RÉSUMÉS

Your résumé should be redone whenever additional credits in TV, film, or stage are added or you have mastered another important skill. There are different opinions on how résumés should be set up. I like to list either feature films or theatre first—whichever is your stronger credit. List television second or third. Don't list commercials. List only those special skills in which you excel. These should include dialects. The résumé should be the size of the picture (8" x 10") or slightly larger (8-1/2" x 11"). It should be printed on good-quality paper, but stay away from colors that are difficult to read. I prefer a very light slate grey or off-white color. The picture and résumé are stapled back-to-back at the upper left-hand corner. The résumé should be whittled down as your career progresses, so that your more significant credits remain and your less significant or representative ones are left out. It is very important that you keep your résumé updated with your current agent and phone number. If you change agents, it may be difficult to track you down since agents frequently don't have time to pass information on about former clients, especially when there's no commission involved.

In formatting your credits:

1) If it's THEATRE, list the TITLE OF THE PLAY, the CHARACTER you played, the NAME OF THE THEATRE, the DATE/YEAR it played (optional).

2) If it's a FEATURE FILM, list the TITLE OF THE FILM, the ROLE you played, the STUDIO, and the PRODUCER/DIRECTOR of the film.

3) If it's TELEVISION, list the TV SHOW or SERIES, the ROLE you played, the NETWORK the show appeared on, the DIRECTOR, and the STAR(S) (optional).

Directors' names should be listed as often as possible, since they establish a track record. Putting the studio down makes it easier later on to find tape on the actor. It's important to be honest about the size of the role—"featured," "co-star," "star" billing, etc., should only be used where appropriate. Each of the billing terms indicate a number of things: money, the length of time on the screen or the amount of dialogue, and the efficacy of the agent/manager in deal making.

Training and special skills are important, especially if your professional credits are few. It also helps if you have trained with prestigious teachers, such as Stella Adler, Lee Strasberg, Uta Hagen, Sanford Meisner, etc., so be sure to list them if you've studied with them.

Résumés can be typeset, but, keep in mind that unless the printing company has a free updating service, it can be costly to have it redone each time. I have a typist redo my clients' résumés as soon as they need updating, which is cheaper than typesetting in the long run. Having a résumé typed will cost $10 at the most, probably less, and is a good investment. If you have it typed, an additional credit can be inserted or written in, so you can use up some of the résumés before going to the cost of having them redone entirely. When you do update your résumé, make sure you provide your agent with the most recent résumé and that he throws away all the old ones, even if you have to go in yourself and collect them.

The résumé must include height, weight, hair, and eye color. So many calls go back and forth between casting director and producer over silly things like height (the star of the project may be very tall or very short) or coloring (they want to match you with a set of parents), so having the correct information immediately available on the résumé indicates professionalism and saves time. Changes in height or weight probably mean more for child or adolescent actors than adults.

Don't list your age or age range, although actors under eighteen should list their birthdate. Don't emphasize your singing and dancing credits unless you want to be considered only as a dancer or singer. Avoid cutesy or autobiographical information on résumés. Keep them businesslike. Never list your home phone number. List your agent's, manager's, or an answering service number. Your résumé should have your agent or manager's logo on it or be on their stationery. You should also be current with SAG and AFTRA computers, as well as the *Academy Players Directory*. Actors don't realize how easy it is to get lost—or how widely those computers or the *Directory* are used. Desperate producers in casting sessions will leaf through the directory hunting for the right face and look.

On the following page is a sample résumé for the actor Ross Harris. Its layout reflects the preferred format outlined above:

Terrance Hines Management
6542 Fulcher Ave., No. Hollywood, CA 91606

ROSS   HARRIS

HT. : 6'   AGENT: PROGRESSIVE ARTISTS
WT.: 146 lbs.   BEL ZWERDLING
HAIR: BROWN   400 S. BEVERLY DR. SUITE 216
EYES: BLUE   BEVERLY HILLS, CA 90212
                          (213) 553-8561

FILM

"Centurian Odyssey" – Starring as "Eric" – Music 33 –Michael
      Phylegar, Dir.
"Testament" – Starring Role – American Playhouse – Lynn
      Littman, Dir.
"Another Man, Another Chance" – Co-Star – Claude Lalouche, Dir.
"Airplane" – Co-Star – Paramount – Zucker, Abrams, Dirs.
"Once in Every Three Million Years" – Co-Star

THEATRE

"Four Corners" – Starred as "Jimmy" – Odyssey Theatre, 1985,
      Gina Wendkos, Dir.

TELEVISION

"Home Sweet Homeless" – Starring Role – CBS – Kevin Hooks, Dir.
"Wild West" – Starring Role – WDR-TV Germany – Dieter
      Wedel, Dir.
"Together We Stand" – Guest Star – Universal
"Young Harry Houdini" – Co-Star – MOW – Disney – James Orr, Dir.
"Penalty Phase" – Co-Star – MOW – Tony Richardson, Dir.
"Under One Roof" – Starring Role – NBC
"United States" – Series Regular – NBC
"Two Kinds of Love" – Co-Star – Universal
"Fire on the Mountain" – Starring Role – MOW – ABC
"In the Custody of Strangers" – Co-Star – MOW – Filmways
"Amber Waves" – Co-Star – MOW – NBC – Joseph Sargent, Dir.
"Miracle in Caulfield" – Starring Role – MOW – NBC
"The Dog Days of Arthur Caine" – Starring Role – ABC

THE VIDEOTAPE AUDITION CASSETTE

While the 1/2-inch videotape is certainly not an uncommon format, the vast majority of casting people, producers, and directors have 3/4-inch machines in their offices. 3/4-inch tape is wider and the signal maintains itself better, therefore giving you better visual quality.

Companies that put together a professional 3/4-inch audition reel usually charge for videotaping shows off the air (called an "air check"). Sometimes the company will store your master in their library, so if something happens to your copy, you can go back and very quickly have another copy dubbed off the master. You definitely need to have duplicate copies of your tapes because sometimes people don't send them back for long periods of time or the machines they play them in aren't clean and might spoil the tape. It is important for your agent and manager to each have one tape. And you should have at least one copy, too, in case all the rest are tied up for some reason and you can't get to them. At least you'll have one tape to take to the audition or producer.

Your reel should be three to ten minutes long and contain your best work. It's like a résumé and needs to be updated as soon as you start to change physically. If you've done a wide variety of roles, you may need two demo reels—one with comedy and one with only serious material. If you have two reels, you have an option of presenting yourself in two different ways. You can also set up a reel with contrasting scenes throughout, so you can show your versatility. Approximately two minutes of each role should be on the tape. The material should be arranged so that you put the larger and more important roles first.

If you need a scene from a feature which hasn't been released yet, the producer's office might be willing to give you a piece of it. Certainly, once it's on cable or home video, it's easy enough to get your scene on cassette. If you absolutely have to show someone a piece of that unreleased feature in which you are "fabulous," it is sometimes possible—if you beg and cry, or if the request is from Steven Spielberg—that the studio will set up a screening. Studios want to keep important casting directors, producers, and directors happy.

If you don't have major credits, but you did a large role in an AFI, USC, or UCLA student film, put it on videotape. Sometimes the school will provide you with a copy of the film for your participation in it. This assumes, of course, that the student film was properly lit and shot. Taped scenes from showcases and acting classes, however excellent the acting, usually are not properly lit. Your work looks amateurish, overshadowed by the bad production values, and this kind of videotape will definitely work against you.

You need to label the tape correctly with your name, your contact phone number, the order of the clips, as well as with the approximate running time of both the whole tape and of each segment. This allows the viewer who has neither time nor interest in viewing the entire tape to easily cue up whichever segment is appropriate. This is also why your best material should be at the beginning of the tape—in case the viewer does not watch the whole thing. Be sure and clear all of the material with your agent or manager before you put it on the reel to make sure someone else agrees with you that the material you've chosen will work to your advantage. Tape can work against you in some situations where a piece of tape isn't as current as you need it to be or isn't the right quality for the role they're casting. It's a real guessing game in some cases, but the best thing to do is to have your agent/manager talk to the casting people and find out what they're looking for so that you know whether you have a piece of tape that's useful.

A SENSE OF HUMOR

Along with pictures, résumés, and videotapes, you will have constant need of a working, well-oiled sense of humor. In order to help you keep it in good running order, listed below is a brief glossary of casting directors' often-used criticisms and their translations:

NOT SPECIAL ENOUGH — This means you don't look like Robert Redford, have the versatility of Robert DeNiro, or the sense of humor of Woody Allen. Otherwise, you're fine.

BORING — You didn't really want to be there, or the casting director is tired and wants to go home, or he's late to a screening.

TOO ETHNIC — Your hair is black and your eyes are brown and your name might have been Spanish or Russian or Italian at one time.

NOT ETHNIC ENOUGH — You don't have the one-quarter Indian, Eskimo, or black blood required by the SAG rules for this role. Go home and get your birth certificate.

NOT HANDSOME ENOUGH — They're looking for Rob Lowe look-alikes who will work for scale. You're not it.

NOT SEXY ENOUGH — The casting director is a leg man and you're all bosom. Or if it's a woman casting director, you remind her of the football player she had a bad experience with when she was fifteen.

SORRY, WE HAVE SOMEONE LIKE YOU ALREADY — But they thought they might want to get rid of that person, so they brought you in and then changed their minds.

I DON'T KNOW WHAT TO DO WITH YOU — You are so versatile and can play so many roles that I'm too lazy to categorize you.

YOU HAVE THE WRONG LOOK — I don't know what I'm looking for, but I will when I see it . . . and you're not it.

YOU'RE TOO TIMID — Your sudden attack of shyness didn't cheer us up or make our day. Better luck next time.

CRAZY — Maybe you thought it was clever, but don't you ever, EVER, come to an interview again chewing that trick gum that forces you to salivate fake red blood down your chin and onto the papers on my desk!

TOO SHORT — We're casting NIGHTRIDER with David Hasselhoff, who's 6'5" and you'd look silly next to him at 4'10" tall.

WORK HOURS — You're under eighteen, so we have to follow the rules. We want someone we can work cheaply twenty-four hours a day.

OUT OF STATE — We can take advantage of the rule and work you as above.

UNFINISHED — This means I don't have the heart to tell you that your acting at its best is a bad impression of a wooden Indian.

SIT-COM-EY — Stop mugging at the casting director and posing while you wait for laughs.

STAGEY — Don't ever stand on my desk again to make a point! And do something about those continuously working eyebrows; you look like the wolf in LITTLE RED RIDING HOOD.

COACHED — You did it so perfectly that we can't come up with any suggestions.

YOU STUNK — You can't act and should go back to cleaning the animal cages at the St. Louis Zoo. (This has been said to stars who are now making millions!)

WE WENT ANOTHER DIRECTION — They already hired someone and didn't tell us. She's the director's girlfriend.

PART TWO

CHOOSING
THE
JOBS

CHAPTER 5

WHAT DOES A MANAGER DO?

A personal manager is someone whose job is to develop and guide an actor's career along the road to eventual stardom. Along the way, the manager must decide which projects will benefit his client and help to expand the artistic and business growth of the partnership. The manager often becomes friend and confidante.

A personal manager is a gambler. Very few agents are in the position to turn down work because it doesn't advance an actor's long-term career goals. A personal manager might and should. The manager's job is not to develop "day players." The agent often works on the ten-percent philosophy, while the manager is more interested in the long-term gain—and that may require years of sacrifice and hard work for both the actor and the manager. The manager may have to advise the client to turn down well-paying television roles that overexpose the client, or that only allow the client to continue being regarded in a category which has become too limiting. The manager's advice may be to skip the money this time and, in its place, do theatre, even non-paid waiver theatre, so that another side of the actor's talent can be shown and eventually used as a springboard to feature roles of a wider range.

The careers of actresses such as Sally Field, Farrah Fawcett, and Bruce Dern are examples of how such transitions can and do occur. Fawcett felt she was being exploited for her beauty, not her acting, and it took the role of a rape victim who eventually fights back, which she played on stage in EXTREMI-TIES, to turn around the industry's image of her as the blonde head of hair on CHARLIE'S ANGELS, the series which had first

brought her to prominence. The television movies THE BURN-
ING BED and THE BEATE KLARSFELD STORY have now solidi-
fied the image her as that of a powerful actress. Because of her
success in the TV series THE FLYING NUN, Sally Field was only
being considered for "cute" roles consistent with the industry's
image of her as Gidget in a habit. Not until after SYBIL, a
television movie of the true story of one woman splintered into
nineteen personalities, was Field considered for the kind of
feature roles in which she would eventually triumph and for
which she received her Academy Awards—NORMA RAE and
PLACES IN THE HEART. Bruce Dern made his first mark playing
disturbed villains in "B" pictures. He then went through a period
where the only roles that were offered to him were those of
psychotics. Through wonderful performances in THEY SHOOT
HORSES, DON'T THEY?, SILENT RUNNING, THE GREAT
GATSBY, and COMING HOME, he became known as an actor of
range and varied appeal. Now, when he does choose to play the
disturbed villain, it is because the role interests him. And it's in an
"A" picture. If the actor is always and only in the position of
saying yes to each job that is offered, this kind of growth and
success is virtually impossible.

A good manager can be of criticial importance in helping
the client time these choices properly. There was a time in
Hollywood—and it may still be true of the very largest Hollywood agencies—wherein an actor's entire career was considered, his life was handled, and even his personal tastes taken care
of first by the studio, then by the agency. This is no longer true.
Most agents—while making an attempt to gauge whether a part
will advance an actor's career or not—basically try to get an actor
work, and they don't have the time to focus on the total career of
the actor. If you are the kind of actor who needs someone to take
a good overall look at your career in order to focus it, to help you
handle the thousands of details, perhaps you need a manager as
well as an agent. The reason child actors so often fall into this
category is because agents for children don't have time to
prepare the child for the interview, and, in most cases, the parent
doesn't know how to properly coach and prepare an actor for a
reading. A manager becomes invaluable. When a career becomes

established very successfully, the details only multiply, as have the number of people around you who are unwilling to disagree with you about the potential or consequences of what you're being offered. By that time, a solid relationship with a manager who has an overview of you and the business, and who is not afraid to tell you the truth, can be even more invaluable.

Keep in mind that an agent gets ten percent of your salary. A manager gets ten or fifteen percent more. So any money you make will be minus up to twenty-five percent. Is this expenditure necessary to your career and at what point? To help you understand and decide, are three interviews with personal managers handling a variety of successful careers in a variety of ways. By way of introduction, here follows an "interview" between a manager and a prospective client, which sets out some of the basic vocabulary and responsibilities of personal management.

AN ACTRESS INTERVIEWS A MANAGER
Suzanne Vaughan / Terrance Hines

WHAT QUALITIES SHOULD I LOOK FOR IN MY MANAGER?

You should make sure your manager has time to talk with you about problems and will be available to you after 6:00 p.m. Your manager should be someone you like and respect, someone who's intelligent and has a track record and contacts in the business. He should be someone with whom you agree on the direction your career should take, someone who is respected by people in the business, and someone who takes care of logistics and conflicts for you, so that you can arrive at the right place and the right time with the right material.

Your manager should be aware that each client needs to be treated differently, since they're all individual people. Management is like any other relationship. There are certain clients who are going to want certain services and others who will want something different. No manager is a mind reader, so it's important for you as an actor to communicate with your manager—on a daily basis, if necessary—as to what services you need. Some actors require a tremendous amount of hand-holding. Other actors, especially when they are coming out of adolescence, want to cut the moorings and make some of their own decisions—and the manager, at that point, becomes someone who guides and consults. Some clients love to have that personal attention while others resent it because they want to make their own decisions. It's important for the manager to be prepared to be there for these clients, too, in case they fall.

WHAT DO YOU THINK A MANAGER SHOULD DO FOR ME AS AN ACTOR?

He should have the time to talk to you on the phone to work out a problem and should keep the relationship between actor-manager-agent tight and working as a team. He should keep track of your interviews and make notes of changes that might be necessary, or watch for patterns. He should make sure you are provided with a script—or at least "sides" of the scene to be prepared—and proper time to prepare. The manager's function is the guidance and long-range planning of your career and, consequently, he should be watching the tools (pictures, résumés, tape, and training) closely to determine when it is time to update them again.

Your manager should aid in negotiating the contract, having participated in your previous deals and knowing your needs. He can also serve as someone off whom the agent can bounce ideas. (In California, the manager cannot actually negotiate the deal on his own since contracts may only be negotiated by franchised agents who are licensed and under the jurisdiction of the Labor Board.) The manager must keep in mind the concerns of all the parties and work with them as a team to get a deal that serves everyone's needs.

He should be able to offer an objective look at situations where a lot of non-objective personalities are involved. You should be able to invite him or her to rehearsals, so, again, you can get objective feedback on your work, which often because of your deep involvement you cannot possibly view with objectivity.

LET'S SAY I DON'T WANT AN OBJECTIVE, HONEST OPINION. MAYBE SOMETIMES I JUST WANT SUPPORT. DO YOU OBJECT TO THAT?

Providing support is essential, but a good manager cannot agree with his clients simply to keep the waters smooth. He needs to be able to stand back and take a look at all the ramifications of certain decisions—whether they be the actor's choice or the agent's suggestion. It's important that your manager be able to look at all aspects of a problem and give advice, but it's vital that he does not make the final decision. The decision should come by agreement between all parties as a result of providing the actor with the information needed to make the best possible decision. It's better to have too much information than not to have enough or none at all. While we're trying to build your career, my job often involves trying to keep you happy, but that's not the same thing as keeping you ignorant.

SHOULD MY MANAGER GO ON AN INTERVIEW WITH ME?

It is a good policy—especially with child actors—for the manager to escort the client to the interview whenever possible. The physical and emotional support and hand-holding is often necessary. With adult actors, the manager is a presence, and he must keep in mind when not to hand-hold. The manager should get together with the actor ahead of time and work on preparation for the interview—go over the material, make choices, discuss wardrobe, dressing for the character, etc.

I have found from my experience that escorting even my adult clients to occasional interviews has proven very successful—although I never go in to the reading with them. That little push of extra support can frequently be the thing that pushes the actor over the edge into getting the role. It is also a wonderful oppportunity for the manager to be visible with casting people and renew his relationships with them. Often casting directors will call me at my office to ask me for a recommendation for talent for future projects or the capabilities of my client—and sometimes even ask if there's anybody new I'm representing whom they should meet.

From my standpoint as a manager, one of my biggest advantages is that I teach acting. I can watch, train, and encourage my clients in the specific aspects of what they're trying to do. They're not all alike. Not all of my clients study with me. I encourage them to take classes in other areas with other teachers.

HOW MANY CLIENTS SHOULD MY MANAGER BE HANDLING TO AVOID LOSING ME IN THE SHUFFLE?

If a manager handles only adults, he can handle more clients, because, on the whole, they require fewer services than minors. If a manager is working principally with minors, not only must the manager be prepared to arrange for such things as transportation, a set-sitter, and coaching, but he must also be prepared to make many of his clients' career decisions which adult clients decide for themselves.

If your manager has more than fifteen adult clients whom he's handling alone, you should find another one—because he won't have time for you. If you're a minor and your manager has more than ten minor clients, find another manager.

DO I LOOK LIKE A MINOR TO YOU?

Well, . . . you could certainly play young. You could definitely play under—

IT'S FUNNY YOU'D SAY THAT. CASTING PEOPLE ARE ALWAYS TRYING TO CAST ME IN JUST ONE KIND OF ROLE. I CAN PLAY MEDEA AS WELL AS GIDGET. WHAT'S WRONG WITH VERSATILITY?

During the early period of your career, it's dangerous to be seen as "too versatile." Unfortunately, the "versatile" people don't come to mind for specific roles when productions are casting. Put versatile on the shelf to be brought down when you're better established. At this point, people still have to think of you for roles, certain types of roles, to consider you at all.

HOW WILL YOU DECIDE IF A PROJECT IS A GOOD CHOICE FOR ME?

As far as television is concerned, I think it's important to be aware of what network the project is on. If it's on a network that needs this kind of show, then the project may get episodes ordered and be put in a time slot much quicker than on another network. Check out the director working on the project. If he is someone you admire or someone you have worked with before, it could be an element that could help move you along in the casting process. On the other hand, it might be someone with whom you previously had an unpleasant experience and whom you want to avoid. If you read a lot, watch TV and go to a lot of films, then you get a good sense of what is a good piece of material, what reads well, what tells a story. It must have a beginning, a middle, and an end. I read five or six scripts a week.

WHAT SHOULD I LOOK AT WHEN I SUDDENLY HAVE TO MAKE AN IMPORTANT CAREER DECISION?

The type of role you're playing—how much of an opportunity it will give you to explore your craft. Because, after all, the acting has to be the most important. If all goes right, someday, that's all you'll have. What can the role teach you about yourself, others around you, the world you live in . . . If you're in it for the money, the decision is easier! How much are you getting paid? If you're not getting what you want, turn it down. However, more often than not, if the role or the project is something you really want to do, then you will probably settle for less money. There is next to no negotiating leverage when you love a project and don't want to lose it. In TV series work, you are often offered sacrilegious amounts of money to do something you don't want to do, but you may find yourself in a position where you need to take advantage of the money or the exposure. The money will tide you over so that you can wait for those roles you really want, the real stretch pieces, so that you can still feed your soul and at the same time pay your rent. If a script reads badly, it's not going to get any better. This is true in features as well as TV. The script is the most important element in your decision-making process. If the writers don't have a track record from other shows, don't care about the actors or the characters, they will probably just set up jokes for the actors to deliver . . . something that is not conducive to growth as an actor. When you have multiple projects to look at, many of these things come into play. You have to sit down and put it on paper and really think about it. I use pro and con columns and try to play the devil's advocate as well. I want to open up all the possibilities that might be there. If you're a minor at a difficult age when you're not going to work a lot since there isn't a need for that age group, you might consider a series as a real possibility because it may give you the visibility and longevity you want. Michael J. Fox (FAMILY TIES) and Kirk Cameron (GROWING PAINS) are good examples of what TV visibility can accomplish.

SO TELEVISION SERIES ROLES ARE HOW TO DEVELOP

MY CAREER?

It's important to take a good look at what kind of project it is—whether it's a series that is four-camera with a live audience, or whether it's a series filmed without a live audience. If you like theatre and enjoy the response of a live audience, then you should be looking for four-camera live series such as GROWING PAINS, THE COSBY SHOW, MR. BELVEDERE, or IT'S GARRY SHANDLING'S SHOW, all of which thrive on laughter and the excitment generated from the reactions of a live audience. In choosing a major project for television, consider—if you're a minor—how many other kids are there in the show? If it's about a large family, how much opportunity will there be for episodes to be developed specifically around your character?

If you are recognizable from a TV series, it opens up other possibilities for work during the downtime in a series (hiatus). Also, a series provides a regular—and often quite large—paycheck. It pays more than anything else except twelve national commercials at once! The series is like a regular job with hours that can approximate, but sometimes go way past an 8-to-5 job. Some days you may be going to work so early it's still dark outside. If you're a minor, you need to decide how you would feel about being on the set every day, getting your education there instead of a regular high school or grade school, and being able to see your friends only on weekends. The role has to be something you want to do before you put yourself in that situation, because you're going to be playing this same character, if all goes well, week after week after week, and it's through this character, at least for now, that the public will know you.

WHAT ABOUT MOVIES-OF-THE-WEEK?

If you prefer serious material, you might want to consider movies-of-the-week. MOWs tend to be based more on fact and will give you the chance to explore the serious side of your craft and the more emotional side of your instrument.

The attitude I respect is the one prevalent in Europe and in repertory theatre and, unfortunately, not common in Hollywood, and that is you can be playing a leading role one day and a small supporting one the next. I believe you can step into a MOW or feature film and do a small role, and do a wonderful job. It might be enjoyable and the role might not be one you ordinarily would be cast in. This may not pay immediate benefits, but, in the years to come, it may get you something you really want, and will certainly develop your talent further.

SO YOU PLACE A LOT OF VALUE ON SMALL ROLES IN FEATURES?

It depends on the role. If the role is right for you and it looks as though the film might turn out to be a special film, you should do it. An example of this was TESTAMENT, in which I had two clients, Ross Harris and Roxana Zal, and later handled Lukas Haas, the little boy. This was a PBS/American Playhouse Production and didn't pay a lot (around $800 a week). It was shot during the rainy season, which was a miserably cold experience. BUT . . . the director was the wonderful Lynne Littman who brought the best out of her actors and out of the film, which got a lot of acclaim and in the long run helped all the other actors' careers immensely. A project like this is very important to watch and push for. Keep your eyes open and see where the material is going to go in the future. Maybe the project will be a cult film, or it will play film festivals, or it's going to give you a wonderful piece of tape that you can use to engineer interviews as well as give you clout when you start to meet studio execs. It might also give you the opportunity to work with more experienced and respected actors.

OTHER THAN BAD WEATHER ON LOCATION, ARE THERE ANY OTHER KINDS OF DRAWBACKS TO DOING FEATURES?

Many times feature films are shot overseas. Obviously this presents wonderful opportunities—experiencing other cultures, learning new languages and foods and ways of thinking, working with actors you wouldn't otherwise meet. On the other hand, it can also mean time away from families and friends, and your at-home relationships can and do suffer. If you are a minor, you must consider the time away from regular school. Sometimes even straight-A students will drop a letter grade because of missing the labs and P.E. requirements. Can you handle this full work week and go to school at the same time?

When you do film, there is a big gap between when you shoot and when it arrives at a neighborhood theatre—sometimes as much as a year. In the meantime, if you're young, you may have physically changed by the time the film comes out. So the usefulness of a film in terms of career advancement may not be as strong as doing television, which will be on the air in less than three months and in which you're visible every week, or in some cases, every day. The audience sees what you look like and becomes very familiar with you. Also, what if you turn down other things for a feature film that you think will do wonders for your career, and the film finally comes out—and it's a bomb! Or there is the possibility of it being shelved. Or the film comes out, is a hit, but your work has been whittled down to insignificance. When you're considering a feature, keep in mind who's already cast for it. Do you respect the lead actors? Do they always do their best? Do you want to associate yourself with these people?

LET'S SAY I'M VERY CLEAR ON MY GOAL: I'M GOING TO BE A REGULAR ON A TV SERIES BY TWO YEARS FROM TODAY. IT'S A 24-HOUR-A-DAY JOB. WOULDN'T TRYING TO TACKLE THE THEATRE SCENE AS WELL BE A DISTRACTION? AND COULDN'T IT MAKE MY FILM WORK "STAGEY?"

Theatre is extremely important to any actor, whether it be in Los Angeles, New York, Chicago, or Turtle Creek. Actors should be encouraged to do as much theatre as possible because in the theatre an actor has the opportunity to give a sustained performance and also to work in front of a live audience. Check *Variety*, *Drama-Logue*, and the *Breakdowns*, as well as your agent or manager and your own sources to keep searching out good directors and plays that you can read for, even if you get nothing

more than the experience of reading for the play. It's different
from reading for TV and film because the actor is usually reading
in front of a group of actors. Equity or Equity waiver (no pay)—
it's still an opportunity for the actor to grow and tackle roles that
he might not get in film or television because he is still too young
and not the right type. It gives him an opportunity to stretch his
craft beyond where his life has yet to take him. When Laurence
Olivier played Lear and Othello in his twenties, he played
through pure imagination. Later he performed these roles at the
National Theatre when he approximated the character's true age,
allowing him to bring a knowledge and experience to bear on his
interpretations. They were landmark performances. Even if yours
aren't, encourage your agent and manager to come and see your
work. They can judge whether you should invite casting people,
which will also depend on the quality of the other actors and the
quality of the play itself.

WHAT IF I ACTUALLY LAND A SERIES AND IT'S SUCCESSFUL. WHAT DO I DO SO THE MONEY DOESN'T ALL GO TO TAXES?

Series deals provide some of the best money available to an
actor, but Uncle Sam assumes your weekly salary will be paid all
year long, even though the network only ordered ten episodes.
With this in mind, Uncle Sam will take between fifty to fifty-four
percent of your check. When you total this up, along with the
agent's ten percent and the manager's fifteen percent, it is costing
you a lot of what you earn to do the series. This will not be as
much of a problem if the actor has established a track record with
commercials running, or a small bank account of working capital.
You can claim nine to thirteen deductions, but, if you go over this
or claim an exempt category, it will trigger a notice to the IRS,
who will cast an eye at your accounting. The only way to prepare
financially for a series deal is to incorporate. You'll need a good
entertainment lawyer. This can cost you $1,000 and up. But as a
corporation, your taxes can be estimated quarterly and paid that
way to stop the weekly tax bite. If you're a minor, you'll want to
consider emancipation, which means that you legally become an

adult before you are eighteen years old. In the state of California, this will exempt you from the Coogan Law, which in order to protect child actors requires that twenty-five percent of their weekly earnings be placed in a trust account by the courts and cannot be touched by them or their parents until the child is legally of age. The Coogan Law does not apply to commercials or episodic television—only to long-term feature roles and on-going series roles. The reasonable assumption for an emancipated minor on a series is that for the first few years, as in any small business, you won't be able to take anything out of it. The profit will be in the blocked account, earning interest, until you are eighteen. Of course, the series may well generate additional capital by leading to commercials, movies-of-the-week, features, after-school specials, supermarket openings, etc.

I'VE BEEN REPRESENTED BY THE SAME AGENT OR MANAGER FOR SEVERAL YEARS, AND I'VE STARTED TO HIT BIG. I'M BEING WOOED BY A LARGE AGENCY. SHOULD I KEEP MY CURRENT REPRESENTATION?

It takes years for a manager and a client to get to know each other. You need to keep that in mind when you think about going with the larger, more glamorous agent or manager. The people you're with now got you started and know you very well. They've devoted their time and energy to someone who only had a possibility of making them any money at the beginning. On the other hand, the big agency may represent directors, producers, writers, and actors and may be able to service your needs more effectively. You have to make critical decisions at this point. The manager has to keep this in mind when he decides who and how many and what kind of clients to handle. Having an age span to a client list can protect the manager in many respects and allow him to groom the younger actors into adulthood and be able to take advantage of all the time, effort, and money he has put into their careers.

ISN'T IT A CONFLICT OF INTEREST WHEN AGENTS, MANAGERS, AND CASTING DIRECTORS SEEM TO

WEAR SO MANY HATS AT ONCE?

Multiple hat-wearing is the normal order of business in Hollywood. Casting people often manage and teach. Producers write and manage, and somehow all this intermingling adds more opportunities to open doors for everyone.

It seems like a natural evolution for personal managers, agents, and lawyers to expand their influence into the producing and writing areas to accelerate the careers of their clients, especially in a business that relies on the development and nuturing of personal relationships. Jay Bernstein, who started as a personal manager, now wears the hats of personal manager, producer, writer, and director. Bernie Brillstein produces, manages, writes and develops. Ron Howard, Henry Winkler, and Anson Williams, alums of HAPPY DAYS, act, produce, direct, write, and package for their own banners.

Smart personal managers know they have to keep up with their clients as they grow. As the actor reaches a new plateau, the manager has to reach it at the same time, and his services for that level can then be tailored to the client's needs. On the other hand, sometimes being both manager and producer can pose a conflict of interest, for instance, when the personal manager as producer earns more money when his client participates in one of his projects rather than someone else's—although the outside project might be a better role for his client. Or the personal manager-producer may find himself in a time quandary, since both roles demand a lot of time and may cause the manager to neglect management or producer duties in trying to be all things to all men. The solution to this has been for personal managers to become executive producers, hire a line producer, and only oversee the film. Another choice has been to become a full-time producer and stop managing.

WHAT IF I WERE TO HAVE AN "OVERNIGHT SUCCESS"? IT CAN HAPPEN. COULDN'T I THEN JUST BYPASS ALL THIS CAREER BUILDING?

One of the most important things once you're successful is

exactly the same when you're coming up the line and that is to have a very good, strong support system or "base." If you're a younger actor, your support base may very well be your family, secondarily your agent, and then your manager if you have one. As you begin to get more successful, obviously your team is going to increase in size and scope based on your particular needs. Overnight success tends to work against you, simply because you don't have an opportunity to put the support system in place, define the duties, develop the relationship so you can sit down and talk about problems that come along.

If you're too successful too quickly and you don't have a very strong base, you tend to wonder who your friends are and if they should be your friends anymore—simply because you're more successful now than they are. You often see the ramifications of it in broken marriages, in affairs on the set, a lack of respect for other people whose jobs you may not feel are as important as yours. We're all familiar with the worst-case scenarios of enourmous talents who end up dead, from Marilyn Monroe to John Belushi, because, in some fundamental way, they have no idea who they are in relation to the community that surrounds them.

Sid Caesar is a prime example of someone who has taken years to sort himself out. He was the *enfant terrible* of '50's television—he wrote, produced, directed, and everyone thought he was wonderful, and he couldn't cope with it. He was so frightened of being a success and had such a fear of being a phony that he drank for fifteen years. Now he's making a comeback because he's able to accept himself and give up the alcohol. He can admit what kind of talent he was and is. On top of all the success, even if you've worked hard for it, you might start to wonder if you're really as good as everyone says you are. Or if you can keep doing it. You get to feeling unworthy, and that's when you start to sabotage your career, both on a conscious and subconscious level. And if you haven't worked hard for it, the problem is magnified.

Another classic case is Dennis Hopper who, after directing, producing, and acting in EASY RIDER and being highly acclaimed, drank, smoked, and drugged his way into oblivion.

Only after APOCALYPSE NOW has he been able to work again in films such as BLUE VELVET, HOOSIERS, and THE RIVER'S EDGE. The popularity of drugs in the '60's made it easy for him to lose his perspective since they tend to completely skew you out of balance. Because of this, Dennis got a reputation for being "difficult," and so for a long time no one would work with him. He's had to prove that he's straight and serious.

BUT DON'T YOU THINK THAT NOWADAYS ACTORS ARE MORE BALANCED AND TOGETHER?

You'd hope so, but no one is ever prepared for the distortions and loss of privacy that enormous media attention and success actually bring. And if you try fight it in a way that generates more publicity, such as slugging photographers who shove themselves in the path of your family, there can be a limit as to how much the public tolerates before there's a backlash among your fans. The real problem is that no matter who you are as an actor, you're never going to be prepared for what it's like to not be able to go to the grocery store without being mobbed, or what it's like to have so much money that you're able to do or buy anything you want. You're never going to be able to imagine, try as you will, what it's like to be surrounded by people who are there just to serve you, and who are all dependent upon you for their jobs. It's going to be a shock when it does happen, and, if it happens to you overnight, the shock can be crippling.

Not to mention that if it comes overnight, it can all evaporate overnight as well. One of the things to keep in mind is that actors are basically a product. In this town, there are the sellers and the buyers. The sellers are the agents and managers, and the buyers are the producers, the networks, and the film companies. The actors are the basic fodder, the commodity, and therefore they have to understand their careers can be very short-lived. What often happens is you can have a meteoric rise in your career, and all of a sudden it bottoms out after two or three years, and no one wants to hear from you again. They're embarrassed to be around you. They don't even want you on the studio lot or at a party because the sight of you makes them uncomfortable, reminding them of the possibility of failure, which is something certainly that does exist. So you must be capable of looking at your career and realizing that your career is not as important as who you are as a person—a person with goals, who can even look beyond his career. It's imperative to have people around you with whom you've built a base of trust, so that as everything seems to be changing, you can rely on a support system that is well enough in place to withstand these growth spurts.

BEYOND MY AGENT AND MANAGER AND PERSONAL RELATIONSHIPS, WHO ELSE SHOULD BE A PART OF MY SUPPORT SYSTEM?

The really fine acting teachers can certainly be a part of the support system for a lot of actors, especially the actors who have stayed close to the theatre and/or studied with the excellent teachers, like Sanford Meisner at the Neighborhood Playhouse, Stella Adler, Uta Hagen, or at Yale Rep and places like that. These are actors who have really been on the boards and have had to deal with success and failure on an immediate level. They are not studying with this or that teacher to make more money; you can't get paid a lot in the theatre, anyway. They use the class and the teacher to develop what is within—their talent, their art. The good acting teachers in many cases spend very little time talking about the business as a business from the standpoint of money or cars or condominiums. They try to establish a basis for the actor to understand that if he's in it for the money, he should do something else. If he's in it because he loves to act, then that's the right reason for being there. Therefore, if they have really been worked over by a few good acting teachers, when they go out in the business, they don't tend to behave inappropriately.

As far as teachers go, it's also important for an actor to have access to a good voice teacher and dialect coach. If you're faced with a character who is angry, you're going to find that, without the proper training, your voice will get stuck up in the higher registers and that it will tend to stay up in that angry tone. Even if this is realistic, no one will be willing to listen to it in a film for two hours. Actors have lost roles in films because of annoying voice qualities that a producer or director believed would be detrimental to the film holding a paying audience. Actors should take to heart the career of John Gilbert, the Clark Gable of the silent-film era, who appeared in many films with Greta Garbo. His career came to a quick and painful end when "talkies" came in and it was alleged that this masculine star recorded as high and squeaky. Believe it or not, this kind of situation still occurs on a much smaller scale in casting sessions all over Hollywood today.

I HEAR A LOT ABOUT PACKAGING AND POWERBROKERS. IS THERE SOME RULING CLIQUE?

In the days of the studio star system, the powerbrokers were studio moguls such as Louis B. Mayer at MGM, Jack Warner at Warner Bros., and Harry Cohn at Columbia. At the beginning of each year, they decided what films they were going to make for what stars, and who was going to be hired to direct and write them. And that was that.

While the moguls ran the studios, .agents had very little leverage or negotiating power. When the star system disintegrated in the '50s and the studios lost much of their power, the agent began to come into a position of strength. Once all projects were up for grabs, agents discovered they could put together packages, which would include a star or stars, a writer, and a director, and maybe a producer. Given that they had the principal components for a project, they could force the studios to accept their terms and became "powerbrokers" in their own right. Agents then began to tire of putting together an entire project from the beginning and then having to relinquish the power and control as soon as the project went into production. Soon, many of them segued into the position of personal manager, which allowed them to produce projects for their star clients as well as continue to manage them. (Agents are not allowed to do this). By becoming manager-producers or "hyphenates," they kept their power and control. Sometimes they moved over into the producer area completely, and some were called on to chair the studio. After a couple of years as the head of the studio, and after acquiring the requisite ulcers, they would go back into independent production (called "indie prod"), gaining more money, less responsibility, and they would not have to look over their shoulder as often.

So the powerbrokers now encompass everyone from agents and managers to producers, heads of studios, and heads of networks. The power is shifted from one to the other. The only thing you can be sure of is that just when you thought you had it figured out as to who is playing on what team, the whole structure changes. Barry Diller was president of Paramount, and then he suddenly went to Twentieth Century Fox. Richard Frank, who was at Paramount almost as long as his mentor, Diller, went to Disney. David Puttnam, producer of such artistically successful films as CHARIOTS OF FIRE, was hired as president of Columbia, but, even before any of his projects were released, he was replaced by Dawn Steel, previously president of production at Paramount with a nine-year tenure there. B. Donald (Bud) Grant spent fourteen years at NBC, was president of CBS from 1971 to 1987, and then resigned to go into independent production during the period when CBS was the third-ranking network.

Many of these powerbroker types are also lawyers, who moved from the business affairs departments at studios or from being agents into managing and from there into production, and who have the added advantage of being superior negotiators who can read contracts. A Louis B. Mayer would sigh as he looked at the current crop of executives and producers and ask about creativity. Very few of these people have degrees or hands-on experience in cinema and television. Since they come from legal and business-affairs backgrounds, their view tends to be one of making a good deal and the profit margin. The biggest success is the one that breaks box office records.

BUT I'M AN ACTOR. I'M CONCERNED WITH IMMEDIATE THINGS—THE CASTING DIRECTOR, MY AGENT, AND THE PART. I'LL PROBABLY NEVER MEET BARRY DILLER.

Acting teaches you to focus on your feelings, but we all know extremely talented actors who study and work and somehow never seem to become successful. Part of what makes an actor successful is to remember that this is show "business" and to have a sense of the structure of the business itself, who runs it and how, where they came from, and what motivates their decisions and use that to help you. (Besides, if you have the career you say you want to have, you very well may be meeting Barry Diller.)

SO WHAT YOU'RE SAYING IS THAT IT'S WHO YOU KNOW, NOT WHAT YOU KNOW?

It's definitely who you know and how you know them. Working in this business is the business of developing relationships. If you work with a director and he likes your work, chances are he'll remember and ask for you to work with him again. When managers look at the *Breakdowns* for a part, they are looking at whether the director of that project is listed on any of their clients' résumés. The fact that a client worked with Richard Donner once, for example, is good leverage to get that actor in to read for another Donner project. When managers visit actors on the set, the actors are sometimes surprised at the amount of time the manager spends in conversation with people other than the actor. It's from these seemingly innocuous conversations that the manager develops the relationships that lead to the actor's next job. Often these conversations revolve around future projects of the director or producer. It's not unusual for a manager to place several of his clients in a film after having visited one of his clients on the set of the producer or director's last project.

This is also true with casting directors, who, if they hired you once, won't forget you and will certainly bring you back again. It is said that Lynn Stalmaster had a young Richard Dreyfuss in to read and was very impressed by his talent. He then sent him on many interviews before Richard got hired, but Richard got many opportunities to be seen and to get work because of Stalmaster's interest in him. Debra Winger was an actress who was pushed by casting directors Mike Fenton and Jane Feinberg, who believed in her talent, and they were proved to be good judges of who will succeed.

In this business, it is important to feel part of a community and to relate to your fellow actors, but it is even more important to create relationships with the people in power who can hire you, such as casting directors, directors, producers, agents. Other actors, as a general rule (unless they are Sylvester Stallone), cannot get you work. They are too busy trying to get themselves work. This does not mean sucking up to powerful people. But neither does it mean being afraid to create a relationship with people in different jobs and positions than yourself, and sometimes knowing a little or a lot about these people can make it easier to create this relationship when you finally do meet them, especially if you, too, come from the same place or went to the same school. But if that closeness isn't immediately available (you don't know anyone who went to Colorado School of Mines with you), just having a sense of who these people are and what they come from proves helpful in making you feel more comfortable when you meet them. For example, producers Robert Chartoff and Irwin Winkler, who've produced many of Sylvester Stallone's movies, come from New York and seem to prefer to work with very strong actors who have multiple skills as well as "New York" actors such as Stallone, Al Pacino, and Robert DeNiro. Producers Richard Zanuck and David Brown, who are responsible for THE VERDICT, THE STING, and JAWS and JAWS II, are both Stanford graduates. Brown's background is in journalism, and his wife is Helen Gurley Brown of *Cosmopolitan* magazine. Zanuck, the son of Darryl F. Zanuck (who ran Twentieth Century Fox for thirty years), produced his first film, the successful COMPULSION, when he was twenty-four years old. During his eight-year tenure as president of Fox, which began when he was only thirty-four, his studio won Best Picture Awards for THE SOUND OF MUSIC, PATTON, and THE FRENCH CONNECTION. Both men went "indie prod" in the early 1970s. If you are expecting people in these power positions to take the time to look at your film and skills, doesn't it make sense that you should know something about them? When you meet someone who has the power to hire you, it's helpful to know the kind of product they generate. Are they the kind of people who stick to a project to the end? Are they people who do offbeat material which takes great dedication to get produced? Or do they do exploitation stuff? If you get to the position of reading for Steven Spielberg, it can't hurt to know that when he was a kid his mother supported him in skipping school to make films, or that he used to "borrow" empty offices on the Universal lot to get his start. It's information that may give you some some sense of how to relate to him.

Obviously, if you're young or new to the business, you won't walk in knowing all this background. But your manager should either be able to educate you or send you in the direction of this kind of undertstanding of who runs what and the web of relationships in which so much of this business takes place. On a very practical level, knowledge of how the business is changing helps you in making choices that may determine how widely you'll be seen in a project and where. In the late '80's, the trend in entertainment strategy was vertical integration. The major studios—and even some of the mini-majors—have been making and distributing movies, screening them in their own theatres, manufacturing and selling the videocassettes six months later, then syndicating their product to their own television stations, bypassing the networks, and, in the case of Walt Disney, playing them on a studio-owned, pay cable channel. Warner Communications shares ownership of MTV and Nickelodeon cable channels. Even series that were once produced for network television, such as CAGNEY AND LACEY or MIAMI VICE, have now been bought by cable stations. Art films get produced by hungry videocassette companies who need product and are willing to underwrite a filmmaker with one or two million dollars to greenlight the project. Though a movie has to play in the theatres in order to make it worth something for home-video sales, the exhibitors book everything for as little time as possible. The result for the working actor is that there's more product in the market place than ever before. And, it's possible to be widely seen in a film that plays only briefly in a theatre but has terrific home-video sales or extensive cable showings.

WHAT IF I GET OFFERED A GREAT PART WITH A NON-NEGOTIABLE, EXTREMELY EROTIC NUDE SCENE? WHAT WOULD YOU ADVISE ME?

I'm often asked if I were still managing Lisa Bonet's career, would

I have advised her to do ANGEL HEART? Bottom line—yes. If I had weighed it out then, the opportunity to work with two of our most talented actors, Robert DeNiro and Mickey Rourke, and the chance to break out of the mold of teen actress would have swayed my vote. Lisa was eighteen and trying to break out of her teen years as America's child on the immensely popular COSBY SHOW. She needed an adult role, and the opportunities for adult film roles for a young black actress are almost nonexistent. I would have fought against some of the excessive nudity, but decisions on a project like this are painful and difficult at best. You might regret turning down the role of a career just on the question of film content or an objection to nudity.

Strangely enough, nudity in a mainstream, big-budget film is often acceptable in Hollywood and will not shortcircuit a career. (Appearances that come to mind in this regard are Tim Curry in THE ROCKY HORROR PICTURE SHOW, Jamie Lee Curtis in TRADING PLACES, Kim Bassinger in 9 1/2 WEEKS, Brooke Shields in PRETTY BABY, Glenn Close in THE BIG CHILL, Natassia Kinski in CAT PEOPLE, and Isabella Rossellini in BLUE VELVET—all of them mainstream product.) However, nudity in a low-budget, teen-exploitation, horror or comedy movie will often mark an actress as an easy target for additional films of a similar nature, in a situation where producers or directors might say, "Well . . . you disrobed for that last film. Why are you demanding a no-nudity clause in mine?" You end up being continually hired for the one character in the *Breakdowns* that specifies "nudity required" because of your previous track record. Every script that needs breasts exposed, a naked shower scene, or just a girl in bed will be yours for the asking, even when you don't want it . Of course, it's unfair and obviously typecasting of the worst kind. Once you agree to do nudity for a film, it is difficult to re-cross that bridge.

If you must agree to do the nudity, make sure you have accepted its necessity to the script and the development of your character. Decide if you can handle the sequence and if it will be shot in good taste. Videocassettes make the performance live forever. Can you live with that later in your career? Last, but not least, do you have the body for it and the physical conditioning to make it tasteful? And is it something you could actually go through with—taking off your clothes in front of fifty actors and studio technicians? Thinking about it and doing it are two separate things. Ultimately, it's your personal decision. The best example of the "B" film transition would be Darryl Hannah segueing from the bomb SUMMER LOVERS to her casting as the half-nude mermaid in SPLASH, where her career took off.

The requirements for the European film market are totally different. Nudity is accepted, even commmonplace.

What's more difficult to gauge in 1990 is the fall-out from a role where the character uses drugs or participates in them in some way. If you've just completed an anti-drug short, or public service announcement, or have vocally taken a strong anti-drug stance, your playing such a role might be construed as hypocritical by a public which often cannot distinguish an actor from the role. But who's the character? Is it someone who comes to a change, an acceptance of responsibility? In this case, you may have no problem. Actors worry about this with playing characters who are homosexual—that Hollywood typecasts actors in roles in which they're successful. So the actor wants to know what happens if you get great reviews and everybody then only thinks of you for gay roles. For actors with previous credits, this doesn't seem to be the pattern. The industry appeared to appreciate William Hurt's performance in KISS OF THE SPIDER WOMAN as an excellent opportunity for him to stretch as an actor. He won the Academy Award. A Hal Holbrook doesn't encounter typecasting as a result of his role as the homosexual father in THAT CERTAIN SUMMER. If actors have not yet established names, they do run the risk of being typecast based on an early success. But it didn't prove true for Matthew Broderick after the play of TORCH SONG TRILOGY or for Aidan Quinn in the TV movie AN EARLY FROST. Both performances were honest and illuminating portrayals of very well-written characters, and in both projects these actors were surrounded by other excellent actors. Before accepting a homosexual role, one thing you should consider, if you are not homosexual, is how well you will handle it. Even if you have no problem with the relationship being depicted, it can be a shock to find yourself in front of a camera in bed with someone of the same sex or kissing someone of the same sex. It may have read perfectly fine to you off the script page, but, if it's something you have no personal experience with or desire for, don't assume that it is something you can do instantly or without difficulty. If reading the scene in the script makes you in any way uncomfortable, imagine how you'll look on the screen forcing yourself to do it. Be sure you are applying the same considerations you would to any role: Is this something I can play honestly? Is this a character I can learn to believe in and commit to? What's the quality of the script? What is the caliber of the other actors who are involved in the project?

WHAT ABOUT GETTING TRAPPED IN "B" FILMS? THERE ARE A LOT OF HORROR MOVIES AND TEEN COMEDIES NOW, SO THERE ARE A LOT OF CHANCES BECAUSE THEY'RE WILLING TO GO WITH NON-NAMES, BUT I DON'T WANT TO BE STUCK IN THEM FOREVER AND NOT CONSIDERED FOR OTHER KINDS OF FILMS.

The teen years for an actor are often engulfed in playing the teen heartthrob hero or heroine, nerd, or victim. Be patient and keep growing as an actor. These may be the only film companies willing to give the untested artist a chance. This brings to mind Michael J. Fox in TEEN WOLF and Tom Cruise in ALL THE RIGHT MOVES. It is quite possible to negotiate star billing in the main titles and perhaps paid ads while accepting scale salary and less-than-quality writing. This sacrifice may make your talent more accessible to the mainstream product. Your "B" film might turn out to be that sleeper like DIRTY DANCING or CROCODILE DUNDEE.

Look at the first films of Bruce Dern, Jack Nicholson, Robert Duvall or, more recently, Anthony Edwards (TUFF TURF) or Jamie Lee Curtis (HALLOWEEN). All these artists used their low-budget films to gain visibility and experience and then employed their talent to rise above and grow beyond them. If you can make this material work, then all things are possible.

Often in the long run little attention is paid to a film that is so bad it disappears from the box office in two weeks. But if you bring something special to a bad film or box office bomb, then your performance tends to be remembered in a positive way.

HOW WOULD I BECOME MY OWN MANAGER?

The first step is to put yourself in the manager's position and take a close look at the players and the tools of the business . . . how they do and don't work for you.

Set up a game plan which might include the acquisition of a series of episodic credits and roles in feature films, no matter how small, that will give you the visibility and a track record with certain casting directors and producers who know you are serious—until you have a résumé that expresses this.

In order to help you formulate your own game plan, the next chapter interviews three different levels of management, offering advice, opinions, and information on a variety of questions and issues:

1. **Mimi Weber**
2. **Helen Sugland**
3. **Diane Hardin and Nora Eckstein**

CHAPTER 6

INTERVIEWS WITH MANAGERS

1. MIMI WEBER

MIMI WEBER MANAGEMENT, MANAGING
PAM DAWBER AND HARRY GUARDINO;
CONSULTANT AND PARTNER IN PONY
PRODUCTIONS, PRODUCING *MY SISTER SAM*

I graduated from high school at sixteen during World War II. I went to work for the Quartermaster Corps. in the legal division. I married a serviceman, lived in Muskogee, Oklahoma, and had a child by the time I was nineteen. I worked for an attorney until I gave birth and then was a housewife for a short time. After that, I went back to work at everything from a secretary to a hat model to a dance teacher. Finally, after four marriages and raising a child by myself, I decided it was time that I really got involved with something.

I was reading Earl Wilson's column in a New York paper and saw Freddie Fields' name. He and I had gone to Erasmus Hall High School together. He was a senior when I was a freshman. So I got dressed and went to MCA in New York and got in to see him without an appointment, although his secretary tried not to let me through. I told him I needed a job, and he told me that he would get me into the company one way or another, even as a floater. By the end of May, 1958, I got a call to report to work.

I worked on a summer replacement show for the whole summer, put in over 300 hours overtime in three months, and then I was absorbed by the company. I started out as a "secretarial assistant." It was like an agent trainee. They made me an agent in December of '58. I had a lot of fun. It was a great company. Lew Wasserman also was a man who hired a lot of women, as did David Susskind. I think Lew had more women working in the company than anyone else in town. After Freddie left, I had a big fight with the head of the department. He hated me because Freddie hired me and he didn't like Freddie. I had closed a very big deal that he wanted, and I wouldn't let him have it. I showed up at work on the Jewish holiday. I should never have gone in because he said, "I would like you to resign." I said, "I won't. Fire me because I've just moved to New York, and I'm going to need unemployment insurance since I just took an apartment to be near the office." It caused a furor from some of the biggest stars. They called Lew Wasserman, who was not happy that I'd been fired, but, in order to rehire me, he would have had to fire the other guy. He said, "I'm doing you a favor. The government's going to put us out of business. You'll be out on the street faster than all the men in the company." That was October of '61. The Justice Department stepped in, and MCA was out of it in July. [AUTHOR'S NOTE: In 1961, the Justice Department stepped in to break up what they considered a monopoly by MCA of television, film, and the record business in the areas of acquisition, development, creation, and eventual distribution of production to the exclusion of others. MCA not only ran a talent agency but made the films and distributed them. MCA opted to stay in the filmmaking and distribution business and sell its theatrical agency.] They all congregated in my office like it was a memorial.

George Chasin, Herman Citron, Ned Tannen—all
of them. They all tried to help me. They were the ones
who told me I should become a personal manager.
So I got Myrna Loy right away, and Carole Bruce
and Larry Kert and George Maharis, so I didn't do
too badly. Even Jerry Lewis went to bat for me. They
all called Lew—Tony Martin and Cary Grant and
Myra Loy. They all called him, but he couldn't rehire
me. It broke my heart. I loved the company. Had I
stayed, I'm sure I'd probably still be at Universal.

WHAT QUALITIES DO YOU LOOK FOR IN TALENT?

I have always gone strictly on intuition. When somebody has walked into my office, it was a look, a style, a mannerism, personality, intelligence. I never asked for film on them. If they were in a play, I'd go to see them. A lot of young actors starting out don't have film. That's a big problem in this business. They want to see film. Pam was already in MORK AND MINDY for two years when I started representing her. Harry Guardino had been in the business for many years and had been nominated for Oscars, Tonys, Emmys. I knew his quality. A lot of the actors and actresses who came in to see me through these years—I just had a feeling about them. I went on that feeling. I have to say I've never been wrong. Anybody that I ever got involved with made it. Those that didn't make it—it wasn't because they didn't have talent but because of the nature of the business.

ARE THERE CERTAIN QUALITIES YOU FIND MORE ATTRACTIVE THAN OTHERS?

A sense of humor is important. There's something that comes through when a person sits down and starts to talk to you. I don't normally start an interview with, "Now tell me what you've done." Or what you're about to do or what you want to do. I usually talk about who they are, where they come from, where their family is. Some of them are very angry. I find that a total turn-off. Even if

I couldn't represent them, I have tried to help them get jobs. I've been very honest. "I can't represent you, but if I can do anything to help you, I will." I've helped a lot of actors and actresses whom I did not represent.

ARE THERE OTHER REASONS WHY YOU WOULDN'T TAKE ON A CLIENT?

In many cases, I've had to turn down people who I knew were very talented because I didn't have the time to represent them. I think it's very dishonest to take people on and shortchange them. Because there's only one of me. So what happens is you have to divide yourself up and, if you have more people than you can really handle, it's unfair to represent them. Now I was geared to represent a lot of people because I was an agent for MCA. When I went to work for them in 1958 in the dramatic television department, we were given as many as twenty or thirty people on our responsibility list. So there is a way to represent a number of people, but as people start to emerge, a lot more of your time is required. You go to meetings, read scripts. You get into their personal lives. So there's just so much of you. There are people I've had to turn down—very important people. There was nothing I could do. Rather than do anything to damage my name or my integrity, I would rather not represent them.

WHAT DOES A MANAGER'S JOB ENCOMPASS?

It's different for each talent. We advise, guide and counsel. We direct. But it's much more than that. We're all spokes of the wheel. It's the actor in the center, and then we're all spokes on that wheel, all part of making that wheel run. If a couple of those break, then the wheel doesn't roll. You might get embroiled in the personal problems. Maybe he's having problems with his wife or she's having trouble with her husband. Or a boyfriend or a girlfriend or their mother is sick. I can't even begin to tell you the things that you run into that are expected of you. Other than the day-to-day "I need a job," "I can't pay my rent," "My phone bill . . ." I mean, it goes right down to the nitty gritty. You finally get them a job, and they're so behind that they pay everybody but you. You're the one that they depend on, and yet they feel that you can wait. I've always gone along with that.

I had very good training to become a personal manager. I was an agent. I worked for one of the greatest talent agencies in the world. There will never be another MCA. Agents really cared about what they were doing. They weren't busy being stars like a lot of them today, and we really learned our craft. I don't negotiate the deals, since it's against the law in the state of California, but it's okay for agents and managers to sit and discuss it. In Pam's case, she has a business manager. I have a wonderful working relationship with her agents at the William Morris office, so we discuss it. Harry Guardino, whom I also represent, is with Morris. It worked out better for me that way. He has a business manager. The bottom line is that Harry will say, "What do you think?" He doesn't care what anyone else thinks. Interestingly enough, Pam cares what other people think, but she puts great stock in what I think. So whether it's a deal, billing, the role, or even decorating an office, we discuss it.

Pam and I have been together for seven years. She was very much on her way when I started representing her. I represented Harry Guardino as an agent twenty-nine years ago. When I was no longer an agent and went into personal management, I didn't represent him for many years. He called me and asked, "How come you never asked to represent me?" I said, "I never ask anybody." He said, "Well, would you meet me for lunch?" I went and met him for lunch. He started to tell me what was happening at that time. He was being offered a series at Universal, and his agents were telling him one thing and he was very frightened. Harry is probably one of the most underrated actors in the business and probably one of the finest. We sat down and had lunch, and he gave me the script. I went in to see some of the guys at the studio and then went home and read it. I called him and said it was a piece of junk. He said, "Good. Will you take over from here?" He had called his agents and told them. They thought I had a contract with him. I didn't. I don't think we had a contract ready for weeks. So it's a trust. I knew everybody who was involved. I said, "He's too good for this." Harry and I have been together so long we're like family. I remember when his first child was born. She's now twenty-seven or twenty-eight. He remarried a couple of years ago, they had a baby in July of 1987, and I'm a godmother. That's part of what it is. You have to really care. When Pam was arranging this very secret wedding because she and Mark Harmon didn't want it to become a three-ring circus, I was part of making those arrangements. It was a great joy. We have an unusual relationship. She is like the daughter I never had. I have a son who is older than she is.

WHAT DO YOU ENJOY MOST IN THE RELATIONSHIP WITH YOUR CLIENTS PAST AND PRESENT? AND, WHAT DO YOU ENJOY LEAST?

With Pam, what I enjoy the most is her happiness. It makes me feel good to see her so happy. We have spent a lot of time together. We've traveled around the world together, and we spent a lot of time talking, kind of telling about our inner souls. When the times were painful, we would cry in the planes when it was dark so no one could see us. She is from such a totally different background than I am and obviously a lot younger. But she is so much like me that when I see things in her that, I don't want to have happen because I don't want her to have the pain I've had, I share it with her. It's really so hard to explain what a lovely, special person she is, totally apart from her talent—because that has nothing to do with being a human being. There are people who are very talented and who are terrible people. Terrible. I think they threw away the mold when they made her.

I never represented a lot of women, but most of them were just great. One young woman went to Europe with her husband, and when she came back, it was a whole new bunch of casting directors. Today she is a very successful real estate agent. Not because she doesn't have talent. It is the nature of the business, the cruelty of the business. I represented another young lady who was a total unknown when she came to me. I started to build her. She was doing very well. Very difficult, unattractive, very neurotic. She would drive me up the wall. But I had great compassion for her, so I stayed with her. And then our contract was drawing to a close.

It was time to renegotiate. I think the contract ran seven years. She told her business managers that the new contract that she wanted was one in which she would pick up my option up every year. I told the business managers to tell her in three or four words what she could do and that was it. Years later, when I was very successful with another actor who became a superstar, she had the unmitigated gall to come to me and ask me to represent her again. I told her no.

As far as the guys are concerned, I had some confrontations with a couple. The big thing I have going now is the lawsuit with Nick Nolte. When an actor comes into town with three pairs of jeans to his name and a truck and he's doing free theatre and his first job is $250 on a MEDICAL CENTER teaser, and a couple of years later, he's doing RICH MAN, POOR MAN because of his manager. . . I don't have to tell you the millions that he's made, but I'm never going to have that problem again. I could say a lot more, but I'm going to save that for the trial.

Most of my clients, however, are still very much a part of my life, and we remain friends. I represented Jayne Meadows for a long time. She is a very busy lady, always traveling. It drove me crazy because I could never find her when I had something for her. So we had lunch and I said,"Jayne, I love you and I think you're a big talent. But I'm going to have a nervous breakdown trying to find you. You're either in New York or some place else. So why don't we just stay good friends?" Which we have. When I had to close down the large management business, they all understood. Pam felt very badly about it—that they would not have me. But they understood. In fact, Art Metrano was a client of mine, and he said to me, "I am going to miss you desperately. I don't know what I'll do, but I'm giving you the opportunity that you deserve, an opportunity that should have been given to you by a superstar actor that you built, and so therefore I wish you all the luck in the world."

Part of the reason I closed up that large Mimi Weber Management was that I didn't like moving eight clients around from agency to agency. I like to have relationshops with all the different agents. Every once in a while, actors get very neurotic and think that if they leave this agent and go to another agent, it's going to be better. Sometimes it's better. Sometimes I think it's worse. I haven't really lost that many clients. I usually kept clients a very long time. I had Christopher Stone when he first started in the business. I think he was with me for sixteen years when I closed down the office. I represented Paul Peterson for a very long time. Logan Ramsey was a brilliant character actor, and he was my client for many years. I still hear from Logan. I still hear from Art Metrano. He's now had a second baby, and I'm involved with the family. I had an actor by the name of Bryan O'Byrne whom I represented for seventeen years. To this day, we're not only close, but whenever I have to go out of town, he moves into my house. When I can, if I hear of something, I try to help him. My actors always knew they could call me. If they weren't working and didn't get paid, I kept working. If they worked and did get paid and they couldn't pay me, they paid everybody but me. What other fool would sit around working seven days a week, be on call all the time and not always get paid for it?

WHAT HAVE YOU LEARNED ALL THESE YEARS ABOUT THE BUSINESS?

I feel sorry for all the young people in the business today. I would never want to start in the business today. It's a business of mogulettes and tight pants. They're all stars and drive fancy cars. They're not the agents of yesterday. The studios aren't run by creative men in many cases. They're run by companies. Those who are still around at the very end of that wonderful era are what makes it wonderful to be in the business. I hate to tell you how many people hate this business today who are still in it.

I find a sixteen million dollar salary to an actor a disgrace. A total, utter disgrace. When for sixteen million dollars you can make two feature films and give more work to more people. The "stars!" To me, there's only a handful of leading men left, and they're not kids anymore. The new leading men that are around today, I don't like the way they conduct their lives. I'm not telling you that they didn't live in the fast lane in the days of Myrna Loy, Cary Grant (may his soul rest in peace), Sinatra. But when they walked out, you knew they were stars. They didn't walk around with dirty clothes and matted hair.

There are still a number of people left at the various companies, at the networks, the studios, the agencies. They call us old-timers. But once we're totally gone, I hate to think of the legacy I'm leaving for the younger people. I don't know what they'll do to themselves. I really don't. See, I consider Barry Diller an old-timer, even though he's a young man. He's a very hard-working man. He knows what he's doing. Because they do come out of a certain period. But we have men in our business who are in their sixties who are brilliant. I mean, you're never going to replace the great minds of some of these people—ever. Or the ability to know how to build a star. There are no more Gary Coopers or Cary Grants or Ronald Colmans or Clark Gables or Robert Taylors—and there are never going to be. The only ones who are around today that mean anything to me are Paul Newman and Robert Redford. That's it. No, excuse me, there's also those wonderful kind of people like Michael Caine, Clint Eastwood, Warren Beatty. I think Warren Beatty is sensational. Dustin Hoffman is a very talented man. I mean, extremely talented. Pacino, DeNiro are terrific too. Jimmy Caan. Now, he's not what you'd call a gorgeous man, but he's a man. His presence on-screen is wonderful. But you can count them on one hand. I remember when you couldn't count them on your hands and toes. I mean, the Errol Flynns and men that had such great style. They may not always have been great actors, but they had style and a quality. The same with the actresses. Fortunately, I got into the business at a time when I got to know a lot of these people. As I say, I still will go any place to see Sinatra, who is a good friend. I also like Tony Bennett and Vic Damone. When they're gone, there's nobody to replace them. Who am I going to listen to? Those people who have dirty clothes on with their hair sticking out of their chest and pony tails? So I really stay in my own little world unless there's a big premiere or a big party where I know that I'm still going to rub elbows. Mark Rydell, Sydney Pollack—they're old friends. I still want to be with them. I don't like going to things that the other people are at because I have nothing in common with them. If I were an agent today, I don't know how I would represent these people.

I am just delighted that I represent Pam Dawber and that she's married to a doll like Mark Harmon, who's a comer. I mean, Mark Harmon is going to be a big star. He looks good and he's talented.

TELL ME SOMETHING ABOUT PONY PRODUCTIONS, PAM'S COMPANY.

Pony was originally Rabbit Productions, but a couple of years ago, we were advised by Eddie Rabbitt's attorneys that, if we didn't stop using the name Rabbit Productions, we were going to be sued. Stupid idiot. I mean, number one, how can anyone mix up beautiful, delicious, adorable, petite Pam Dawber (who spelled "Rabbit" differently) with Eddie Rabbitt?

I said to her, "Let's let it go. Why spend a lot of money on attorneys? Let's feed sick and hungry people instead." So she kept trying to think of a new name and came up with Pony. Pony comes from the story about the two boys, the pessimist, and the optimist. The boys have a father who fills up one room with lots of toys and fills up another room with a lot of horse manure. The kid who's the pessimist can't understand why he's got a room full of toys for the holiday—there had to be some kind of catch. The kid who's the optimist is pushing his way through all the horse manure. The father asks, "What are you doing?" The kid says, "Well, with all this horse manure, there must be a pony somewhere." It's part of what Hollywood is. There must be a pony with all this crap. So she came up with the name.

WHATEVER COMES FROM YOUR MOUTH IS PAM'S VOICE? YOU SPEAK FOR HER?

Yes, she authorizes that. If I go to a meeting—when we were pitching this new series—all the top people at the studios and networks knew that Pam was not going to come because she was tired of pitches or whatever. They all knew that my presence indicated that I was there for us both. If there's something I have to fight, I will say to her, "Is this 'us'?" And she'll say, "It's us." So I never assume it. I always ask her. If I ever write a letter, it will read "Pam and I support you." That's very important. The same with Harry. You're as important as your client, and your client is as important as you are. You do represent your client out there. It's very important because there are managers and agents who are a disgrace, who shouldn't even be in the business. When I'm out there representing Pam Dawber, I damn well better behave myself and know what I'm doing. Who you are reflects who your client is.

In the beginning, Pam and I—we had a really hard time. We were at Paramount for two years trying to develop this show, and then we were at Columbia for a year. We would have meetings, and, as soon as they were through, I had all these other clients, you know? It was a responsibility. I used to have to work into the night to make sure that they got covered with everything. So a couple of years later when it started to get very hard, I sat down with her and said, "What do you think?" She said, "I would love it. I just feel that I would be very responsible. I would feel bad about the other clients." I said, "Well, I can handle that. I'll just meet with all of them, because I feel that you need so much of me right now, I don't know how I can do everything and do you justice." We're so deep into everything with trying to develop shows and going to pitch meetings and trying to develop TV movies and miniseries . . ." I think she was also worried because she thought it was like that old saying, "putting all your eggs in one basket." So I made a joke out of it. I said, "Pam, I started out as a legal secretary and, if something happened to your career, I guess I could always get a job. Now tell me, how is your shorthand? . . . Don't worry. We'll go through great times together and if we have hard times (which we did because work was not abundant) we'll manage together." And that's what we did.

In fact, July is three years that I closed down the big office. I have to tell you, it's wonderful! It really is. I love doing this. The creating of it. We're developing quite a few movies for television, so I'm always reading and looking for things for her. As far as the show itself, it's wonderful because I go over there, and, even when I have things to do for her, I always try to make sure that I do it for all the other actors. Maybe that's what an executive consultant is. Pam said to somebody yesterday, "Tell Mimi to do it. She's like a mongoose, she never lets go!" I always say, "I'm twenty-five trapped in a more mature body." However, I think I am the senior member. There's a few other people who might be equally senior members. But they're all younger and it's always a lot of fun to be that smart, that secure. When you get to a certain age and you're a woman, something happens and nothing frightens you. Nothing frightens me. I don't have any trouble meeting with anybody and talking to anybody.

Speaking of being a woman in this business, I have to tell you very honestly that it has been a wonderful experience. I was never treated chauvinistically, so maybe I was just lucky. I started twenty-nine years ago, and as far as the men in the business ever not helping, I think some of the most important men extended their hands to help. So my experience as a female in the entertainment business is a very pleasant one, and probably the only reason I didn't make it bigger in corporate structure is that my timing wasn't right. Like Renee Valente. She was the first female president of the Producers Guild. She should have been president of any studio in town. Maybe her timing wasn't great. Maybe I was already too mature to become president for a studio. Who can say?

Considering what's going on, I am happy that I was born early enough to enjoy what was left of the business in the '50s. Because I'd been around it and got to meet those beautiful, talented people. I was a New Yorker, so I got to Broadway and saw the greats. We really had to learn our craft in those days. I was in the television department, but I made it my business to know what was going on in every department. I spent my own money coming out here. Being an MCA agent opened all the doors, and I observed everything. I went to every studio, I got to meet lots of people. The vice presidents of MCA would take me with them to introduce me to the network and studio executives, so I've been trained. I have wonderful memories, wonderful. Whenever I get a chance to sit down and write my book, I'll put them all in there. Because I have kept everything I ever had that had to do with the business since I started.

HOW DOES THE ACTOR TAKE PERSONAL RESPONSIBILITY FOR HIS CAREER?

By working at it. He needs to study, be involved. He has to really care. A lot of the guys and girls are becoming actors to become super stars because they read about all the goings on of the Bruce Willises and Don Johnsons. If an actor has financial problems, he should figure out a way to get a job, to subsidize himself so that he doesn't become desperate. They go into an interview and they want the job so badly, not only because they want it but because they need the money. They should know that it is a business and it is difficult, and be realistic enough to realize that they may not be that talented. They should work very hard to find out if they are that talented. So if they aren't, then it would be better to pursue another career. I see a lot of young actors, even people in middle-age, who out of the clear blue sky decide, "Hey, I like that lifestyle. I want a big house and a big car and gorgeous clothes and I want to go to all the parties." They're not equipped for it; they're dreamers. This is not dreaming, it's hard work. If you're lucky enough to get a shot, then you have to work very hard for it. There are times when it can be hurtful but you have to know how to deal with it, if you want it badly enough, and you have the talent—that you're not just another pretty face. You're leaving yourself wide open for rejection, pain, and hard times because it doesn't happen overnight.

2. HELEN SUGLAND
LANDMARK ARTISTS MANAGEMENT, PERSONAL MANAGER FOR ADULT AND YOUNG ADULT ACTORS

I was born in Washington, D.C,. and grew up in Old Saybrook, Connecticut, a small town on the shore of the Connecticut River. I graduated from high school there and went to college in Boston, Massachusetts. I graduated from the Boston Conservatory of Music, where I majored in music education and minored in voice in theatre. I taught school at Saybrook Junior High School, taught music and theatre for three years, then I moved to New York. I pursued the business for a very short period of time and decided that I wanted to get in on the backstage side. The next morning I picked up a local free newspaper in Manhattan, and there was a little ad in there for a management company who was looking for someone to work part-time, with a background in the industry. I got the job and segued to full-time. Then they asked me if I wanted to move to the West Coast to open up an office here. I did and brought several of their clients out here, who are doing quite well now. Four years ago I made the decision to go into partnership with Gary Goddard. Some of our clients include Eric Stoltz, Larry B. Scott, Dean Cameron and Diane Ladd.

HOW DO YOU ACQUIRE YOUR CLIENTS?

I acquire all my clients through recommendations. The recommendations come from casting directors, agents, producers, directors, and even some studio people. I've gotten clients from going to tapings and plays. There are an awful lot of Equity waiver plays in this town that I attend. Believe it or not, I even pay attention to pictures and résumés in the mail. So for all of you actors who think you're beating a dead horse when you mail out a hundred pictures and résumés to various agents and managers in this town, I can at least say that, in this case, I actually do pay attention. I read résumés and, if, in fact, there's a market for that type of person in my company, you will get a phone call from my secretary. I have also attended several high-school productions, looking for younger people. I think that's happening more and more here, too. There are a lot of very fine music and theatre programs going on within the high-school system.

WHAT DOES A MANAGER'S JOB ENCOMPASS?

The job encompasses numerous things depending on where the actor's career is at the moment. The responsibility of management grows as the actor grows. If you're talking about actors in the beginning stages, you're talking about such things as studying, the right kind of classes, how experienced they are in terms of their acting abilities at that point, dress, preparation of material, how to deal with casting people, who are the casting people, how to deal with studio people, directors, and producers. These are your responsibilities as a manager.

The job function grows as the actor's career starts to grow and you deal with the right type of project as they start to develop their credits. You read scripts, develop material, and produce projects for clients.

First and foremost, the personal manager and the actor have to have a clear understanding of what the goals are. What you want initially and what you want five years from now. I believe in game plans. Ultimately, what is it you want to have accomplished as an actor, given this is your lifelong career? It is a career, meaning it does have to deal with longevity. When you deal with it that way, it is difficult sometimes to see the trees through the forest because you take mini-steps, as I call them, as opposed to big jumps. Ultimately, in the long run, I think it's much more beneficial. You truly have a career that you can be talking about and that can be functioning for years and years to come.

Actors have to put themselves in a position where they are no longer actors for hire, which is what I call them. That is something that I think managers need to discuss with their clients right from the beginning. Acting is a difficult business because of the inconsistency of it. You need to work toward putting yourself in a position where you can ultimately do the kinds of projects you would like to do. That is a long way down the road. You have to do a lot of homework ahead of time, but I think management should help you understand that and help you plan toward that.

ONCE YOU AND AN ACTOR MAP OUT A CLEAR UNDERSTANDING OF WHERE YOU'RE BOTH HEADED, WHAT IS IT THAT THE MANAGER DOES?

With respect to day-to-day things, I believe in preparation for auditions. I spend a great deal of time making sure that clients have prepared the material, have an understanding of the character they're going to read, know who they're going to see, where they're going to go, and the personalities of the people they're going to meet.

A great deal of my time is spent attending screenings, tapings of TV shows, and visiting sets. I do a lot of traveling. It behooves managers to take the opportunity to visit your client while they are working to develop the relationships with the producers and directors and to maneuver this into more work for the actor. That's part of the manager's homework on behalf of the actor. Work does breed work.

You have to make the right choices with respect to material for the actor, and the only way you can do that is to read scripts. And now there are more than ever with the high number of low-budget projects that go on in this town. And there are a lot of distributors out there who will deal with these movies. That's a way you, as a manager, can assist your actors in moving in the direction of not being actors for hire: get into development under the banner of the actor's own corporation. Actors, save your money. Do not get caught up in the hype of this town. It's longevity we're talking about. Incorporate yourself, start to develop your own properties; let your money work for you, not you work for the money.

DO YOUR CLIENTS FALL INTO CERTAIN CATEGORIES?

They move from category to category, but at some point, they belong in a certain category, and you function differently for actors depending on the category. There are actors who are beginning and who need certain kinds of guidance with respect to preparation, to getting the job, to building the résumé and the credits. You move from the beginning category to what I call the "middle-of-the-road" category, which is where you start to deal with visibility on a more consistent basis. If you're talking TV, if you're talking film, there is a certain kind of visibility that I call "commercialism," and that's a nasty word for a lot of actors in this town in 1989, but I think you have to understand that this is a business. It's very difficult when you think about producers, studios, the money people, the investors—it's very difficult to convince them a lot of times, no matter how talented an actor you are—that you're going to be box office for their movie when they've invested millions of dollars, if you have not proven to them that you are capable of bringing in the audience. So you must at some point bite the bullet, if that's the kind of career you want. If you want the studio picture, a big picture, you must bite the bullet. You move from that category into many other categories, depending on what you want.

WHAT QUALITIES DO YOU LOOK FOR IN AN ACTOR OR ACTRESS?

The first thing I look for is ability, because my philosophy about management is longevity. If there isn't ability there—and it doesn't have to have finesse or be polished or trained to its ultimate—but I have to be able to see that there is some place to go with that talent. Once I get past that necessity, I have to deal with the personality and disposition and the human being. Management is personal. Management is a marriage for me, and, if we are absolutely on the opposite sides of the fence in the areas of temperament and philosophy of life, then we will never survive. I've been fortunate. The clients that I represent have been good solid human beings. Without that, I couldn't function on their behalf. I think that actors have to have their feet nailed solid to the ground, and they cannot be swayed by the "show" part of the show business. If I feel that they are, I can be assured that we will have a problem down the road. We're talking about the human qualities and the importance of being a human being in the madness of this wonderful industry. I mean that in the most honest way. I love this business. However, it is a business that can totally destroy you as a human being if your feet are not solid on the ground.

TALK ABOUT LOYALTY AS IT DESCRIBES YOUR RELATIONSHIP WITH YOUR CLIENTS AND YOUR EXPECTATIONS.

I think loyalty is an important human factor for all of us to acquire and achieve. There is certainly loyalty between my clients and myself within the company, but I think that sometimes loyalty gets confused with reality. This is going to sound strange coming from a manager, someone on the business side of the business, but if, in fact, you are not acquiring what you set out to acquire from a relationship, you are within your rights to terminate that relationship. The key is how you terminate that relationship. I think if you have a problem with your agent and/or manager, you should be loyal enough and care enough about that relationship to walk in the door, sit down, and say you have a problem. If there is no way to resolve the problem, then you should terminate the business relationship. I am not an advocate of maintaining a business relationship with anyone when that relationship is not serving its purpose.

AS A MANAGER, DO YOU GET CALLED IN ON "EMERGENCIES"?

I don't know that there are any managers who haven't experienced problems. I can remember getting a phone call from a client at some ungodly hour of the morning. He had a very early call, and I'm not good when you wake me up. He was working in town on a movie and it was a very strenuous movie and he had hurt his back. He had been dealing with the pain for a couple of days, unknown to me. Actors, please don't be martyrs about that. There are such things as insurance and, ultimately, your life and your health are more important than your job. They wanted him to work that day, and he literally was in too much pain to do so. They wanted him to do it anyway. I got called, I got up, and went down to the set. I refused to let him work. I talked to the producers, and they shipped him off to the emergency room and discovered that something was wrong with his back. He had some treatments for that, and he didn't work for a few days. Make use of your manager in that respect. I have dealt with physical problems to small things in contracts, which are not so small to the actor. I mean small perks such as hotel rooms. I had a client who was doing a movie out of the state. We had negotiated a deal whereby she was to have first-class hotel accommodations equal to all other stars and a full-size trailer, not a motor home. For those of you who don't know the difference, the only difference is the motor homes require a teamster driver and a trailer does not, but it's full-size, which means you have all of the amenities: shower, refrigerator, stove, bed, the little lounge area where you have your couch and your radio. She dicovered that she did not have that. So I got on the phone, and I had to threaten that she would not work until they took care of it. I can't think of any incidents where things were not resolved. I can remember an incident with a motor home for a client. It had been promised in the contract, it was to be equal to, once again, all the other stars. My client had been given the motor home for the first two weeks of rehearsal. The first day of shoot there was something else there. I had to meet with the producers that evening when they wrapped on the lot to look at all of the motor homes that they had available. I had to walk through and pick one that was comparable to what they had promised. It was resolved— so unnecessary, but, unfortunately, that's part of the business.

I THINK WORKING OVERSEAS PRESENTS PROBLEMS THAT HAVE TO BE CAREFULLY ANTICIPATED SO THAT THEY DON'T TURN INTO EMERGENCIES, BECAUSE, WHEN THEY DO ARISE, THEY'RE ALMOST ALWAYS COMPLICATED BY THE DIFFERENCES IN TIME ZONES AND LANGUAGE.

In Europe, they don't have the same kind of amenities that we have here. So you have to deal with something that is comparable to what we are normally accustomed to seeing. That is hard to come by. We are also talking per diems. It's important that managers and actors understand that there's truly a difference in the value of the dollar, and what we assume we're getting is not necessarily what you do get when you transfer that over into their currency. Their concept of first-class amenities, of first-class hotel accommodations, is certainly not ours. It becomes extremely difficult to communicate with the powers-that-be overseas. It has forced me to try and become a little more bilingual, something I've never been very good at, but I am discovering I can pick up some of the language if it's necessary. My favorite is calling hotels in Hungary. First of all, you can hardly hear. Second of all, you can't understand them. They can't understand you. But you live through it, folks, you just live through it! It's important, and I discovered this very much the hard way many years ago, that you do your best to get your monies paid out of the United States. You're talking about monies coming out of a foreign bank. How long does it take it to get here? How long does it take it then to clear with the bank of the production company before you ever see your dollar? And by the time you realize, by the time you learn whether or not the check actually has cleared, you could be half way through your movie and your checks could be rubber. Get your money in escrow, and, if you can't, get it drawn off on an American bank.

I had a client who was doing a movie in Europe and the production had been moving from one location to another. Two days before they were to move to the new location, they were being given their per diem for that week and they all noticed that they had money that was deducted from it. They asked why, and they were told that the money was being deducted because the refrigerators that had been placed in each one of their hotel rooms. Mind you, no one had ever requested the refrigerators in the hotel room, and, when someone finds a refrigerator in the hotel room, they think it's part of the accommodation of the hotel. Well, apparently that was not the case. The production company had been charged additional monies on a weekly basis by the hotel and obviously they wanted to pass down that expense to the actor. My actor and all the rest of them received the small amount of money that had been taken out of their per diem after we made some noise about it.

WHAT HAVE YOU LEARNED ALL THESE YEARS ABOUT THE BUSINESS?

I've learned that this is a business whereby you can accomplish anything you want to accomplish if you understand the system and how to play within it. That's probably the hardest thing I had to learn. I'm a child of the '60s who grew up with rebellion in her soul and believing in a cause and taking it to the limit. There is still a part of me that does that. However, the best way to achieve success is to deal with that cause within the system. That has been established long before I came and will be here long after I die. There are people who have influenced me, some of them who don't even know that they've influenced me. In this business. I've learned from several actors about the right and wrong things to do by watching them make the right and the wrong decisions. I have admired a couple of managers in this town for years in the business. I have watched from a distance one manager specifically—his name is Bernie Brillstein. Over the years, the thing that I have learned from watching his progress, the big thing, is that management is a complete, full-service business. If you service the actor at every stage of his career, if you segue with them and take them to the next level, you will have your clients and you will all have success together. I think in a town where there is so much flux, where you have a client today and you don't have that client tomorrow, that is a very valuable lesson for me to learn. He doesn't have a clue that I learned that from him. I've also learned that power and its proper use are the greatest tools in this town. How to make it work for you, to support you. You don't have to be vicious. People on the outside perceive Hollywood as vicious. You don't have to be that way, but you do have to know how to use your relationships and your abilities to move along. I think I make a concerted effort to try to impart that to my actors. Make what you learn work for you.

A long time ago, before I learned a great deal about the business, I'd learned about the importance of music, theatre, and art, and about the importance of working hard. I learned from my parents and from an old music and theatre teacher that I had many years ago in junior high school and high school. You can accomplish anything when you work hard and put the energy into what you want. They programmed me to think that way and then I was afforded the opportunity to surround myself with people who I saw doing it. And that gave me the encouragement to proceed.

IS THERE ANY ONE ASPECT OF PRESENTING THEMSELVES PROFESSIONALLY THAT YOU THINK ACTORS SHOULD PAY PARTICULAR ATTENTION TO?

Your job function—the way you sell yourself—is via your work. And if you don't have it on tape and you can't present it, you've lost your best tool. You must be able to have a composite tape. It's your best friend. Actors, you must tape your work. I can talk from here until I'm a hundred years old, but, unless you are a star and everybody knows you, you will always find people who don't know who you are. I can show them credits, I can tap dance, I can do it all, but nothing quite speaks like seeing your work.

3. DIANE HARDIN AND NORA ECKSTEIN
HARDIN-ECKSTEIN MANAGEMENT COMPANY,
PERSONAL MANAGEMENT FOR YOUNG ACTORS

DIANE HARDIN: I went to college at the University of North Carolina, and then went to the Barter Theatre in Virginia for six years. I went on two tours of one-night stands, bus and truck, all over the country. I lived in New York from 1959 when I married actor Jerry Hardin, till 1965 when we left New York and went to the Alley Theatre in Houston, Texas. Then the Manitoba Theatre Center in Winnepeg, Canada; Front Street Theatre in Memphis, Tennessee; Brandeis University Theatre. We performed in regional theatres for ten years all over the country, doing winter and summer stock. I played leads in over a hundred plays. We came to L.A. in 1972 because we had two young children, and we were moving them around so much that we had to either go to New York or California. I had my first teaching experience at the Will Rogers School in Santa Monica with a group of disturbed children, who the principal said were incorrigible until I started improvising with them. I was also in an improv company called Public Works in Santa Monica. I performed with them for two and a half years, and it was so satisfying that I wanted to continue to teach, so I worked in the gifted program at the Marquez Elementary School in Westwood for four years.

I started teaching acting classes in a friend's den. The classes grew so much that I realized I needed someone to help me, so Nora Eckstein came with me in 1981, and we became partners in a management venture. I now run the Young Actors Space and have approximately 200 students at any given time. I have four teachers on my staff, and we do improvisation and scene study. I was acting coach on SANTA BARBARA for several months, and then I worked on HELP

WANTED: KIDS, the Disney film, and was also the set coach on FANTASY ISLAND. I'm married to actor Jerry Hardin and my daughter, Melora Hardin, is an actress. My son just graduated from USC film school.

NORA ECKSTEIN: I was born in Texas, moved to California shortly thereafter, and grew up in the entertainment industry. I started taking acting classes when I was eleven years old. I took acting classes all through high school and went to Antioch College in Ohio. I have a degree in Creative Dramatics from Cal State Northridge. I worked at a school in Berkeley, at a camp in New Jersey for inner-city kids as a drama specialist, and then at UC Santa Barbara working in children's theatre. I was a member of the American Theatre Arts in Hollywood for ten years, acting, doing costumes, and teaching improvisation and scene study. I taught through the L.A. City Schools, piloting a creative dramatics program in the schools, incorporating improvisation into the academic structure, and teaching the teachers how to teach improvisation. I was an apprentice with the Improvisational Theatre Project at the Mark Taper Forum for a season and also at the Taper Two. I was a member of the Odyssey Theatre. I was introduced to Diane Hardin at American Theatre Arts and started working with her five years ago in teaching young professionals. I've worked as an acting coach on RAGS TO RICHES and a couple of Disney movies-of-the-week. My father is producer/writer George Eckstein, and my mother is actress Ann Gilbert, who's now married to Guy Raymond. They're actors doing regional theatre. My sister is actress Hallie Todd on the BROTHERS TV series on Showtime.

WHAT DOES YOUR JOB ENCOMPASS?

NORA: Our first job is to make sure that our clients are prepared for auditions—to make creative choices, take risks, have fun. For young people, that's especially important. If it's not fun, there's no point to being in this business. We oversee their craft, their agents, their long-term commitments. We help them decide whether a particular project is in line with their long-term career goals. Management is nuturing and being there to catch them when things go badly. It's our job to see what went wrong and prevent it from happening again if possible. Sometimes we're dealing with clients who are new in the business. We inform clients of the nature of the business and not to take things personally. All our clients take classes at the Young Actors Space, and we make sure they're trained. If we find that they need more help, we encourage them to take classes elsewhere—to seek voice work or dance classes— so they're well-rounded and prepared for whatever happens emotionally or creatively.

DIANE: One of our clients is a young man, Chad Allen, on OUR HOUSE. We are on the lookout for other projects that are going to expand his career and might even develop projects ourselves. We expose our clients to theatre and suggest books for them to read. I think every one of our clients has a copy of Uta Hagen's *Respect for Acting*, and they've all read it. Many of them have discussed it with us. We do help them decide how to dress for a role. For example, one of our clients, Krista Denton, got a role because of the way she dressed. While it's her talent, her personality, and her look that got the job, one of her first big breaks was THE BURNING BED. Nora took her on this appointment. The casting people felt she was too pretty for the part, so we dressed her in a long, dirty T-shirt dress and put a little makeup under her eyes, very light to give her little blue circles under her eyes. And we spritzed her hair with water just before she went in. The casting people saw a totally different person. They saw her character. And she got the job.

NORA: We really try to keep it fun. One of the things we do on the way to interviews or at interviews is to make sure, because there's so much waiting involved, to keep our clients' spirits up, keep them involved, and keep their energy high during some of these long waits before auditions or in tense situations when it comes to final callbacks.

DIANE: Sometimes that means keeping them down the hall a little bit from what's going on, and with the younger ones it may just mean playing TicTacToe. Or running around the block if they're tense. It may mean telling jokes, whatever it takes to get that energy focused, so they haven't been socializing so much that they've forgotten why they are there.

NORA: When they get a role, especially when they're first starting out, we try to spend as much time on the set as possible. To keep them coached so that their nerves don't get the better of them. We want them to be relaxed enough to be able to take risks so they can give an interesting performance.

DIANE: We want them to bring a great deal of themselves to the director, and hopefully the director will say, "Yeah! That's a great idea!"

NORA: I think most actors wait for a director to bring them out. Directors, especially in TV, will work with what they see because they don't have the time. I think that's where we as managers/ coaches can really help is by getting them to be brave and creative right off the bat.

HOW DO YOU ACQUIRE YOUR CLIENTS?

DIANE: All of our client acquisitions have been here at the Young Actors Space. We are very particular because we have to feel that they are extremely talented and have star quality—that undefine-able thing, charisma. It makes people want to stare and listen and stare some more. Where that comes from is not always clear. Unless we feel that a person has that, we really are not interested in managing them at this point because our energies are limited. We can only put in a certain amount of energy on each client. We have to be very excited in that way. We also have to like the person because of the time we spend with them. The few times when we have jumped and taken someone a little too quickly, we've been brought up short. We realized we do need to watch, look, care, and work with an artist for a long time before we make a management decision. We take that "personal" very seriously. We find our clients primarily through the school. That doesn't mean that if we went out and saw a play with a young person in it, and we were just blown away, we wouldn't go up to that person and say, "Would you come to the Young Actors Space, and we'll give you classes while we watch you work for a while with the idea of management in mind?"

WHAT QUALITIES DO YOU LOOK FOR IN AN ACTOR OR AN ACTRESS?

DIANE: First thing that Nora and I look for is talent. Talent is an energy and a vulnerability. A willingness to be open to the stimuli around a person, not only all the sensory things but to the other people as well. It's a person's personal energy. It is the energy and vulnerability together that make an interesting actor. The best actors are people who look at the world a little differently than the average person. An energy, a vulnerability, and a sense of humor are qualities that we look for, and we do search for a look. We're not going to sell someone who doesn't have an interesting look— be it beautiful or character, it doesn't matter, just a look that will sell. We look for a voice that goes with the look. If someone has a voice that is off from the way they look, it's going to hurt them. Vulnerability, energy, talent, openness, voice, look . . .

NORA: A nice person, nice parents—we do look for that. Parents are our clients when we're dealing with young people as much as the actor. We look for parents who are supportive of their careers and people that we can work with. We look for actors who are disciplined. They have to be in love with acting. That promotes their discipline. Our clients are able to come to classes as much as they want. We have one client, Thomas Wilson Brown, who comes to four or five acting classes a week. He's a young fourteen-year-old boy who does scene work in every single class, and his growth has been just tremendous. It's extremely exciting for us to see that kind of commitment and love of it and discipline. He's an extremely attractive young man and that's something that we look for a lot, an attraction. When you see other young people being attracted by a client's charisma, it's a good sign. I would say that all of our most successful clients and students are extremely attractive young people. People notice them, like them, like to be with them. That likability and magic that they have is extremely important. I was talking to Diane the other day about a young actress, Mare Winningham, whom I saw in high school in a camp situation at USC Idlewild. She had such a charisma about her, it was just astounding. It was before she had ever worked professionally, but there was just something about her that all of these people were just compelled by her, and she's that kind of fabulous actress today. That's the kind of quality we look for, somebody that has that magnitude.

WOULD YOU TALK A LITTLE ABOUT THE KIND OF DAY TO DAY PROBLEMS THAT CROP UP AS PART OF YOUR WORK?

DIANE: This instance was a real team effort with Thomas Brown's agent, Ro Diamond. He got a ST. ELSEWHERE, and at the same time he got a Del Monte commercial. And through our efforts and Ro's—and I must say Ro was absolutely fabulous in this effort and also his commercial agents, Herb Tannen—it was worked out so Tom could do the episode of ST. ELSEWHERE and be picked up on the set at noon and be able to do the Del Monte commercial. It took a lot of effort on everybody's part, including the producers of ST. ELSEWHERE and the commercial, but it was everybody really pulling for Tom, and we were able to work that out.

NORA: It was an incredible week for him. He had gotten DADDY, a miniseries, and another guest-star role. Four jobs all in one week. And he could do only one of them technically, but, between all of us, we made it fly so he could do two. It was very exciting because that role on ST. ELSEWHERE was a real break for him.

DIANE: Chad Allen got a job literally overnight in a TV movie called CODE OF VENGEANCE. He went on the interview at 4:00 and was on a plane by 7:00 p.m. He was replacing a young actor who didn't quite work out, and Chad hadn't done a lot of theatrical at that time. Now, the guy is a seasoned professional, but he wanted one of us to coach him on the script. So Nora flew to Arizona and stayed there.

NORA: Since he was replacing somebody who had not worked out, everybody was really on pins and needles as to whether this child and his mother were going to work out. There was a lot of tension. I was there two or three days. They had never been on location before, so I got them accustomed to what location shooting was all about. I got him coached for the role, which was quite a heavy dramatic one. It was quite an adventure for them. Now, of course, they've been all over the place, but it really called for teamwork on their part.

DIANE: Another situation where we really helped out at the last minute was a client whose work permit was going to be up that day, and we were able to go down and get the work permit taken care of and over to the Office of Labor and save the situation when no one else was available.

NORA: We have a client who is a very religious woman, and we have to be very careful about what projects to submit and push for. She's very selective about her work, which is actually quite moving. She's incorporated her beliefs into her work. We often will read scripts for her, and there are certain things we know that she's not interested in doing and other things maybe are more question-able. Chad Allen is very successful, and he started getting more fan mail than he could possibly handle. The teen magazines have been featuring him very heavily, and so we did research and looked into developing a fan club for him. That was something we learned about just recently—how to handle fan mail and get organized. We took care of that for him and actually footed the bill for some of the set-up fees. Another client was very interested in taking guitar lessons, and we thought that would add to his career. So for Thomas Brown's birthday, we rented a guitar and gave him guitar lessons.

DIANE: Elizabeth Berkeley, who lives in Detroit, Michigan, has been one of our clients for about a year now. She came out here and landed a small film called PLATINUM BLONDE for the National Association of Children of Alcoholics. Everything was donated. The studio, the props, the actors all donated their time, but we all got together and felt this would be a good break for Elizabeth. She would have some nice film on her. She would be doing the lead as Karen Black's daughter. The fact that there was a star in it like Karen Black gave it a great deal of credibility. Elizabeth came out and we put her up for six weeks, coached her, and she took classes. Then she went home and was back and forth all year to read for projects. She got very close on several projects, and we're there for her just as much as we're there for any of our L.A. clients.

DEFINE LOYALTY.

DIANE: Loyalty in many ways can be boiled down to respect. You respect someone, and you want to do what is best for them. You want them to respect you and trust you. In trusting someone, you know they won't do anything that is going to purposefully hurt you and, yet, if I'm not doing the job for someone, we'll be the first to admit it and say, "Go elsewhere." But if we're doing the job for someone, we would trust them to come to us if there's any problem in the relationship and be up front with us about that and discuss problems along the way. Being loyal to someone is being up front with them—and all that comes out of respect and trust.

NORA: It's difficult to talk about because each case is so individual. I think the only thing you can do as a manager or as a client is to establish an open relationship so that, from the beginning, problems are handled as they come up and things are not brewing and stewing. Problems do come up, and I think what you're getting at is in terms of people leaving to go to someone bigger—a manager taking a child from an agent and putting him with a different agent or a client dropping a manager and going with a bigger team. A management team may grow faster than its clients. I've seen both happen. It's such an unpredictable business that it's hard to make generalizations about loyalty. I think appreciation and open communications are important. I think people have to bring up positive things. Everybody needs strokes, and it's important for people to know when they're doing a good job as well as a bad job.

DIANE: Contracts should be honored. We have contracts that are legal and binding, and even though minors have an easier time getting out of contracts, why do we have them if they're not to be honored? We've been in several situations where we would have loved to have torn up a contract. We didn't, because we felt that just as we hope our clients will honor the written contract with us, we honor the written contract with them. That means that they can continue to have classes here, it means that they will be included in client affairs and given attention.

WHAT ABOUT WHEN THINGS DON'T WORK OUT AND THEY BREAK THE CONTRACT? OR IT'S JUST A CASE WHERE THE CONTRACT HAS EXPIRED, AND YOU AND/ OR THE CLIENT ARE READY FOR A PARTING OF THE WAYS. HOW DO YOU DEAL WITH THAT AND KEEP IT IN PERSPECTIVE?

NORA: That's the biggest problem that you take on in working with young people. When you take people who are very young, they grow up and they change. What you saw in a young perspon may not be true in a few years down the line. Our contracts are three-year contracts, and children change enormously over a period of three years. I would say that has been our biggest problem. A child may grow and end up not liking it as much as they liked it when they were quite young. We are loyal to our clients, and we do stick by them although they may not grow up into what we had envisioned. Their interests change, and they get a little too pat with their work.

DIANE: We have taken on some clients who have had no previous professional experience at all. In two cases, this has turned out to be very frustrating. They just don't come through professionally the way they do in class or they don't want to. They really enjoy acting, but they don't enjoy interviewing. Or they don't enjoy preparing for the interview. It's a big difference. We have found that extremely frustrating in several cases. From now on, we're going to be more aware of that and be sure that these people know what the word "professional" means. We are going to work with people on a verbal basis for a while before we sign them in order to see how they translate from the classroom into the professional world because of how strongly we feel about our contracts!

NORA: I think it's difficult when you're dealing with people who are green in the business and may not understand what is involved in maintaining a professional career. They may not know about the business, so there's no trust. They didn't have the trust or respect because they didn't really know what they had. I think that's why it's important to talk to people in the business. There's a fine line between educating yourself about the business and being in on the "grapevine" where people are gossiping and worrying about every single little bitty thing. There's a fine line in terms of information gathering that's important. We deal with children, so I'm talking about parents, and I think that when it didn't work out was when people were just a little too green to appreciate us. It's worked out better for us when people have been in the business for a while and have been frustrated and, when they come to us, they can really see the difference we make. We're very good at what we do, and we work very hard. And we have made a difference in everybody's career. We see their résumés grow and grow. When people don't have an appreciation of that, it's because they don't have anything to compare it to.

HOW CAN THE ACTOR TAKE RESPONSIBILITY FOR HIS CAREER?

DIANE: It is very difficult for an actor to take responsibility because his career in the long run is up to the people who are going to hire him. Luck is when preparation and opportunity meet. Take control by getting good training, so that it's not hit and miss. When you audition, do the best that you can possibly do at that moment. It's not an accident that you give a good reading. Never leave readings up to chance, whether it's a two-line part or a lead. You need to show your best colors every time you go in. Classes keep creative juices going. An actor can never feel, "Ah, now I know it all, I can sit back and rest on my laurels." He should go around to different teachers. I don't think any one teacher can give a young actor everything he needs. Stay in class and keep your skills honed and your creative juices going. You have control of the pictures you hand out, how you look when you go to an interview, whether you're going to be on time or not—those things show that you're responsible. Are you going to be a friendly person? You have control over whether you bring your problems to the set or into the casting offices with you. You don't have control over whether you get the job because they may want someone with one pink eye and one purple eye. You may be cut out of a script because the part may not have been important enough to the story. You do have control over time, energy, appearance, skills, voice, body. Take dance classes. Above all, be sure that you're not a mumbler.

NORA: Taking control of your craft means developing a discipline. It's extremely difficult in this town for an actor to really have discipline because acting is an ensemble effort, and a lot of actors have difficulty maintaining that discipline in a solo situation. It 's vital to keep your studies going. Develop a support system for yourself because it's lonely and tough out there. Find friends who really believe in you, coaches, a manager—develop a team around you that really supports you. That's vital. I see so many people succeed because of this support . . . you're able to go out one more time and bang your head against the wall.

[AUTHOR'S NOTE: *Since this interview was completed, several of the clients mentioned have added considerably to their résumés. Chad Allen is now a regular on the television series MY TWO DADS. Thomas Wilson Brown has moved into feature films with roles in HONEY, I SHRUNK THE KIDS and WELCOME HOME after appearing in a recurring role on the television series OUR HOUSE. Elizabeth Berkeley is now in the NBC series SAVED BY THE BELL.]*

PART THREE

Making
The
Deals

CHAPTER 7

DEAL MAKING

NEGOTIATIONS FROM THE OTHER SIDE

The deal is the interim agreement, either verbal or written in deal memo form, between the people who represent you (agent/lawyer/manager) and the people who represent the production company (casting director, producer, business affairs). The deal specifies the agreement on salary, billing, length of employment, per diem, transportation, and any other special perks you might be entitled to. The deal concludes in lengthy contract form to be signed by the actor, or the parent or guardian if the actor is a minor.

Although the deal is usually put together over the telephone, there are times—for example, on the second season of THE COSBY SHOW—where sit-down discussions must take place between lawyers, agents and managers. Meetings of this kind occur when careers have reached a certain level of complexity or when phone negotiations have broken down and face-to-face negotiations become necessary. Also, the typical phone negotiation can be interrupted by other calls, which can cause your agent to lose track of where he was or lose the pressure he might be applying successfully. In the COSBY situation, the show was shot in New York, but the production company and network executives were in Los Angeles. The power struggle is frequently affected by where the sit-down discussions are taking place— your office or theirs. Are you the host or the guest? Is your ultimage option to walk out or to throw out? Sit-down negotiations tend to make solving the problems more urgent, but also more expensive—lawyers cost money.

When the casting director is the one negotiating the deal for the production company, he is in the interesting position of having already dealt with the talent on a creative level, and now he must switch hats and deal with the talent's representation on a business level. Reading actors and negotiating with their agents are two different sets of skills. Do casting directors enjoy this aspect of their work, or is it an obligatory headache? How do they feel about your representatives on the other side of the fence?

"IF THEY CAN GET AWAY WITH IT, THEY LOVE IT . . ."

"There is a big difference in the negotiating style of a large agency versus a small agency, a lawyer versus an agent. A lawyer and large agencies have so many minor details that they want to work through and have set in the contract. Because they're working with a star, they're going to have a lot more in the deal than someone starting out. It's not that they're inventing it—it exists because they're handling talent of that stature. I negotiate with big agencies in which the agent comes to me with absolutely unrealistic things. If they can get away with it, they love it. I usually don't let them. I will say, 'That's the most ridiculous thing I've ever heard!' I have this agent who's hysterical to make deals with. This person makes me laugh a lot because she will come in with all these demands. I'll say, 'This is so ridiculous,' and she'll immediately back off. It's a big challenge for this person to come in and ask for all these things. She'll know she's absolutely out of her mind, but she'll do it anyway. Some people will give it away. So why not? You get better after you negotiate a while.

"There's always a question about making test deals—whether the lowest money makes a difference, and, if you ask for too much money, can you lose the deal? If there's a decision that's being made between two actors and they can't really decide who they want because both bring interesting things to the role, and one is going to cost the producer less money, then, sure, every producer wants to save money. They're going to want the best person, and I would say in the case of a real tie between two artists, that might have something to do with it. Sometimes an actor will be so expensive that you just can't make a deal. The company doesn't have that kind of money in the budget, and the actor is going to lose the part if the actor's quote and the money budgeted is so far apart. Producers feel they can find someone else for less money. If they are dying to have that actor, they'll probably find the money somewhere."

Rene Rousselot
Formerly Director of Talent & Casting, CBS

"I AM REALLY NOT CRAZY ABOUT MAKING DEALS . . ."

"I used to like deal making. Early on, it was kind of fun to get into the whole thing, but now it's gotten so complicated. I feel like I'm a lawyer. It's not the creative side, and once I get out of the creative side, I get bored. I am really not crazy about making deals, although I am very good at it—and I have very good relationships with agents. Over the years now, they've learned they can trust me, so I usually don't have huge problems closing deals. But I get really mad when certain agents lead me to believe we're close to a deal and all of a sudden turn around and start asking for more things. It makes my life more difficult, but it also makes me look like an idiot when I have to go back to the producer.

"Because I do a lot of smaller-budget films, very often I will put it right out in the *Breakdowns* what we've got in the budget for the actors, which a lot of times is scale plus ten percent for anything other than the leads. When we set up the appointments, we say, 'You are aware that this is scale plus ten?' And then we get to the deal making and it's, 'Oh, our actor won't work for scale plus ten!' We've gone through all this time and everything. I wish agents would pay more attention to the *Breakdowns* because I think there are now more casting directors that do that sort of thing, since, if we don't, we're wasting everybody's time. There are deals where there's really not much to negotiate. I know that's part of the agent's job to try to get the best deal possible. I have agents saying, 'Well, there's nothing we can negotiate on!' They get so upset. I just figure, 'Hey relax! The clients will either want to do the film or they won't. They're not going to think you're a bad agent, especially if we said up front that there weren't going to be a lot of negotiations. Just relax!' I'm honest with agents and very up front, and I wish they would be as up front with me, because sometimes they give me quotes that aren't correct. I do check up on quotes. I'll check the last couple with other casting directors or producers of some of the bigger roles."

> Stanzi Stokes
> Independent Casting Director

"I'M NOT GOING TO WRESTLE THE AGENT TO THE GROUND . . ."

"I just went through a negotiation that was so difficult. Until there are television phones, nobody is ever going to know who is sitting in the room with you when you are negotiating a deal. This deal was difficult because of the agent. This agent proceeded to tell me that the actor that I'd already hired for first-star position in my movie—and who was signed, sealed, and delivered—was an asshole, a loser. Why was I giving this person the first card? This was none of this agent's business. I was calling about a totally different role. This agent also believed that his client should have first-star billing, and since first-star billing was already given away, he was hoping that by demeaning this other actor or demeaning me it would give him some movement on the deal. Wrong! He then proceeded to say, 'Well, who are you dealing with at the network?' When I told him, he said, 'You're dealing with the wrong person. I'm going to call up so-and-so.' I said, 'What are you doing? We're doing everything but talking about your client and why I telephoned you.' The two producers on this project and the director were in the conference room sitting around the table, listening to me. I am being the most gracious that I've ever been because with them listening, I can't be real loose. I can't go, 'Let me check and see if there's more money.' I can't. The person who can tell me that is sitting right across from me. I can't really lose my temper because they're liable to say, 'Well, she really flies off the handle.' If my producers are very interested in an actor, I will call the agent and ask for quotes—that is, 'How much money did your client make on his last project?' For example, I call you and you say, 'Okay, my client did a movie-of-the-week for CBS and he received $27,000 for three weeks.' I call CBS and say, 'How much did Johnny Jones get for such and such?' and they say that it was $27,000 for four and three-quarter weeks! So the agent lied to me to the tune of about $16,000.

"I was being pushed to the max and finally the agent said to me, 'What's the matter with you, Mary? Do you have your head up your ass?' And I said, 'Hold on! Let me check.' And I put the person on hold, realizing that I had three people sitting in the room, looking at me, all waiting. And they said, 'What are you checking on?' and I thought, oh hell! I said, 'I'm checking to see if I have my head up my ass.' And the director leaped from his chair and said, 'I will kill him!' At this point, this actor—who did not know this was going on—was in the process of having a dead agent because the director was going to kill him, and I was doing my damndest to not let on there was anything going on. I was prepared to never hire this actor again and never deal with this agent, who happens to be an excellent agent with an excellent eye. Dealing with this individual is like spitting into the wind. It is so hard. I get submissions from this agency, and I die because every single person that is submitted is so perfect for my pictures. And I go, oh, my God—and my partner won't deal with this agent, either. Anything I have to say in a deal is not a big secret. Before I have an actor in, I always tell the agent how much money I've got, because why bring an actor in if I can't afford him? It should take very little time. I'm not going to wrestle the agent to the ground. One key thing is I always have a back-up. I will never get into the negotiations unless I have a good second-position person, which a lot of agents have been surprised about . . . I never threaten. I just say, 'Look, it's your prerogative.' If I don't have a good second-position, person, more than likely I will not call an agent and make an offer."

Mary West
Independent Casting Director

"I DON'T WANT AN ACTOR WORKING FOR SLAVE WAGE..."

"I have no personal investment in the deal. If I save my production company money, I don't get a kickback. I am aware of the budgetary restraints—when you're working in a production company like this, you get to sit in on the staff meetings, you get to see the beginning of the process, the evolution of the project and the kind of problems that are associated with above-the-line costs, below-the-line costs, low licensing fees from the network, and deficit financing because of the studio. When you get the final budget, you understand. I've gotten budgets that I can't work with. They're just too low. And it will put a constraint on me as far as the kind of actor I can have in the role and that's when you have to be creative. My attitude is that it should be fair. I don't want an actor working for slave wages. I know a lot of times that agents or managers will pass on a project on the basis of not being able to make the deal. This town is turning into the deal becoming more important than the job. I've had screaming arguments with agents over this because we were very close in a negotiation that I was conducting. I keep tabs on what's going on, I goose the agent a little bit if I think he's being a little too hard-nosed, and the same thing in business affairs. If I think they're taking too hard a line and the actor is very important and they're offering an unfair amount of money, I will address that as well. In fact, that's usually the case. It's me beating up the business affairs people.

"I understand the agent's problem. On the rare occasion that I've had to make a deal and I couldn't close a deal on an actor that I knew was perfect for the role, I had a screaming argument with an agent saying, 'Listen, you don't give a shit about the actor. All you care about is the deal, and that's the bottom line, and you'd better reassess why you're in this business.' It was an important role for the actor and I knew he wanted to do it—it was a project he was excited about and it was a good career move for him, but the agent wouldn't close the deal. The reason we're in this business is to make movies, to make TV, or whatever—good TV—that is the primary goal. People in this business make pretty good livings. When it gets to the point that the deal comes before the job—like the tail wags the dog—it's when you've got to go, 'Wait a minute, we better reassess what's going on here and reevaluate our participation in it.' I think that an agent and a manager have to sit down with their client and say, 'Listen, we can't get you as much money as you might want or we might want to get for you on this, but this is a positive growth step for you. This is a breakthrough role. And it's important that you do it.' That's a manager's responsibility. A lot of times, though, I find managers are not doing that. They're more interested in the fifteen percent or the ten percent than they are in the welfare of the client, and they're looking for the short haul, as opposed to the long haul. I think that's unfortunate, and it has to change."

Marc Hirschfeld
Liberman/Hirschfeld Casting

"NEGOTIATING TO ME IS BASICALLY LOGIC . . ."

"Seventy-five percent of my job is deal making. I like doing it. I saw fewer actors than all of the other casting directors at Cannon Films because a lot of my time is spent in making deals with top stars. They're complex and complicated and we weren't real flexible. We were pretty honest about what was in the budget, and if it was a scale part you'd know it before you came in. I'm at an advantage because I've been an agent. I always advise a director to have a second or third choice. Second or third choices are usually the people who end up starring in the movies. AN OFFICER AND A GENTLEMAN was offered to Elizabeth McGovern. She turned it down. Deborah Winger did it and became a star. RUNAWAY TRAIN was supposed to be Gene Hackman and Sean Penn. It turned out to be John Voight and Eric Roberts, and they were both nominated for Oscars. More often than not, the second choice works out for the best. I always like to prepare. I tell directors, 'Do not tell an actor that he has the part,' because then I have absolutely no power at all in negotiating.

"There are so many perks that the majors give them that they expect to get them at Cannon. There are points and there are

extra plane tickets and there are arguments over per diem and
there are deferments. It's so creative. There are different schedules of players that if they make a certain amount of money they
get so many free hours of overtime through SAG. The only thing
that my economics classes taught me is that a liberal arts
education doesn't train you to do anything. But it will teach you
how to think. And negotiating to me is basically logic. If the
person needs the role, if he wants the role, if he hasn't done a
film, you're in the driver's seat. I was a much harder agent than
most of the agents that I deal with. I will play down to the last
card if I can. And I usually win. I can't even think offhand of one
that I lost. As an agent, you have to prepare the client to lose the
job. They have to totally accept that. If they say they want this
amount of money yet they still want the job, don't blow it but get
me this money, I mean you can't have it both ways. So you have
to have really great relationships with the client. Do you really
want to do a series for five years or be on a soap for three years
and do this part in this movie and have like five options of low
money at Paramount? And with the directors, you have to be
willing to lose, too. They must have second choices. And of
course it all depends on the director. A great script you can get
almost anybody to do for less money. People will work for Andre
Konchalovsky for less money than they would for someone else.
He's an actor's director. So you have that to your advantage.
Some of the deals that I've made for him have been incredible.

  "Actors are offered parts in films and never even knew
about it. The offers were not taken to them. And they wanted to
do the parts. For example, a particular part was a female lead in
a scale-plus-ten film. The actress had never done a feature
before. I will see any actor or actress who stars in a movie—I
don't care what it is—as will most casting directors, because
there's some reason why they were cast. They may be terrible,
but you'll see them anyway. Someone trusted them to carry the
film. It will get you in on anything to say, 'My client just starred in
this movie.' Well, this particular agency had gotten an offer for
this particular client to do some syndicated thing, a silly sitcom
kind of thing, and it was more money. And the client was never
ever informed that she had been offered this feature. And they

called back and said that we couldn't get through to her. She was so protected by her manager and the big agency that we believed them. You can only go so far. We don't go and call actors at home because we have to continue relationships with the agencies. You never know if you'll need someone at some point. I always say, be nice, no matter who it is. If you leave an agency, be nice about it. I had an actress whom I liked, who was marginally talented but very beautiful. In two years, she had a series. She starred in a couple of films, she guest-starred in a lot of episodic television, and she came in to me and said, 'Now I need a real agent—I'm leaving you.' Well, she hasn't worked since. This was six years ago. I just got a phone call from her yesterday. I can't believe she's calling me. She insulted me so badly, and I worked so hard for her and made her a lot of money. I don't forget things. Don't ever burn bridges no matter where you are. I have made that mistake. I told someone to drop dead, and the next day a director insisted on hiring one of his clients. They're asking for this over-priced kind of thing and they have complete control over the client. The agents that deal with Cannon are trained to know Cannon just doesn't pay like the majors do. Cannon does a lot of movies and puts a lot of people to work. No one will hold a Cannon quote against anybody."

Bob MacDonald
Independent Casting Director,
MacDonald/Bullington Casting

"NEGOTIATING CAN BE FUN ON BOTH SIDES . . . "

"When I'm negotiating with agents on the phone, I like to be as up front as I can be and save as many back-and-forth phone calls as I can. I will usually say—depending on who the client is—how close I am. If I'm very far apart, I will say that up front. 'I don't know if we're going to be able to make this work. I've only got X amount of dollars . . .' I will ask them for quotes on their client. I'll be able to tell instantly, if I don't know already, how unrealistic it is and then I'll just try to cut right to it and say,

'I think at best it's going to be a compromise situation. How badly does your client want to do this job? We want him desperately. Are you going to be able to make this work, or are we kidding ourselves?' And if we're a few thousand dollars away, then I'll say, 'Tell me your bottom line. I know what my bottom line is, so let's save having five or six phone calls back and forth and see if we can do it.' I also like agents to tell me all the parameters. If it's a big deal that's going to involve what kind of dressing room or how many transportations, I appreciate it when the agent asks me everything up front because a lot of times it's hard to get your producer on the phone. To go back and finally have the money, the billing settled and then they say,'Oh, now we have to talk about expenses . . . ' I say, 'Oh, I have to go back in again and is this everything?' So I like to get everything discussed in the first or second conversation so that it saves calls to the producer. On a smaller deal, I'm guided a lot on who I bring in. Hopefully, I've already got a cast budget, and I know if I got $1,000 a day and it's a good character part. I know not to go to somebody who's going to cost me $2,500 a day, and it's just going to waste my producer's time and the actor's time, unless I know I have flexibility with that agent or that actor. You say to them, 'Look, I've only got $1,000 a day. I know he gets $2,500 a day, but it's really a lovely scene. Maybe I can get you an extra $100, or something.' I'm not into game playing. I'm sure there's a certain amount of that that we all have to do at certain times, but the ideal situation is where you just get all your cards on the table up front . . . and that saves a lot of time.

"I enjoy deal making. I think it's a challenge, especially when you have budgets that are not as realistic as you would like them to be and yet you want to get the best talent possible for your director and for the piece you're working on. You really have to do some dancing. And I think where the agent has to be flexible is in determing when it's okay for a client to work for less money than they've established, and when it's appropriate to demand a little bit of a raise. I don't think that's an easy thing to do. I'm sure that agents work differently with different casting directors. I'm sure they get a bead on how certain casting directors work. I think it's important for them to know when it's okay to make certain concessions. Maybe when a separate card isn't as important in one case as it might be in another and when getting their client maybe $1,000 less a week is okay and when it's not. I don't think there's any cut and dried answer to that. You have to look at a role for your client in terms of whether it's going to be a good career move. If it's a quality project that's going to put them in another league, maybe you're more willing to make certain concessions. If it's a part that they've done before, and everyone already envisions them in the role, then it's more important for the agent to make it worth his client's while by getting him extra bucks. We're all very aware of those situations. I think negotiating can be fun on both sides, and I'd like to think our office in particular wants to be fair. Even though we're working for our producer and we want to get the best talent possible and still save him some money, I would want people to know that we're the first ones to speak up if a budget is so unrealistic that it's just not possible to be creative. 'If you producers want this, then you can't look at it in terms of this amount of money. It's not going to happen, and there's no reason why the actor should work for this amount of money for this size part.' If there's a compromise to be made, you'll go back and do your damnedest to make it work. You want to be fair, and yet you want to do the best job possible."

> Judy Taylor
> Fenton-Feinberg & Taylor Casting

CREDITS

Your deal will also determine what form your credit will take, and credits should be looked at from several standpoints. Credit serves the purpose of feeding an artist's ego. Credit informs potential employers and the public that the artist is responsible for a specific contribution to a project. Also, the level of credit an artist is able to obtain can serve as an indicium of how highly the artist is regarded by those seeking his or her services, and the greater the perceived demand for an artist, the greater the salary the artist can command. Moreover, the greater the quantity

and quality of an artist's credits, the greater the impact on stature
and salary.

For motion picture artists, the two most important types
of credit in connection with a picture are: 1) screen credit and 2)
credit in paid advertisements, such as newspaper and periodical,
billboard, radio ads, and theatrical and television trailers.

In theatrical pictures, screen credit is given to practically
every individual and entity, including the caterer. In television,
however, because of network limitations on the length and
composition of the opening and end titles, it is typical for relatively fewer of the individuals and entities involved with the
picture to receive credit.

SALARY

"Determining how much you will be paid usually begins
with a request from the casting director for the current salary
quote—how much the actor makes per day, per week, per
episode, per film, on a given type of project. The agent presents
the quote that is applicable to the type of job in question—a
MOW quote for a MOW, last feature quote for a feature, etc. If the
deal is for a television series pilot and the artist has no previous
pilot quote, then the agent would offer the highest quotes for
other similar work in order to establish a track record in this new
area.   When Henry Thomas finished E.T. and it was mega-
successful at the box office, his feature quote got him high
weekly salary offers from several television series, which he
refused. On the other hand, Michael J. Fox, out of a hit series,
FAMILY TIES, was able to demand a large feature salary because
of his high visibility and large weekly television salary.

Once the casting director or the business affairs people
have received the actor's current quote, he would then take this
quote or no quote—if the actor has not worked at all or has only
SAG scale—to the producer or network business affairs to
prepare an offer.

"Actors can be priced out of the market in terms of agent/
casting director negotiations. The monetary situations are pre-

dicted upon facts and figures. You don't make a million dollars a picture if you're not going to bring it back at the box office. So if your actor is bringing that kind of money in for one reason or another, then you deserve that money. If, however, you're asking for that kind of money based on nothing, you as an agent with unreasonable demands can put an actor out of business. I enjoy the negotiating aspect of casting. However, it is time consuming. When we casting directors used to do all of the negotiations for all of the series people, with the options for seven years on everybody that was testing in the next two weeks, the time element was frantic, just frantic, so therefore, business affairs people are very welcome in that instance where you don't have the time. But for myself, I do like to negotiate my own deals."

Caro Jones
Independent Casting Director

"If it isn't in the budget, then we'll have trouble closing the deal—that's the bottom line. I don't know of any awards being given out to casting directors who come in phenomenally under budget. If the money is there and you have quotes or work to prove that you have gotten that money for your actor before, I'm not there to screw you. If you have $1,500 quotes and I get you for $1,000, first of all, production people will probably never know it unless I call to tell them, and, secondly, I don't get the $500 difference. If it's there and I have it, you get it. But if I'm told not to exceed a certain amount and that's it, neither you nor I can do anything about it. It's a business. I hope we can make it work, and if it doesn't, you say, 'Sorry, maybe next time.' More times than not, I get day players that have a $600 quote and an agent will say, 'God, they've been making $600 for the past year.' Well, if I can, I'll bump them on every occasion. You know, $50. Big deal, but at least next time they have a $650 quote."

Bob Harbin
L.A. LAW Casting;
Formerly Manager of Casting, NBC

PER DIEM

Per diem is Latin for "per day," and per diem is the amount of money given an actor per day on an out-of-town location to cover meals, taxis, etc. SAG has established a minimum of $42 a day (breakfast $8.00, lunch $12.00, dinner $22.00) but this is negotiable because, for example, in New York the cost of taxis, food, and tipping is much higher, so the minimum might go as high as $100 a day to cover the essentials. Make sure that your agent specifies the amount of per diem for each on-location shoot. SAG also specifies that for actors who must be accompanied by a parent, both parent and child are given equal per diem amounts. However, the producer has no obligation to pay more than one per diem if the actor is over eighteen or is emancipated. In foreign countries, per diem is often paid in the currency of the country to save money on the exchange. If the exchange rate is not in your favor, ask for it in American dollars. Always be sure to exchange your money at a bank. Hotels and stores and even airports change money, but they will not give you as good a rate as a bank.

Per diem does not cover lodging. Per diem should be paid in cash the day you arrive for the entire week. This should be handled by the Second or Third Assistant Director or other production personnel. Per diem should not be included in your check because the check often goes directly to your agent or, if it is given to you, you don't have time to cash it, or the bank it is drawn on is out of state. It is sometimes useful to hold on to your per diem cash and use a credit card instead for many purchases here and overseas because it is an excellent record for tax purposes. Asking for and saving cash receipts can be tedious to the already overburdened actor.

ACCOMMODATIONS

Even though it's your agent who is making the deal, it's you who will be living through the actual conditions which the deal sets up. Consider carefully, beyond the role itself and what you'll be paid, questions such as does the role require travel? Is it out of the state or the country? Will you need a passport? Who will set up travel arrangements? What kind of room arrangements will be set up for you and/or your family?

Never feel foolish about making whatever fuss is necessary to arrange for accommodations that will allow you to do your best work. Make sure you have a separate hotel room. If you are told one is not available, call SAG and they will help the producer find one for you. If you are traveling with family members, you may still require a separate room in order to insure sufficient privacy. The actor may have an early call while the relative may want to sleep late or stay up later. Visitors such as agents or family members or friends may come for a short stay. This extra space can make it more affordable and convenient. As a minor, when you are not working on the set, you might want to have the studio teacher come to your room for classes, which means a parent can't be there, since the hotel room has now become a classroom. Accommodations for the young artist should be equal to adults with the same importance to the film—same billing, etc. If you're not happy with your room, say something. The production company cannot force you to share a room with another actor. When in doubt, call your agent and find out what was negotiated. A long distance call from your agent or manager may have more effect than your complaining to the First A.D. Frequently, production companies are housed in several hotels due to the number of people involved. The quality of accommodations may vary from hotel to hotel. Being concerned with this may seem petty, but you as an actor cannot do your best creative work if you are worrying about your hotel, or kept up all night by paper-thin walls. Ross Harris, one of my clients, was on location in Germany filming CENTURIAN ODYSSEY and discovered that, while his hotel was of very high quality, he had arrived during a period of massive renovation—which necessitated his carrying suitcases up five flights of stairs because the elevators didn't work. Nor was there any food, since neither kitchen nor room service were working. A minor point, unless you're starving and exhausted at 2:00 a.m., and there's nowhere around to get food and you have to be up in four hours. (You'll be happy to know that the production manager resolved the problem by moving the actor to another hotel as soon as he learned of the problem.)

First-class hotels are generally the accepted rule when you are working overseas, although, depending upon the location and duration, consider the possibility of staying at a neighborhood hotel that will allow you to get to know the locals and that is near the populated centers for shopping, or perhaps in a small nearby village where you can actually be part of a foreign culture. American hotels have Americans on vacation.

All valuables should be kept in safety deposit boxes at the hotel desk. More than one actor has lost a week's per diem, watch, or cameras to thieves. The safety deposit boxes are free, and you can use them ten times a day if necessary. They always give you a numbered key, which you should give to the A.D. for safekeeping while you are on the set.

The purchase of a Texas Instruments calculator that has foreign exchange tables into which you can feed the current rate each day can be invaluable. When the exchange rate (which is listed in hotels, banks, and even on the wall of McDonald's overseas) is in your favor, purchase items that you know are deals—leather, furs, jewelry, ceramics for future gifts—because you may regret it if you never have the opportunity to go back and because these items can often be resold later for a good profit.

You may grow weary of the food in any locale, overseas or stateside, so it is often a good idea to ask for accommodations that include a full kitchen—so that on occasion you can reacquaint yourself with such staples as the hamburger, hot dog, pizza, or steak and baked potato. Homemade spaghetti is excellent at dispelling homesickness and/or loneliness!

If your stay on location is more than five weeks, the request to rent a house or a furnished condo may be a more practical venture for you, especially if you need a more quiet environment to return to after a long day's shoot. It makes sense if you are traveling with a small entourage or expect many visitors during the shoot. Obviously, if the house is unfurnished, the set-up and return of furniture and kitchen utensils may be too time-consuming for you to consider, unless the production company will be responsible for the set-up and return. Often the cost to the production company for a house or condo is less than the cost of a similar period of time in a first-class hotel.

(On a nearby overnight location, if you drive, keep a record of the miles. You will be entitled to re-imbursement at the rate of 30¢ per mile. When you get your check, compare the mileage rate. If there is a discrepancy, call the Guild and it will put in a claim for the whole cast. Also, keep in mind that, on a nearby location, you will be entitled to a twelve-hour rest period between the first and second day of shooting. This is called a "twelve-hour turnaround." Anything less than twelve hours will constitute a "forced call" and will entitle you to an extra day's pay.)

RELOCATION FOR SERIES WORK

If you have to move in order to do a television series, the costs of relocation for you and your family can be very expensive. One of the reasons that the second season of THE COSBY SHOW involved the aforementioned complexity of negotiation was due to the issue of relocation and what it had meant for the actors during the first season. During the negotiations for the Cosby pilot, the company Carsey-Werner and the network NBC attempted to go to court in Los Angeles to have the contracts for the series court-approved. In their appearance on the scheduled court day, all the petitioners (children, agents, managers, parents, and lawyers) were invited into the judge's chambers. The judge said to us, "What I'm being asked to do is to court approve contracts which, in essence, state that of the weekly salary of $5,000 [a fictitious figure], 10% will go to the agent, 15% to the manager, 25% will go into a blocked account [per the California Coogan Law requirement], and approximately 54% will go the IRS." The IRS makes the assumption that the weekly salary of $5,000 is made 52 weeks a year, even if only 22 episodes are ordered. This amount will be removed each week until the year-end tax bite is fulfilled. The judge said somewhat facetiously to the kids, "Why don't you just get rid of your agent, manager, lawyer, and parent—the people taking your money?" At that point, the lawyers for Carsey-Werner and NBC went white. The judge refused to court-approve the contracts as they stood. The network and the producers could of course go forward with the series without court approval, but the problem was compounded by the fact that all of the Cosby Kids were under eighteen (minors), and without a court-approved contract could disaffirm the contract and leave the series at any time and not be sued successfully. Obviously, the networks could not put themselves in that situation, and the meeting ended without a court-approved contract.

To send these kids to New York cost each parent several hundred dollars each week out of their own pocket for the privilege of doing the series and being in New York. A number of the children were from single-family households whose parent had to work to keep the family unit together. It became necessary for the parent to give up their jobs to go with the child to New York to supervise. The rents in New York at that point were between $1,400 and $1,600 a month. First, last, and a one month security deposit were demanded up front—totalling almost $5,000. This was for a two-bedroom apartment in a safe part of the city close to the Brooklyn Studios where THE COSBY SHOW was filmed. The first half of the season no transportation was provided to the children—leaving parent and child to use the subway or pay for cabs—one a dangerous avenue (especially for someone with TV visibility), and the second an expensive alternative. A small one-time relocation allowance of $3,000 was given to each child.

In the ensuing months, conversations were held in an attempt to find a way out of this dilemma. Eventually, Carsey-Werner decided to deposit in each childs account, out of the producers' pocket, an amount of money equal to 25% of the weekly episodic salary to meet the Coogan Law requirement for each individual family. In essence, the child and parent could then have the 25% to operate on and not have this money deducted from the weekly check (except for commissions and the IRS). This extra 25% left in the check allowed the parent to defray expenses in order to make surviving in New York possible for the families and secured the court-approved contracts.

What should have been done in retrospect was to allow the agent to successfully negotiate perks such as housing assistance, living expenses, transportation, even per diem so that the actor can afford to do the series. Relocation should not have to mean penal servitude or looking for someone to dump from the actor's team who may have been responsible for the opportunity being presented in the first place.

The second season saw all transportation provided, an allowance each month in excess of several thousand dollars for living expenses, help with private schooling, etc.

"LOOK AT WHY THE ARTIST IS DOING THE PROJECT . . ."

When a deal is ready to close, the actor should feel that all of the people who represent him have been communicating with each other frequently, with every point being written down and understood, including the future ramifications of all decisions. The actor should be kept apprised of the process, so that there can be no regrets once a decision is made to close the deal, and so that there is no lingering dissension that can be exploited by any of the involved parties in the future. Did you get what you wanted? And, if you didn't get everything that you'd wanted, can you live with what you got?

The person to whom it usually falls to negotiate on your behalf is your agent. Richard Berman, senior partner of the full-service agency, The Agency, describes how he sees his job in negotiation:

"From my standpoint, in making a deal, it is important to me to look at why the artist is doing the project. Are they doing it because they need to do it in terms of career? Has their career been in the doldrums for a while and they now have this offer— a major coup? I look at it as a deal they cannot afford to lose. What I would not want to happen is for the artist not to do the job. If that, in fact, is the case, then I have to go in on the philosophy that, no matter what happens, no matter if they offer me garbage money and no billing and lousy working conditions,

I must still close the deal. I look at the role and I say, 'This is a terrific role and, no matter what the case is, this person has to do this.' And the same thing with a writer or a director.

"If it's a situation where they're growing and it's absolutely imperative that their monies and their billing be bumped and that their stature in the industry is going to be viewed very, very importantly with a jaundiced eye by everybody in town, then I think it's real important that everything be up to par or the deal not be made. Otherwise, I will lose the client. When they come out with an important role and can't get the money or billing or whatever, that's exactly what the other agents are going to come to them and say, 'You mean your current agent couldn't get you more money on this? Look at this role! Look at where your career has been going. You are so hot!' What is important is that no matter how bad the deal is, if the client says, 'I have to do this role, I must do this part, I don't care what it is,' then I will go on record as saying this is something I don't advise, but I certainly would never ever try to come between an actor or any artist's gut feeling about a particular project. I've seen it happen too many times where they felt this is something they need to do, and the agent turns the project down—the project becomes successful and then they blame the agent for not having done it.

"I've seen a situation where an individual had an opportunity to resurrect his entire career with a movie, and the money was bad. The agent suggested that they pass on the project so casting will come back to them with more money. The actor was a little reticent about it, and the agent said, 'Trust me. No problem!' They passed, and a day went by, and the actor called back and said, 'Well, did they call with the other offer?' 'No, let me call them.' The agent called the casting director who told him, 'Well, no, you passed, so I just went on to my next choice. He accepted it for exactly that money, and he's doing it.' I won't tell you what the role was, but it was a role in a famous film that became a series of films, and it totally resurrected somebody else's career. It could have been his. So after that experience, I would never ever do that with an actor or director who says to me, 'I really feel I must do this role.' I would be honest and say, 'Okay, you've basically taken away everything I have at the poker table . . .' I usually follow it up with some kind of friendly but informational letter because artists have a habit of not remembering certain phone conversations and even one-to-one conversations, so that's when I say to them, 'Don't you remember you said you had to do it?' 'I don't remember that conversation.' Well, they conveniently tune it out. But when I pull out a letter and I say, 'Just want you to remember . . . this was the letter I sent you and it acknowledges that I condone this project and I support you. I support you in everything you do, even though I have misgivings about certain projects.' So I try to cover my backside . . . I sit there in amazement, staring this person in the face and saying, 'You don't remember this conversation we had?' They say, probably as honestly as the day is long (because they've totally blocked it out), 'I do not remember this conversation. I just remember that you wanted me to do this project, and you made a bad deal for me.' It's not a letter saying, 'I want to go on record,' but that, in essence, is what the letter says."

> Richard Berman
> The Agency

THE VOCABULARY OF DEAL MAKING

Arbitration: A process of hearing and determination of a case in controversy by an impartial person chosen by both parties.

Billing (Screen Credit): The relative prominence that an actor's name receives in positioning in the crawl of the film or TV show, which includes the card, its position (first, second, or last card), whether it's to be shared with another actor (shared card) or not (single card). This will include screen credit and credit on paid ads.

Exclusivity: A limitation of possession, control, or use of an actor's services by a production company for a specified period.

Favored Nations: A clause providing that if any other actor is given a term or condition of employment more favorable relating to credit, compensation, guarantee, exclusivity, or other specified matter than your agreement, then your contract will be automatically upgraded to equal that favorable term or condition.

First Refusal: A clause that gives a production company that has just employed you an opportunity to match offers made by other production companies for future projects. If you must agree to any first refusal provision, attempt to negotiate a clause which requires: 1) that your current employer must give you an answer as to whether it will match another job offer in not more than forty-eight hours; 2) that your current employer must match not only the compensation being offered but billing, vacation, rehearsals schedules, minimum of guaranteed programs, and site of production; 3) that your current employer's right of first refusal expires sixty days after the expiration of your employment agreement, so that if you are offered employment on another serial at least sixty days after the termination of your present employment on a serial, the right of first refusal is no longer applicable.

Force Majeure: A term used to describe a situation that arises where neither side can perform the contract due to circumstances beyond their control—acts of God, natural disasters, death of the director, etc.

No-Quote: When you have a situation where a client wants to do a show very badly and there isn't the budget to pay what the actor is worth, the casting director will offer a no-quote—you'll do the favor of working for less in exchange for a promise that, if anyone calls the casting director for your last quote, they will not divulge the fact you worked for less than your established quote.

Offer: The amount of money and specific terms offered by the production company based on the budget of their show and the quotes of the individual artist.

Options: Agreements within a contract to extend the contract's terms past its termination, contingent upon certain eventualities. For example, an actor's contract for the first season of a television series will contain options covering the actor's services for subsequent seasons of the series if the series succeeds; by exercising the options within an agreed upon period of time, the employer is spared having to re-begin negotiations from scratch each season. The option's provisions will specify, among other things, salary, number of episodes, the length of time covered by the option, when and how the option must be executed, etc.

Paid Ads: The artist's name on billboards, trades, press releases.

Pass: A term that designates that the artist wishes to decline an offer presented by management.

Pay or Play: A negotiating point. If an artist's services are contracted for on this basis and the show is not finished, sold, or distributed or you are fired, the full salary must be paid to the artist.

Per Diem: "By the day." Money paid the artist in cash for food and extra expenses on location filming. The SAG minimum is $42 per day. (Breakfast $8.00, lunch $12.00, dinner $22.00.) This is always negotiable depending on the costs of living for that location or city and your negotiating prowess.

Quote: The artist's previous salary history on MOWs, pilots,

features, including daily and/or weekly, rates usually given by the seller (agent) to the buyer (casting
director).

Scale Plus 10: The most frequent bottom-line salary offer. Scale
is the weekly or daily payment established by the
guild for an artist. The "plus 10" refers to the agent's
commission added on top because agents can't take
commission on scale jobs and must negotiate their
commission on top of the salary.

Sequels: A commitment for additional films based on the original
at a predetermined price.

Stop Date: A date is given by a studio or production company as
the last date the artist's services are required. A very
difficult negotiation point to win. If you're given a
verbal stop date, always ask for the date of the
completion bond. It is generally the outside date for
finishing the project.

Top of the Show: The largest amount of money paid for TV
episodic work for non-regulars on a weekly basis—
half-hour show/$2,060, one-hour show/$3,650.

SCENARIO FOR A TV DEAL

The artist—let's call her Tina Maxwell—is up for the part
of Wendy Dalton, the eldest daughter in a new series about the
life of an urban yuppie couple who move their whole family to a
small town and open a bakery. The series is tentatively entitled
DOLLARS TO DONUTS.

Tina has the following quotes:
(1) $1,000/day for a movie on which she worked three
days (an excellent daily quote!)
(2) $20,000 for MOW (movie-of-the-week) that shot for

for four weeks (average $5,000/week)

(3) A pilot deal that went to series but was later canceled. $15,000 for shooting the pilot (usually two weeks or less for tape shows—$6,000 per episode, first year)

(4) A feature quote in a starring role that paid $50,000 for 8 weeks of work.

(5) Many guest episodes on sitcoms such as SILVER SPOONS (half hour) that paid "top of show" ($1,500) or a guest shot on an hour show that paid $2,500/week.

After having submitted her quote to the casting director, Tina's agent meets with her manager to put together their "ideal deal." (The series will be shot in the same city Tina lives in, so relocation is not involved.) Her agent and manager use the following considerations as a basis for negotiations:

(1) Tina is valuable to the series because of a special look the producers need and want.

(2) Tina has performed as a semi-regular in a canceled series.

(3) She has a feature credit in a starring role and has made $50,000 for eight weeks of work.

(4) She has six to ten guest starring roles at top of show ($1,500 for half-hour, $2,500 for hour).

Tina is certainly in an excellent position because of her track record to structure a good deal. Tina's agent believes the pilot will have to pay at least $15,000 for the one to two weeks of shooting. The weekly episode rate will have to be at least $7,500/week, but he will ask for $10,000/week on the strength of previous quotes and the size of the roles or billing, figuring that he may have to compromise. At this point, Tina's manager may suggest that they ask for star billing, at the head of the show, in no less than third position, since the series has a mother and father and other minor children. Tina's manager also adds that the should request a "separate card" (no other names) to read "Starring Tina Maxwell." The agent points out that if they can't get that, it would be better to skip fourth billing and secure the last position, with a single card that reads "Introducing Tina Maxwell as Wendy Dalton."

The casting director calls back and opens with an offer based on the quotes from Tina's group and the money in the budget for this role (known as above-the-line money). The casting director has been authorized to offer $10,500 for the pilot and $7,500 per episode with ten-percent "bumps" (prearranged cost of living increases) for the subsequent years of the run—which could total seven years on a typical contract. The casting director readily accepts the third-position billing for Tina, thereby letting her representatives know that they are interested in Tina and thereby eliminating billing as a negotiating point.

Tina's group takes the offer and compares it with the ideal deal. They now know that the production company doesn't want to lose her because of the tone of their first offer and their acceptance of billing, and the back door appears to be open for further negotiating. Feedback from other sources has also pointed out the strong desire for Tina as first choice of producer or network . . . either from casting directors or other agents and managers who have clients up for other roles and share valuable information. Tina's group comes back with $12,500 for the pilot and $8,500 per episode, and it is accepted. Tina gives them permission to close the deal.

Deal making can be more complex if there are two networks interested in Tina at the same time. Then deals can be negotiated with both networks, forcing each to raise the pilot and weekly episode money by using the "highest bidder" lever. If there are several excellent actors being considered, then the bidding becomes more tricky because Tina's people don't want to put her out of a job. They gain access to competitors' names and, through sources, find out how much they might be worth and how badly they want the role. Pieces of information are constantly traded for future favors. Just as casting directors call other casting directors to check on actor quotes, so do agents and managers gather information on the other players and their strengths and weaknesses. Many times the actor won't take part in the actual negotiations. The agent will call him to get a "thumbs up" or "thumbs down" on the deal. However, actors should be included in most of the necessary steps of the negotiating process, or an "ideal deal" should be discussed, step by step, with the actor ahead of time. It is important for the actor to learn the business aspects and to develop the business acumen to evaluate the information.

SCENARIO FOR A FEATURE FILM DEAL ON A STARRING ROLE

Paula Agent uses the Checklist below to structure a feature deal for her client, "Tommy Superstar":

TYPE OF EMPLOYMENT
Paula negotiates Tommy a three-picture movie deal.

DIRECT EMPLOYMENT OR LOAN-OUT
Tommy, advised by his manager to incorporate to take advantage of the tax benefits, forms Lionhart Productions, Inc., which then loans out Tommy's services to the production company.

LOCATION OF EMPLOYMENT
The first picture in his deal will shoot on location in Florence, Italy, and New York City.

LENGTH OF EMPLOYMENT
Fifteen weeks of location shooting. Five weeks of studio work in New York.

(a) Start date: June 5

(b) Services required prior to start date (rehearsals, photos, public appearances, costume fitting, makeup tests): Paula agrees that Tommy will give one week of free rehearsal plus one photo day, one public appearance, one costume fitting, one makeup day (prosthetic special effects).

(c) Limitations (availability, minimum notice, specific period preceding start date): All free services subject to Tommy's availability with a three-day notice and all services must be completed one week before location shooting begins.

POSTPRODUCTION SERVICES
(looping, dubbing, retakes, added scenes, foreign versions)
Paula agrees that Tommy can do two free looping or dubbing days, but that retakes, added scenes, and foreign versions will be negotiated when those services are deemed necessary.

LIMITATIONS
(availability, minimum notice, special period)
All of the above are subject to Tommy's availability with one week's notice, within three weeks after the picture wraps principal photography.

COMPENSATION
(for this picture, additional compensation beyond guaranteed period deferments, overscale residuals, gross or net participation)
Tommy is getting $375,000 for twenty weeks ($18,000/week). Any shooting after twenty weeks will be prorated on the weekly basis of $18,000. Nothing is deferred since Tommy's tax status is not yet a problem. If the film is released to TV, Tommy will get double scale residual payments.

(a) Compensation due date: Tommy will be paid 1/3 of his salary on the first day of work, 1/3 at midpoint, and 1/3 at the end of the picture.

(b) Payment guarantee (escrow, third-party guarantee, letter of credit): Since most of the shooting is in a foreign country, Paula demands that all of Tommy's salary be put in escrow in order to guarantee payment.

FIRST REFUSALS
(sequels, terms of future employment)
Tommy agrees to first refusal on the sequels to the film but will only negotiate compensation at a future date, since his career is

on the rise.

APPROVALS/CONSULATIONS
(final script, script changes, final budget, director,
performer's makeup person, hair-dresser, wardrobe,
stand-in, stunt double, publicist, stills)

Tommy has consultation on script changes and approval on personal makeup, hair, wardrobe, stand-in, and stunt-double persons, but no approval or consultation on director or final budget.

CREDIT
(form, media, size and prominence, placement)

Paula has negotiated star billing, single card, first position main titles. Tommy will get credit in both the film and any paid advertising in size and prominence no less than any other star's credit, and in paid ads he will be in a box containing no other performers.

RIGHTS GRANTED
(use of results, use of performer's name, voice and
likeness, photographic likenesses, commercial tie-ins,
use of voice in soundtrack sound recordings)

Use of Tommy's name and likeness is limited to in-character use. He refuses to give out-of-character use because he wishes to maintain his rights to posters. Tommy has agreed that the song he sings in the film may be released as a single, and he will get a percentage of the soundtrack album.

TRANSPORTATION AND ACCOMMODATION
(class, additional person, per diem, force
majeure/disability, local transportation, location
accommodations, travel insurance)

Tommy will get a first-class, roundtrip ticket on TWA to Florence, plus two coach tickets for his wife and his manager. He will get a $150 per diem while in Florence and, when they shoot in New York for five weeks, he will get $100/day. In case the director gets fired or an act of God causes the production to halt (force majeure), he will continue to be paid his salary and his per diem if he has to remain in Florence. He will be provided with a rental car in Florence and a car and driver in New York. He has opted to stay in a local hotel in order to visit his Italian relatives (instead of a first-class American hotel). His hotel is a large suite of rooms including a full kitchen. The production will take out $100,000 worth of travel insurance on Tommy (family will be beneficiary).

PROMOTION
(public interviews, appearances, limitations)

Tommy will go to New York for one week to promote the film on TV and will also attend the Cannes Film Festival where the film is to be exhibited. He will attend the opening-night party. He will be provided with first-class transportation and accommodations, for he and his wife and manager, including limousine to and from his commitments. He will require a two-week notice prior to these commitments.

FAVORED NATIONS CLAUSE

Tommy's agent invokes the favored nations clause in order to gain additional perks that other stars have in their contracts (i.e., two additional plane tickets, additional per diem beyond SAG scale).

PERKS
(wardrobe, video of picture, security personnel,
others desired by performer)

Tommy gets to keep all his wardrobe with the exception of rental clothing, a 3/4-inch videotape of his film, a bodyguard while in Cannes, and can take his manager and his wife.

RESTRICTIONS
(nudity and sex acts, doubling, dubbing)

Tommy will refuse to do any frontal nudity and lets the producers know that they need to get written consent and double approval for any sex scenes in which they wish to double him. Tommy can speak fluent Italian and has first refusal in dubbing the Italian version (for which he will negotiate additional compensation).

CHAPTER 8

INTERVIEW WITH AN AGENT

BOOH SCHUT
THE BOOH SCHUT AGENCY
(with a special Boutique for children
and young adults)

I wanted to be an actress as all little kids want to do—to put on shows and plays. I was president of the Drama Society at a private all-girl high school in New Jersey. I went to the Pasadena Playhouse, then moved to New York City, where I studied acting, singing and dance. I did one show on Broadway, worked in stock and community theatre, and then lived in Europe for five years. I moved back to the United States and went to work for Kent Wakeford and Associates, a production company that produced commercials. I left it for a job as a children's agent at Sutton, Barth, and Vennari. They stuck me in a little closet with a bunch of shelves and said, "Okay, go ahead and do this." I worked there for several years and then eventually opened my own agency.

In the beginning, I was shocked when anyone came into that little closet I was working in and actually said they would sign with me! I began my agency with six or seven clients whom I had started out with at SBV. It was because of them that I started my own agency. They said to me, "We want to be with you, Booh. Start your own agency." And I said, "Sure, okay!" I had no idea what I was getting into—what the ramifications were. I was full of total stupidity and naiveté. I started my own agency with no money, just gut instinct, but with great belief in these people. I opened up an office and went to work. People started mailing in pictures. I looked at them and, if I thought they would be interesting, I called them in, interviewed, and read them. In the beginning, I ran a commercial and theatrical department myself. Work begets work, and clients beget clients. Word of mouth spread, and people started to hear about me. I went to classes, plays, talked to a lot of people, and my clients talked to people because they started getting work. There were a few managers I worked with who brought me clients, and their clients began working. Then casting people started recommending me to people. It escalated to a point where I would now say most of my clients come from recommendations from casting directors, producers, and managers. I still bring people in through the mail. I do not ever solicit other agency's clients, period. That's it, the end. I don't believe in it. I do have situations where people are with other agencies and call me or come in and ask to speak with me. And so I have taken on people who have left other agencies and come to me. I do ask if they have confronted the problems at the other agencies and tried to work them out. I have always been very reluctant to take on a client who has been working steadily and doing quite well with another agent. They will not be too long with me if that's the case. I try to be very careful in that regard. I'm at a point now where people have been leaving large agencies and coming to me because they have found that the large agencies have been misrepresenting them. They're not doing well or have gotten lost. They want more individual attention.

WHAT IS AN AGENT'S JOB?

To meet actors and determine if they are talented and salable. To sign the talent and begin the job of getting them seen. People who have credits may not need certain kinds of guidance. Part of what I do is to read everyone who comes into my office on scene work and cold reading. I also look at tape. I have them do scene work for me if none of those happen to work. I recommend classes and coaching if I feel that it's necessary. I don't always recommend the same coach or the same classes. It depends on what I feel the talent might need or is looking for. I make suggestions on how actors can take responsibility if they're beginners. I talk to them about pictures. I ask them how they see themselves and what they want to do. It's very important that I know how they picture themselves, the kind of roles or work they want to do—because if I see something totally different from what they see, it's not going to work. It doesn't mean that I'm right. It means that an agent should represent his talent well. Then my job is to do whatever it takes to get that particular actor or actress, child or adult, out on the interviews that would be right for them. If they don't do well, I try to get them back in again if I'm convinced they can do a better job and weren't appreciated the first time. I give them advice if they're offered a job they should take or shouldn't take, if it's good material or not, and then hopefully make a deal that is beneficial. I don't always look at the money. I look at the importance of the project or the role before I look at the money. I will not turn down a job for a client based on money. I think that's silly. I talk to producers, directors, writers, casting people, network people, sometimes other agents, their managers, their parents—their mothers, fathers, sisters, and brothers, or whoever else I need to talk to. Acting coaches. I also coach them if need be. Whatever it takes.

WHAT IS IT YOU ENJOY MOST ABOUT BEING AN AGENT?

I enjoy developing and watching the growth process of the actors. I like the people I work with and most of the people I deal with. I enjoy reading scripts and viewing films. I have a great affinity for material, and I think I have an actress's insight when I approach it. Having my own agency for five years has afforded me a good feeling about myself.

WHAT IS IT YOU ENJOY THE LEAST?

My pet peeves include the negative attitudes of casting directors, network executives, actors, parents of actors, and managers . . . the old complaint about loyalty, ethics, and honesty.

WHAT'S YOUR BOTTOM LINE WHEN YOU PUT TOGETHER A DEAL?

What's important in structuring a deal is that you come up with something that makes your client happy, period, the end. Because it doesn't matter how hard you work or what the end result of it is if the client is not pleased with it. That doesn't necessarily mean a lot of money. It could mean that a particular job is a good deal because it's a job that the client wants desperately.

TALK ABOUT TELEVISION MONEY AND HOW YOU DETERMINE WHAT IS ACCEPTABLE IN SPECIFIC SITUATIONS.

Well, when someone gets a first job you obviously are happy that they got a job, period. I will give you an example of something that just happened a few weeks ago. I had an ex-client who got a job one day on an episodic. The client had a quote of $500 a day. He had a weekly quote for a movie-of-the-week of $2,000 a week. He was hired for one day on an episodic with a top of the show, meaning the highest that guest stars are paid on that particular show is $1,500. The casting director called me to make the deal and ask for the actor's quotes. Now what an actor needs to know is the first thing that happens when a deal is to be made is that they will ask for an actor's quotes, which means what is the most he has made previous to this job coming up. If it's television, they want a television quote, if it's a feature, they want a feature quote, and so forth and so on. And then they go back and look at their budget and come back and make you an offer based on the quotes that you've had. Now, generally speaking, if it's a first job, and you get a casting director or a producer who wants to be great and terrific, they'll give you $500 a day for the day, or, "We've got a big budget on the show, let's give them $600." Generally, you'll get scale plus 10 and be very happy that they've taken the trouble to give the actor the first job. You got a job. Hurrah! If only the actor would remember to be as excited everytime he gets another job, as he was the first time. Forget the money; be happy that you're working. So here's this young adult, who gets a job one day and his quote is $500, and his manager says to me, "Well, Booh, what do you think we can get for this?" I raise people's quotes all the time in the deals that I do. I say, "Gee, so-and-so, what would you like me to ask for then?" "Well, what do you think?" And I say, "Well, I think basically he has a $500 quote. This is not a large role. It's one day. Top of the show is $1,500. I think I'll ask them for $650." "Well, I want $1,000," the manager says. And I say nothing, because if that's what I'm being told by the manager to ask for, especially since the manager has just removed the client from my agency anyway, I decide not to argue. I know exactly what will happen as a result of my going to the casting person with this request. Nevertheless, I feel that I have to do what I am asked. So the casting director from Lorimar calls me and says, "Okay, I have so-and-so's quotes—so what do you think?" And I say, "Well, I'll be very honest with you. I have been told by the manager that they want $1,000 for the job." "What?! How do I justify $1,000 when our top of the show is . . ." And I say, "Forgive me, I think this is embarrassing. I apologize. This person should thank you for getting the job," because, frankly, what they don't know is he went into the producers and blew the reading . . . Anyway, to make a long story short, because the manager of this particular client ordered me to demand $1,000, this guy lost what could have been a nice raise in his day quote.

There are shows with large budgets, DALLAS, DYNASTY, KNOT'S LANDING, L.A. LAW. Those shows aren't necessarily locked in to one particular fee. So that if you have a client who has worked quite a bit and has good quotes, you can get good money for them. But if you're talking about half-hour sitcoms, where top of the show is $1,500, unless you are a name they're not going to pay over the top of the show for you. Basically you're limited. If you're going in as a guest role it's $1,500, and if you work less than a guest role you can't make any more. You're not doing it for the money, you're doing it for the work, and that's just the way it is. If you're doing L.A. LAW and you have a small role, they will pay $1,000 for the day, if your previous work and quotes warrant that much money. There are situations where if you have a client who wants to do a show very badly and there isn't the budget to pay what the client is worth, sometimes the casting director will offer to give a "no-quote" quote, which means that if you'll do them the favor of agreeing to have your client do their show for less money than he usually makes for that particular role, then when someone calls to hire your client on the next job, and they want a quote for the last job, the party in question who has just hired them is not going to divulge the fact that the talent worked for less money than he's worth, therefore, not hindering you in trying to raise their day quote or three-day quote or a guest quote. I don't see any harm in letting people know so-and-so did this for no money because he wanted to do the project and loved it. When you know the money is there and you know that they can afford to pay, and you know that your client warrants that money, then you fight for it. If it's not there, why bitch and moan? Take the work if it's important work and you think that it is something that your client can do. The actor has to understand things. It's not always your agent's fault. Some agents turn down work without telling their clients because they don't have the $1,000 and the client never knows that the offer came in, because all they are concerned about is the money and not the work.

ARE THERE SPECIAL CONSIDERATIONS IN NEGOTIATING A DEAL FOR CHILDREN?

If you're talking about kids, what you hear when you're making a deal for a minor is, "Well, he's only a kid. How many kids make da-da-da amount of dollars?" That immediately makes me crazy, because what I say is, "Who cares if he's a kid? He's an integral part of the show. If you don't have a kid in it, what good is it anyway?" So I hate that. But people use it all the time. It is true that, generally speaking, children are not paid as much as adults for pilots and episodic TV. I do think it's getting better. You have to consider whether it's a cable or syndicated show, where it's often scale plus 10 percent. Does your client want to do it? If you want to be hard nosed and press for money, then they have to be willing to take a chance. The actor has to be willing to lose it. If you give your agent the leverage and the freedom to be able to deal hard, to better the deal points, then an agent can go in and fight hard and be tough. I can't tell you how many actors have said to me, "Now go in, but I don't want you to lose this, so don't be too hard, and don't scare them too much, and I want to do this job, and even if they don't have the money, I want to do it anyway. So be careful." When you have a client who is that scared about not getting the job, you can't go in and do your best work. You go in and you fight as hard as you can without fighting. I will tell my clients that that is the situation they're putting me in, so it may not be the best deal that I could get. If I can't take a risk, then I can't take a risk. There are times when I don't think I should take the risk. There are times when I feel that I could but my hands are tied. Talent has to realize that down the road they should not come back and say, "Well, so-and-so at the BIG agency said I should have had MUCH more money when you negotiated that deal for da-da-da." Because they forget that they told you back then, when they weren't big, that they didn't want to lose the job. As far as dealing with pilots, you have to look if it's an hour, if it's a half hour, are there previous quotes? If there aren't previous quotes, you do the best you can possibly do. If you're brand new and you haven't done a thing, be thankful that you got the job, period, for whatever can be negotiated. I don't think it's really fair to throw out figures. Companies come in anywhere from scale plus 10 to starting at $3,500 a week to $6,000 a week to $7,500 for a series weekly.

I WOULD HAVE SAID $3,500 TO $5,000 A WEEK IF YOU'RE A KID WITH NO PREVIOUS QUOTES OR VERY

LITTLE, DEPENDING UPON THE SHOW.

I've seen $2,500 a show. Look at YOU CAN'T TAKE IT WITH YOU. For people with credits, with quotes, $2,500—that was it. Take it or leave it. Period. That's really what the bottom line is, not the money but the project. A lot of agents would disagree with me and say, "Oh, that's terrible money, turn it down!" Ultimately it must be the talent's decision with advice from a manager or an agent. And when they do make that decision, they must take the responsibility for having made that decision. Period. Go to the Screen Actors Guild and look at the percentage of people who are working and be thankful. It's a miracle when anybody gets work. As far as movie-of-the-week deals go, they look for quotes. You can start with a larger quote on a movie-of-the-week just because it's a movie-of-the-week. And they have a budget. Feature quotes mean nothing in television, although it's nice to throw them in. When you have a good feature quote, you can always demand more money for television. However, the other way around television quotes don't mean much when you're going into a feature film. The more visibility, the better chance of a stronger deal.

ARE PAID ADVERTISEMENTS OUT OF LINE UNTIL YOU'VE REACHED A CERTAIN POINT IN YOUR CAREER?

Paid advertisements are always important. If you're doing two days on a feature film as a feature player, you're not going to get the main title, separate card, billing—you know, over the title with points and merchandising and paid ads. If you are doing a first film, for instance, and if it is a starring role, billing is very important. There's a whole flow that happens when you're talking and negotiating a deal. You listen to what the other person says and then you respond. Position is important, but so are size and type. If it's your first feature, you want to suggest if you can't have first billing, last billing with "Introducing." Of course you would like to have paid advertisements, because that means except for the "usual exclusion" on one sheets and on most press releases, your name is going to be there. The more people see your name the more valuable you become. The more viable a commodity you become, the easier you are to sell and the more money you can make. Casting people are reluctant to give paid ads—but you fight like hell anyway.

WHY ARE THEY RELUCTANT? IS IT BECAUSE OF THE EXPENSE INVOLVED IN THE ADDITIONAL TYPESETTING AND —

I don't know why. Everyone wants paid ads, so they try to give that prize to as few people as possible in order to get concessions in another area. You'll find situations where you do a deal with someone on a feature and they're more than generous. You don't have to beg and moan for any of this stuff. These people are FAIR. They offer you something and you say, "My God, this is extraordinary! I don't really have to fight for a hell of a lot here . . . a little more money here, an extra plane ticket there or more per diem." These people are not bullshitting around! They're saying, "We appreciate this person who's going to do a good job, we appreciate that we need this person's talent. This is an important role in this project and we're going to give you what you deserve!" Wow! Pretty amazing! That has happened on a few deals that I've had and I really appreciated it. There's a situation I'm involved in now, someone who wants to hire a client for a first feature. They want to pay scale plus 10 percent. It's a starring role, no paid ads, no merchandising, three sequels, okay? They say it's a starring role, but they won't offer starring billing. It's an important role, so they want three sequels but there are no paid ads, see? They expect it will be a huge film, but they won't give merchandising because there won't be anything to merchandise. Now ask me if my client will turn this down. Of course not. It's a first film. If I lean on them hard enough, I might get a little thing here, a little thing there, and maybe I won't because it's take it or leave it. There's no way the actor would want me to jeopardize this opportunity. Period. Everything is fine except I don't really understand why, if someone is trying to convince me that it is an unimportant role in a feature film only worth scale plus 10, that they would want three sequel films.

WOULD THE STRATEGY BE IN THAT SITUATION, THOUGH, SIMPLY BECAUSE IT'S MEDIOCRE ALL THE WAY DOWN THE LINE, TO PICK THAT ONE AREA YOU THINK IS THE WEAKNESS AND GO AFTER THAT AND TRY TO GET ONE SOLID COMMITMENT FROM THESE PEOPLE, WHETHER IT BE IN THE BILLING OR IN THE PAID ADS? *SOMETHING* SO THAT YOU CAN COME OUT OF IT FEELING THAT YOU MADE AN EFFORT?

Here is the problem. The talent has had a discussion with these people. She wants this role badly, she has told the producer and director this and, of course, they've said, "Well, we only have scale," and she said, "Oh that's fine!" So she has already agreed to scale. Of course I found out after the fact that they're paying other people who have the same track record that she has more than scale. She has already agreed to that, as did her manager. They never said anything prior to the development deal about three sequels, but they mentioned it to her. They said, "We're doing a couple of sequels." She responded, "Well, I'll do one, but I won't do three." So she's already agreed to at least one sequel. Coming in, I said I did not want to agree to any sequels. I would agree to negotiate in good faith for any sequels, giving them the right of first refusal, but she already agreed to one, as did her manager. I am now put in a position where my client and manager have agreed to terms that I find ridiculous, and I look like a total idiot on the phone with the lawyer. They would offer scale plus 10, but she could ask for scale plus maybe 13 or scale plus 20. I said, "What? There's no such thing as scale plus 13! Where did they come up with this?" "Well, it's the first deal that these people are making." "Oh, I see, and you agreed to this!" Now this is a manager and client! The manager is saying, "You could ask for scale plus 13." And I said, "What is that?" So, I'm on the phone with business affairs really sounding intelligent, and one of the producers is giving my client and manager this information. It's scale plus 10, it's no position, no anything, and because everyone looks like such a complete idiot, that's what it's going to be. I would assume that there are probably people who negotiate for their clients who have never read a script, who have no idea what the size of the role is, the importance of the role, so when you go to negotiate, you're talking a deal and that's all you're talking. You really have no idea what your client is going to do. So I don't understand how one can make a deal without having read the material, but people do it all the time. I know that agents get contracts and just sign them or have their clients sign them, and don't read them, because it's work and it's money. Sign it, and that's the end. A good agent tries to find things that can be changed, negotiated, compromised, or improved upon. Go through every single one of those little points, from the dressing room to requesting a teacher, to helping pay for a guardian if it's a minor.

WHAT'S A STOP DATE?

A stop date is a day or a date that is the last day that a particular actor/actress is required to work on a project. So if you're shooting a movie and the last day is February 2, 1988, then that is the stop date and, as of that date they are no longer under any obligation to work in that production and can go on to something else.

Michael Caine on JAWS. They have trouble with the water and with the shark, and he's already committed to doing SWITCHING CHANNELS in Canada, so they're already having to push their dates. They're in deep trouble, mainly because Universal didn't or wouldn't give him a stop date for JAWS. And Burt Reynolds moves in to do the role.

It is very rare to be given a written stop date. People might be given a verbal stop date, but they don't bother to ask what's the date on the completion bond for the project, because you will find that that is generally the outside date for finishing the project. So, if people give a date before the bond, generally speaking, it's not even valid, or if you go to them afterwards and say, "You gave me a date," they'll tell you, "Well, the person who told you that didn't have the authority to do so." So the first thing to ask for is, "Oh, by the way, do you have a completion bond? What's the date on it?" It's almost impossible because there is no way to know what might occur. I have gotten stop dates. I just got one a couple of days ago. And I'm proud of myself when I do that because it's like, "Wow, I've done the impossible," because people are reluctant to give it. I do understand it, because it can get you in a lot of trouble. People will schedule—it depends on how important you are, if they can change boards around to help work the character. If you're doing a starring role and working every scene, there's no way they can change everything without completely re-boarding the entire picture.

WHAT'S FIRST REFUSAL?

Well, let's say I'm a producer and I'm hiring you to act in my movie. First refusal means that in your contract it will say that once I've finished this movie with you, if I am interested in using you in my next project, and you've already been offered another job, if I match or better these other people's offer, you must take mine. It's writing into the actor's contract that on my next project, if I can match and/or better the offer currently in front of you, you are obligated to take my project over this other one. Options, however, are different. Options are already negotiated and you don't get to play. You don't have a choice.

HOW ABOUT A FIRST REFUSAL IN REFERENCE TO PILOTS? SUPPOSE YOU HAVE A PILOT AT ONE NETWORK . . . CAN YOU HAVE FIRST AND SECOND AND THIRD REFUSAL?

Okay, you have a client who has gone to network on a pilot and the network says, "We like your client." There's another production company who calls and says, "Gee, we'd like to see your client on this pilot," and we say, "Gee, I don't know, we went to network the other day and she's doing their pilot." "Well, but it doesn't conflict with our shooting schedule and we'd like to take her to network on ours as well." Well, okay, you have to take her then in second position, which means that if the first pilot gets a pick up and goes and the second pilot gets a pick up and goes, the people who were in second position lose my client and have to re-cast. But they like the actor so much they're willing to take that risk that the first project will die and won't get sold.

Sometimes you can have people in first, second, and third position. It means that you can work different people on different projects, and you still may end up ultimately not doing any of them. You can go to network on three pilots and three positions and get none of them. It affords wonderful negotiating power in terms of deals. When three people want your client, for three different projects, the more you're wanted, the better the money and the better the deal. Nothing is more attractive than an actor who is working or can't do the job because of other work.

IS IT DIFFICULT TO NEGOTIATE PER DIEM PAST THE SAG MINIMUM?

It's a real open figure, depending on the importance and size of the role and the budget of the project. If you are doing a starring role in a major motion picture, then your per diem is based on what your needs might be or on the particular requirements of the location. If you have a guardian that has to go, if you have children that you have to pay for here, if the guy wants to take his wife, or stuff like that. People are generally pretty fair. I doubt if it ever costs an actor money to do a job in terms of the per diem.

IN NEGOTIATING A SOAP SALARY, YOU HAVE TO BE VERY CAUTIOUS, ESPECIALLY WHERE IT INVOLVES RELOCATION.

You should be realistic and know that if you're going to relocate to New York City, they're very stingy, they pay for practically nothing, and that it's going to be real tough, and hope that your actor knows somebody in New York as far as housing.

WOULD YOU DISCUSS LOYALTY AS IT APPLIES TO THE AGENT/CLIENT RELATIONSHIP?

A talent will ask me, "Well, how long will you send me out? Will you believe in me if I don't get work? Will you release me then? How many interviews do I have to go on? If I don't do well, does that mean you won't think I'm talented?"

Loyalty to the client is two- or three-fold. If you believe in somebody, you take them on to handle. You believe they're going to work. I don't think there's any time frame to put on it, but if you're dealing with someone whom you believe in strongly, it can take a long time for them to get a first job or a second or a third. But as long as you're able to get them out there and get the exposure and they are doing well, then I don't see losing excitement or enthusiasm about the client. Sometimes I have brought in people who I thought were very good. I thought I could service them very well. I found out that despite my excitement and enthusiasm, they were not out on a lot of interviews and were not getting work. I call them in and say, "Listen, I'm not servicing you well. I'm not doing you any good here because, for some reason, I'm not able to do a job for you."

Just to say you have representation doesn't mean anything. Often they don't care. They'd just as soon stay, and not leave and find other representation, but it's not to their advantage. I think I'm being loyal and honest with them by letting them know I'm not really doing a good job. That is loyalty to the client. Loyalty to the client who is doing well is to really and truly look out for their interests in the choice of projects—career building rather than looking at the dollars. I tend to be managerial, to my own disadvantage at times, by not looking at the dollar first but at their career. I am loyal to the client in the sense that if they trust me with information that is not so nice, or a point of view that's not real pleasant, or make a choice that I don't agree with, then I do have to listen to that client because that's where my loyalty lies. I may not agree with what they have to say, but I am, in fact, bottom-line working for them. I will always give them my opinion, but bottom-line is that I have to do what they want to do, which is not always what I think would be the right thing. Sometimes that backfires. I think loyalty is being honest. That has lost me clients. Honesty to the point of not being political. There are times when there may be answers that people expect to hear or points of view they expect to hear, be it an actor or a manager. I'm still honest. I have lost clients because I didn't like their views on racial prejudice, or religious prejudice, which I won't stand for or abide. I would rather lose the money and the client than deal with someone who has that frame of reference.

I expect a client to understand my job just as I try to understand what they do. They realize that I'm a person, a human being. I have a point of view, but I'm not always right. But I'm very opinionated and they don't have to agree with me. However, I will tell them what I think.

In the beginning, talent will choose an agent, ask a lot of questions, and want a lot of information. You volunteer the information. That might include choosing a teacher, a coach, material—"take this project and not that one," or a way of approaching casting, getting an interview, changing the tone. When someone is new, they trust you implicitly. But once there's some sort of visibility, all of a sudden the judgement or the advice or the point of view that they trusted in the beginning erodes. This is not true in every case. Questions suddenly come up, and, where there was a lot of trust in a point of view, it starts to seem like an attack from me. They don't see the support system. The egos seem to get more frail rather than stronger, so when there is constructive criticism, talent starts to perceive it as being critical. "You don't care about me" or "You don't think I'm good." They might suddenly hear from somewhere over there that there is a) another agent who thinks they're wonderful and b) they're on a project they have visibility with and people start soliciting them. They are given information that is all "yes" information. These people obviously don't know how they started, don't know what the growth process was, don't know any of that. "You're wonderful, and you should be doing this and making that," and all of a sudden the trust turns to, "Well, I met somebody who can do a lot more for me because they say this and they say that and I believe them because . . ." Not having any history with the new agency or whomever, it's easy for the client to walk in cold and hear people only say wonderful things about them. It's easy to believe that. So I have lost clients who I felt should be loyal. The easiest thing to do is to take someone who has established a list of credits and has started to accumulate a bulk of nice representative work that is easily salable. It's very easy to turn that over to someone who really doesn't have to do anything but pick up the phone and answer calls.

The hardest thing to do is to build that bulk of work. I would expect the talent to realize what it takes and how much time and effort went into building that bulk of work so that there is interest from the outside, either from the other agents who are bigger, larger, better, whatever. Because if that bulk wasn't there and that person walked into that larger agent's office, none of these people would spend the time, energy, opinions, advice, or anything else to create that amount of work. They wouldn't care. So it hurts a lot when you spend the time, help build the credits, and try to guide the client and then suddenly he will walk in and say, "I've been with you a long time, so I think it's time for a change. Because you're the only agent I've ever had, and even though I'm doing great, I should move on because you're really like a) my mother or b) my mentor. But thanks a lot for starting me off and working your ass off. And now that I'm really doing well, I'm going to turn over all of that money that I can now generate because of you to someone who doesn't know me at all."

So loyalty from a client to an agent is recognizing how hard an agent worked. But those people that I have worked very hard for hopefully will appreciate how many hours I've put in, how much I believed in them, and the sacrifices I've made on their behalf doing my job. But I also hope they will allow me the benefits of my hard work by staying with me past the point of being able to "make it big" or be important to the industry or make a lot of money so that I can also share it. That's loyalty. You can have a great affinity and caring for the actor. You get very frustrated because when it comes right down to it, you often feel they really don't care about you, but, on the other hand, they want to be cared for constantly. Sometimes we need to be cared for, too. We need to be validated and appreciated and "thank-you'd" because the only "thank you" basically that I get, the only real reward that I get is recognition and loyalty from the actor.

AGAIN, AS IT RELATES TO THE ACTOR/AGENT RELATIONSHIP, HOW CAN AN ACTOR TAKE PERSONAL RESPONSIBILITY FOR HIS CAREER?

When an actor signs with an agency, I believe he is obligated to trust his representation. They are involved in shaping the actor's career. The actor should be responsible for giving the agent and manager the tools from which they must work: proper résumés, updated pictures, being available, being on time for interviews, being prepared, getting material, reading it, coaching if necessary, buying *Drama-Logue* if you're a beginner, checking out AFI and Screen Actor's Guild's programs for films, Equity waiver, graduate films, getting yourself on tape, making yourself visible. And an actor who bitches and moans all the time about doing nothing and can't get involved, who is sitting and waiting for work rather than going to AFI, USC, UCLA, Pepperdine—you should get a job, make some money, rent space, put yourself in a scene, get some tape. If you need to borrow money or get a job, do it. An agent can't do everything for you. Actors come in and ask me, "Do I need a manager?" What do you expect from a manager? Decide that and then go shopping. An actor should take responsibility for making certain choices in his career. Sometimes the actor must learn to take the blame. It isn't always someone else's fault when an actor doesn't get a role or does not read well. It is not always the casting director or producer or agent's fault. Sometimes they just didn't cut it and they have to be able to take responsibility to understand, to listen to criticism and encouragement, and understand that criticism doesn't always mean, "We don't love you—you're no good." It means that we're here to help you solve the problem and make you better for the next time.

CHAPTER 9

INTERVIEW WITH AN ATTORNEY

ALAN FELDSTEIN
ENTERTAINMENT LAWYER

After graduating from UCLA, I became very active in the arts. I became a music agent for three years. I did a lot of negotiations for artists on concert tours, both internationally and nationally, and I did a lot of negotiations with concert promoters. Unfortunately, at the time I was a music agent, the music business was suffering terrible business downfalls. I got out of it.

I met a gentleman who had lived with Lana Turner for ten years and wanted to do a book about his life with her and approached me about putting the deal together for him. I negotiated a contract with Bantam Books. About two weeks before the book came out, Lana Turner's lawyer, Melvin Belli, sent a letter to Bantam Books threatening to sue if they didn't get to see the galleys ahead of time and approve everything. Bantam Books was quite concerned about libel and defamation and asked us to start verifying everything in the book with regard to truth and accuracy. Well, we started meeting and dealing with a lot of lawyers. I realized that I could probably do as good a job as they could and decided to go to law school. Currently, I have my own firm in Century

City doing both business and personal litigation and with a particularly active entertainment division.

My practice involves actors, actresses, producers, writers, and musicians. I do just about everything for the client. I am involved in negotiating contracts, overseeing their other private business dealings, and litigation as it arises.

WHAT DOES AN ENTERTAINMENT ATTORNEY DO FOR THE CLIENTS HE REPRESENTS?

A lot of it depends on the client's needs. If we're speaking in the context of actors and actresses, most of them have agents who are out on the front line, contacting people and trying to find them work. As an entertainment lawyer, I'm involved in trying to make deals for my clients. I've also been involved in situations where the major deal points have been negotiated by the agent, but a more formalized document has now been prepared and the agent and the client have requested me to read that document and make sure that it comports with their agreement and to make sure the finer points are in my client's favor. An entertainment lawyer tends to give a lot of emotional support and advice. I have clients call me excited about some project that they're working on and just want to hear that I am enthusiastic. Clients will call up and say, "I've just met somebody and we want to get together and we want to do some work," and the entertainment lawyer will point out, "Here's what to be careful of, here are the pitfalls to avoid." There are a lot of ideas floating around and not a lot of money, and everybody wants to do something together, and then, when all of a sudden it hits and there's a lot of money at stake, there seems to be a dispute as to what was agreed on.

A lawyer may be involved in preparing some simple documents to protect those beginning fledgling relations or, at another time, he may just be involved in saying, "Well, if you're going to work with this person, make sure that this is clear, and that this is understood." You don't want to hinder an artist's creativity, but this is show business and it's part show and it's part business, and you want to make sure that the business part of it is covered and protected for the client.

IN A CONTRACT, WHAT ARE THE THINGS THAT THE ARTIST SHOULD LOOK AT CAREFULLY, IN TERMS OF DEAL POINTS?

Besides the obvious points of salary and length of employment, per diem, I think the most important point is net profit participation for an artist. It could be the most important aspect of a document. An artist may receive a salary for a motion picture and, if he's well enough along in his career, he's entitled to some profit participation. The definition of that profit participation can become extremely important. The other important points are the ancillary rights, especially in this day and age. Will the artist participate in cable, videocassette, merchandising, soundtrack recordings, endorsements? They are extremely important and are not always thought of in the beginning of a negotiation because the main purpose of the negotiation is to hire the artist for a particular job at a particular salary. A lot of these areas, while covered by the SAG agreement, are also subject to negotiations. I represent some minors, and there are some other deal points that become extremely important—making sure that the production entity will at least follow the SAG and the California labor guidelines as far as safety, hours, time worked, and also schooling for the minor.

Credit is a very important thing for an artist. It's one of the most important and major sticking points in negotiations because credit not only involves what's going to appear on the screen but whether you're going to be in what are called "paid ads." If the producers take out ads in the trades, are you going to be included in those ads so that your name is spread around to people in the industry? I think credit is as important sometimes as salary because that credit and the type of credit that you get can have a large impact on the type of deal you make on your next project. If you're seen as someone who's always starring in films, people are going to realize that that's the kind of roles you want, and that's also going to be the kind of money that you expect to command. No one is going to come back and try to insult you with a co-starring salary.

Comfort is important also. Are first-class dressing rooms going to be provided? Are you going to get first-class travel? An artist needs to be in a nuturing environment when they're performing. I had a client who shot a film in Rome, Italy. It was a very difficult shoot. They got to the hotel, and the hotel was a cheap hotel in Italy that was totally inappropriate for anybody to stay in, let alone an artist of this caliber. I had to get on the phone at 3:00 a.m., which was 8:00 or 10:00 in the morning Italian time, to straighten those matters out, so that's the kind of services I think a good lawyer provides for his client.

Per diems while you're on location. Is there going to be enough money so that the money that an artist is earning isn't coming out of his pocket and being eaten up by spending it on living expenses while on the set? Is the artist going to be required to do talk shows or interviews? Does the artist want to do interviews? Making sure that they're subject to availability, also making sure that they're provided first-class travel and arrangements when those are done.

When a lawyer or an agent negotiates a deal, a lot of it is going to depend on the kind of leverage that they have. I represent a musician who just signed a deal with one of the major record labels. This is a gentleman who has never had a deal before. He has no track record—nothing. They just happen to like his music and want to sign him. The terms of the deal are going to be dictated to me, just as with a new actor who's having a role in a film for the first time. What you try to do in these situations is appeal to their sense of fairness and try to grab as much as you possibly can. Once this deal is over, your client will have a track record, more leverage, and you'll be able to extract a little more next time. A client who has a track record makes negotiating much more pleasurable because you're holding more of the cards. It's a question of power and leverage. When I'm negotiating deals for those clients, I'll be negotiating with a business affairs person or a casting director, and they'll say, "That's it, that's the best we can do," and a lot of times what I like to do is say, "Okay, tell me, is this a take-it-or-leave-it offer?" In other words, are you telling me that if I don't take your offer right now that we don't have a deal? Nine times out of ten, they'll say, "No, that's not what I'm saying." And then I know there's more money at stake or there's more deal points that can be negotiated. And if they say, "Yes, that's it," my comeback to them is to say, "Okay, you'd better be telling me the truth because if I hang up this phone and then call you back and tell you we don't take it, or tell you right now that we don't take it, I mean don't take it." And that's an important thing for a reputation for a lawyer to establish, that when he says something he means it. And once people begin to believe you when you say that and they don't try to play those games with you anymore, I think that's real important.

A star with leverage, I go back to the net profit participation situation. Where an artist can be taken advantage of, and where the real serious money is to be made, is in the area of profit participation. If you're talking about producers' net profits as opposed to net profits, as opposed to a modified net profit definition, or a gross profit participation—any one of those can mean a difference of millions of dollars on a major hit. This is the one area where I think lawyers service their clients particularly well. There are a lot of legal definitions and mumbo jumbo in the agreements with which lawyers are far more familiar. A lawyer does a service to a client by reviewing the deal memos and the formal documents, reading the fine print. We're trained to look for ambiguities, vagueness, and words that appear to mean one thing and may, in turn, mean something entirely different.

Lawyers' and agents' responsibilities tend to overlap, especially in the area of actors. For the majority of actors, an agent is certainly qualified to negotiate a deal as well as a lawyer can.

BUT CAN THERE BE ADVANTAGES TO HAVING A LAWYER DO THE NEGOTIATING, OR AT LEAST PARTICIPATE?

Bringing in your lawyer has an effect on a deal. People tend to be intimidated when they find out that you're a lawyer. I've seen situations where an agent has negotiated a deal and I get called in, and what the agent couldn't get, I can, not because the agent was not doing his job, but just because I'm a lawyer and all of a sudden it's, "Oh-oh, this must mean they're really serious." A lot of times when you're dealing with people who aren't lawyers and you're able to negotiate contract language that sounds one way and means another, it can be effective. I had a client who did a film with three other stars of equal stature, and I wanted top billing. They said, "No, we're going to do it alphabetically," which would have meant my client went last, and I said, "No, that's not acceptable," and we went back and forth on it, and finally they came back to me and said, "Look, here's our problem. The producer wants to leave credits open because he doesn't know how he's going to end the picture. He may show their faces at the end and just flash their names under their faces, or he may just put the names on a list. We have to be open." So I said, "I'll tell you what. I'll leave the billing open, but I want a clause in the contract that states my client's billing will be no worse than anybody else's," which sounded fair. In other words, if they went with the idea of putting their faces on the screen, everybody's face would be on the screen and their names would be underneath it and that would be acceptable. They really didn't know how they were going to do it at that time. So they agreed to that term. Well, lo and behold, what happened was that what you mean by "no worse than anybody else's" essentially means that you have to be at least first in position of billing because, if anybody else is before you, you'd be worse. So what eventually happened is my client got top billing on all the paid ads, on all the advertisements, and on the credits at the end of the film only because I was able to put a clause in the contract that dealt with their needs and also dealt with my needs at the same time. And I am sure when it came time to do the credits and review the clauses in all the contracts, they realized that they had no option but to put my client at first billing. For this particular picture, it launched my client's career and it was very, very important for my client to have top billing.

There have been times in deals where I've just gotten up and walked out of the room without saying another word, and,

nine times out of ten, someone came running after me to bring
me back in. When I was an agent in the music business, I was a
great yeller and screamer. I tend to find that doesn't work as
much anymore. There was a time when an agent would pick up
the phone and just rip someone's ear right off, yelling and
screaming and basically intimidating. I guess with being a lawyer
and having clients with leverage, I'm able to sit there in a non-
yelling and non-screaming way and intimidate by saying, "Look,
here's the way the deal has to work, and, if we can't do it this
way, then it's not going to work, and you're going to have to
answer to a lot of people as to why this deal didn't work."

HOW DO YOU BILL FOR YOUR SERVICES?

For some of my clients, I bill on a straight hourly rate. Hourly
rates can range anywhere from $100 to $250 an hour. Many times
with a new artist we discount our rate in the hopes that we're
going to establish a long-term relationship with the client. If it's
someone who just comes in and needs a contract read or
something like that, most of the time we'll do it on an hourly rate.

There are other agreements where you're sharing in the
profits of the deals that you make for your clients. You take a
percentage like an agent would. Lawyers have to be very careful
when they participate in an executive producer capacity and take
profits from the production because at times you may have a
conflict of interest. This is usually taken care of by consent from
the client and it doesn't seem to be a major problem in the
entertainment industry as it may be in other areas of practice of
law.

**THE MORALS CLAUSE—TO WHAT EXTENT ARE YOU, AND
YOUR CLIENTS, CONCERNED WITH IT?**

Quite honestly, it has never come up with me because I'm
particular about the clients that I represent and I don't have to
worry about that. Big name stars do have an obligation, and I
think you have to read that morals clause very carefully. People
are free to live their own life as they see fit. I think a morals clause

should only apply if you're arrested for crimes of moral turpitude or things like that. A morals clause is another excuse to get out of a contract, and I've never actually seen one tried to be asserted against any one of my clients. And if I saw one come, I would want it to be extremely restrictive in what would constitute a violation of that clause for termination of a contract, and I would probably take the position that it's not necessary and shouldn't be included in the contract.

Another thing to look for, which really would only apply in long-term contracts that are not SAG related, is the law in California that someone has to be guaranteed a minimum compensation of $6,000 a year if he's being signed to a year's contract or longer. That's something that comes up a lot in recording contracts. Nowadays, I'm finding clauses in the recording contracts that essentially state that if you don't earn $6,000 a year, let us know and we'll make up the difference because otherwise, essentially the contract is voidable.

HOW DOES AN ACTOR CHOOSE AN ATTORNEY?

Number one is a referral from somebody else who has had a good experience. A lot of people pick lawyers on the basis of the lawyer's fame or fortune as opposed to the artist's fame and fortune. I'm not so sure for a new artist that's the best way to go because a powerful, established lawyer has a responsibility to the clients that put him in that position, and therefore a new artist may not get the attention that he needs in a young career.

When you're looking for a lawyer, sit and talk with three or four referrals, and ask whom they represent. Look at their negotiating style. Do you like their personality? Do you like the way they operate? Do they have good references? If you can't communicate with your lawyer, or you don't like the way he practices, it doesn't matter if he can do the job or not, because the issue becomes that you can't get along or communicate with him.

It's important for an artist to tell a lawyer what he wants out of a deal. Artists come to me at times and say, "Look, this is my first big shot at an acting job, I'm willing to do it for free, so just get me the best deal you can but don't go crazy with them."

I'll get the best deal I can but make sure we make the deal. There are other people who'll say, "I want every nickle out of those mothers I can get, let's go to war!" That's what they want, and that's what we'll do. And, if we don't make the deal, they'll have to understand that. A lawyer can be helpful in avoiding litigation, and that's an ultimate goal. Litigation is time-consuming, it's expensive, and it's an emotionally upsetting thing to go through. A lot of litigation can be avoided in the beginning if things are well documented and there's good communication between the lawyer and the client.

WHAT IS FORCE MAJEURE?

Force majeure is a situation that arises where neither side can perform the contract due to circumstances beyond their control, acts of God. For example, if there's a war declared by the U.S. and all production gets shut down on the film, or there's a labor strike and the production gets shut down because of the labor strike—these situations invoke the provision of force majeure that traditionally appears in every contract that I've seen, and it allows each side to suspend their obligations under the contract. If there's a Directors Guild strike, then anything that's in production during that time will be suspended, and there'll be no obligation for the studio to pay the artist under a force majeure provision. Those provisions need to be looked at closely because, if a force majeure situation extends for a certain period of time, then the artist may have the right to terminate the contract or at least not be under an exclusive obligation to that particular project if he has the opportunity to go work somewhere else.

HOW ABOUT PAY OR PLAY?

An artist is contracted to perform in a film, but for some reason the financing falls through and the film is not going to be made. Well, the artist blocked out that period of time, didn't audition for anything else, maybe even turned down some other jobs. Under a pay or play provision, that artist is still obligated to be paid according to the contract, even though the film is not being made. Pay or play would also apply to a situation where, if all the money has not been paid up front, and no distribution for a film has been made it doesn't matter—the artist still gets paid regardless of whether the film is distributed, whether the film is ever made. An artist will come in to a project, and two other offers will come in and the artist has to turn those other offers down. Well, there's no reason why the artist should suffer if for some reason this project falls through and it's too late to go back to those other two projects—he should at least be compensated for the money he expected to earn from the initial job to which he made a full commitment.

WOULD YOU EVER PREFER TO BE REPRESENTING THE OTHER SIDE—THE BUYERS (PRODUCTION COMPANIES, NETWORKS, ETC.)—AS OPPOSED TO THE SELLERS OF THE TALENT?

I like working with artists as opposed to representing studios and being in business affairs. I have to answer to a client and if I have good relationships with the client, I can sit there and say to the client, "Look, this is the best deal I can get you. We either take it or we don't take it," and the client feels comfortable that I did a good job for him. A casting director can lose actors. Business affairs can lose their job over not making a deal. There are a lot more worries that they have that I don't have to deal with, and I use that to my advantage. The important thing is to realize what's livable. I think lawyers tend to have their egos get in the way at times, and they want to impress their clients that they've made the absolute most incredible deal in the world. Ninety-nine percent of the time that means there wasn't a deal made, that the deal was lost. And that's detrimental, not beneficial, to an artist's career.

Lawyers have to know what your parameters are for syndicated television series and what's the budget of the film. If I am negotiating a movie deal, I want to know the budget for the film, who else is appearing in the film, who's directing. What are the distribution deals like? If it's an independent production company, they may have to give up a lot, so there may not be a lot of money there to make a deal. Where is the film being made? Is it being shot in Los Angeles or on location? Is it being shot in an area where labor is cheap or in an area like New York City where unions are very expensive? I like to get as much of that information ahead of time, which I normally get from the agent, for lawyers have to be careful that they make a deal that everyone can live with. If you fail to do that, then you fail to do your job.

Your job is to make deals, not break deals. There are times where I've called the client up and said, "Here's the deal, I don't think you should take it," and my client will say, "But I want to do it," or the agent will say, "I think we should do it for a career decision," and it's not my decision then to say no.

CHAPTER 10

"A HOLLYWOOD FABLE"

A TALE OF DEAL MAKING BY TERRANCE HINES

ONCE UPON A TIME, not so very long ago, in a town called Wood of Holly, there lived two clans, whose favorite sport was to best each other in a sort of jousting they called deal making.

One clan was called McAgent and sometimes McManager, while the other clan was called FitzCasting.

Each morning the heads of each clan would get up and go to their offices prepared to do battle with members of the other clan. Each day, one of them would win and one would lose. The loser always vowed revenge at some later date.

Always, there would come young people from outlying towns and valleys to try for the privilege of joining the various clans—not just McAgent or FitzCasting, but also O'Actor and O'Actress.

Sam, a young man from the small city of Muddy Brook, had found it impossible to get anyone from any clan to pay any attention to him at all. So finally in desperation, because he was cold, hungry, and had no place else to go, he sneaked into the offices of one of the McAgents and spent the night. He awoke the next morning too late to escape before Ben McAgent showed up for work. Sam hid behind a large cabinet against the wall, trying not to breathe hard, for to listen to the conversations in these hallowed halls between the two feuding factions was forbidden . . .but oh so exciting. And here is what he heard . . .

BEN IS SITTING AT HIS DESK IN HIS OFFICE, A SMALL
COTTAGE DEEP IN THE WOODS. PHONE IN FOREGROUND.
SFX: RING - RING - RING - RING.

> BEN
>
> I'll let it ring. I don't want to appear too
> anxious. After all, I've got zero leverage.
> > (picks up phone)
> Star Talent — Ben speaking.

> RUTH
>
> Ben, it's Ruth in Business Affairs at FitzCasting.

> BEN
>
> How are you, Ruth? I saw you lunching at
> the McGrill yesterday. Loved that blue dress.
> You looked ten years younger.

> RUTH
>
> Let's cut the bull, Ben, and get to the point.
> I'm going to make your day! My network,
> Castle Moat Corporation, number one in the
> ratings, has agreed to hire your untested,
> somewhat-talented newcomer. . .What's his
> name again?

> BEN
>
> David McMoon.

> RUTH
>
> If you say so. . . Darling, look, I'm going to be
> honest —

> BEN
> > (sotto voce)
> That'll be a first.

> RUTH
>
> I'm going to overlook that. . . Our budget is

blown on the thespians playing the mother and
father. So let me tell you what we're going to
do for you today. . .

                BEN
Ruth, look — Darling, this is called deal making,
and, as I recall, it involves an offer and counter-
offer — not an ultimatum.

                RUTH
Cute! I've got 10,000 ducats for the pilot —
nine days. I'm reaching deep becauseI like
you — 5,000 per episode. Hey, he's got no
credits. He's a waiter, for God's sake! I can
guarantee seven episodes, first season. Billing
in main titles, separate card no less than fourth
position. I'd offer third position, but the
network wants to hold out for a star name
for the ten-year-old brother. Ten-percent
bumps, five-percent net merchandising, twelve
episodes the second year, all episodes the third
year. Fifteen-day option period after tomorrow's
test. If the show is cancelled after two to three
years, then CMC has the right to produce it
or syndication without prior actor approval.

                BEN
Ruth, stop, I'm getting a migraine. I can't
sit still for this. David's got potential.
He's been studying with Uta McSchmidt — the
German acting teacher — for two years. He
did some waiver, two grad films. He's got
incredible potential. He oozes it.

                RUTH
He's a waiter at Friar Jim's! You know this,
I know this, and the network knows this!
5,000 ducats a week is more money than

this twenty-year-old bumpkin has seen since
he fell off the turnip cart. He's untried . . .That's
the deal — take it or leave it. If this kid's got
potential, then he'll make up for it down the line.

                    BEN
Look, Ruth, we go back a long way. I know you
have us. The kid has no track record — but
the deal is terrible.

                    RUTH
Maybe Friar Jim's restaurant will hire him back?

                    BEN
You're heartless, Ruth . . . I'll call you back.

TWO HOURS LATER. SFX: PHONE RING - RING - RING.

                    SECRETARY
CMC Television.   Ruth Brown's cottage.

                    BEN
This is Ben from Star Talent for Ruth Brown.

                    SECRETARY
Hold, please.

                    RUTH
            (coming on phone)
So — do we have a deal, Ben?

                    BEN
Look, Ruth, Dave can live with the pilot
money, but you've got to come to 7,500
for the weekly — third position, main titles,
guaranteed separate card — no non-network
play without the actor's approval. Test option
period — five business days.

RUTH

All right, Ben, you're making me feel bad. I
think we can put this deal to bed . . . As far as
the billing, I'll give you third position — only
if we don't hire an actor of stature over your
client. I'll accept the 7,500 fee per episode.
The rest as we discussed.

BEN

All right, we have a deal, Ruth. But I'm
going to be like a snake hiding in the brush,
and down the line when my client is mega-
successful, I'll be back to see you.

RUTH
(playful)
Oooh, vindictive. . . Let's get together at next
week's clan gathering for a drink.

BEN

You got it.

*Of course, Sam was so excited by this conversation that he uttered
a gasp and was quickly discovered by Ben, who took him in as an
apprentice because he couldn't afford to let him leave. He knew
too much.*

*For three years, he trained Sam in the ways of the McAgents.
Finally, at the end of three years, when David McMoon was a
huge star, Ben told Sam the time was right for revenge. Sam could
hardly stand the excitement as Ben dialed Ruth FitzCasting.*

NARY THREE YEARS LATER.   RUTH BROWN'S COTTAGE AT
FITZCASTING. SFX: RING - RING - RING.

BEN
(on phone)
Ben of Star Talent for Ruth, please.

SECRETARY

Hold, please . . . Ruth, it's Ben at Star Talent.

RUTH
(sotto voce)

Oh, God, I've been afraid of this call. All right,
put him through.
(to Ben)

Ben, how are you? I saw you a week ago in
front of the Gray Moustache, and it looks like
you lost twenty pounds. Your client, David,
is just doing terrific. I hope we don't have
a problem, Ben.

BEN

Ruth, darling, let me cut to the point.

RUTH
(sotto voce)

I was afraid of this. God, how bad can it be?

BEN

Remember three seasons ago when you took
my client — now superstar David McMoon —
and dropped him off the castle parapet? Oh, by
the way, did you happen to catch David's
movie? It's at 175,000,000 at the box office,
and he's got the cover of *Time* next week.

RUTH

No, I haven't had time.

BEN

Well, we'd like to sweeten the pot a little.
We didn't come after you at the end of the
first or second seasons as you know.

RUTH

So now you're going to make up for it and

drain my blood?

> BEN
>
> That's funny, Ruth . . . Let's begin putting it
> on the table. With current bumps, our episodic
> is at 9,075 a week. I'd like a raise from that to
> 75,000 for the fourth season, 90,000 for the fifth,
> 125,000 for the sixth and 150,000 for the seventh
> season per episode. I'd also like to move David
> from third position in the billing to first
> position — so I'd like you to call the agents of
> the actors in first and second position and let
> them know the new billing . . . David would
> like to have six weeks off at Christmas and ten
> weeks during the summer for a feature we're
> developing. His personal manager will be
> coming aboard as executive producer at 10,000
> a week. We want a movie-of-the-week for
> David —

> RUTH
>
> Pay or play, no doubt —

> BEN
>
> Actually, Ruth, in your case, it'll be pay or
> pay. He wants a series, thirteen on the air, for
> his own company. He will only executive pro
> duce. Seventh year — a mutual option if he
> agrees to it and a 500,000 ducat bonus as an
> advance against syndication profits. Twenty-five
> percent of all merchandising . . .

> RUTH
>
> Ben, you're killing me. I feel a stroke
> coming on.

> BEN
>
> David might go dragon slaying — accidents do
> happen.

> RUTH
> Are you saying he'll conveniently get lost in
> the forest if he doesn't get what he wants?

> BEN
> No, just that unhappy thespians spell
> production holdups.

> RUTH
> I'll have to call Networkson to get some help.
> We're deficiting the show to the tune of 150,000
> ducats a week. I don't know that we'll be able
> to make this deal roll on wooden wheels.

> BEN
> Ah, give it a try, Ruth. Talk to Cousin
> Merlin. He can work wonders. I know that.

> RUTH
> I'll get back to you. I have to go to the
> bathroom now and throw up my brains.
> (to secretary)
> Get me Merlin Jenkins at Castle Moat
> Corporation.

SFX: RING - RING - RING.

Ben smiled at Sam in satisfaction. He and Sam both knew that Ruth would have to check with someone at Networkson to make sure she could make the deal with Ben, but they both knew they had won. Of course, it was only one battle in this continuing saga of warring clans, but it would be sung by bards for times to come that Ben had finally bested FitzCasting. There would be feasting in the McAgent cottage tonight. And they all lived happily and pugnaciously ever after until . . .

THE END

PART FOUR

Maximizing
The
Deals

CHAPTER 11

INTERVIEW WITH AN ACCOUNTANT

PHILIP KAL
ENROLLED AGENT SPECIALIZING IN
ENTERTAINMENT TAXES

I was born April 20, 1927. I attended Roosevelt University in Chicago, Illinois, graduated in January, 1951, with a degree in accounting, and passed the Federal exam for Enrolled Agent to Practice Before the Treasury Department in 1969. I have specialized since arriving in California six years ago in entertainment taxes, and since it's a field that is constantly changing, I find it a continuous challenge. I have my own practice in Beverly Hills.

SHOULD OUT OF WORK ACTORS BE COLLECTING UNEMPLOYMENT?

Yes. Absolutely. The unemployment law is designed for the person who is out of work. The employer paid a percentage of your salary into a state fund when you were working, so it's your money. Just be aware, however, that when you receive unemployment, under the current law you are receiving income that is taxable.

I AM AN ACTOR. I HAVE NEVER BEEN AUDITED BY THE IRS, AND I WANT TO KEEP IT THIS WAY. WHAT ARE THE THINGS MOST LIKELY TO TRIGGER AN AUDIT?

One of the things that accountants do to avoid audits for their clients is to compare tax returns from year to year and make sure that the deductions taken are consistent with what has taken place in the past and consistent with what is projected for the future. People have a lot of misconceptions about what is allowable. I get into heated discussions with clients who feel that they're entitled to things like food, makeup, and clothing. Even though the law says you're not entitled to them, people want to insist that they be allowed them. I pride myself in being able to do tax returns and not have them audited. What this means is that I'll always push the deductions that a tax payer is entitled to, but up the limit of the law. The best advice that I can give any actor who is making a substantial income is to go and get himself a good tax accountant to do his return. I'm talking about a good entertainment accountant who knows the the current laws and who has a consistent record.

SOMETIMES WHEN I WORK AS AN ACTOR, I GET W-4 FORMS, AND OTHER TIMES I'LL RECEIVE 1099 FORMS. WHAT'S THE DIFFERENCE?

When you are hired, if you are asked to fill out a form listing the number of deductions to want to take for your your taxes, you're filling out a W-4 form. It means that you are being considered as an employee and that your employer will be subtracting from your salary federal taxes, state taxes, state disability, and unemployment insurance, and issuing you a check for the balance. At the end of the year, the employer will send you a W-2 form that states the total amount you were paid and the total amount that was sent to taxes and unemployment insurance. Using the information on this W-2 form, you figure your income tax payments.

A 1099 form, however, means that you have not been hired as an employee but as an independent contractor. When you are issued a 1099 form, no unemployment insurance or disability or taxes are witheld from you by the employer, and you are responsible for the payment to the government of whatever is owed on this income. A copy of the 1099 form is sent by the employer to the government, and if you don't pay the tax you owe and you can't be located when the IRS comes after you to pay it, the employer then becomes liable for it. This is why employers are so reluctant to treat anyone as an independent contractor unless he or she falls under one of the widely recognized categories for independent contractors—such as a manager, a model, or an unincorporated agent. By dealing with you as an employee now, the employer avoids future complications if you fall short of your tax-paying responsibilities.

WHICH IS BETTER FOR THE ACTOR—TO BE CONSIDERED AN EMPLOYEE OR AN INDEPENDENT CONTRACTOR?

I've always considered an actor an independent contractor, even when he's received a W-2. The IRS looks at a person who gets a W-2 as an employee. The couple of times that I've had audits and I've gotten into this with the IRS, I've maintained that when an actor winds up with fifteen or twenty W-2s, he's obviously not anybody's steady employee. He is an independent contractor, and I've always filed tax returns that way. I will take his W-2 income and put it on a Schedule C, which is the self-employed individuals' schedule, and I file it that way. I always have. The law up through '86 had been very grey in this area, in terms of "what is an employee?" So therefore I haven't had too much of a problem with it. But now under the '87 law, the actors have more or less been led up the garden path. The '87 law said okay, yes, okay, if you make less than $16,000, then you can claim all of your actors' expenses, such as agents' and managers' commissions. But as soon as you make more than $16,000, then you are subject to a 2% floor, which means you automatically lose the first 2% of your deductions. Most of the actors that I'm dealing with make much more than this $16,000. Under the '87 law, I can no longer file them under a Schedule C; I have to put them under a different schedule. If an actor's adjusted gross income, let us say, is $40,000, his commissions to his agents and managers now go on a schedule as miscellaneous deductions right along with his personal deductions—medical and dental and his contributions and so forth—of which he's automatically losing $800 because they are only deductible insofar as they exceed 2% of his adjusted gross income. And if he's being taxed in the 28% bracket, he's losing $2,000 to $3,000 in actual cash. He would have been a lot better off if he'd stayed an independent contractor under 1099 and never gone in as an employee.

In past years that's exactly how I did it. The actor's expenses were separate and the personal schedule was separate. Now under the law I have no choice. I'm an accountant that firmly believes that an actor's expenses, his agents' and managers' commissions, and his auto expenses and everything else should be against his gross income and not as a personal deduction. So, as it stands now, the only other choice that I have, once I've got an actor making, let's say, over $80,000, is for him to become incorporated.

WHY?

Oversimplifying it, when a production company or studio wants to hire an actor's services, the studio or production company pays the corporation, of which the actor is an employee, a fee, and the corporation "loans out" the actor. As long as this kind of loan-out corporation gets rid of its taxable income through payroll and withholding taxes, qualified retirement plan contributions, and business expenses, it can be a very good vehicle through which the actor can handle these expenses. The corporation's business expenses are not subject to the 2% floor and may include such things as the actor's publicity, pictures, résumés, tapes, business travel, business entertainment, managers' and agents' fees, and accounting and legal fees. Additionally, a loan-out corporation, or "personal service" corporation as it's also called, can maintain a medical insurance plan covering the employee/owner, allowing the corporation to pay and deduct the cost of premiums. A loan-out can also provide some life insurance coverage, tax-free. A corporation can provide the actor with a profit-sharing pension plan, for which you're not eligible if you're receiving a W-2 from someone else, and you can borrow up to $50,000 from the corporate pension plan. What your personal service corporation must *not* do, however, is to accumulate undesignated income that will be viewed as profit. There used to be a range for corporate taxation, but this kind of personal service corporation is now taxed at a flat 34%, so some of the other benefits of incorporating have fallen by the wayside.

AT WHAT POINT SHOULD THE ACTOR CONSIDER INCORPORATING?

Generally, once an actor's income is in excess of $80,000, it may well prove useful to him, but it's going to depend on other specific factors. And remember that there are extra costs involved in using a corporation—additional taxes and fees.

ALL RIGHT, LET'S SAY I'M A MINOR. I HAVE A SUPPORT TEAM WITH AN AGENT AND A MANAGER, AND OCCASIONALLY I USE A LAWYER. I JUST GOT A SERIES AND, AFTER I PAY EVERYBODY INCLUDING THE GOVERNMENT, I'M FINDING MYSELF NOT HAVING ANY MONEY LEFT. IN FACT, IT COSTS ME TO BE ON THE SERIES. WHAT CAN I DO ABOUT THIS, ASSUMING THAT THE SERIES IS GOING TO GO SEVERAL YEARS?

Cash flow is a problem. It's not an unusual problem, especially with minors. I've known of some that have had to even borrow money out of savings in order to pay manager's fees. The thing that can be done is to try to project the amount of deductions that you're going to have and to set up exemptions based on those deductions so that it will lessen the amount that's being withheld for taxes. Basically, you should figure one exemption for each $2,000 to $2,500 in deductions, even if you have to claim ten-twelve-fifteen exemptions to eliminate the income taxes withheld. That is the answer as far as cash flow, though establishing this number of exemptions will require an explanation to the IRS. Unless it's necessary for cash-flow purposes, under normal circumstances, you don't want to claim more than nine exemptions on your W-4, since the IRS will immediately demand a justification as to why. And you want to avoid having to make explanations and justifications to the IRS. At any and all times. If you do have to take more than nine, the strongest justification is the previous season's record. "Look, I'm taking $2,000 for every single deduction, and X number of episodes have been ordered, so it appears I'm going to make the same amount this year I made last year . . ." If you're claiming exemptions for the coming year based on what is a matter of record for the previous year, it can't be disallowed. And if things turn out differently, there's nothing the IRS can do until you file this year's tax return.

WHEN I AM ENTERING THE SECOND YEAR OF A SERIES, AND A CERTAIN NUMBER OF EPISODES HAVE DEFINITELY BEEN ORDERED, COULD I TAKE THAT STUDIO CONTRACT AND GO DOWN TO THE BANK AND BORROW MONEY?

That's a very good question. Whether or not a bank would loan money on a contract such as that is hard to say, especially here in Southern California.

But by the second year in which there is a sustained income of $75,000 to $100,000, there are certainly other things to do besides borrowing. By now I'd suggest incorporating, and, if need be, you can draw a salary from the corporation. As a member of the Screen Actors Guild, the actor already has a pension fund, but as an employee of your own corporation and no longer a self-employed person, you can also be setting up a pension or profit-sharing trust. This becomes a very useful tool for the actor in that it can set up the money for the future while simultaneously taking a deduction on it as well.

To some extent, real estate will also shelter your income. In the long run, it is still a very good investment and has a lot less risk involved in terms of internal revenue laws.

On the whole, what I would do is take 40% of my usable income and put it in a good growth mutual fund, keep another 30-40% in cash or money markets (which are the same thing as cash), and then the other 20% could be gambled in some type of penny stocks.

A DIFFERENT SCENARIO: I'M AN ACTRESS. I'M NOT A REGULAR ON A SERIES, BUT I WORK STEADILY. I LIVE

IN WESTWOOD, AND I'M PAYING $750 A MONTH FOR A STUDIO APARTMENT. I HAVE ABOUT $20,000 THAT I SAVED UP IN A BANK THROUGHOUT MY CAREER. I HAVE THAT IN CASH. IF I CAN GET A LOAN, SHOULD I CONSIDER PURCHASING A CONDO IN WHICH I MIGHT RENT OUT ONE OF THE ROOMS AND LIVE IN THE OTHER ONE?

I would definitely agree that if your career has reached the point where your income is steady, I would definitely look toward buying. This would shelter part of your income. The mortgage payment is 95% interest in the first couple of years, and that would shelter a big portion of your income since it's deductible.

IF I COULDN'T AFFORD THE FULL DOWN PAYMENT, WOULD YOU SUGGEST I APPROACH MY PARENTS AS A CO-SIGNER OR PERHAPS EVEN BORROW MONEY FROM THEM IN SOME KIND OF LIMITED PARTNERSHIP IN ORDER TO AFFORD TO BUY THE CONDOMINIUM?

Very definitely. Real estate is excellent from the standpoint that it is nothing that the IRS can get into. You own it, it's simple. The only thing you have to prove is that you've actually paid the expenses that you're deducting on your tax return. It is cut-and-dried; there's no law against it. The recent change in the law still has real estate as an investment. It is good as long as, of course, the real estate itself is solid, and that's something else again.

IN THE STATE OF CALIFORNIA WE HAVE THE COOGAN LAW. HOW DOES IT RELATE TO TAXES?

It is my understanding that under the Coogan law a portion of the money earned by a minor has to be set aside and can only be put into a savings account, period. Today, savings accounts earn interest at under 5%. There are all kinds of things you can do today with this money where it will earn anywhere from 7% up to 12%. The way in which the Coogan law forces the money to be set aside is a little bit foolish. I think it should be far more flexible in allowing investments. Obviously, one of the things we try to do is have as little as possible set aside. It is senseless not to change the law to assign a trustee to develop and guide the portfolio. If the client is fourteen years old and I run into this situation where I know he's going to get a series invoking the Coogan law, I'll recommend that he get emancipated and then incorporate. He doesn't find himself in a situation where he has to go borrow money in order to do the series. That way he doesn't necessarily have to incorporate. You have to be careful because the corporation becomes an individual under the law. It files its own tax return. The only way that you can get income out of a corporation is you either have to take a salary or declare a dividend. And you definitely don't want to declare a dividend in a corporation because that results in double taxation: the corporation has to pay the tax on the dividend and, then, when the individual picks up the dividend, he has to pay taxes on it again. So, you have to be careful not to get into a situation where the corporation starts to accumulate money. By law, the corporation can't be amassing money unless it has clearly stated plans for that money. You have to be careful to have some idea in the back of your head just exactly what you're going to do with the corporation once you have it.

WHAT MIGHT YOU DO WITH IT IN ORDER TO KEEP FROM ACCUMULATING MONEY?

You want to make sure that your charter gives you under the law a wide range of what you can do with the money once you're accumulating it so that the IRS can't come in and beat you on the head. The corporation can invest in real estate, the money market, and IRAs. It used to be you could purchase a car, and you still can, but under the new law there is such a huge restriction in terms of what you can write off to depreciation that the corporation is better off leasing the car instead of buying it because the present law is a little more advantageous with leasing.

The main problem with the corporation is not as it's developing but when the actor needs to take a salary. If it's possible, you want to avoid payroll taxes. The corporation can pay directly for all the expenses that the actor has as opposed to paying the actor. One of the other things that I try to do with minors where there is a corporation is to pay the mother a weekly draw as a manager in the form of a 1099 salary. I have her file as an independent contractor, avoiding to some extent the payroll taxes, but you still have her self-employment tax.

IS IT STILL WISE TO PAY THE MOTHER A SALARY WHEN THERE'S ALREADY AN AGENT AND A MANAGER WHO ARE RECEIVING TWENTY-FIVE PERCENT OF THE ACTOR'S EARNINGS?

It depends on how much the mother is actually involved in the child's career. If she drives him to interviews, sits on the set with him, or coaches him, then she is entitled to take a salary as a driver, set-sitter, coach—or all three. The amount she is paid has to be tailored to the child's income and the income of the parents. What you're talking about is a question of planning. It comes back to trying to spread the income around in some manner, shape, or form. Within the law, the IRS cannot come to you and say, "How come you're paying the mother a 1099 salary?" The mother in many cases *is* the manager. I have never seen the IRS attack that. The whole purpose of trying to spread this income around is to lower the tax burden. If putting the mother on a salary increases your tax burden, then it doesn't make sense. You may still want the mother to draw, but maybe lessen the draw.

I have a couple of situations where I've got a lady with three kids, and each one of them is working. We've got a corporation. The corporation is hiring her, we're pulling income out of the corporation. The tax rate for the corporation is 15% up to $50,000. What I'm doing is having this mother draw her 1099 income out of that corporation, but I'm having her pay the car expenses personally, since without these deductions she'll probably wind up in a higher bracket than the corporation. I'm having her take some of the expense and having the corporation take some of the expense. Keep people below the ceiling.

It means I have to stay abreast during the year of what's taking place. But, unfortunately, people don't like accountants.

They don't want to deal with them or talk to them. Even after you do all this planning, you've got to look to see what's happening. They're paying me a fee to help them. They've got to help themselves by allowing me to take a look at what they're doing. Too many times people come in only at the end of the year. They're ready to sit and talk to me when and it's finished and there's nothing I can do about it. We talk to some people about incorporating. They're making this big money, and they're going to wind up paying out a lot of money which they might not have had to. But instead of taking the time to hire a lawyer to incorporate and do the whole routine and lower their tax bite, they don't deal with it until it's after the fact. So it's sad.

DOES IT MATTER WHAT YOU CALL YOUR PERSONAL SERVICE CORPORATION?

Just make sure your name is not the same name as the corporation. This is one of those things that sends up the red flag.

CHAPTER 12

INTERVIEW WITH A PUBLICIST

MICHAEL CASEY
PUBLIC RELATIONS, FLAHERTY AND
WINTERS; FORMER DIRECTOR OF PUBLICITY
FOR WARNER BROS., NBC PRODUCTIONS,
AND LORIMAR TELEPICTURES

*I was a contract player at Fox in the '50s, I was
there for a year and didn't become a movie star
right away so . . . I think I was making $117 a
week, and I was impatient, so I walked out on my
contract. Those were the days when it was kind of
popular to be nervy like that. I was in eighteen
pictures in these small parts. After I walked out of
my contract at Fox, I went to the Pasadena Playhouse and did two years at UCLA.*

*I became a page at CBS, and then a prop shopper
and a set decorator and then a cue-card holder on
PLAYHOUSE 90 and STUDIO ONE, THE RED
SKELTON SHOW, and BOB CROSBY SHOW during the day. I became a stage manager and assistant director, and then I went to Erwin Wasey Advertising Agency, producing and directing commercials. I went to work for the Chargers football
team and fulfilled a boyhood dream of being
assistant to Frank Lahey, the great Notre Dame
football coach.*

As a press agent, my first job was on CAPE FEAR

with Gregory Peck and Robert Mitchum. I walked in very nervous to the dressing room of Gregory Peck, interviewed him and he was really very nice. I went from Universal to Rogers and Cowan, then to Twentieth Century Fox to directing and producing. I went to KTLA Channel 5 as a director of publicity and then to producing and directing. I opened my own management company and had it for four or five years at the 9000 Sunset building.

I closed my agency and helped make Bob Dornan a congressman. One of my shows I directed was The BOB DORNAN SHOW. I moved to Washington with Bob as his Chief of Staff and had eighteen people working for me in Washington and Los Angeles. Four years later, Warner Bros. called me in Washington one day and asked me if I wanted to come there to be director of publicity. I went to Warner Bros., and after four years NBC called and said they had this experimental company that was expanding called NBC Productions, and did I want to head up the publicity there? From NBC Productions, I recently made a move to Lorimar Telepictures.

WHY DO I NEED A PUBLICIST?

You don't need a publicist unless you have something going. A publicist can't publicize somebody unless they have some kind of hook. A lot of people think, "Well, I'm going to hire this publicist, and then I'll get my child or myself in the newspapers," but it doesn't work like that. No publicist, no matter how well connected, can call a reporter and say, "I'd like you to interview someone" or "I'd like you to put something in" and have it appear. It just doesn't work that way.

ARE "PUBLICIST" AND "PRESS AGENT" THE SAME THING?

Public relations executive, press agent, press rep.—all the same. Publicist is a little fancier way of saying press agent. Press agent is a word out of the '30s and '40s, but I like it better. If the actor is just beginning, the publicity work can be done by that actor or that parent. If the actor is in a number of things in a row and looks like he's going to continue his momentum without long dry spells, then a publicist can be hired. But until that time comes, the actor can write these stories themselves and send them to the trade papers. The main objective is to have yourself before the industry. You should be in *The Hollywood Reporter, Daily Variety* and *The Electronic Media.*

YOU SAY I DON'T NEED A PRESS AGENT UNTIL I'VE GOT "SOMETHING GOING." CAN YOU GIVE AN EXAMPLE?

You need a press agent when you have enough momentum that the press agent has something to work with. Generally, that's when a person gets on a series or a big picture that's going to take three to six months to shoot. The average actor coming up gets his first part and then he might not get a second part for another six weeks.

Here's a sample release: "Jane Wyatt has been signed by Executive Producer William Kaidan to Guest Star with Mare Winningham in the two-hour TV Motion Picture, WHERE ARE MY CHILDREN? slated to Air on CBS." In the first paragraph you take the name of the actor and say "has been signed by (title of executive producer) to guest star with (whoever else is in the project) in the (what it is) two-hour TV Motion Picture (and then the title) and then, if you have an air date, you say that, scheduled to air on CBS. In the next paragraph it's the Kaidan Gleason Production in Association with Warner Bros. TV, and it began filming this week on a Southern California location. When you start with a television film you always have an airdate. You take this little formula and just substitute the facts that you're working with. You send it to Dave Kaufman at the *Daily Variety* at 5700 Wilshire Boulevard, Los Angeles 90036, and you send it also to the *Hollywood Reporter* to Lou Chunovic, 6715 Sunset Boulevard, Hollywood 90028. Then you call to follow up on it the day you know that he's going to get it. The editor who gets this wants to look at it and see whom to call in case they need to check facts. The parents can take it over the night before and put it in the mailbox of both *Variety* and *Hollywood Reporter*.

When I was starting in the business, I use to have a little one-two punch of putting it in the night before and then the next day, around 10:30 to 11:00 a.m., I would call Dave Kaufman directly at (213) 469-1141 and Lou Chunovic at (213) 464-7411. They're on deadline around 3:00 or 4:00 p.m., so they're very impatient and abrupt with you if you call them at that time. Let's say a parent calls at 4:00 or 5:00 p.m. and goes, "Uhhhhh, Mr. Chunovic, uhhhhhhh . . ." he will throw the release away rather than doing anything for you. You call and say, "Dave" or "Lou" and try to be as relaxed as possible. Take a deep breath before you call. Have on a piece of paper about four points—what you would want to say if he were to ask you anything more so you don't have a mental block. "Hello, Dave? This is so-and-so, I'm just calling to check to see if you've got the release on my son, so-and-so, who is appearing in, blah-blah-blah, and was just signed . . ." And then he might say, "Well, no," and then you can say, "I'll send a xerox over to you right away."

It's important, and I don't know why but it is, not to send them copies the first time. Type it up, send the original to Dave Kaufman. Type another original and send it to Lou Chunovic. Even though Lou and Dave know that this is probably going to the other paper as well, they don't like to think, "Well, you sent the original to the other guy and I got the copy," or they might think, "Mmmmmmm, I am the only one getting this." They want to feel it came right out of your typewriter.

When I was a beginning press agent, I would use the technique of making intentional mistakes on copy that I typed, I would "x" out stuff, then the people I sent it to had a feeling that this was right out of Mike Casey's typewriter to them. Fresh. And maybe exclusive. So they would want to get it right in their paper. The reason I know it is because I went to *Variety* and *The Hollywood Reporter* and worked two or three days for free in their city rooms, on my own stuff; I mean, I just used their desk and did stories. I asked them if I could do it so I could learn to service them properly and give them what they wanted. I remember them saying things to me such as, "The first thing I want to do is see who it's from," because they respect who it comes from. You must be dead honest and have the reputation of being real with your copy. If you are inclined to hyperbole or to exaggerate to the point of lying and they find out, you're dead with them forever. It's important not to use adjectives. If any adjectives appear in any copy that is printed, it's for them to do, their editorial license. It's not for us to say, "Jimmy Johnson, the great actor has been . . . and so-and-so producer said, 'We're so *glad* to get this young actor because he was so wonderful in PELHAM ONE, TWO, THREE.'" This might even be true, but the editors at *Variety* and *Hollywood Reporter* want to throw up. When they see these adjectives, it's a little bit like saying as you introduce your wife, "And this is my lovely wife." Well, it's really not for you to say. It's really for others to decide whether she's lovely. So, it's not really for the press agent or for the parent writing about their child to brag. You're a professional person, you're handling managing your child, and you're also doing publicity. So you call and say, "This is Bob Jones checking to see if you got my release on Jack Jones, who has been signed with NBC or CBS or ABC or Warner Bros.," you know, and you use that big name. And then you shut up and let him answer. Don't go into a long thing about how great the kid is in it or how great the story is or anything like that.

IF I'M UP AND COMING, WOULD IT HELP TO HAVE A PUBLICIST TO GET ME MORE WORK?

Let's define "up and coming." Let's say you get Lisa Bonet started on THE COSBY SHOW. But THE COSBY SHOW hasn't made it big yet. Still, if it's a network series, with a known star, you go forward with a press agent right away. He would be part of the team with Cosby's personal press agent. I think it's an excellent idea if you have that kind of thing going. If you have a little part here and there, the press agent is probably not going to be able to make money for you. And it's going to be tough on you making those payments. If you're a wealthy person, you live in

Bel Air and have a 450SL convertible, sure, put him on from the beginning, and then he can help to do a lot of spade work trying to figure out how to get your name in print.

HOW MUCH DO PUBLICISTS COST?

Rogers & Cowan is the biggest entertainment public relations firm in the world. I don't think they'll take anyone for less than $1,000 a week. The more successful you are, the more money you make, the more you pay. They will charge $10,000 a month to a Bill Cosby because there's so much more work. There's a lot of work for Kirk Cameron in GROWING PAINS because it's a very successful series, but it isn't the scope of the Cosby client. They're going to bill you for basic time, $1,000 a week. Then above that they're going to charge you for overhead—telegrams, messengers, stamps. I haven't been in independent publicity for so many years, I can only give you some good guesses. I would say Rogers & Cowan is number one, and Solters & Roskin is number two, I worked for both. Lee Solters is a hustler. Almost an ambulance chaser. He is so frenzied about his clients! But he has Frank Sinatra. When I worked for him, I had Paul McCartney, Sinatra, and a lot of big names. I would say that you could get with Lee for probably his rock-bottom price at about $500 a week. And maybe Warren Cowan and Henry Rogers would come down from their $1,000 if they felt like it. But they're in a position where they can just about demand first-cabin clients and get $1,000 a week. PMK is another good agency. They're real hustlers and they're strong. I would say PMK would be at least $3,000 a month. Michael Levine is probably around there, too. Levine is very hungry for clients. He's building.

WHAT ABOUT CONTRACT LENGTH? IS IT VARIABLE?

Let's say PMK, for instance, has William Friedkin on a temporary basis. They have him while he's doing something. And they had him for CAT SQUAD when I was working with him on an NBC Production. They had him for six or eight weeks. During the crucial time. Someone like Rogers & Cowan, they want a year's contract, but then you drop down to PMKs and Levines, who'll go for six weeks.

WHAT DO THEY DO FOR THE MONEY THEY CHARGE YOU?

First they interview the client for three or four hours and find out everything they can about him. They'll arrange a photo session for that client and get the very best pictures. Then they'll write an in-depth bio and have the best 8 x 10s with that bio sent out to everybody. NBC is not crazy about sharing their art with independent press agents. But they'll do it. CBS will, too. So, if the client wants to save money he can say, "Well, let's let the NBC photo department do that." The NBC Still Department has a still man on the set shooting. On a one-hour show, NBC will cover two days. If you have a two-hour movie, NBC will cover four days. The network is obliged to cover the movie and so is the production company. So if NBC network is doing something in association with Warner Bros., then you'll have eight days covered for a two-hour movie.

DO YOU MEAN PEOPLE ARE JUST STANDING THERE, SHOOTING PHOTOGRAPHS ALL THAT TIME?

From early morning until they finish. Your client should call Thelma Lewis when the photography has been shot at (818) 840-3641. She's NBC's photo coordinator and takes photo requests. You say, "My client is so-and-so, and I would like to make an appointment to come in and look at the proof sheets and select some art," and you try to finesse her and see if you can't get them for free. Maybe you can if you're the main thing in a movie or something. They'll give you color if you order it, but you've got to come in and look at it. It's laborious to look through all that stuff but it's worth it.

They start priming editors around the country about this actor. The editors won't interview anybody unless you have an airdate because they don't want to waste their time. The thing may never air. It's got to have a good hook, and, if a client has been a Broadway star and this is their debut TV movie, that's a hook. A good press agent will call me up as Director of Media Relations at a studio or network. They will say, "Are you going to have an industry screening? Or a party?" They will try to stir things up and make you go out and have parties and invite press in. We will have a number of screening and little parties.

The Golden Globes is very important. The independent press agent should encourage the head of publicity at a production company or a network to have an individual party for the Hollywood Foreign Press Association members. If you really want to go first-cabin, you'll put the money out, or you'll share the money with the network or the production company, to send cassettes of the movie that your actor is in to all the Foreign Press members. You're pushing the Foreign Press and romancing, wining, and dining them. I did this for Loretta Young. NBC Productions never had a Hollywood Foreign Press Association party in its life until I came in. We had a wonderful party in the executive dining room at the network, and I brought Loretta in and introduced her and she charmed them for about two hours. They went home feeling pretty good about her, and, when she up against formidable competition, she was a winner. She went home that night with a Golden Globe.

I've always considered it a kind of sleazy press agentry to put so-and-so together with so-and-so seen at so-and-so restaurant. I've never cared about putting people in *The Star* or *The National Enquirer.* They're treacherous.

In *Variety* they have a TV log every Thursday or Friday. They have "Telecastings," "Feature Castings," "Agent Castings," and "Who's There." For *The Hollywood Reporter* it's "Travelogue." In *Variety*, Army Archerd is the most important columnist—he is widely read. Army's been a friend of mine for twenty-five years. I found the penetration and feedback of Army's readership to be of greater quality.

HOW ABOUT GOING ON SHOWS LIKE *AM LOS ANGELES*, *TODAY SHOW*, *GOOD MORNING AMERICA*, OR GOING ON A TOUR TO PROMOTE THE FILM? ARE THOSE THINGS THAT CAN BE DEVELOPED BY A PUBLICIST?

Going on tour is prohibitively expensive for the client. Networks used to finance those things, but they don't anymore. The independent press agent should do everything he can to convince the network to include their client in what they call the press tour, which is in N.Y. at the Waldorf or the Plaza four times a year. In L.A. they have electronic and media press days at The Century Plaza, and you go over there and you're interrogated by about a hundred reporters. You sit up on a riser along with your producer and one or two actors, and the writer, and they ask these questions. You go from room to room in these little TV things. They have their TV cameras set up, you're interviewed and then you go to the next room where somebody else from another part of the country is located. All these people go back to their home states and present them on the air in their papers and magazines: AM LOS ANGELES, etc. That's all good stuff, but it's pretty hard to get in to that unless you have an airdate. If you're an unknown actor, it's almost impossible to get on.

SUPPOSE YOU'RE ON A SERIES AND YOU HAVE A GOOD PUBLIC RELATIONS PERSON, SOMEONE WHO'S GOTTEN A LOT OF LETTERS COMING INTO FOR YOU. WHAT KIND OF BARGAINING CHIP DOES THIS TURN OUT TO BE FOR UPPING YOUR SALARY?

When it comes time to renegotiate your contract, this outpouring makes you more desirable. The volume of mail will make a difference. When I was in the rock 'n' roll business, I would put a bank of phones in a room, and I would hire thirty girls. They would call radio stations just after my records had been delivered to them and say, "I heard this on such-and-such radio station in such-and-such city. Do you have it? I want to hear it again." You have them go into the shops and call the record shops. To build an audience, to build record buyers, to do whatever is necessary in business. If we put thirty girls with a bank of phones in a room and have them call the networks exclaiming about how great so-and-so was last night on such-and-such, I would say that if you got twenty calls about somebody, they log them in. All of them are logged in at NBC. And if you get twenty calls, Brandon

Tartikoff's eyes are going to bug out. I mean, this is really going to cause attention. And if you get five or ten critical calls, it worries people around there.

WHEN MICHAEL J. FOX FIRST STARTED ON HIS SERIES, HE SURFACED AS A MAJOR STAR VERY QUICKLY AND GOT A LARGE AMOUNT OF LETTERS EVERY WEEK. WAS THIS A RESULT OF PUBLICITY?

I had him on a movie and I did a campaign with him. He didn't have a press agent at that time. FAMILY TIES almost went off the air. Then they put it after COSBY and it became a success. If they hadn't put it there, it would have been off a couple of years ago. Now, it's a good show, but he would just be another good actor on a hit show. His breakthrough, as he told me himself, was BACK TO THE FUTURE. "I thought it might be a good little movie, but I didn't think it was going to be anything like what happened," he'd said. BACK TO THE FUTURE was the momentum that made Michael J. Fox. Sylvester Stallone didn't have a press agent, but ROCKY captured the imagination of the country, and nothing could stop it.

SAMPLE PUBLIC RELATIONS RELEASES

Date:
From: Name of Parent or Manager or Agent
Phone:

EXCLUSIVE TO ARMY ARCHERD

Figure skater Astrid White has been hired by
executive producer Ben Picilo to portray a
skater, natch, on the first episode of WX-TV's
ICE PRINCESS. Starring Jim Benton, Lisa Webb,
and Rick More. The series debuts on XBC in
February.

Date:
From: Name of Parent or Manager or Agent
Phone:

MARY FORD TO GUEST-STAR IN
WHERE ARE MY DOLLS?

Mary Ford has been signed by executive producer
Bill Wise to guest-star with Paul Markam in the
two-hour TV motion picture WHERE ARE MY DOLLS?
slated to air on CBT.

The Lion/Glow Production in association with
Capitol Bros. Television began filming this
week at a Southern California location. The
producer is Paul Brown. Liz Dahl directs the
teleplay by Nancy Brown and Jay Stone.

PART FIVE

CHAPTER 13

CHANGING YOUR AGENT

TYPES OF AGENCIES

There are two kinds of agents—commercial (for commercials) and theatrical (for film, television, and theatre). Agencies that include theatrical agents fall into three categories—full-service, boutique, and Broadway/New York agencies:

A FULL-SERVICE agency usually handles not only stars but major directors, writers, and producers and can package a whole film from that agency alone. If you're Robert Redford, you have a full-service agency. Examples of full-service agencies include Creative Artists Agency (CAA), International Creative Management (ICM), William Morris Agency (WMA), Triad Artists, and The Agency.

A BOUTIQUE agency handles big stars but isn't as large as a full-service agency. BOUTIQUE AGENCIES include Paul Kohner, Kurt Frings, Agency for the Performing Arts (APA), McCartt, Oreck, Barrett, Mishkin Agency, and Sandy Bresler.

The BROADWAY/NEW YORK agencies handle up-and-coming stars, fine New York stage actors, and character actors who work all the time. Examples include The Gersh Agency, Smith-Friedman, Abrams, Harris-Goldberg, Writers and Artists Agency, The Artists Agency, STE Representation, and J. Michael Bloom.

The rest of the agencies offering theatrical representation on the whole tend to handle day players and are top-heavy with newcomers.

There are also YOUNG-PEOPLE AGENCIES with strong track records and which are staffed by agents with many years experience, some owning the agency itself. Several deal with the major power brokers, a step above casting director relationships. These include Booh Schut Agency, Iris Burton Agency, The Savage Agency, Harry Gold, 20th Century Artists, and Kelman/Arletta Agency.

It's best to sign with the biggest agency that will take you but won't bury you. Agents merge and change all the time, so it's hard to keep track of what's going on. If you're getting work, you have a good agency, even if you're not with William Morris.

A WORKING RELATIONSHIP

This is a business . . . "show business." The bottom line in the business relationship between the actor and the agent is if they are making each other money. The agent's job, from the actor's viewpoint, is to submit the actor for jobs, and if the actor is cast, to negotiate the deal. The actor's job, from the agent's viewpoint, is to get the job. From the agent's commission on the client's pay, the agency pays its bills and the agent eats. Ideally, there comes that point when the actor need no longer "get" the job because the actor is now being sought for the jobs. But the good agent understands that developing an actor's career to that point involves periods of time in which the actor does not pay his way in terms of bringing into the agency anywhere near the amount of money the agent is expending in time and effort on the actor's behalf. The agent also understands that, although the actor-agent partnership is a business relationship, it assumes personal aspects even when the two individuals are not friends, since it's the agent who finds himself advising the actor on why, for example, someone didn't want the actor because of his looks or attitude, or why a résumé photo doesn't bring out the "real you" in the actor, or why the agent doesn't see the actor in a part the actor desperately wants to be submitted for, etc. Even when processed with the greatest professional objectivity, this feedback will be taken in by the actor personally. This is unavoidable—it's the actor's "person" which is the commodity. So it is essential that the actor and the agent have good communication between them. A long-term relationship cannot develop if you are maintaining a private grievance list or if you don't feel you can speak honestly with your agent.

Even with excellent communication, however, there are transition points in any career, and you may find your career at the point where you need to change agents, or the agency may feel that you should move on without them. It is always a difficult, and often painful, decision. It never happens without a certain amount of suffering during the transition. But if it is necessary, and if there has been a history of open and direct communication, the change can be accomplished with the belief that it's nobody's fault. Anger and resentment are powerful motivations for some people, but they fall under the category of "personal" and not "business" considerations. Changing agents is a business decision. Business decisions are not allowed to leave strewn bodies in their wake, even if they accelerate one's destined rise to the top. You never stay at the top without collaboration and assistance, and you will find it hard to locate these if you are known as someone who makes business decisions—such as dispensing with others' services—because you simply felt like it.

THE AGENT'S WORK

How do you know if you have a good agent—if the agent is doing his job? Consider:

—Is your agent submitting you frequently for roles? Is he submitting you on parts you think you could do?

—Do you feel your agent has any idea of who you really are and the work you are capable of? Does he come to see you perform or watch your TV work? Did he read you in his office when you first signed to get a sense of the range of what you can do?

—Has he had any direct involvement with your "look," hair, pictures, résumé, classes?

—Does he deal comfortably with your manager, your parents if you're a minor, your attorney, your accountant, or your publicist if they are an active part of your support team?

—Has he made certain to see you in person often enough that he knows what you look like now if it's different than what you looked like a month ago?

—Does he follow up your submissions with a call to the casting director to push for you or to obtain information to help you on the next reading? Does he obtain scripts for most or all projects you're interested in and does he read them?

"Yes" answers to any of these questions don't guarantee that you'll get submitted for every project that interests you, or that if you are submitted you'll be seen, or that if you are seen you'll be received in the way that you want. And none of these eventualities may have anything to do with the agent performing his job properly—it may have nothing to do with the agent. You may feel like blaming your agent, but that doesn't mean that what feels unsatisfactory to you is in any way his fault. For example, your agent subscribes to a publication called *Breakdown Services*, which provides talent representatives with a role breakdown for parts being currently cast by casting directors and producers. Let us say that your agent saw something perfect for you in *Breakdowns* and has sent in your picture and résumé. The casting person has never seen you before, and your credits are not yet impressive, so the casting director is unwilling to set up an appointment. Your agent has called the casting director and pleaded for you to be seen. Your agent doesn't know the casting director all that well, but has really gone out on a limb and told the casting director that if she misses you in the Equity-waiver play you're currently performing in, she'll regret it for the rest of her life. She attends the play. She's dazzled at your work. But her producers on the project you're interested in have told her, absolutely, that they are unwilling to see anybody for the second lead who doesn't have a certain line-up of credits. You don't have these credits. She goes to bat for you, and they remain adamant. On this project, you're not going to go further, and it is not the fault of either your agent or the casting director.

In theory, this is easy enough to understand, but it can become very difficult to accept when you find out that your actor friends are going in on projects on which you're not. Here again, it may have nothing to do with your agent. Perhaps a casting director sees something in your friend's picture that sparks her interest. Perhaps the casting director owes your friend's agent a favor. Perhaps the casting agent remembers your friend from one of *his* Equity-waiver plays. Perhaps the director has worked with your friend before. Perhaps your friend is a member of an acting family, and the director has worked with your friend's brother or sister before and is interested in meeting the rest of the family. Perhaps any of the above are true and this is only the first series of readings and you will receive your call to come in a few days later. Perhaps a few weeks or months later, if the casting has started in L.A., where you are, and is scheduled to jump to New York for a while before returning to L.A. Perhaps the casting director knows you, likes you, and realizes that it's going to take a push to get the director to see you, and you'll have a much better chance after the director has seen a bunch of actors who are exactly what he mistakenly think he's looking for. If your agent has a track record of missed opportunities, you will want to question why you can't get in to see the casting people. Or, if you've been with the same agent for three years and you're still having trouble being seen for under-fives, the problem may indeed be with the agent. But if neither of these are the case, then it is important that you have enough confidence in your agent to stay out of his way and let him do his job. You have to be willing to not get crazy over each and every inexplicable obstacle or rejection. Perhaps when the casting jumped to New York the principal roles in the project were all re-cast and your look, the same as your friend's, is no longer appropriate and your appointment is canceled. None of it has anything to do with you or your agent. A series of hysterical phone calls to your agent not only isn't going to do any good, it's going to steal time from your agent's working day and keep him from doing his work to get you and his other clients other jobs.

Your agent is not your therapist. Because some actors refuse to accept this, they find themselves changing agents almost as frequently as they change underwear. They insist on relating to their agent as an on-call psychotherapist, leaving him little recourse but to avoid the calls. Since one of the primary criterion by which to judge whether or not a business relationship is working successfully is if the other person will take your call, these actors have arranged a situation in which they feel they have no choice but to change agents. If they arrive at an interview and everyone else has the script that they were told was unavailable, immediately it's the agent's fault. If the agent gives them frank feedback from the casting director, they are offended by the agent who brings them the message, determine that the agent is hostile to them, and decide to change agents. If the agent has no coaching skills and suggests a particular class to strengthen the actor in the area the casting director found weak, these actors assume the agent is getting a kickback from the recommended teacher. Or if the agent recommends a specific photographer with whom he's had success, these actors suspect a kickback. (And there generally is one, but it's for the actor, because this photographer usually re-shoots for free if the agent isn't satisfied with the photos, whereas many other photographers won't.) When these actors' egos have grown too large to fit through the agency door, it's the agent's fault for not appreciating them sufficiently. If they can't immediately reach their agent by phone, it's because their agent has lost interest in them or is ignoring them, and, once again, it's time to change agents. Repeated agent-hopping, now matter how justified the actor feels, bespeaks a lack of judgment on the part of the actor. If you can reach your agent soon enough for good business, but not soon enough to soothe your ego when it's been bruised, remember that a good agent is working extremely hard and putting in very long hours to get his clients work. He wants you to work—it's how he makes his living. Beyond submissions, the typical agent's day is crammed with hours of phone calls, videotape viewing, reading of contracts and scripts, juggling shooting commitments and audition appointments so actors don't have to be unemployed before they can read for their next job, strategy meetings for clients' careers, meetings with prospective clients, attendance at showcases, etc. Then, at the end of the day, when normal people have gone home, agents begin the hours of making deals over the telephone. Then, at night, come the television shows, and attendance at the plays and the screenings of features in which their clients' are working. On weekends come the rest of the scripts they haven't yet had time to read. Your agent may, indeed, have to get back to you.

THE ACTOR'S WORK

From the agent's point of view, are you doing everything you should to support his work?

—Have you followed his recommendation on photographers and classes?

—Do you keep yourself alive, fit, and growing as an actor by working out in class or in plays?

—If you are newly signed with him, are you allowing enough time for you to demonstrate your worth to his agency, or was your last agency such an unhappy experience for you that you automatically assumed any change would instantly result in an improvement?

—Do you take the feedback your agent gives you from casting directors and do something with it other than be angry at him?

—When there are roles of a type in which he's never seen you, but in which you are interested, have you clearly let your agent know—or do you expect that part of his job is to be aware of your range, even if there's never been any evidence of it?

—Are your feedback expectations realistic to the kind of representation he is offering? For example, are you expecting your commercial agent to supply the level of feedback provided by your theatrical agent? Commercial agents tend to have less contact with their clients and give almost no feedback. A good commercial agent will send you on interviews several times a week, and the feedback is that you get a callback or land the commercial.

—If you are going to be late for a scheduled appointment, do you call your agent so it can be handled through his office, or do you call the appointment directly, which normally only further complicates their day and makes your agent look like he's not on top of your schedule?

—Do you make sure that you are sufficiently organized that, once you've been told where and when you have an appointment, you're not repeatedly telephoning your agent to get the address (which you've lost) or directions (which a good city map could supply you)?

—If you finish an appointment early enough to be available for another interview, do you let your agent know?

—Do you call your agent about business during regular business hours or at his home?

—When an interview has been set up for you, do you do everything within your power to keep that appointment, or do you require multiple re-schedulings so that the agent and casting director are spending a great deal of time just trying to re-schedule your appointment?

—If you have a legitimate concern, such as you're working the next day but haven't heard anything about your work call, and you call the agent's office and can't get through, do you leave a clear and specific message so that the office can act upon it even if the agent can't immediately call you back, or do you just say, "Tell him to call me immediately!" and hang up?

—Do you keep a record in a notebook of all interviews and jobs so that it isn't your agent's responsibility to remind you of where you've been and who you've already met?

—Do you always let your agent know if you are going to be out of town or unavailable?

—If residual checks are mailed directly to you—or any checks, for that matter, from ad agencies, networks, studies, etc.—do you always send these checks directly to your agent so that his office can deduct the proper commission and then pay you, thereby insuring that the your agent has received his commission and has a record that you've been paid your salary? Are you aware that you must pay your agent a commission on your residuals for network primetime reruns, up to and including two reruns?

—If you are a minor, do you or your parent make sure that your work permit hasn't expired? If you're not a minor, do you have the other necessary documents to determine your identity and employment eligibility? (*See CHAPTER 16*)

—Have you made sure that when it is time to renew your agency contract that you don't let it expire just because you haven't heard anything yet from the agency?

IT'S TIME TO CHANGE

Let's say your answers to all the above are "yes" and your career is suffering not because of you but because your agent is doing a lousy job. You've tried talking about it, and you get back a lot of malarky and double talk—for example, the agency has a "conflict" between you and several of their other actors with regard to type. If an agency has several actors of the same physical type, then, when one is hired, the casting director is more than likely to call that agency knowing that others of that type are also available. Besides, if you represented a "conflict," why did they sign you or the additional others in the first place? You agree with the agent's analysis that you're not getting jobs, but you always get called back, and if you're not getting sent out, you're satisfied it's because the agency has lost faith in you. It's time to change agents. Under the standard Screen Actors Guild agreement (which is the same for AFTRA), if your agent doesn't get you fifteen days of work within ninety-one days, you have the right to break the agreement. Some agents don't even bother with agreements until you get a job, figuring the paperwork isn't worth the time involved. If you feel you have a problem with your agent, a representative at Screen Actors Guild or AFTRA will be able to answer your questions.

To present you with an agent's point of view on how and why actors choose, keep, and change agents, as well as on several other aspects of the agent/client relationship, there follows an interview with Richard Berman, senior partner in The Agency.

CHAPTER 14

INTERVIEW WITH AN AGENT

RICHARD BERMAN
SENIOR PARTNER, THE AGENCY

I was born in Columbus, Ohio. I graduated from Ohio State University with an arts education . . . actually, a blended major and minor in Communications and in Speech and Spanish from the education college. Then I taught high school for two years—drama, speech, radio, and television. At the same time, I was the associate producer for a local television show and did all of its casting. Meanwhile, I was also on the board of the Columbus Junior Theatre of the Arts.

I left teaching, but teaching didn't leave me. I got involved in industrial communications doing training films and cassettes and multi-media presentations. When I came out here, I started as an agent trainee for Joan Scott. That's where I got my "Marine Basic Training"—I had to bring an extra undershirt with me every day. I then served as an assistant agent or in an agent trainee capacity at a number of other agencies, then as a sub-agent. When I met Laurence Becsey, we became partners and together we formed Talent Management International. Six years ago we merged with Jerome Zeitman Associates to form The Agency.

*Education has continued to play an impor-
tant part in my life, well past my own early
training. It figures significantly into my philosophy of agenting. I think often businesses
aren't successful or clients aren't successful because they don't have the proper education or
training for what it is that they are actually
trying to do.*

THE AGENCY IS A FULL-SERVICE COMPANY. WHOM DO YOU REPRESENT?

We represent writers, producers, directors, actors, cinematogra-
phers, and choreographers.

WHAT DOES AN AGENT'S JOB ENCOMPASS?

I break it down to the Three S's. An agent "selects" his clients,
then the agent "sells" his clients, and then the agent "services" his
clients. That's what we do. We pick the ones we want to
represent, whether it's signing people or going after established
clients or finding someone new. We sell them and introduce
them to the buyers. Once we get them the job, then we service
them, whatever that takes, whether it means going to visit them
on the set, meeting with attorneys—whatever.

WHAT DO YOU ENJOY MOST?

The fulfillment of discovering a young talent and having the
feeling that this artist is a winner, and then the realization and
recognition of the artist by the industry. To be able to sit there
and say, "I've been telling this to you for so long and now all of
you must agree." It is so exciting to be able to make that call and
tell an actor he got the job. It takes away all the bad days when no
one gets a job or clients leave you or you get beaten up by the
buyers.

IS THE MONEY IMPORTANT?

Of course, the money is important. But that isn't the reason that I got into the business. There's a lot of other things out there that I could be doing that would make me just as much money, if not more, but I love the business. I love talent. I love art and the written word. I love to create and, as agents, we are involved in the creative process without really getting in the trenches and doing the actual production.

WHAT'S THE DIFFERENCE BETWEEN A LARGE AGENCY AND A SMALL ONE?

The difference is that smaller agencies at least have the ability to give the personal attention to the client. You wouldn't have it in a larger agency where there are so many people to be watched over.

I'm not so sure that small agencies don't have the power. If it's a small agency that has strong agents and a lot of clout in the industry, it's as good as any agency at the point. Just because you're with a large agency doesn't mean you have clout. The large agency probably has clout, but do they use it for you? You can only find that out after being there, and usually after it's too late. The larger agency has access to more information. It's only by numbers. It's not by ability or strength. It's just that if you have fifty people out there gathering information, you're going to get more information than if you had two people out there. That's not saying that those two people who are gathering information wouldn't be bringing back a lot. But there's just so much that two people can do. Even if they're very good.

IS IT VERY DIFFERENT REPRESENTING ACTORS FROM, LET US SAY, WRITERS?

The main thing about writers is that they're usually a little less social than actors. You don't run the risk of them gossiping back and forth like you do with actors. Actors don't have anything to do. When writers don't have anything to do, they'll sit down and write a script. Or they'll think about ideas, or they'll go out and try to get stimulated. If actors can't think of anything to do, they'll think of something destructive to do to themselves. Like go out and meet a friend and talk about all the projects they're not up for. Or compare notes and get each other more upset and aggravated. They'll gossip about who is doing what. Of course, this is all misinformation. They'll come back and call their agents and spend thirty minutes on the phone going through all kinds of crazy paranoia, talking about projects that probably they're not even right for. This was the price we end up paying for their lunch or drinks at Joe Allen's.

HOW ABOUT REPRESENTING PRODUCERS?

The biggest problem with producers is that they love to take a lot of time with you. When they're not working or when they're trying to get a project off the ground, they will drain you for as much time as possible because they look at you as their partner. You're running with them. In some cases, you are. But in a lot of cases, all you are doing is trying to get the material out and make the deal for them. That's why we generally don't like to represent producers. Unless they are writer-producers. They drain you for time and energy, and then you don't have anything to show for it at the end. When they're working, they have no time to talk to you at all because they're too busy.

AND WHAT ABOUT REPRESENTING DIRECTORS AS OPPOSED TO ACTORS?

The most frustrating thing about directors is that after they've done a project and it's basically successful, until they find a new project that absolutely excites them, you could offer them GONE WITH THE WIND and they wouldn't accept it. They will pass on everything. It becomes very frustrating. You can send them reams of material from every studio in town, and they will pass and pass and pass. Part of it is insecurity. They're afraid to take the next step. They feel that they've got to have a studio blockbuster script, and who are they to decide what that is? If they knew that, then they should be running the studio. Enough time goes by where it suddenly dawns on them one night when they're getting ready to go to bed, "I haven't worked in a long time. I wonder what the studios are thinking about me. Will I ever be able to get another job now?" And then all of a sudden, they call up the next day, panicked, and say, "I've got to go to work!" You say, "Well, fine, how about these 200 scripts you just passed up?" It's the timing. It's their feeling of the moment.

Directors are a strange lot. They run much more autonomously. They're a little more rebellious than actors. They feel that they can make their own decisions. Often we end up having to make a decision for them without their knowing it, or we have to beat them into making a decision—so that they do go back to work. If the project doesn't work out, then they can always come back to us and tell us, "You know you pushed me into this project and it's your fault." But the bottom line is that if they don't go to work, they'll look at us and say, "You never got me anything, and I'm going somewhere else."

DEFINE LOYALTY: AGENT TO CLIENT, CLIENT TO AGENT.

The agent's loyalty is to continue to fight and to get an actor on the "A" projects and the "A" parts and sell him as if he were working constantly, even though he may not have worked in a long time and consistently gets mediocre feedback. An agent does this because he feels that the terrific job that will resurrect his client and put him back on the map is right around the corner.

In terms of client to agent, I feel that when a client works consistently and all of a sudden has a dry period, he shouldn't lose confidence in his agent because the agent may temporarily have run out of his bag of tricks and needs a little time to replenish that bag. The client gives him the opportunity and time to regroup. Maybe it's not even the agent's fault. Maybe it's the fact that there are no roles out there for him. He has to consider the marketplace. When a client gets to a certain level in his career, he should evaluate his agent. "Did this agent get me here, and will he be able to take me any further? Did we learn together, and is he continuing to learn?" A client should give it a lot of thought and try to analyze the situation with an unbiased person who may be knowledgeable in the business and who's not prejudiced toward any agent.

HOW DO YOU ACQUIRE A CLIENT?

Any number of ways. If it's someone who's basically undiscovered, it's by finding them somewhere or referrals from publicists, attorneys, personal managers, or other clients. Whether it's going out visiting a client on a set and meeting other clients and trying to develop a relationship with them or whether it's going to a party or screening and just going up and introducing yourself to a prospective client. Telling them how much you admire them, how good you think they are. Eventually, it leads to a meeting or lunch, discussing their career. Maybe it's a situation where you admire someone tremendously, and you make an effort to get to them—a campaign to sign the client. I knew one agency that had five agents going after this client. They camped out on his doorstep, day and night, gave him scripts, called him on the phone, took him out. That's the way they do it. Eventually, someone like that has to fall. It's like chopping a big tree down. You just keep chopping and chopping and the tree will fall. I don't care how loyal the client is. An agent invariably makes a mistake somewhere. They're only human. And if that army of agents is there at the right time, they'll probably get the client.

WHAT QUALITIES DO YOU LOOK FOR IN AN ACTOR OR AN ACTRESS?

Besides talent, I search for a look and a personality that's appealing, unique, and where there's a certain kind of mystique. You can almost sense that there's a kind of aura about them, a magic. When you put a camera in front of them, they're a totally different person in terms of look and style. When you see them walking down the street, they would not stand out in a crowd. They could be someone who would blend right into the crowd, but the camera is going to pick up certain things that are very special. The camera just loves them and reaches out and kisses them. They talk about screen magic—that's what it is.

WHEN YOU'RE LOOKING AT A PROSPECTIVE CLIENT'S RÉSUMÉ, WHAT'S THE FIRST THING YOU TAKE NOTE OF?

On a résumé, my eye goes to film first. Then I go to theatre credits. If an actor has done film only and no theatre, I question his discipline. He may be terrific on film and a great film star, but I wonder, when it's all said and done, if he ultimately falls into the category of "Life is too short to deal with whatever this is." I often find that, with the theatre people, there's already a discipline planted. They know how to work within that discipline when they get to film and television. They understand the pecking order, although stardom does strange things to people. I've always had much better luck with people who are trained in the the theatre than people who've just gotten off the bus and never been on a stage before and think that they're movie stars or that they want to do nothing but be in the movies and television.

DO YOU HAVE ANY PET PEEVES ABOUT TALENT?

Yes, when talent is told exactly how to do something and they don't do it. Whether it's clothes to wear, an attitude, or a way to play the part. "In order to get this role, this is what you have to do. Don't play it this way. This is what everyone else has been doing and this is what they don't want." And then they'll come in and do it exactly the opposite of what you told them. Exactly. If you tell them, "Don't wear what you're wearing, you look old. Wear something that will make you look younger," they'll go in exactly the way they did before, or they will decide themselves what is more appropriate. Even though they have been told specifically what to wear, they will wear something else, thinking that they know more, and they will lose the role. That aggravates me. Or when they are told to just go in and do the job and get out and they stand there and talk and talk themselves out of the role. They oversell themselves. Pure and simple. I just had that happen yesterday. We had an actor who went in for a particular role, but they asked him to read for another role because it was larger. The scene had more substance. The actor went in and read and was terrific. The director decided to hire him. The actor went out, came back in two minutes later, and proceeded to scold them. "If you're bringing someone in for one role, you shouldn't have them read for another and confuse them." He stood there for about three minutes and lectured them as to how they should run their operation. The casting director called us and said, "Your client just talked himself out of the role." The director felt the actor was telling him how to run the casting session. What would happen when they're out on location somewhere? The actor would tell him how to run the whole production.

ANY PET PEEVES AS FAR AS THE BUYERS ARE CONCERNED?

With a casting person, my biggest pet peeve is when there is something very simple and they make it into a federal case. The casting director says, "We lost your submission. Can you send another picture please?" They create so many snags and so much additional busy work that you wonder why you got into it in the first place. It's stupid extra work because someone doesn't know how to just put it through. Maybe it's an assistant who doesn't get it right the first time or maybe it's a casting director who's not convinced or is afraid for his job. He's insecure or doesn't know the person. Maybe they were told, "Please make sure your people know who this person is." You send in a person of a certain stature, and they're going to be upset if they're not acknowledged and not treated on the level they've earned in the industry. The response is, "No problem, no problem." Then the actor walks in and the first thing the director says is, "Now who are you again? Aren't you on—are you on a series or did you do that movie?" Right away, the actor looks at the casting director like "you didn't do your job." At that point, the actor is turned off. He's not going to do a good reading. He's pissed off. Then he gets back home and calls me and reads me the riot act. Then I call the casting director and read him the riot act. He makes up all kinds of excuses. It takes forever to get the thing back on track. It's because this person didn't do his homework.

DO YOU INCLUDE THE ARTIST AS PART OF THE CHAIN OF COMMAND WHEN YOU ARE TRYING TO PUT TOGETHER A DEAL FOR HIM?

If he's the type of person who can handle it, and be comfortable with it, I do. If he's the type who cannot handle it, and, if I feel that by letting him in on certain kinds of information that he's going to get more nervous and uncomfortable and feel that the deal is going away, then I don't think it's really healthy for him to hear everything. Certain ones will tell you, right up front, "I don't want to hear about it. I don't want to know about it. Just tell me when the deal is done, and tell me when to go to work." That's the easiest. I always say, "I just want you to know what we're asking for here. You could lose the deal. I just want you to know that. If you have a problem with that or if you feel that is where it's going, do you want me to stop?"

If we feel that we have to be held back all the time, or if we feel that we have to be walking on egg shells all the time, we can't do our best negotiating. And if it's a situation where the artist has an opportunity to call up the negotiator himself and get in the middle, that's a nightmare. That's happened. Or where the negotiator calls up the artist prior to the negotiation and discusses certain points of what the deal is going to be and the artist agrees to it or says, "That sounds all right." Then you get the job of trying to pull it out and make it all sound reasonable.

HOW DO YOU WORK WITH THE BREAKDOWNS?

Basically, we only use the breakdowns for episodic and independent feature films. For pilots, feature films, and movies-of-the-week, we've usually had the scripts at least a couple of weeks before, sometimes months before. We've already created our own breakdown in-house. We've planted our initial suggestions and have been talking to the buyers, whether it's the producer or the director or an executive on the project. We tell our agents not to rely on breakdowns. We don't like them to wait for the breakdowns to come out before they cover a project. By the time the breakdown comes out, those key roles are gone. Independent films come from everywhere. It's impossible to cover all of them, so we look at the breakdowns for them and also for episodic. It's just not worth it for our agents to read every episodic script that's out there.

TALK ABOUT THE IMPORTANCE OF STUDYING.

I think training is important for discipline. The best training ground is New York. Not just for training, but for the overall experience of getting to know oneself as an artist. To be able to kind of wheel and deal on your own. New York is a tough city and it kind of builds a nice crust around people so that when they come out here, it's a sort of an additional insurance. A lot of people don't know what to make of it out here because it's kind of nondescript. The city is very deceiving in that it just kind of lies sleeping with palm trees and beaches and pretty buildings and sunshine. There's an energy in New York. It's a human freeway. The energy and the feeling of the city just embraces you, sometimes squeezes you to death. It's built in. You have no choice but to go with it or get the hell out. To be able to bring that energy here and maintain it is really the only way of surviving in this city. I've always told New York actors when they come out here—if you were in a dance class in New York, find a dance class here. Or an exercise class. If you had a certain routine you followed in New York, get into that routine out here. Don't get into a situation where you lie by the pool and wait for the phone to ring. Don't become lethargic. Because the city will work on you. You'll start to go crazy. I've seen it happen over and over again. I tell actors when they come out here, if they're not working right away, don't live at the beach. Try to live in as close to a city atmosphere as possible. Maybe one that's not so wonderful, but one that will give them the feeling of wanting to work. With no work to go to and no auditions, it's very easy to say, "I'll stay home and I'll sit around and think." Ultimately, the head trip takes over.

HOW CAN AN ACTOR ASSUME PERSONAL RESPONSIBILITY FOR HIS CAREER?

An actor has to constantly be looking and re-evaluating himself without becoming neurotic. Is he growing—being fulfilled? What does it take for him to be fulfilled? Is it realistic? He must say to himself, "Am I really this kind of an actor? Am I right for these roles? Am I a leading man? Should I be doing character roles? And if I'm not a leading man, why am I fooling myself thinking that I should be a leading man?" The same thing with women. In terms of age, look, and style, there's nothing more frustrating than to deal with an actor who the industry and the agents feel is one thing but the actor thinks he's something else. If he can prove that he is something else, that's great. But it's difficult. Actors should be making sure that they are staying in shape in terms of abilities, continuing education and training, and that they are accessible to the buyer. Are they professional in every way? It's nice when they hear about a project and then call us and let us know about it, but I don't think it's necessary for them to be their own agents or to stick their noses in and maybe screw up negotiations. This is a pet peeve of mine—when an artist gets in the middle of a negotiation and takes all the power away from the agent.

HOW DO YOU VALIDATE YOURSELF?

After I make a deal, I look at it and I say, "Did I do as good a job as I could have?" Or if I didn't, "What could I do better?" I'll make a note of that for the next situation. Before I sign someone, I will say to myself, "Is this right? Is this someone I can really do a job for, even though he may be a name?" Ultimately, I will not sign someone if I don't feel that I can really get in there and make that commitment to him.

CHAPTER 15

CHANGING YOUR NAME

THE NOM DE THESP

In the 1930s, '40s, and '50s, during the "star system" days, studios changing an actor's name was so common that film actors almost never kept their real names. Names were automatically changed "for the sake of the marquee." A stage name, or *nom de thesp* (name of the thespian, or actor) was chosen by the studio. Famous nom de thesps such as Rock Hudson, Marilyn Monroe, John Wayne, and Cary Grant have become household words, standing in for people whose real names were Roy Harold Scherer Fitzgerald, Norma Jean Baker, Marion Michael Morrison, and Archibald Leach.

In prior centuries, many actors took new names so as not to disgrace their families. Acting, not considered respectable as a profession, ranked with pickpocketing and worse. "Nice" hotels didn't rent to actors and, even in Hollywood, country clubs refused entrance to such "gypsies." Not too long before, actors couldn't even be buried in churchyards. But during the 1960s, partly from the realistic emphasis of the prevailing interpretation of "method" acting, partly from the rise of pride and identification with ethnic origins, this name changing phenomenon was reversed, and it became significant to actors to use their real names.

Nowadays, though things have loosened up, some of the old considerations still apply. If your name really is Omar Sharif, and if you are very Arab-looking, changing your name to Mark West is not going to help you get more roles. On the other hand, if your name is Ramon Estevez and your looks could as readily type you as Irish as they could Latin, you may wish to change your name to Martin Sheen. You couldn't, however, use either of these names, since they are already taken. SAG and AFTRA rules require that you must change your professional name, even if it is your real name, if that name already belongs to a SAG or AFTRA member. If your real name was Jimmy Stewart, but there already was a Jimmy Stewart, then you had to become Stewart Granger. It used to be that you had the option of merely adding a different initial, and that Stewart Granger could have become James L. Stewart. But SAG no longer accepts initials, although AFTRA still does, so Jimmy L. Stewart would have had to become James Lablanche Stewart. Both SAG and AFTRA will change your name for the first time for free. Second and consecutive changes cost $15 per guild per change ($30 a throw). At the time of this writing, both unions permit you to change your nom de thesp as often as you like, providing the name is not already being used and you can afford the fee.

One purposeful reason for changing your professional name may be that you are known as a young actor, and your name is identified with you as a young person, but you are no longer that young. The change from "Ronnie" Howard to "Ron" Howard has accompanied a change in the public's perception of a child actor into the image of an adult actor and a director. "Rossie" Harris, the little boy in AIRPLANE, is now nineteen and has become "Ross" to move on from the image that he is still eleven years old. He is, in fact, six feet tall. Morgan Brittany made a career and a lot of money as child actress "Suzanne Caputo," but when she went into her teens she couldn't get work at that awkward stage of transition. One day she got on an airplane, found the name "Morgan Brittany" in a novel, got off the plane with that as her new name, and started a very successful new career. "Morgan Brittany" is an unusual name, but it's neither hard to spell nor understand, which is a primary consideration in choosing a nom de thesp. It used to be that certain names sounded obviously made up and adopted . . . "a stage name if I ever heard one." But here again, nowadays, it can be difficult to tell. "River Phoenix" is the actor's real name, and his distinguished work in films such as STAND BY ME, MOSQUITO COAST, and RUNNING ON EMPTY has helped create interest in the considerable talents of his siblings, who are carving out their own careers under their real names—Leaf, Liberty, and Rainbow.

If you plan to change your name, whether to something more or less unusual, check with SAG and AFTRA's membership departments as your first step.

CHAPTER 16

DOCUMENTATION

QUALIFYING FOR EMPLOYMENT

Under the Immigration Reform Act, to qualify for employment you now must be able to present either one item from List A below, or one item each from List B and List C. All documents must be original.

LIST A (Establish Identity AND Employment Eligibility)
- United States Passport
- Certificate of U.S. Citizenship
- Certificate of Naturalization
- Unexpired foreign passport which contains authorization to work
- Resident Alien Card, Temporary Resident Card or Employment Authorization Card

LIST B (Establish Identity)
- Driver's License or State I.D. Card
- School I.D. Card
- Voter Registration Card
- U.S. Military Card
- Native American documents
- Other I.D. accepted by the Attorney General

LIST C (Establish Employment Eligibility)
- Valid Social Security Card
- U.S. Birth Certificate

- INS Employment Authorization
- Any accepted certificate that establishes U.S.
  citizenship at birth
- Other I.D. accepted by the Attorney General

To obtain new documents:
- SOCIAL SECURITY CARDS may be replaced at any
  Social Security Office. Obtain a receipt stating
  that application for a new card has been made.
- VOTER REGISTRATION CARDS may be obtained at
  your local Registrar of Voters Office. Inquire at
  your local election board for details. In Los
  Angeles County, call (213) 721-1100. In
  Manhattan, (212) 924-8228.
- I.D. CARDS may be obtained from the Department of
  Motor Vehicles if you do not have a Driver's
  License. These cards may be used as documents
  under List B. Apply in person with verification
  of birth at your local Motor Vehicle Office.

(If your legal and professional names differ, present your Social Security Card with your legal name and your SAG card with your professional name. The same Social Security number on both will prove you are the same person. The SAG card, however, is not a substitute for an official document.)

QUALIFYING FOR UNEMPLOYMENT

If you work as an actor, you are entitled to unemployment benefits regardless of age—because money is subtracted from your salary for these benefits. (This is not true if you are incorporated.)

Even if you're making good money from your acting when you're working, the unemployment can be used in various creative ways to foster your career. It can be used for classes, pictures, transportation costs, etc. It's not as complicated as it seems at first, because, once you sign up for it, your checks are mailed to you and all you need to do is fill out a form (whenever the Employement Development Department requires it—about every ten weeks). You must specify what you are doing to get work—meaning what interviews you have been on. The professional actor keeps a logbook of his interviews, but if you're unsure, you can contact your agent or manager to find out what you might have been submitted for. Also, you will need the address, phone number, and zip code of the production companies you list.

An actor's residuals must be credited against unemployment benefits only in the week the residual payment was received by the actor. Unemployment considers residual, rerun, reuse, and holding fees the same for unemployment insurance purposes—they are all monies generated by the use of the commercial and are wages within the Code's meaning (See *Commerical Codes and Payments* in the Glossary). Contact the Screen Actors Guild or AFTRA for assistance if your claim is denied.

The optimal time to file for unemployment is during the four month period in which you've generated the most money, since this way you can collect the largest weekly claim amount. The usual extent of a claim is six months, although extensions are possible under certain circumstances. The E.D.D. can let you know whether you are eligible for an extension.

Allow two hours for your first visit to the E.D.D. office. Office hours are 8:00 a.m. to 5:00 p.m. You need to file your claim between Monday and Wednesday. If you wait till Thursday, you will have to wait an additional week beyond the normal two-week waiting period before you can collect your first check.

On your first visit, you'll fill out certain forms to help the E.D.D. determine whether you're eligible for unemployment and how much. They will then set an appointment for you to come back for an "orientation class" in which the whole process is explained to a large group of people, rather than having each person briefed individually. Unfortunately, though this frees E.D.D. workers from repeating the same explanation over and over again, frequently there are so many languages being spoken that communication gets worse, not better. If you have a Korean lecturing Latinos and Iranians, you can imagine how confused things can get. You will then be sent off with forms which you will mail in every two weeks (after your initial two-week waiting period). Keep a log of interviews you've been sent on, because about every ten weeks they set an appointment for you to come in and ask you for a list of places contacted. Sometimes they call and double check, so be careful in the interviews you invent.

If you tell them you are also a secretary, they will expect you to look for work in that area, too. You must declare the money you make, which will be subtracted from that week's benefit. If you don't declare it and they catch you (and they can!), you will have to pay it back, lose your current unemployment, and possibly be fined.

Providing you abide by the rules, there is no reason not to apply for unemployment to cover the periods in which you've not been employed. The only time you shouldn't apply for unemployment is if you feel it's necessary to have your limo wait for you in the parking lot!

PASSPORTS

Passports should be applied for as soon as you know that you will be going overseas because they frequently take a couple of weeks. The best policy is to have a current passport so you are ready if you get a job which will require you to have one. If it is very short notice, the Passport Office will cooperate by speeding yours though, but it's better to allow plenty of time. Passports can be applied for at some post offices, local county courts, and in Los Angeles at the L.A. Passport Agency at the Federal Courthouse, 11000 Wilshire Blvd., 13th Floor, West Los Angeles. A taped recording will give you all the information you need at (213) 209-7070. Should you have some specific question, you can call (213) 209-7075 and talk to a real person. The office is open from 8:00 a.m. to 4:00 p.m., Monday through Friday. Call Directory Assistance in your city for the location there.

Getting a passport, as you may guess, involves standing in a line. In order to avoid several trips, it is important that you bring the right documents with you. First of all, you must fill out the Passport Office's own forms, which are obtainable through the mail or at the office. Secondly, you will need a certified copy of your birth certificate, stamped individually with the seal of the Custodian of Records in your birthplace. A xerox copy will not be acceptable. The Passport Office can give you a list of places where you may obtain a certified copy of your birth certificate for a nominal fee if you do not have one. Thirdly, you will need two photos, full-face, two-inches square, color or black and white. Many facilities have machines on the premises that will take these photos for you. But if you want to look good on your passport, be prepared to go to a photo studio that makes passport photos and have them taken there. The odds of the machine photos being good ones are very slim. Fourthly, you will be required to show evidence of American citizenship (a previous U.S. passport or naturalization papers) as well as personal identification (driver's license, military I.D. card, etc.—see List B above). If you have changed your name or the name on your driver's license differs from your birth certificate, you have to have friends or relatives fill out affidavits that you are who you say you are. While the Passport Office is usually very cooperative in speeding up your passport should you need one in a hurry, be aware if there is a problem—with affidavits, for example—which have to be signed and notarized and may have to be sent to someone in another city— it could take longer than you plan. So make sure you have enough time to do the paperwork.

The cost of an adult passport is $42 and it is good for ten years. If you are under eighteen, your passport will be good for five years and will cost $27. If you are thirteen years of age or older, you must appear in person at the Passport Office. The Passport Office will accept cash or your personal check in payment with your application, and it will keep your birth certificate. Your passport will then be mailed to you, along with your birth certificate, within a couple of days.

Once you have a passport, make several xeroxes of the front page where your signature appears. If you should lose the passport, the xerox will make getting a new one at a U.S. Consulate much faster.

REPORTING EMPLOYMENT

A W-4 tax form is given to you at the onset of your employment to determine your withholding for income tax purposes. It should be given to you your first day on the set. If you don't get one, ask for it—you won't get paid until you fill it out and sign it.

A W-2 tax form is sent out by an employer (no later than the last week in January) stating how much money you earned and how much tax was withheld from your salary over the previous year. These must be sent in by you with your Federal and State income tax forms.

A 1099 tax form is sent out by the employer (no later than the last week of February) if there was no withholding. It lists the total amount of salary which you earned, all of which you were paid. 1099s also must accompany your Federal and State income tax forms. Your employer will have sent copies of either your W-2s or your 1099s to the IRS.

The following sample income tax deduction worksheet is offered only as a guideline for what expenses may possibly be tax deductible. You must check with your own accountant, who will advise you of which items in your case may and may not be deductible for personal use.

INCOME TAX DEDUCTIONS WORKSHEET

YEAR_____

NAME _____

SOC. SEC. # _____

CATEGORY   TOTAL $

Advertising/Promotion (Zed cards, variety mailouts) _____

Business Cards/Stationery _____

Computer Supplies _____

Office Supplies _____

Photos _____

Film Processing/Lab Touch-up _____

Postage/UPS/Messengers _____

Professional Publications/Trades/ Books/ Magazines
_____ (*Variety, Drama-Logue, Premier, Calendar,* **Not** *L.A. Times*)
_____ Résumés/Copying/Scripts _____

Storage Expenses _____

Videotapes/Supplies _____

Finance Charges/Interest Expense (home mortgage, automobile
_____ loans, credit card finance charges) _____

Fees for Tax Planning and Preparation _____

Cable TV (ON, SELECT, DISNEY, HBO, etc.) _____

Answering Service/Answering Machine/Beeper _____

Equipment Repairs (Phone, VCR, TV, Answering Machine) _____

Music/Records/Tapes _____

Telephones/Pay Phones/ Car Phone _____

Industry-related Equipment Purchase (TV, VCR, Audio Equipment,
_____ Computer, Telephone [less personal use]) _____

Commission/Agents _____

Commission/Managers _____

Commission/Publicist _____

Commission/Business Manager

Professional Services/Attorney/Psychiatrist

Subcontractors (1099s)

Union/Professional Dues (SAG, AFTRA, AGVA, Equity)

Directory Listings/*Academy Players*

Entertainment Dinners/Parties (Agent, Manager, Casting Directors,
Producers — Business-related)

Set-Sitters (Minors)

Travel Expenses (Out-of-pocket, including Taxis)

Auto Expenses (Out-of-pocket, including gas, repair, registration,
lease insurance, mileage at $0.21 per mile [less personal])

Parking Charges

Coaching/Dance/Voice/Accompanist/Acting/
Special skills private lessons

Dance/Rehearsal Clothes

Education/Seminars/Conferences

Reference Materials/Newspapers/Books

Theatres/Plays/ Movies

Wardrobe/Maintenance

Gifts/Flowers ($25 maximum ded. per individual)

Donations (Charity)

RA Contributions

Rentals/Studios/Equipment/Limousine/Tuxedo

Medical (Out-of-pocket)

Casualty Losses (due to theft or damage to property)

CHAPTER 17

WHEN TO SAY NO

SAFETY IN HAZARDOUS STUNTWORK

A great deal of this book counsels the actor to be flexible, to adapt, to roll with the punches. There are occasions, however, where the punches are not safe, and the actor should refuse to participate. No role, no shot, no one's lunch hour nor budget concern is worth your life or any of your limbs.

By SAG definition, hazardous work is defined as:

No player shall be required to perform a stunt, a stunt-related activity, or any other hazardous activity without prior consultation. The player's consent shall be a prerequisite to performing stunts or hazardous activity. An individual qualified by training and/or experience in planning the stunt must be engaged or present on the set.

This applies not just to things such as fights and car chases, but also to working with animals. I have had clients work with crocodiles, snakes, rhinos, lions, and wild horses. It is imperative that proper consultation is held prior to the shooting of the stunt. The various escape routes should be discussed. Someone from the production company should be assigned to watch any minors, and if there is imminent danger, to pull the child to safety by the pre-arranged escape plan. The exact actions of the animal and the distance to the actor should be discussed beforehand and compromises made, if necessary.

The nature of the animal's movement and the animal's

temperament should be discussed beforehand by the trainer. For example, alligators can be tamed and often scared off by being tapped with a stick. Crocodiles, on the other hand, are extremely dangerous and aggressive and cannot be bluffed by the same tactic. Even the smallest crocodile is capable of inflicting a major wound.

When working with poisonous snakes, you need to make sure that a qualified snake handler, nurse, and an antidote are nearby. There are modern surgical techniques that render a poisonous snake harmless by tying off or removing the venom glands. If a snake has had this surgery, the area in front of the eyes is sunken.

Primates such as chimpanzees, monkeys, orangutans, and baboons are extremely emotional and powerful animals. A ninety-pound female chimp once curled 1,200 pounds. Most male monkeys are very possessive, jealous, and tend to regard all females (human included) as possible members of their harem. Primates have very quirky personalities, and the only way to learn what behaviors can upset the animal is by a discussion beforehand with the trainer.

When working with large wind machines, it is necessary to see and examine the size of the projectiles and the distance from where actors will be to the blades. Particles can be thrown into eyes, bruise skin, and clog windpipes. It is difficult to be in a wind scene and not receive some small bruises. Test rehearsals should be run with the fan at the speed of the take. Protection of the eyes is extremely important. I had a client dressed in a miniskirt for a wind scene in MONSTER SQUAD, and when she went home she found leaves and pebbles up her underwear from the force of the wind.

Needless to say, stunt work with guns and explosives is often one of the most dangerous situations, even if the presence seems like only a minor detail on the set. A handgun loaded only with blanks nonetheless killed John Erik Hexum when he was handling the weapon between takes and the gun wadding exploded, striking his skull and penetrating his brain at point-blank range. If you are to handle a firearm in a scene, great caution should be taken to have proper rehearsal and training, and thereafter it should only be handled by you when absolutely necessary. Children should not be asked to handle a gun loaded with live ammunition, or even with blanks, even under supervision. The off-camera firing of a gun can create the horror necessary for the effect without the child having to fire the gun or be seen firing the gun. The use of explosives in the making of TWILIGHT ZONE led to the tragic deaths of Vic Morrow and two small children. Whether proper planning was really done will never be known, but explosives and children just don't mix because even the best technicians couldn't avert this tragedy. If explosives are involved, then it may be best and prudent to say no, if you are the parent of a minor, to allowing your child in the stunt.

If after the discussions and rehearsals are held the stunt still appears too improvised, so much so that any rational person would refuse to do it, then so should you. Unfortunately, pressure may be applied. You may hear:

"Your stubbornness and lack of professionalism are holding up all these people."

"Look how much this is costing the company because you won't do this stunt."

"The other actors are doing stunts, why not you?"

"It's not that dangerous."

"I guess we won't have this shot in the movie and it will suffer because of you."

No matter how much pressure is applied, you should refuse!

Pressure can often be applied on overseas locations especially well. They 1) have you out of the U.S., 2) in a strange and uncomfortable situation, 3) away from your support base of agent, manager, parent, 4) English may be a second language to them, 5) they can speak to one another in a language that you don't understand and 6) differences in culture, work habits, and ethics may be used to make your American behavior seem unreasonable.

Don't be pressured into putting yourself or your child in jeopardy. If you are starting to feel cornered, you might reply, "This is not the way we discussed this stunt in our meeting. It looks very dangerous. It's getting dark and you're losing light, so the longer you take trying to pressure me into a decision which jeopardizes this young actor [or me], the less time you will have to reblock it and shoot this stunt the way it should be safely done." Stand your ground.

Still stumped? Call your agent or manager.

Are you scared? Trust your instinct!

PART SIX

GLOSSARY

Academy Players Directory: A pictorial directory of actors and actresses, published three times a year in Los Angeles by the Academy of Motion Picture Arts and Sciences. Each listing includes one picture and up to two agency representatives, unless the actor has no agent, in which case the listing may refer to a manager or other contact number. Listings are divided into categories such as leading men and women, young leading men, ingenues, children, character actors, etc. To be listed, an actor must have a franchised agent or be a member of one of the actor's unions. A single annual fee of $45 covers inclusion in all three issues. The Directory serves as a reference guide for casting directors, producers, and directors searching for new faces or trying to identify unknown names belonging to familiar faces.

AFTRA: American Federation of Television and Radio Artists. Union with jurisdiction over performers in live and taped radio and television shows (includes newscasters and announcers), taped commericals, and phonograph records. AFTRA is an "open union," meaning that one need not have worked previously under AFTRA's jurisdiction to qualify. (*See SAG*)

Breakdown Services: A company founded by Gary Marsh in 1971 that publishes condensations of scripts to be

produced and lists the roles in them to be cast.
Separate New York and Los Angeles editions cover
upcoming available parts in theatre, film, and television productions. In addition to noting start dates,
producers, studios, etc., for each project, the lists
"break down" available parts in terms of sex, age,
and brief character description. Designed for the
use of franchised agents and managers to set up
auditions for their clients

Callback: After the first audition, the invitation to return for a
second (or third or fourth) audition until the field of
contenders has been narrowed down to one final
choice. Technically, commercial calls are allowed a
maximum of two callbacks, after which the actor
must be paid for his time, whereas there is no limit
to the number of theatrical callbacks.

Commercials (Television): Short advertising messages made
as motion pictures, three minutes or less in length
and intended for showing on television.

Commercial Representation: Agents representing actors exclusively for work in commercials.

Cold Reading: Technically, the reading of a scene from a script,
aloud, instantly on first viewing, as in sight-reading
music, with no advance preparation. In practice,
however, the term refers to the practice by which
most actors are chosen for roles, or callbacks, by
their reading of a scene with which they are familiar, but which they have not memorized. Advance
preparation may range from five minutes to overnight, in which case the reading is not totally cold.

Composites: A group of lithographed photos, almost always in
black and white, of one actor or model in different
situations and poses, arranged on both sides of an

81/2 x 11-inch pictures, used especially for gaining roles in commercials. The front side shows a single, full-size headshot, very jolly, and the reverse side arranges usually four different photos of the actor as various "types" or in various activities.

Coogan Law: The Child Actor's Bill, passed in California on May 4, 1939, requiring court approval of contracts for minors to be submitted by the child's guardian, and placing one half of the child's earnings in trust until the child reaches the age of majority. Named for Jackie Coogan, child star of the movie THE KID, who earned $4,000,000, but whose account at the age of eighteen years old only contained $535,932 and whose final settlement in the case was only $126,000.

Dealer Commercial: A commercial made and paid for by the manufacturer or distributor of a product or service, delivered to the dealers in such product or service, and where the air time is contracted and paid for by the dealer(s).

Downgrading: Reducing an actor's presence—and hence his residual—in a commercial from what it was at the time the commercial was originally made. Where downgrading is permitted, players must be notified of the change in classification and must be paid an additional session fee. Performers may not be downgraded so long as their face appears recognizably in the commercial. Stuntmen may not be downgraded as long as the stunt is identifiable and in some way relating to the narration of commercial message. If the actor disagrees with the downgrading, the issue is arbitrated by the Screen Actors Guild.

Equity: Actors' Equity Association. Union with jurisdiction over stage performers and stage managers. An actor qualifies for membership in Equity by 1) being signed to one of the standard Equity contracts or, 2) accumulating fifty weeks in the Membership Candidate Program at an accredited theater or, 3) having been a paid-up member in one of the affiliated unions for at least one year and having worked under that union's jurisdiction on either one principal, one "under five" (*See UNDER FIVES*), or three days of extra contracts. The affiliated unions include AFTRA, SAG, AGMA, AGVA (*See SAG for full titles of these acronyms*), SEG (Screen Extras Guild), and HAU, IAU, and APATE (the Hebrew, Italian, and Puerto Rican Actors'Unions).

Fixed Cycle: The agreed-upon standard unit of time for running commercials by which payment of use fees to actors are figured: Each period of thirteen consecutive weeks beginning with the date of actor's employment in the making of the commercial. Distinguished from *USE CYCLE*, which refers to the thirteen consecutive weeks period dating from first use of commercial.

Franchise: Signed contracts between a union and an agent authorizing the agent to negotiate on behalf of actors for jobs falling under the jurisdiction of that union. They are difficult and expensive to obtain, so their possession assumes a legitimacy on the part of the agent, and without them an agent cannot submit or negotiate for actors' contracts on productions covered by the actors' unions.

General Interview: Interviews set up by casting directors to "meet and greet" new talent, or to meet talent whose work is unfamiliar to them, but not for the purpose of casting any specific roles in specific projects.

Holding Fee: A separate fee in an amount equal to a session fee, payable to the actor 12 working days after commencement of fixed cycle, whereby a producer maintains exclusive right over the actor's participating in any other commercial for a similar product while deciding whether or not to continue use of the commercial into another use cycle. Holding fees may be credited toward use fees if the use cycle commences during the fixed cycle for which the holding fee was paid. Separate and individual holding fees shall be paid for each commercial made.

IATSE: International Alliance of Theatrical and Stage Employes [*sic*] and Moving Picture Machine Operators of United States and Canada. Union with jurisdiction over non-performance craft jobs in production, such as scenic artists, hairstylists, set painters, costumers, grips, film technicians, publicists, model makers, camera operators, etc.

Local Programs: A classification of program for which commercial use fees are payable to the artist, as in the manner of Class A commercials, per use, and fifteen working days after commencement of use cycle. (*See PROGRAM COMMERCIALS*)

Majors: Industry term for the long-standing, established studios—such as Columbia, Paramount, Twentieth Century Fox, Disney—with film libraries and with their own facilities for production, including capital, sound stages, and backlots. Once the pioneers of the movie-making business, many are now owned by parent corporations, in some cases having little or no experience with the business of making movies.

Mini-Majors: Industry term for those smaller independent production companies—such as the Ladd Company, Orion, Lorimar, Chartoff/Winkler, Imagine Films, Rastar—more recently formed than the majors, and with greater flexibility in developing product, but which, by the same token, do not maintain their own physical production facilities and must usually—though not always—go outside to arrange capital and distribution.

MOW: Movie-of-the-Week. A film made exclusively to be aired on network television. Often dealing with current events or diseases of current interest.

Outgrading: Removal of any portion of a performer's image of services from a commercial. Upon prompt notification, players will not receive additional payment by reason of the outgrade.

Program Commercials—Class A, B, and C: Program commercials are generally commercials used in conjunction with or in sponsorship of a specific program (*See WILD SPOT USE*). Fees for actors who appear in them are determined by the "class" of program commercial, which is a designation of the number of markets in which it plays. Class A program use, designating markets in twenty cities or more, is paid per use of the commercial, and payment for all uses within a single week shall be made not later than fifteen working days after the end of that week. Class B (six to twenty markets) and C (one to six markets) program uses are paid at a set fee for unlimited used within each thirteen-week cycle.

Residuals: A payment made to an actor each time a film, television show, or commercial in which that actor appears is re-broadcast after its initial airing. (Does not apply to extras.)

SAG: Screen Actors Guild. Union with jurisdiction over performers in films, filmed television shows, and filmed commercials. An actor qualifies for membership by 1) being employed under a SAG contract; or, 2) having been a member of an affiliated union for at least one year, and having worked at least once as a principal performer in that affiliated union's jurisidiction, in addition to being a currently paid up member of that affiliated union. The affiliated unions are Equity, AFTRA, AGVA (American Guild of Variety Artists), AGMA (American Guild of Musical Artists), and ACTRA (Association of Canadian Television and Radio Artists). Joining fee equals current initiation fee plus one half annual dues.

Session Fee: Payment made for actual services in the performance of a commercial (usually a day's pay), payable twelve working days after services rendered.

Sides: Originally, "in the olden days," the term referred to pages containing just the lines and cues for a single role, which were used to avoid the time and expense of hand-copying a full script for every actor. Now, the term refers to typed sheets or photocopied pages from scripts containing just the material to be read in the audition. Since sides don't contain any of the other information usually necessary to giving a good audition, such as where the character comes from or ends up, SAG rules now specify that actors have the opportunity to at least look at a full script if it's written.

Story Board: A schematic drawing, often cartoon-like, designing a sequence of shots as they are intended to be filmed. Designating frames and the direction of action within the frame, storyboards are often used in film and almost always in commercials.

Submission: An agent sending a picture/résumé of an actor to a casting director in the hope of getting that actor a reading or interview for a specific part being cast. If the agent represents several actors appropriate for several roles on an individual project listed in *Breakdowns*, the agent will put them together into a single package and submit them—usually by messenger—to the casting director.

Test Deal: The prospective deal which a network makes with an actor, once the field has been narrowed down to the final contenders, before bringing each of these actors in for the final reading before all the network executives. Once the choice of actor is made, the deal for that actor has then already been "tested" with regard to such terms as salary, option period, start date, number of episodes per season, number of seasons, etc. Not usually covered in test deals are terms such as exclusivity, dressing rooms, additional perks, etc.

Theatrical Representation: Representing actors for work in film, television, and theatre.

Under Fives: A specific category in AFTRA contracts designating a role with five or fewer speaking lines. Rate of pay is determined by such designations in SAG and AFTRA contracts, but SAG roles fall into only one of two categories—principals and extras, with extras falling under the Screen Extras Guild. AFTRA, however, designates two categories between the principal and extra under fives and special business.

Wild Spot Use: A commercial shall be deemed to be used as a "wild spot" if it is broadcast by non-interconnected single stations and is used independently of any program or is used on local participating programs. Payments for "wild spot" use are based on thirteen-week cycles of unlimited use and are determined by the number of markets in which the commercial is broadcast. All markets in the U.S. are assigned a unit value with Los Angeles, New York, and Chicago being treated separately as major markets in recognition of their hiring market and extensive populations. The amount of compensation due for a given thirteen-week cycle is computed by determining the total number of major and other markets, totaling the combined units, and applying the applicable dollar value to the units so totaled. Use payments are due fifteen working days after commencement of use cycle.

About the Authors

TERRANCE HINES

Michael Terrance Hines was born in Alliance, Ohio, one of six children in a struggling, Irish-Catholic family. His B.A. in Creative Writing from Walsh College in North Canton, Ohio, was followed by an M.A. in Acting and Directing from Kent State University in Kent, Ohio.

He served in the Navy in Vietnam from 1965 to 1967 aboard a destroyer doing shore bombardment. When he returned from the war, he taught at a Catholic elementary school in Palo Alto, California, and then became Head of the Drama Department at Los Altos High School for five years. During this period, he founded an innovative and highly successful Shakespeare Festival, as well as directing and producing over forty plays, ranging from MARAT/SADE to Irwin Shaw's BURY THE DEAD. He then joined the faculty of West Valley Junior College in Saratoga, California, where he taught film production, acting, and directing. He produced and directed several 16mm short films while doing graduate work in film at Stanford University, and went on to study at both the American Conservatory Theatre and the American Film Institute.

He currently teaches private lessons in auditioning, cold reading, and scene study for young professionals at The Shop in Burbank, California, with fellow instructor and Neighborhood Playhouse alumnus Andrew Magarian. He spent two seasons as acting coach on KIDS INCORPORATED and as monologue coach for contestants in the MISS HOLLYWOOD CONTEST.

In addition, for the last twelve years, he has maintained

an active career in personal management His clients have included Roxana Zal (TESTAMENT and Emmy Award-winner for SOMETHING ABOUT AMELIA); Lukas Haas (WITNESS); Ross Harris (TESTAMENT, UNDER ONE ROOF); Lisa Bonet (THE COSBY SHOW); Susan Rinnell (JUST BETWEEN FRIENDS, ONE TERRIFIC GUY); Amanda Petersen (CAN'T BUY ME LOVE, A YEAR IN THE LIFE); and Tina Caspary (CAN'T BUY ME LOVE, MAC AND ME).

He also coached and trained Tim Gibbs (ROUSTERS, FATHER MURPHY, DEAD WRONG); Tonya Crowe (KNOT'S LANDING); Philip Tanzini (GENERAL HOSPITAL, HOOPER-MAN); Melissa Michaelson (GOLDIE AND THE BOXER, OR-PHAN TRAIN); and Moosie Dryer (KIDS, INCORPORATED), who is now a television director.

He is currently managing, teaching, and developing feature and television scripts, as well as working on a second book.

SUZANNE VAUGHAN

Suzanne Vaughan was born and raised in Texas, where her family has lived since 1797. She received a B.A. in Theatre from Texas Western College at the age of nineteen and then won a Woodrow Wilson National Fellowship to do graduate work in theatre at Stanford University.

She appeared in numerous theatre productions in the San Francisco Bay Area, including at the Actors Workshop and the American Conservatory Theatre. She also worked as a technical writer and editor for various electronic firms and earned an M.A. in English Literature from San Jose State University.

Her continuing dream of working professionally as an actress drew her to the Los Angeles area, where she has spent the last fifteen years, first as a performer on such television shows as ALL IN THE FAMILY and GENERAL HOSPITAL, and then in legal clearance and business affairs on such shows as ENTERTAIN-MENT TONIGHT, LIFESTYLES OF THE RICH AND FAMOUS, THE STUNTMEN AWARDS, and THE LEGEND CONTINUES: MICHAEL JACKSON.

She recently served as Associate Producer on the television series THE STORY OF ROCK AND ROLL as well as on the videocassette series THE BEST OF THE TELEPHONE HOUR for Henry Jaffe Enterprises.

She has also written situation comedy and teaches dialect classes, and, while her daughter and son attend the University of Southern California, she is currently in her second year of study at Loyola Law School.